PRESERVING THE *Self*

IN THE SOUTH SEAS, 1680–1840

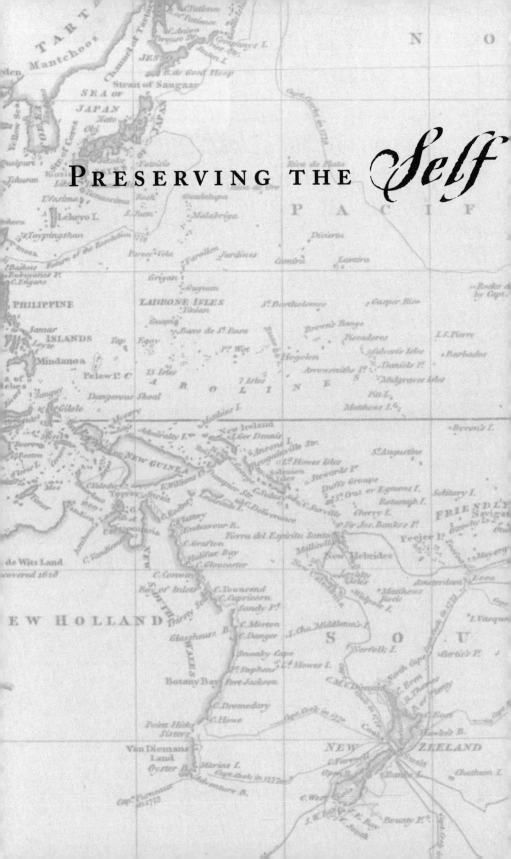

Preserving the *Self*

IN THE SOUTH SEAS
1680–1840

Jonathan Lamb

THE UNIVERSITY OF CHICAGO PRESS   CHICAGO AND LONDON

JONATHAN LAMB is professor of English at Princeton University. His articles and essays have appeared in journals such as *Huntington Library Quarterly, Journal of Maritime Research,* and *The Eighteenth Century,* among others, and in edited collections. He is the author of *Sterne's Fiction and the Double Principle* (Cambridge University Press, 1989) and *The Rhetoric of Suffering: Reading the Book of Job in the Eighteenth Century* (Oxford University Press, 1995). Among his coedited works is *Exploration and Exchange: A South Seas Anthology, 1680–1900* (University of Chicago Press, 2001).

The University of Chicago Press, Chicago 60637
The University of Chicago Press, Ltd., London
© 2001 by The University of Chicago
All rights reserved. Published 2001
Printed in the United States of America

10 09 08 07 06 05 04 03 02 01   1 2 3 4 5
ISBN: 0-226-46848-8 (cloth)
ISBN: 0-226-46849-6 (paper)

Library of Congress Cataloging-in-Publication Data

Lamb, Jonathan, 1945–
    Preserving the self in the south seas, 1680–1840 / Jonathan Lamb.
        p.   cm.
    Includes bibliographical references and index.
    ISBN 0-226-46848-8 (cloth : alk. paper) — ISBN 0-226-46849-6 (pbk. : alk. paper)
        1. Travelers' writings, English—History and criticism.   2. British—Travel—
    Oceania—History.   3. Oceania—Description and travel.   4. Travel—Oceania—
    History.   5. Oceania—In literature.   6. Self in literature.   I. Title.
    PR756.T72 L36 2001
    820.9′355—dc21   00-011809

⊗ The paper used in this publication meets the minimum requirements of the American National Standard for Information Sciences—Permanence of Paper for Printed Library Materials, ANSI Z39.48-1992.

This book is printed on acid-free paper.

For Esther and Becky

Contents

Illustrations

Acknowledgments

The bulk of this book was written during 1998 with the aid of sabbatical leave from Princeton University, a fellowship from the American Council of Learned Societies, and fellowships from the Centre for Cross Cultural Studies and the Humanities Research Centre (Australian National University, Canberra). For their timely generosity and hospitality I am most grateful. I am also indebted to the Princeton University Committee on Research in the Humanities and Social Sciences for financial support that allowed me to study in London for the three summers before, and to the dean of the Faculty's Fund for financing my attendance at conferences in New Zealand and Australia. The Committee on Research has also contributed handsomely to the production costs of this book.

While working in Australia, I was given crucial help with ethnographic, historical, and other Oceanian matters by Nicholas Thomas, Greg Dening, Richard Grove, and Richard Eves. Moreover, it was a fascinating as well as an instructive experience to help teach a graduate seminar at the Australian National University on the theme of eighteenth-century voyages to the Pacific. In Canberra, Paul Turnbull, Bronwen Douglas, and Iain McCalman were helpful and steadfast colleagues. While I was there I met Ruth Watson, who since has taught me a great deal about maps and terrestrial paradises. In New Zealand, Alex Calder and Stephen Turner of the University of Auckland, and Donald Kerr of the Auckland Public Library plied me constantly with data and ideas, and listened patiently to my own opinions. Reina Whaitiri, Anne Salmond, Lydia Wevers, Judy Binney, Peter Brunt, Albert Wendt, Mark Williams, Manuka Henare, Bridget McPhail, Andrew Sharp, and Ian Wedde have given me advice and stimulus over the last five years; I also want publicly to thank Bill Pearson and Jocelyn Harris for planting in my head the first idea for such a project.

In Britain, I have benefited more than I can say from the care and attention of Glyndwr Williams, who freely and genially shared his unrivaled knowledge of maritime history. The chapter on scurvy could not have been written without the help of Sir James Watt, who, over several nutritious lunches, explained to me the various types of deficiency that contribute to the symptomatology of that disease. Chris Pinney, Rod

Edmond, David Ellis, Nigel Rigby, Nigel Leask, and Simon Schaffer have always been prepared to listen and to offer advice. Neil Rennie, Steve Clark, and Philip Edwards I met later in the enterprise, and wished it had been earlier. John Pocock made useful comments on an early draft of chapter 6. James Chandler and Robert Markley were not only astute commentators on the first version of the first part of the book, but also proved to be heroic readers of the final draft, giving me suggestions and encouragement throughout, for which I am deeply grateful. Marshall Sahlins has given me guidance, both personally and through his important ethnographic studies of the broad Pacific region. Bernard Smith endows all students of Pacific history with an invaluable legacy of images, and an exemplary method of treating them. Claudia Johnson, Michael McKeon, Claude Rawson, and Simon During have supported the project with good advice and many letters. Mel Humphreys, Richard Wallace, Peter Walker, and Parpie, an African grey parrot, have looked after me in London.

I have talked up, down, and around the issues of this book with April Alliston, Srinivas Aravamudan, Helen Blythe, Paul Carter, Jill Casid, Lennard Davis, Hilary Ericksen, Suvir Kaul, Margarette Lincoln, Greg Maertz, Eun Min, Anna Neill, Felicity Nussbaum, Gordon Orr, Gordon Turnbull, Susan Wolfson, and Michael Wood. Laura Sayre, Julie Park, and Stephanie Smith worked as my research assistants, tirelessly and with great patience; as colleagues, they have exchanged ideas and made suggestions. Sandy Hazel has worked heroically and tirelessly on the manuscript and the proofs. Bridget Orr has never wavered in her support, finding books which seemed entirely lost, and rightly mocking fits of panic that proved to be groundless.

part one

THE ROMANCING OF THE CIVIL SELF

INTRODUCTION

"—My good friend, quoth I—as sure as I am I—and you are you—
—And who are you? said he,—
—Don't puzzle me, said I."
    —Laurence Sterne, *Tristram Shandy*

The period covered by this study contains three interlocking developments in British life: the evolution of a self guarded by certain political rights and duties; the growth of a market economy based on credit and overseas trade; and the completion of the map of the world. The period also covers the transformation of the South Pacific. Hitherto a vast circle whose center was a constellation of islands seldom or never visited by Europeans, and whose circumference was a congeries of unrelated Asian, Chinese, Dutch, Portuguese, and Spanish spheres of influence, it was fully to be incorporated into the world system of trade, chiefly as a result of British (and, to a certain extent, French and American) maritime activity. The simplest but not necessarily the most accurate way of handling these changes is to link them as causes and effects. Thus the emergent individual, whose rights to life and property were guaranteed by the post-revolutionary settlement of 1689, was equipped to embark securely upon transactions in a free market; and this market, growing fast, required fresh opportunities for trade in the form of newly discovered territories. In such an account every datum, whether psychological, political, literary, scientific, or maritime, is consistent with a grand narrative of expansion—in short, the enlargement of Britain's second empire. Compatible with this imperial theme is the history of a civil self whose competence in the market was crowned by the acquisition of social skills, so improved by manners and tastes that the contractual arrangements of the merchant soften into the sociable exchanges of the gentleman.

There is an alternative way of viewing and narrating these matters that is more attentive to the contradictions of nascent capitalism. The growth of the market economy was attended with a new sort of ignorance, productive of a keen anxiety about the tendency of events and the constitution of the self. Instead of relying on Providence for a sense of history, people confronted an engine for social development that they had constructed themselves, but that they could neither govern nor understand. Their anxieties focused not only on the widening gulf between facts and values, as market lore displaced ethical imperatives, but also on the disjunction between private experience and public life. The mass movements of sentiment shaping public opinion and credit were not to be predicted or analyzed; that is to say, they operated in defiance of those social values that had sustained the individual as a conscious civil being. There were two ways of responding to this state of affairs. One was to restore to private life the public and ethical relevance it had allegedly once possessed, as Anthony Ashley Cooper, third earl of Shaftesbury, and the moral sense philosophers attempted to do. The other was to explore the role of the individual isolated in the pursuit of self-satisfactions that could not easily be publicly justified—an alternative chosen by political economists such as Bernard Mandeville, Adam Smith, and Thomas Malthus. Those who followed the first option preferred the generalizing idiom perfected by Alexander Pope for the theodicy of his moral epistles, ultimately implausible but attractive to those in doubt. Those choosing the latter confronted both the hypocrisy of a social world not inclined to have its secrets on display, as well as a species of involuntary pretense arising from the aforementioned ignorance, which prevented even the most candid men and women from ever being able to forecast accurately the consequences of their actions—or even to ascertain that what they said was what they felt or meant.

The upshot of an intrusive world market in the South Pacific was not likely, therefore, to be the consummation of well-laid plans, even if the forerunners of its advent, such as cartographic and scientific expeditions, wore the lineaments of cognitive competence. In fact, confronted with the vastness of the ocean, and the unclassifiable diversity of its people and its plants, its navigators rather redoubled their ignorance than increased their knowledge. The journals of James Cook's three voyages record a mounting bewilderment in the commander's mind, no doubt partly caused by his failure to locate either of the two grand objects of his quests, the Great

Southern Continent and the Northwest Passage. His bafflement culminated in behavior so unaccountable that his colleagues thought him infatuated. Nor is his case singular. George Vancouver, William Bligh, John Byron, and David Cheap acted in ways so far from reasonable that they lost the confidence of their crews, and the thread of their purpose. That such augmented ignorance entailed upon native populations a cognate ignorance, leading to actions also called infatuated—the fetishizing of trade goods, the rise of messianic movements, shamanic raptures—is a fact instructive insofar as it exhibited a common degree of imbecility among mariners and indigenes when confronting the cause and the effect of this intrusion. Europeans spread ignorance before they spread trade routes and disease. The uncertainties that troubled the stability of the European self were intensified in the South Pacific at the same moment that they were being reflected in the Polynesian self, which was in its turn being forced out of its tribal identity into a state more labile and less defended. On both sides of the line of encounter, people became directly interested in the issue of self-preservation.

In using the word *self,* I mean to avoid the implications that attach to *subject.* Although the self I talk about is capable of considerable reflexive agility, it is not constituted by reflection, interpellation, or language. It is merely that bundle of immediate and remembered impressions acquired by an embodied mind on which a sense of personal identity depends, according to John Locke. Just such a contingent collection of desires and inclinations modified the Polynesian self once it was dislodged from an encompassed social existence and driven to locate itself in a material and uncustomary world. I assume, then, no metaphysical division between the European self and its so-called other. There is not on one side an "I" capable of writing a history into which the subaltern "I" on the other side is speechlessly incorporated as its predicate. Although the Europeans started out with great advantages—their guns and their immunity to diseases fatal to natives—they were engaged as exigently as the Polynesians in the struggle to preserve the self.

One way or another, all the pressures of civil society are exerted on the self. This self is the inheritor of all those rights and duties that flow toward human beings capable of asserting that they are who they are, and articulating their own story in the first person singular. The self is also the source of propensities and passions that threaten to disrupt the social, political, and historical continua on which its own identity relies. Although much ingenuity has been expended, in the eighteenth century as well as now, in showing how the self's impulsive interventions on its own behalf serve the cause of social harmony, it is plain that such extenuations are prompted by doubts about an autonomy often characterized as the ignorant pursuit of self-interest. The tension is evident in the "law" of self-preservation, paradoxically construed as the most urgent of instincts and the most imperative of social duties. The self is therefore required to study two different phases of its being, and to see itself at once as the source and product of its own desires. To be fully constituted, it is expected to knit these divisions (which Mandeville referred to as the wishing and the wished-for selves) into a sensually ethical entity, a self spontaneously obedient to a natural and a social law.

Shaftesbury believed the knitting might be so perfect as to leave no trace of the split; Mandeville enjoyed showing that this so-called unity is false, and that the bonds between the interested and the sociable parts of the self are owing only to hypocrisy or pretense. His wilder approach to what he called "the Business of Self-preservation" is more hospitable to symptoms of a loose antisocial energy that Shaftesbury set aside as enthusiasm, and which the architects of civil society had feared—Thomas Hobbes as "gloriation of mind" and Locke as "passionate heats." Enthusiasm, curiosity, virtuoso tastes, and romance all provided pleasure sufficient to dignify the self in its own eyes, without reference to social norms. So too did voyaging. The mariner who told a tale of the wonders of the terra incognita made explicit the division between private excitements and public standards of truth and probability. Shaftesbury disparaged travelers' tales as barbarous and corrupting on this very account, because in opening up the undiscovered world, and all its monsters, they opened up also the terra incognita of the mind, those hidden spaces where ugly and unsociable impulses lie hidden. Mandeville called this the terra incognita of self-love, and commended its exploration both literally and figuratively. The popularity of books of travels, growing to greater heights as the century advanced, must be explained, then, not in terms the truth they produced (for they were broadly regarded as lies) but in terms of their potent dramatization of the feelings incident to the preservation of the self. Like Othello's "travailous history" told to Desdemona, the narrator presented to the reader a story of singular events, so marvelous they could not fully be described, interspersed with feelings so intense they could not adequately be expressed. Here the confusions and passions incident to modern life acquired the glamour of romance by being magnified, not explained and sublimed as a coherent national enterprise. Shaftesbury was right at least to note that this branch of literature added nothing to the sum of politeness or knowledge. It insisted on the ignorance and copiously represented the anxieties that arose with the market.

Even after the 1760s, when voyages of discovery in the South Seas supposedly were put on a scientific footing, the participants are observed not at all times and under all circumstances to present the stable platform for observation needed by an imperial eye measuring its options. The deliberate policy and clairvoyance charged to these explorations in recent postcolonial studies are unconscious adaptations of the language of intentionality and theodicy originating in Pope's and Shaftesbury's polite accounts of the British experience, and rather unsteadily deployed in the work of Johann Reinhold Forster and his son George. The commanders of these expeditions may have been committed to large and comprehensive views, and believed devoutly in systems of classification and cadastral measurement; but their data proved intractable, their experiments prone to failure, and they became periodically distracted, behaving unlike themselves owing to the stress of isolation, disease, fear—and occasionally exquisite pleasure. They exhibited passions deemed uncivil and rude, and their stories admitted episodes and events that struck their readers as improbable. This did no harm at all to their popularity because whether they intended it or not, they joined the genre of voyage literature scorned by Shaftesbury but enjoyed by a reading public curious about the singularities of self-preservation. To insist that the point of such voyages was exclusively the production of truth for imperial purposes is to ignore two things: first, the confusing and sometimes inexpressible experience of extreme conditions endured by the voyagers themselves; and second, the reasons for the currency of their stories in the metropolitan book market.

The South Seas and commercial society are intimately but uneasily connected by the law of self-preservation, all the way from the foundation of the South Sea Company in the early eighteenth century to the researches of Alfred Wallace and Charles Darwin in the midnineteenth. Malthus and tropical islands have things in common because the blend of natural and social law implicit in the original idea of the civil self is proclaimed again in the law of evolution. The theory of natural selection incorporates the history of eighteenth-century political economy, just as the history of political economy incorporates the fable of self-preservation told by Locke in his second *Treatise of Government*, and again by Daniel Defoe in *Robinson Crusoe*. Every phase of this joint exercise in natural and political history refers to the example of a lonely creature adapting to a wild terrain whose generic name was America. How wealth might emerge from this spare and exigent existence—and, at the same time, how a self might take on the form of its own longings for survival and security— is a narrative that combines the miracles of the Robinsonnade with the magic of credit, and anticipates the wonderful metamorphoses exhibited in the adaptations of species. The note that stands for the gold that incarnates the labor that produces the food that preserves the self is the subtlest manifestation of the market, and the last instance of the power of imagination. This abstract form of fundamental desire by no means dissipates its primitive urgency. When the Pacific was raided as an "ocean of fantasy," as Denis Diderot called it later, in order to fuel speculation in South Sea stock in 1720, the business of self-preservation was still the order of the day; and when the speculation in paper wealth failed, this priority became even more alarmingly clear. The experiment of materializing the fantasies of self-extension simply by circulating notes of no intrinsic value was followed by the first serious blow to British national credit. Commentators such as John Trenchard (coauthor of *Cato's Letters*) talked of the disaster as patriacide, an onslaught upon national and personal identity alike, and deserving of the most ferocious retaliation. The metaphors of exotic savagery dominated this first financial crash, named the South Sea Bubble. While the madness lasted, there was a place for the fetish in Exchange Alley as well as on the Guinea coast or a Pacific shore. And when the wreck was complete, people talked of castaways and cannibals, and of self-preservation in its rudest forms.

In trying to establish a more-secure theory of value at the end of the century, Malthus chose land; and by contrasting its limited quantity with the illimitable desire of human beings to reproduce, he restored to civil society its basis in the primordial struggle for life that Hobbes had hypothesized as the state of nature, and that the South Sea Bubble had disclosed. The natural returns to haunt the social as periodically "the mighty law of self-preservation expels all the softer and more exalted emotions of the soul," as Malthus put it. When Wallace and Darwin independently chose Malthus as the model for their explanation of the evolution of varieties into species, they unconsciously recapitulated the chorography of self-preservation by seeking their evidence in the same places where the early navigators had sought gold, paradise, and spices, and where city speculators had expected fabulous profits—in the South Seas, off the coast of South America, and among the eastern archipelagos of Indonesia. When British settlers made a property of land in Australia and New Zealand, Malthus and Darwin had parts to play in the theorization and representation of their efforts; and once more the law of self-preservation loomed large and threatening in the South Seas, not because of a plan but because of a series of exigencies sometimes adapted to a utopian frame.

The passions and sentience of the isolated maritime self are irritated and sharpened by a disease that became epidemic in South Seas voyages. The depletion of vitamins in the bodies of sailors exposed to long stretches of arduous labor and a diet consisting mainly of starch, pulse, and salted meat, caused a battery of ghastly physiological symptoms called the scurvy. At the same time, it provoked a morbid susceptibility to sensations of light, smell, and sound, and an extraordinary alternation of moods that Thomas Trotter named "scorbutic nostalgia." The same phenomenon could strike a victim of scurvy as intensely beautiful and as profoundly depressing. The loneliness of these mariners, and their irrational oscillation between feelings of joy and despair, are well represented in Samuel Taylor Coleridge's *Rime of the Ancient Mariner,* a narrative that borrows largely from tales of the South Seas, and veers as they do between extremes of disgust and pleasure. The poem illustrates both the intense ambivalence of the voyaging self as it encounters unfamiliar phenomena such as albatrosses and phosphorescence, and also the difficult and sometimes combative relation this ambivalence provokes between the narrator and his audience. Often the effects of scorbutic nostalgia have been mistaken as a crude system of differences inaugurating a taxonomy of human types, species, and varieties, of which the noble and ignoble savage and the Wallace Line[1] are the most prominent examples. But the curiously persistent blend of dismay and delight in narratives such as Pedro Fernandez de Quirós's, Willliam Dampier's, George Shelvocke's, Alexander Selkirk's, Cook's, Bligh's—and latterly Herman Melville's and Robert Louis Stevenson's—has little to do with careful observation and discriminate judgment, and much more with an ungovernable yet equivocal emotion, sometimes pathologically intensified, that attaches itself arbitrarily to objects.

Yet it is common to meet with quite contrary estimates of maritime powers of observation, emphasizing the precision and accuracy of the measurements, and the cool management of each succeeding crisis, the better to characterize sailors as instruments of a coherent national policy. Here is an example from a book published recently, Jonathan Raban's

---

1 The Wallace Line, the imaginary boundary dividing species down the Malay Archipelago, was discovered by Alfred Wallace during his researches. He believed that it marked a sharp break between higher and lower forms of development.

Passage to Juneau, a narrative of a voyage taken by the author that traces Vancouver's exploration of the coast of the American Northwest:

> The saloon of my boat was dominated by the memoirs of eighteenth-century white explorers—intruders from the Age of Reason for whom measurement, with their quadrants, chronometers, and magnetic compasses, was a form of taking possession. . . . As part of the century's great communal project of Linnaean taxonomy, they went fossicking for specimens of plants, birds, mammals. They carved their emerging charts of the sea with names . . . shoot! classify! name! describe!—the imperatives of eighteenth-century discovery. (Raban 1999, 25)

So much is taken for granted in these generalizations. It is as if no alarms or mistakes disturbed the collection of specimens, and no terrors smudged the cartographic grid. How easy it is to read the log of George Anson's *Centurion,* perhaps the best known of the British navigations before Cook, and to assume that the laconic references to tempests, freezing rain, and broken equipment, and the daily list of names terminating in D.D. (discharged dead), are heroic reductions of dangers to the level of inconveniences, an impassive assertion of the majesty of a higher purpose. What was Anson's purpose? What was his state of mind? Perhaps they had become indescribable; perhaps he was trying hard to avoid the fate of his colleague Captain David Cheap, so infatuated with pain and scurvy that he forgot his own name. Raban himself discovers in Vancouver a man whose judgment was so disturbed by loneliness and apprehension that he alienated his crew with Bligh's kind of bad language, and had his midshipman Thomas Pitt (cousin of the prime minister) flogged for a trivial offense. Following in Vancouver's wake, Raban acquires some of that loneliness too, ending his narrative with these words: "Wearing a mask for a face, I hurried down the dock to the slip (the word "our," suddenly was no longer mine to use) and hid in the saloon, fitting the hatchboards in place, closing the hatch, and drawing the curtains on the ports" (424). The ego in crisis shuts itself up with the narratives of troubled first persons.

One of the more remarkable polemical debates of the last decade took place between Marshall Sahlins and Gananath Obeyesekere on the subject of Captain Cook's death. They disagreed about the events leading up to the fatal day in Kealakekua Bay in 1779. As anthropologists concerned with the impact on local cultures caused by the arrival of Europeans, they wanted to know why it was reported that the Hawai'ians greeted Cook as a god, and whether this was because his arrival coincided with an annual festival, or because Europeans always expect to be hailed as gods by natives. In the series of replies and rejoinders produced by these experts and their commentators, Cook himself was unimportant. Sahlins wittily sets aside James Watt's suggestion that Cook was suffering from pelagra, and therefore acting in a manner increasingly unlike himself: "Worms done him in. Really there is something faintly heroic in the idea" (Sahlins 1985b, 109; Watt 1979, 155). For his part, Obeyesekere puts Conrad's Kurtz where once Philip James de Loutherbourg had placed a hero of the Enlightenment in order to show how brutally Cook supplanted the intelligible signs of an exotic culture with an imperial lie. The curious elisions and contradictions in the many eyewitness accounts of the death were reviewed only for evidence of ethnographic details, the flair for ritual display, or the practical intelligence evinced by the Hawai'ians when faced with an awkward intrusion. Why Cook should act in a manner that at least two observers identified as infatuated (a state of mind causing what Sahlins himself refers to as the dreamlike quality of Cook's end), and why the events provoked by this infatuation should be so very difficult to narrate, were questions irrelevant to the debate. When Sahlins introduces his essay with William Ellis's judgment of the affair ("a chain of events which could no more be foreseen than prevented" [Sahlins 1985b, 104]) and ends by confirming Bernard Smith's estimate of Cook as "Adam Smith's global agent," (131) he sets aside the *necessary* quality of the ignorance linking Ellis on one side to Mandeville, who had published a scandalous fable about the unpredictable and vile effects of acting upon noble motives, and on the other to Smith, who said the history of Europe's entry into the New World was "a course of accidents which no human wisdom could foresee." Although Obeyesekere believes Sahlins was ornamenting an imperial myth by taking seriously Cook's role as the fertility god Lono in the Makahiki festival, he is equally impatient with Cook as an agent of European expansion, and wishes even more heartily than his opponent to remove him from a place in the story of his own death. It was not germane to their questions to ask whether Cook accepted his role as godhead because he was no longer sure who he was. The urgent problems and questions lay all on the other side of the beach. Yet it is still the death of a man called James Cook that these anthropologists end up hashing and rehashing, and its narrative difficulties that they unintentionally end up perpetuating. Of course, their emphasis on indigenous reactions is important to the understanding of what was happening broadly along the line of contract; but both sides of the encounter demand attention, otherwise the changes each was inflicting on the other will be only partially visible.

If the first paradox of self-preservation is that a propensity asks to be obeyed like a duty, the second is that the self is preserved only by being changed. In civil society, this change is generally regarded as improvement, the acquirement of correct judgment and good manners. In ships and on the beach, it is the reverse: the self suffers a sea change into something odd and strange, subject to moods, passions, and corruptions not easily transmitted to a polite audience. The laboratory in which this transformation is most closely studied is a desert island such as Juan Fernandez, scene of many a stranding and many a Prosperian discovery of new powers of mind and tongue. Although it is usual to identify the island as an infant colony, and simply to brand as exploitation the relations with things and people developed there, there is (as Prospero says) a subtlety in islands that makes such schematism rough and imprecise. Frantz Fanon (1963, 46) has talked powerfully of the importance of trance and possession in the culture of islands. If the agonies and enchantments leading to infatuation can be harnessed by solitaires—that is, if they don't run mad with loneliness and are able, like Selkirk, Crusoe, and Shelvocke, to transform privation into energy of mind—then there is available a fund of pleasures so intense that it causes castaways to fall in love with their islands, and to leave them with great regret. In the course of voyaging, this pleasure is available too, but usually in the milder form of curiosity, and the sharpening of the appetite of a singular person for eyeing and handling unique artifacts, things that are like nothing but themselves.

The sailors who became collectors of singular things and connoisseurs of solitude were exporting another metropolitan mystery into the South Seas, namely the *je ne sais quoi*. This riddling phrase denoting the value of an incommunicable feeling covered the most painful as well as the most pleasurable interludes of navigation, as indeed it did of all travel (Chard 1999, 98). Among the debris of contracts and the ruins of common sense, the self could enjoy a feeling peculiar to itself, with no need of any standard to justify it. The narratives of these moments of private pleasure are really extensions of the je ne sais quoi into a fantastic sequence. Such narratives are utopian in this fundamental respect, namely that a voluptuous egoism projects its pleasure as an imagined society whose purpose is the maximum pleasure for the greatest number. Thomas More's *Utopia* emerges from a maritime je ne sais quoi. Raphael Hythloday's standard affirmation of the voyaging eyewitness frees it from any consensual obligation: "But if you had been with me in Utopia, and had presently seen their fashions and laws, as I did . . . then doubtless you would grant that you never saw people well ordered, but only there" (More 1910, 53). These inexpressible moments enunciated as a distant Utopia are accompanied by a compulsive use of the figure of litotes, where things are located by miss-ing their opposites, and propositions are affirmed by denying their con-traries. This rhetoric is as prominent in real as it is in imaginary voyages, as manifest in Dampier as in Swift, in de Quirós as in Defoe. Its utopian provenance suggests that the emptiness of a new space is a measure of its promise; and its deployment in satire suggests conversely that that what is absent is what ought to be there. But the seesaw between all and noth-ing, sufficiency and deficiency, characterizes experiences that are as in-tense as they are inexpressible; and in the buccaneer utopias of the Carib-bean, and the pirate utopias of the Indian Ocean, the je ne sais quoi materialized as brief immortal commonwealths.

The development of the landscape garden in Britain and the experi-ences of navigators on paradisal islands are likewise a blend of the imag-ined and the real. News of a real terrestrial paradise had been dispatched by Columbus, and then by numerous subsequent expeditions that found the air and vegetation of the New World singularly pleasant. Juan Fer-nandez and Tinian, the islands that figure largely in Selkirk's and Anson's accounts of the South Seas, were expected (like Columbus's Haiti and John Milton's Paradise) to be heavily wooded, and to have cascades of wa-ter silvering their verdant cliffs. They had a double warrant as paradise by Scripture and report, yet these notices scarcely blunted the novelty of landing in paradise, nor did it inhibit gardeners at home from trying to reproduce this natural insular space within the artifice of a created land-scape. The experiences of Cook at Dusky Bay, a part of New Zealand where no European had been before, resonate with a twin sense of the fa-miliar in the unfamiliar, and the intimation of symmetry in a wilderness. The haha, a device invented by gardeners for making seamless the con-nection between artificial and natural spaces, finds an application here, where the thickets of an untouched temperate rainforest are brought within the scope of eyes educated to appreciate the arrangement of pros-pects, clumps, lawns, and streams. In fact, the crew of the *Resolution* set to with hatchets and saws to remake part of the landscape of paradise, joining its ruggedness to the order of the ship. The same bridging of the gap between natural and artificial landscapes is evident in the placing of Cook memorials in those wooded glades of European gardens, generally called the Elysium, which are situated precisely on the border between an uncultivated outside world and a carefully fashioned inside one.

If scurvy renders the decay of the self a physiological fact, sensitiz-ing the nerves to a more vivid spectrum of emotions, then leprosy is its counterpart among native populations. I argue that the change from the civil to the appetent self is matched by a change from tribal "dividuality," or encompassed social being, into a sense of self that includes a taste for vivid sensation and personal pleasure. Leprosy is associated, from the voyage of Louis-Antoine de Bougainville to the establishment of the leper colony on Molokai, with a space divided from mainland society, where the surfaces of things become strange, and the relish of them weirdly focused. In this sense, leprosy compendiously represents a transformation of taste that took place throughout Polynesia in the wake of the voyages of the 1760s. The vast collections of trade goods, far too large ever to be used or consumed, made by Pomare I in Tahiti, Kamehameha in Hawai'i, and Cakobau in Fiji, were expressions of taste and power unparalleled in the history of these islands. Indeed, these curiosities were instrumental in an expansion of chiefly power out of all proportion to the political balance previously sustained between chiefdoms, and between the chiefly and priestly castes in general. This monopolization of power provoked reactions in the form of millenarian prophecies, shamanic possession, and cargo cults. The dynastic form of voluptuousness begot a countervailing politics of local utopianism that emphasized, like its European counterpart, the importance of pleasure. The Hulumanu cult in Hawai'i, and the *arioi* sect in Tahiti, improved their traditional erotic displays into a dissident theatrics that became more extravagant in proportion as the ambitions of the chiefly dynasties grew. This political pursuit of excitement culminated in the festivals of Molokai, where the lepers, often grossly disfigured, reactivated the cult of Lono and embraced pleasures no one outside could deny them or share.

As the landing of highly sentient voyagers on distant shores caused a parallel degree of susceptibility in the local people, their enthusiasm might be expected to meet in a common point of sympathetic ecstasy. In the latter part of the eighteenth century, when narratives of voyages were being published simultaneously with sentimental novels, this was often supposed to be the case. Travelers and indigenes were figured either as united in a cloud of benevolence, or as exploiters and victims whose cruelties and pains had a sentimental value for the reader. In fact, the changes in voyaging and indigenous selves, no matter how parallel they ran in the Pacific, never produced this mutual vibration of hearts, although displays of sorrow, reproach, and remorse were often performed, sometimes quite brilliantly, on both sides of the beach. People possessed by a singular appetite for pleasure are not ambitious for partners. As muskets and land became the commodities of choice for indigene and settler respectively, even the pretense of a *sensus communis* was set aside in the struggle for dominance. In these narratives, sympathy is evident only as that branch of self-preservation defined by Edmund Burke as the longing to put oneself in the place of another, a usurpation of positions rather than an exchange of sentiments. My final examples of Edward Gibbon Wakefield, the inspired architect of New Zealand settlement, and Te Kooti Ariki-rangi te Turuki, a prophet and the last armed defender of Maori land, provide a set piece of a European and a Polynesian working hard at mutual substitution, going to war because they are animated by feelings equally intense for an object equally attractive that only one of them can possess.

I

Political Theories
of the Self

In my dear self I centre everything;
My servants, friends, my mistress, and my King;
Nay, heaven and earth to that one point I bring.
—John Wilmot, earl of Rochester, *A Very Heroical Epistle*

The circumstances of British history that made it necessary to invent the fiction of an original contract—a founding agreement between the individual in a state of nature on the one hand and the embodiment of civil society on the other, aimed at preserving the self within a system of law—had already loosened the "self" from the protocols guaranteeing it an unreflecting, nonassertive place in political life, and forced it to consider itself in some degree of isolation from social structures. Immemorial custom, aristocratic virtue, honor, obligation, and all the other bonds of an encompassed social existence, had been damaged in the Civil War, travestied during the Restoration, and sidelined by the rights confirmed by the Glorious Revolution (Cascardi 1992, 208; Elias 1982, 64; Giddens 1991, 74). To political thinkers for whom the state of nature and the original contract were "true" fictions, they restored some sense of control after a period of civil strife that had divided individuals from inherited bonds of allegiance and forced them to reflect upon themselves as single beings. But the emphasis laid by these foundational myths upon self-preservation as the motive and sole purpose of association indicated a threat as well as a constitutive benefit. When Daniel Defoe wrote "Self-preservation is the only Law / That does involuntary Duty draw" (Defoe 1860, 18), he meant a peremptory instinct independent of social obligation, to which all subsequent laws and duties acted as supplements, not restraints. Like John Locke, he understood the original contract to be an agreement with no other end than that of self-preservation, and terminable as soon as it ceased to answer it. Yet unlike the moral sense philosophers, who construed self-preservation as a common expression of natural affection, an inclination sociable from the very start, he refused to conceive of the self as coming into its own, endowed with what belongs to it by natural right. The self has to act on its own behalf and to adopt a defensive posture toward the world, accumulating the means of its subsistence until a treaty might be struck. This guarded maneuvering toward a contract is the theme (although, oddly, not the outcome) of many of Defoe's novels. In this chapter, I want to consider what kind of boundary divides the active, single self from the social self on whose behalf it is mobilized.

According to Defoe's line of thought, the threat to the preservation of the self does not cease with the contract. The inroads of sovereign power, factional hatred, religious intolerance, commercial greed, and enthusiasm were all proposed by advocates of this philosophy as dangers to the self's integrity. The instinctive duty of self-preservation, they maintained, is not peculiar to a state of nature, but constantly attends a self aware of the boundary of its own interests and the limits of its agency. From beyond and from within the self, the power of self-preservation is depleted: on the one side by a social framework in which inequality is confirmed by law, and on the other by passions incident to an embattled egoism, aggravated by an intuition of personal identity that awkwardly straddles the sense of the self as both a natural entity and a creature of convention. The blurred distinction between nature and culture raises the possibility of two selves—one prior and the other posterior; one wishing and the other fulfilling the preservation of self. This raises in turn the specter of something less than self that participates in its claim to natural integrity, and of something less than social that enters into the civic personality.

As part of this paradox of self-constitution, a number of duties fall to the self that it has no hope of successfully discharging. These chiefly concern the explanation of how events unfold. Previously within the sphere of Providence, but now within the spheres of ethics and politics, narratives of self and state—biography and history—are required by the terms of the contract to reveal how its parties were fulfilling their mutual obligations and acting in the long-term interests of each other. But such accounts are notoriously difficult to compile. Histories of the interregnum, of the Glorious Revolution and of the reign of Anne, follow party lines. Romance was openly rejected and covertly adapted as a model of autobiography. Unsteady narratives of public and private life are involved at the same time in the puzzling phenomenon of opinion in its various chimerical forms, none of them susceptible to political arithmetic or cogent analysis. Bernard Mandeville yielded to the inevitable by outlining "the Necessity there is for a certain Portion of Ignorance in a well ordered Society" (Mandeville 1924, 1:322). Henry Fielding drew the scholium: "Means are always in our power; ends are very seldom so" (Fielding 1996a, 84). If the self cannot connect its actions to a future outcome, or demonstrate that its present circumstances are the fruit of prior purposes, it will be baffled both ethically and historically. It can neither predict nor record a sequence, and therefore remains blind to the true relation between private and public affairs (Smith 1976, 1:25; Pocock 1975, 466). Mandeville provides the broadest overview of this confusion when he sees civil society compounding its limitations with further limitations, and mending "by Inconstancy / Faults, which no Prudence could foresee" (Mandeville 1924: 1:25). Henry St. John, viscount Bolingbroke, gave the poignant close-up, "We are born too late to see the beginning, and we die too soon to see the end of many things" (Bolingbroke 1752a, 35). The best the self can do under these circumstances of a necessary ignorance is to offer vouchers of good intention, signs of civility in the absence of proofs, or simply to concentrate on self-preservation. Politeness, taste, sympathy, and the moral sense are the alleged attributes of a continuous and sociable personal identity, bent on the joint accomplishment of individual and social standards of good. Societies for the reformation of manners stood ready to coerce less disciplined citizens into paths of sociability. But unsentimental estimates of human nature state the limits of such projects by recurring to the original motive for community: "There is nothing more sincere in any Creature than his Will, Wishes and Endeavours to preserve himself . . . which either compel him to crave what he thinks will sustain or please him, or command him to avoid what he imagines might displease, hurt, or destroy him" (Mandeville 1924, 1:200). The multitude of polemics against luxury point out how thinly the coating of sociability was put on.

Indices of the uncertainty of the bond between the self and society were widespread. Apart from the work of political philosophers, who sought to minimize the instability of the self's relation to eligible goals, it was a mystery in physiology (never mind ethics) how an impulse of the mind or nerves passed into an action. Similarly in psychology, a force like gravity was understood to cause the association of simple ideas into

complex ones, but the means by which two ideas were originally associated was (like the original contract) inconceivable as a fact.[1] Theorists of
language, borrowing directly from the contractual model, relied on convention alone as a guarantee of meaning between interlocutors, for want
of a surer method of authorizing the definitions of words. At all levels of
human activity, an opaque medium divided the private motive from its
public outcome, leaving the profession or pretense of good intention to
do the work of visible and indisputable proof. The fear of pretense and
deception looming large in the culture of a people who were inventing
new names for lies ("bite," "sham," and "bubble") and whose former rulers
were now styled Pretenders (James III and his son, Charles Edward
Stuart), made national as well as personal identity a tormenting theme
for reflection and debate. That this should be the fruit of a contract, in
civil life intended as the most binding security for the advantage of the
two parties, is typical of the paradoxes generated from efforts to preserve
the self.

Corresponding to the inner and outer dimensions of these paradoxes
are two principal areas of human activity on which the issue of self-
preservation is played out. The first is pleasure, and the second is voyaging. Francis Hutcheson said, "It is of the greatest importance not to trifle
in the experience and identification of the most lasting lasting pleasures"
(Hutcheson 1725, [iii]). Wanting a means of rational analysis and clear
demonstration, and aware that consensual judgments such as opinion,
sentiment, and taste—immediate registers of what pleases or disgusts—
are the chief determinants of value, political philosophers somewhat reluctantly acknowledged the importance of propensities, as opposed to
principles, in the pursuit of social goals. According to Adam Smith, social institutions are not the result of wisdom, but "the necessary, though
very slow and gradual consequence of a certain propensity in human nature which has in view no such extensive utility" (Smith 1976, 1:25). However, Lord Shaftesbury and Hutcheson led a school of thought that carefully distinguished between "a poor selfish Pleasure" that offers "no rule
of good" and those feelings that are directly productive of social harmony

---

1   David Hartley arrived at the same paradox in psychology that Hobbes coped with in politics; namely,
a power of associating that is at once the effect and the prior condition of association. He said, "The Power
of Association is founded upon, and necessarily requires, the previous Power of forming Ideas, and miniature Vibrations. For Ideas, and miniature Vibrations, must first be generated . . . before they can be associated. . . . But then I (which is very remarkable) this Power of forming Ideas, and their corresponding
miniature Vibrations, does equally presuppose the Power of Association" (Hartley [1749] 1966, 1:70).

(Hutcheson 1971, 387 [149];[2] Shaftesbury 1964, 1:200). Although the tyranny of propensities was widely deprecated as leading either to irregular passions or to corruption of the palate, no one doubted that human beings are guided by them, and the moral sense philosophers believed that the most amiable and benevolent impulses can be developed from them. Bolingbroke beheld a people "dissolved in voluptuousness," entirely given up to "the pursuits of private pleasure," yet he acknowledged the existence of "a sort of intellectual sympathy, better felt than expressed, in characters, by which particular men are sometimes united sooner, and more intimately, than could be by mere esteem, by expectation of good offices, or even by gratitude" (Bolingbroke 1727, 1:244; 1754, 4:10). This aesthetic, extra-ethical form of social bonding is not a principle, therefore, but a pleasurable inclination toward an objective assumed to be social. But David Hume called it an "immediate propensity," antecedent to reflection, and therefore innocent of "all ideas of obligation, and of all views, either to public or private utility" (Hume 1987, 479).

Hutcheson took the lead in identifying the propensity to sympathize with the sufferings of others as convincing evidence of the sociable tendency of the desire to be pleased. He argued that our most pressing feelings are naturally bold and open, appearing in public view as unmistakable signs of a natural language, and easily understood by spectators as bespeaking natural kindness. The occasion most expressive of the production and reception of these natural signs is a spectacle of human suffering. Initiating an intriguing sequence of bloody instances of sympathy among his cohort, Hutcheson produced gladiatorial contests and public executions as specimens of public-spirited pleasure taken in someone else's pain (Hutcheson 1725, 233, 238). As this model of sympathy was successively elaborated by Edmund Burke, Smith, and Adam Ferguson, it became clear that if the language of nature is to excite public compassion, it cannot be too spontaneous or florid: it requires the mediation of art. It also became obvious that the delight it causes is not only artificial, but also belongs to the family of passions connected with self-preservation, not with society (Burke 1987, 45−51). Anyone wishing to argue for the public spirit of compassion first needs to produce a criterion capable of distinguishing between a selfish and a public pleasure, and is therefore stranded on a problem of aesthetics known to the age as the je ne sais quoi.

---

2 Bracketed folios refer to the pagination in the original edition.

It has been observed that the theory of civil society in the early eighteenth century was haunted by the problem of taste (Caygill 1989, 37; Herrnstein Smith 1988, 35–40; Guillory 1993, 308–12). The je ne sais quoi exemplifies the opacity of the medium that keeps a private sensation from knowing its public significance. When Lovelace starts to weep at the sufferings he has inflicted on Clarissa, he writes to his friend Belford of a feeling that can only be known in the experience: "The thing was so strange to me—something choking, as it were, in my throat—I know not how . . . there was something very pretty in it; and I wish I could know it again" (Richardson 1985, 695). As the "charm or enchantment of which the artist can give no account" (Shaftesbury 1964 2:214), the je ne sais quoi dramatizes the embarrassment at the heart of all historical and sympathetic narratives. In none of them is it possible to trace a convincing sequence from sentiment to a corresponding intention or judgment: "The individual [can] identify and pursue the goals proposed to him by his passions and fantasies; but he [cannot] explain himself by locating himself as a real and rational being within it" (Pocock 1975, 466). The je ne sais quoi is a vivid local specimen of the failure experienced by the self when it tries to "comprehend the process of its own historical origination" and is destined to find evidence only of its own enchantment (Cascardi 1992, 32). And the difficulty of establishing a standard of taste that might regulate the social orientation of sentiments of pleasure is paralleled by the difficulty of predicting, nominating, or fixing any value identified by means of sympathy or opinion. Indeed, that a confession of ignorance delivered in the first person singular, in untranslated French, should provide the noun substantive of a peculiarly English embarrassment over the formation of true judgments by forcing an indexical mark to function as a denotative sign, is a solecism in grammar worthy of note (Muehlhaeusler and Harre 1990, 18). The purpose of such a transformation is to impart an appearance of consensual value to a predicament irremediably private (for the "I" of the phrase communicates only that nothing can be communicated); but in proportion as that broader significance is achieved, the more automatic is the reduction of the individual sentiment of pleasure to a cipher standing for a common case, canceling the reality of the "I" in favor of a pretended agreement between a congregation of first persons singular. Contrariwise, the more faithfully the statement refers to a real pleasure of inexpressible intensity, the more forcibly it states the impossibility of consensus. The want of any point of mediation between these two positions indicates the real conflict between them, and the need for self-preservation is renewed by the social appropriation of the very words used to express the privacy of pleasure.

Bernard Mandeville and Jean-Jacques Rousseau, an unlikely pair of Hobbes's disciples, sidestepped this issue by drawing a firm line between propensities and sociable pretensions. In the scene of sympathy, they deployed the terrible circumstances not of public execution but of a child being eaten by a pig, and found no difficulty in granting that every spectator would view it with horror and compassion. However, far from tending toward a moral virtue, such compassion is proof (for Mandeville) of nothing but a self-preservative desire to remove sights that are painful to the viewer; and (for Rousseau) a natural instinct that degenerates as soon as it is socialized (Mandeville 1924, 1:254; Rousseau 1993, 74). There is no species-love here, just an aversion to pain and a desire to restore pleasure to a single spectator. To go any further is either to weaken the instinct and strengthen a taste for barbarity ("revenge became terrible, and men bloody and cruel" [Rousseau 1993, 90]), or to make a lie of out of necessary ignorance, as when people identify compassion as the propensity leading to the foundation of charity schools: "What these People most pretend is the least and what they utterly deny is their greatest Motive" (Mandeville 1924, 1:281). John Trenchard, who shared Mandeville's view of charity schools, entered the same caveat with those who wish to idealize their pity: they are "amused by the play of words, and the sallies of imagination" (Trenchard 1995, 2:766).

Narratives of voyages are delivered as an extended and uncontrolled je ne sais quoi. They tell of paradises, monsters, outrageous sufferings, and miracles. They handle the scarcely expressible intensity of sensations experienced by the single voyager alone in the presence of things utterly new and unparalleled. Here is an autobiography that includes no concession to consensual standards of probability, and operates under no obligation to pretend that the first person singular shares interests with the public at large other than as a market for printed wares (Stewart 1993, 98). Often these narratives emphasize the unbridgeable gulf between the experience of the single self and the history of civil society, not simply by describing remarkable and incomparable things, but also by including accounts of castaways and mutineers, people whose links with the social world were decisively severed, and who had chosen (or been forced) to subsist in a precontractual state of nature.

The rhetoric of a traveler's tale of unknown lands and oceans most closely resembles the je ne sais quoi in its vaunted failure to communicate anything of significance. If solitary pleasure is to be summarized as "I know not what," or an experience comparable to no other, then the various ways of witnessing unparalleled or marvelous things is reducible to the assertion "Nothing you can imagine is equal to what I saw." Both statements, emerging from a first person singular in a state of extreme sensation, are predicated on nothing; yet it is out of that nothing that something is to be made, either as the gesture of sympathy on the part of an imaginative reader or as the fact of certain sensations experienced by a single person in a strange place. Self-cancellation and self-assertion, the two irreconcilable orientations of self-preservation (Greenblatt 1980, 23, 57; Habermas 1971, 276), closely resemble each other in terms of these contradictory juxtapositions of the self with nothing. When wonders are the medium of a daring ego, then the nothing with which these wonders are to be compared menaces the social order in proportion as it celebrates the libido of the traveler. But in its own defense, society wields a large inventory of abusive epithets and traditions, all expressive of the mendacity of sailors and the utter unreliability of their testimony, hurling the nothing back as the sum of their enchantments and lies. Shaftesbury was especially vehement in his contempt for the vacuity of this branch of authorship, where "he is ever completest and of the first rank who is able to speak of things the most unnatural and monstrous" (Shaftesbury 1964 1:223). Nevertheless, his comminations are necessary because the public has a taste for these narratives, not because they mistake them for truth, but because they are pleased by their extravagance.

With their own popularity in mind, narrators of voyages often appealed for sympathy despite acknowledging the odds against winning more solid approval. "Accounts of the manner how our Attempts miscarried," wrote the hapless privateer William Funnell, "I hope cannot but be very acceptable to the inquisitive Reader" (Funnell 1707, [ii]). Between the singular voyager and the public at large, there are ways of avoiding the nullification of the je ne sais quoi preached by Shaftesbury. Travelers' tales are frequently utopian, laced with enchanting descriptions of voluptuous sociality, as if trying to present self-preservation on a new plan, in which the right to personal pleasure might not conflict with a social structure. A first person narrative capable of providing a vivid and detailed eyewitness account of marvelous places, and restoring to salience the utopian promise of civil society (Habermas 1974, 58; Ricoeur 1986, 302), can fascinate an individual reader out of her skepticism. Desdemona gives a world of sighs to Othello's world of wonders, finding them as pitiful as they are strange.

"The tender virgins," said Shaftesbury, typifying Desdemona's response as the female relish for outlandish and superstitious yarns, "assume this tragic passion, of which they are highly susceptible, especially when a suitable kind of eloquence and action attends the character of the narrator . . . and [to indulge it] would frankly resign fathers, relations, countrymen, and country itself" (Shaftesbury 1964, 1:225). In other words, a reader like Desdemona is lost to society because she has become so closely implicated in the aesthetic effects of an assertive self, to the degree that she herself is nothing but its image or print. Shaftesbury allows nothing for her pleasure, or the love she feels in listening to reports from which he himself "takes nothing" (1:209).

I want briefly to trace these arguments about self-preservation in the work of Thomas Hobbes and John Locke, and in their successors (chiefly Mandeville and Shaftesbury), in order to show how the grounds of conflict between the self and civil society form a set of anxieties about the pleasure of traveling to strange places, and about the method of communicating it. The cause of the transition from savagery to civility is, according to contractual doctrine, the common desire for a guarantee of security. "The foresight of their own preservation" was instanced by Hobbes as the reason people choose to end "that miserable condition of Warre, which is necessarily consequent . . . to the natural Passions of men, when there is no visible Power to keep them in awe" (Hobbes 1968, 223). "Every one as he is *bound to preserve himself*," said Locke, "so ought he, as much as he can, to *preserve the rest of Mankind*" (Locke 1963, 311). Civil government commences therefore with "the Consent of the people" (431) and abridges "the passionate heats, or boundless extravagancy" that ventilate when there is no restriction upon the tyranny that one individual might impose upon others (312, 316). In these differing versions of the original contract, passion still yields to reason, and common sense predominates over vehemence and self-will.

Although they both imagined the history of self-preservation as a shift from the indulgence of passion to rational self-restraint, Hobbes and Locke disagreed about its causes. Because the state of nature is one of war in Hobbes's view, where no individual has the right to hold the means of self-preservation, only to fight for them (Hobbes 1841, xviii), a stark division exists between this and the advent of civil society. It is to be bridged only by the intervention of a sovereign power that precedes (although it still represents) the consent of the people. Hobbes knew the turbulence of war persists in civil society, and in some sense is its seal and guarantee

("All society therefore is for gain, or for glory; that is, not so much for love of our fellows, as for the love of ourselves" [5]); but he believed also that the advantage of obedience to the laws ("I mean, Laws living and Armed" [1971b, 59]) can escape no one in their senses. His, therefore, is a revolutionary narrative chronicling the immense change from nature to society. Locke, on the other hand, supposed a transition so smooth it is scarcely visible. In his state of nature, quite complex contractual arrangements already exist to preserve the self before the original contract is signed (Macpherson 1962, 211; Pocock 1975, 436). Each stage is a refinement of preservative art, from the primordial labor of gathering food, which preserves the self; to the property, which preserves labor; to the money, which preserves property; and finally to the government, which preserves the right to property so that it may contractually be acquired and alienated (Locke 1960, 327–44). In this continuum, society merely codifies and empowers "the Common Law of Reason" that operates in a state of nature (Locke 1963, 311, 319), ensuring each individual against the depredations and oppressions of those whose natural passions and political ambitions have become for whatever reason inordinate. "This Freedom from Absolute, Arbitrary Power, is so necessary to, and closely joyned with a Man's Preservation, that he cannot part with it, but by what forfeits his Preservation and Life together" (325). The civil self capable of framing this judgment is not radically different from the primitive or savage self that it replaced by the act of consent; for "he that would have been insolent and injurious in the woods of America, would not probably be much better in a Throne" (371).

By assuming a right to hold property prior to the advent of an armed law to make it good, Locke ran into a criticism that had already been made by Hobbes of those who believe that a contract without a sword will work. "How gottest thou this propriety, but from the magistrate?" he demanded scornfully [Hobbes 1841, 157]). "We would have our Security against all the World, upon Right of Property, without Paying for it: . . . . We may as well Expect that Fish, and Fowl should Boil, Rost, and Dish themselves, and come to the Table; and that Grapes should squeeze themselves into our Mouths, and have all other Contentments and ease which some pleasant Men have Related of the Land of Coquany" (1971b, 66). They who imagine they can appropriate things without authority, enter into a fantastic and utopian relation with material things—as fantastic as the narratives of alehouse braggarts (and mariners from distant seas) "that being met they pass their time in relating some stories . . . [and] if one relate some wonder, the rest will tell you miracles, if they have them; if not, they will feign them" (1841, 4). This interruption of the real history of civil society occurs when the self imagines it can compass its own preservation without the intervention of the law. In Locke's view, individuals are always under the obligation to preserve themselves, obedient to "this Fundamental, Sacred, and unalterable Law of Self-Preservation" (Locke 1960, 413). The same obligation requires them to renounce an original contract that breaches this law and interrupts the orderly progress of civil history—not a revolution so much as a restoration of the evolutionary continuum. Hobbes saw fantasy resulting from the assumption of individual autonomy, and reality from the advent of sovereign power; while Locke maintained quite the opposite opinion, seeing the arbitrary power of monarchs as the nightmare from which the people must awake in order to defend their right of self-preservation, and their sense of what is real.

Locke's fundamental law, however, is not just a law; it is also an instinct that human beings share with irrational animals. "The first and strongest Desire God Planted in Men, and wrought into the very Principles of their Nature [was] that of Self-Preservation" (Locke 1960: 244). In this economy of the passions, the extravagances supposedly controlled by the law are to some extent part of the law, and the reason for its existence. When individuals renounce an imperfect original contract, they recur to the instinctive and desiring side of their natures in order to reestablish the groundwork of self-control. In this respect, their actions may differ in scope and situation from those of a monarch who usurps the rights of the people, but not in kind. The train of "Pretences," "Actings," and "Artifices" (453, 463) that characterize arbitrary power must mingle to some extent in the exertions of those crossing the boundary between a fundamental law and the strongest human instinct. The same paradox informs Locke's theory of property. It is first of all acquired by means of incorporating things so that they are consubstantial with the self: "He hath mixed his Labour with, and joyned to it something that is his own, and thereby makes it his Property" (329). Ultimately, the right to what is literally one's own is disembodied and vindicated in laws and contracts that detach the self from its incorporated part in an exchange for money, whose value is solely determined by a consensual je ne sais quoi, "Fancy or Agreement" (342). Taste alone confirms two widely different forms of ownership, requiring in the end laws to defend a self distributed in discrete material forms. Any contradiction between the preservation of things and the self those things were intended to preserve—and Marxist historians have revealed plenty in the working of the eighteenth-century laws defending property—arises from Locke's belief that passions might prove the bulwark of reason, and that an imagined continuum, based on increasingly abstract representations of value and identity, might forge a real history of civil society.

In arguing for a continuous history of self-preservation, Locke plainly had no intention of making an opening for fantasy. It is precisely in the sober articulation of that history that the reasonableness of an enduring self is tested, and the instruments of political resistance to arbitrary power are forged. To this end, he invested as deeply in a theory of personal identity as in a theory of property, supposing that a self preserved constitutes a narrative, a biography. Personal identity he defined as the continuity of present sensations with the memory of earlier impressions, "[a]nd as far as this consciousness can be extended backwards to any past action of thought, so far reaches the identity of that person; it is the same self now that it was then, and it is by the same self with this present one that now reflects on it, that that action was done" (Locke 1961, 1:281 [2.27.9]). Out of this consciousness arises the self forensically conceived as responsible for its own actions, endowed with rights and obligations (Hacking 1995, 146; Cox 1980). It is legible in what one of Locke's more volatile disciples called "the history-book of what passes in a man's own mind" (Sterne 1983, 70). A false dominion arises in the mind from misremembered biography, trains of associated ideas whose conjunction is accidental, and whose government is compared with madness (Locke 1961, 1:335 [2.33.4]). Under the influence of passion, false memory opens the gates of Bedlam, rousing and tumbling "out of their dark cells into open daylight . . . ideas . . . which had otherwise lain quiet and unregarded" (Locke 1961, 1:120 [2.10.7]; quoted in Hacking 1995, 203). This scene of insanity, run in reverse by Jonathan Swift in his "Digression concerning the Use and Improvement of Madness in a Commonwealth," has recently been explained by Ian Hacking as the beginning of a politics of memory designed to select a civil self from the multiple personalities produced in the trances of passion. If personal identity is to be effective, then it has to expel all symptoms of a self not biographically defined, and suppress all material exorbitant to such a narrative (Hacking 1995, 145–46). On this account, Locke called the substitutions of sympathy mere fantasy, for if a person were truly able to enter into the feelings of another, then "Seth, Ismael, Socrates, Pilate, St. Austin and Caesar Borgia [would be] the same man" (Locke 1961, 1:278 [2.27.6]).

Hobbes treated the threat of alternative selves differently. He adapted the structure of the original contract to an internalization of the power of the sovereign. Self-consistency is acquired by means of a representative self, which governs through the authorization of the represented self: but once such authority is acquired, it can never be relinquished without anarchy. The one body of Leviathan is constituted out of a layer of these "personations," or representative figures, who derive by covenant the immutable right of being delegates: "A Multitude of Men, are made One Person, when they are by one man, or one Person, Represented . . . for it is the Unity of Representer, not the Unity of the Represented, that maketh the Person One" (Hobbes 1968, 220). Finally, in each individual, unity is guaranteed by the level of representation: a mad person can acquire a civil identity by being represented (1968, 219). A person operating outside this system of artificial unity, whose words or actions are entirely his own, is thus "called a Naturall Person," but a person who acquires the right of representing others is "a Feigned or Artificiall person" (217). Hobbes was unafraid of the negative association of representation with feigning, for although "an Idol, or meer Figment of the brain, may be Personated," it is without authority, because "idols cannot be Authors; for an Idol is nothing" (220). By means of an artifice, the natural passions— stimulated by "an irregular Appetite to Riches, to Power, and to sensual Pleasures" (1971a, 57)—are subdued to the rule of reason, and the unity of the self is preserved. However, it is always possible for the natural self to evade these restrictions, and to proclaim its enjoyment of passions such as wonder, revenge, and curiosity in a vainglorious and egoistic way, an enchanted or trancelike condition characterized by Hobbes as triumph: "Internal gloriation or triumph of the mind, is that passion which proceedeth from the imagination or conception of our own power, above the power of him that contendeth with us" (1994, 50).

A reverse symmetry organizes these rival theories of the original contract. Hobbes supposed the process of civility as a single, egoistic self dividing into two, forming a represented and representative self; and the corruption of civility is the reverse, when the civil reflection of represented self is shattered by the singularity of vainglory. Locke, on the other hand, held the unity of the social self to be derived from nature gradually civilizing itself, a process ruined by the fissions of madness and sympathy. These self-divisions corrupt its unity, rather than confirming it. Hobbes redeemed even madness by representation, but Locke's story of insanity requires complete suppression of the nonlucid interval (Locke 1961, 1:339 [2.233.14]). What Hobbes would have called glorious self-assertion, therefore, Locke would have called self-loss. Of course, each had planted the seed of their own kind of corruption, Hobbes with the sheer foundational autonomy of the sovereign, and Locke with original passions outside the law that eventually produce the law. These contradictions range both of them on either side of the je ne sais quoi, Hobbes construing the nothing told by the "I" as an aggressively private fit of glory, and Locke understanding it as an ontological crisis, self-explosion. That is to say, Locke construed the failure of a true narrative of self-preservation to consist in something like Hobbes's state of war, while Hobbes believed that glory arises from a fantastic relation to things characteristic of Locke's notion of property.

These two views of the self isolated by passion would influence the next generation of political thinkers. Locke's pupil, Lord Shaftesbury, identified the unity of the self as the continuity of its natural and civil sides, while Mandeville, following Hobbes, understood the civil self as an equilibrium of two selves. According to the one, the self is lost when it ceases to act like itself; according to the other, this occurs only when the self assumes that it is undivided from itself.

Shaftesbury believed no conflict existed between the propensity for self-preservation and the principles of civil society, for to have "no love of country, community, or anything in common, would be the same as to be insensible even of the plainest means of self-preservation, and most necessary condition of self-enjoyment." He later wondered, with a glance at Hobbes, why "the wit of man should so puzzle this cause as to make civil government and society appear a kind of invention of art" (Shaftesbury 1964, 1:74–75). To imagine prehistory as a condition of life abruptly divided from the social is a useless fiction as far as Shaftesbury was concerned, "a pretended state of nature" (2:80). The natural desire for self-preservation is expressed as a wish for "that which is preservative of the kind itself, and conducing to its welfare and support" (1:74). To be in the desperate condition of Job, where "skin for skin; yea, all that a man hath will he give for his life," is to be destitute of a self to preserve (1:82). For his own part, Shaftesbury disdained to think of himself as divided between a natural and an artificial, or a private and a public self. He instructed himself not to act "two different Persons" but rather to "recollect thy Self wholly within thy Self" (PRO 30/24/27/10, p. 59; quoted in Klein 1994, xii). Thus he aimed to preserve the "genuine, true, and natural self," "a nobler self" distinct from "its representative or counterfeit," whose simple outlines and expressive signs are recognized in the same moment that a public is recognized, and whose interests are wholly served in the disinterested pursuit of benevolence (Shaftesbury 1964, 1:74, 182–83; Cox 1980, 17).

How consistent with this aim of a unitary "uncantonised" self (Shaftesbury 1964, 1:76) is an exhortation delivered by the self in the first person to the self in the second person, where the object—the self to be recollected—must be assumed to be less entire than the subject—the "I" who recollects—is a question posed by Shaftesbury's opponents. He himself imagined a critic asking, "Who can thus multiply himself into two persons and be his own subject?" (1:105). It is important to this way of thinking, therefore, to have a criterion of self-preservation that avoids the perils of a self reflecting upon its own incompleteness. So Francis Hutcheson identified in everyone "some secret Sense, which determines our Approbation without regard to Self-Interest" (Hutcheson 1725, 112), and he called it the moral sense: a propensity that acts like a principle. He emphasized its unreflective secrecy, "so very secret, that many a kind compassionate heart was never conscious of it, but felt . . . a secret bond between us and our fellow-creatures" (1750, 15), a bond preserving the self from doubled and divided assessments. In his emphasis on the immediacy of the moral sense, Hutcheson was laying out the direct connection between sensations of pleasure and social utility, and between the je ne sais quoi and benevolence, with no obscuring medium separating them. In order to establish this unreflective compatibility between the natural and the social affections, he sentimentalized the bonding element of honor in order to explain the action of the moral sense. He said, "Honour presupposes a Sense of something amiable, besides Advantage, a Sense of Excellence in a publick Spirit" (1725, 203), thereby associating his own notion of unreflective secrecy with Hobbes's estimate of honour as "properly of its own nature, secret, and internall in the heart" (Hobbes 1968, 666).

Bernard Mandeville, the formidable antagonist of advocates of the moral sense, relied on Hobbes's division between a natural and an artificial self in order to suppose a difference between self-love and self-liking. This difference later provided the basis of Rousseau's celebrated distinction between the pure motive of self-preservation—*amour de soi*—and its corrupt reflexive variant—*amour propre*. The representation or impersonation of the natural by the artificial man in Hobbes's account of personal identity was imagined by Mandeville as the savage and the social selves entering into a conditional relationship of goodwill. The self wishes the best for the self, and its wishes are answered by an improvement that nevertheless cannot lose the outlines of the wishing self in its wished-for development without suffering self-loss. In a pregnant observation on this relationship, he said, "It is that Self we wish well to; and therefore we cannot wish for any Change in ourselves, but with a Proviso, that . . . that Part of us, that wishes, should still remain: for take away that Consciousness you had of yourself, whilst you was wishing, and tell me pray, what part of you it is, that could be the better for the Alteration you wish'd for?" (Mandeville 1924, 2:137). By giving equal play to Hobbes's idea of the artificial person and to Shaftesbury's (and soon to be Rousseau's) high opinion of the natural or precivil self, Mandeville showed that neither the rebellious natural passions contemned by Hobbes nor the artifice deprecated by Shaftesbury and Rousseau are inimical to "the Business of Self-Preservation" (1:344), which he understood to be the diversifying and intensifying of pleasure. If Hutcheson thought that social virtue is the product of benevolence multiplied by ability (Hutcheson 1725, 168), Mandeville argued that in fact it is the product of the number of our desires multiplied by the arts of circumventing obstacles to their satisfaction (Mandeville 1924, 1:344). In arriving at the sociable craftiness that appreciates the sweetness of deferred pleasure, the self finds a wider range for its propensities: "It seems to be that, which continually furnishes us with that Relish we have for Life, even when it is not worth having . . . it doubles our Happiness in Prosperity . . . it is the Mother of Hopes, and the End as well as the Foundation of our best Wishes" (2:135–36).

Although "there is nothing more sincere in any Creature than his Will, Wishes and Endeavours to preserve himself" (1:200), the human animal is destined to be taught "by Art to consult in an opposite Method the same Self-Preservation" (205). Thus "[M]any of the Calamities that generally attend a too eager Pursuit after Pleasure" are abated while the "luxurious Enjoyment of all worldly Comforts" is considerably enhanced (47). It is, therefore, a maxim with him (as it is certainly not with Shaftesbury and Hutcheson) that "to be at once well-bred and sincere, is no less than a Contradiction" (185). No contradiction exists, however, between the natural and the civil selves, since the wishes of the one circumscribe the pleasures, no matter how oblique, of the other. A propensity hindered is a sociable pleasure heightened, and therefore Mandeville demonstrated that the paradoxes of self-preservation conform to the primordial logic of the human organism, which at its farthest sociable extent is never out of reach of the senses, and always capable of finding a relish in life, even it if is not worth having. In suicide itself, Mandeville maintained, "there is a palpable Intention of Kindness to ones self" (2:136). Here he meant the natural self, the wishing and desiring self whose ends are achieved in the wished and invented self; and not, as Hobbes would have maintained (specifically in the case of suicide [Hobbes 1968, 269, 320]), the artificial self who stands in authority over the interests of the natural one. Mandeville believed the "I" always knows what pleases it; otherwise, its ability to cause itself pleasure would cease.

A fascinating parallel develops between Mandeville and Shaftesbury in their contemplation of these two selves, far-reaching in this study of voyage literature. They are united in believing in a connection between the natural self and the citizen that involves no radical alteration of the primitive personality as it develops civilized attributes. Rather, the instincts for self-gratification are strengthened by the passage from nature to art, so that the objects of public good are deeply implicated in private pleasures. The divergence between them appears to lie simply in emphasis. Shaftesbury wished to affirm that the public objectives of natural propensities— fellowship, sympathy, altruism, patriotism—are the true destinations, both historically and ethically speaking, of the self, and that every worthy individual is conscious of this. Social progress brings about the knowledge of the moral sense, at which point the biography of the self is consummated within the history of civility. On the other hand, Mandeville was always announcing his loyalty to the animal pleasures, for without them the inducement to appear modest, benevolent, and honorable would disappear: "It is impossible that Man, mere fallen Man, should act with any other View but to please himself" (Mandeville 1924, 1:348). This state of affairs cannot produce a narrative of amelioration and virtue. The self wishes itself other only to the degree that it wishes itself well, and therefore cannot be conscious of progressing to a higher stage, only to more interesting "operose Contrivances" of self-delight (2:137, 1:119). By insisting that this is no paradox, Mandeville revealed Shaftesbury's professed loyalty to the self to be absurd because it requires the wishing self to disappear into the wished self, losing all title to pleasure. No matter how vehemently Shaftesbury insisted upon the integrity of the self as it has socially evolved, Mandeville maintained that he suffers from the common limitation of being obliged to express this integrity in a self-divided way: "I tell my Antagonist that his Conscience flies in his Face, while his Tongue is preparing to refute me" (1:349). And as Shaftesbury was intolerant of any imputation of imposture, it is plain (at least to Mandeville, for whom it was axiomatic that a social creature is a hypocrite) that his commitment to self-unity requires one of the two selves to disappear. In a biography such as Shaftesbury's, Mandeville concluded, "[T]he Person wishing, must be destroyed before the Change could be entire" (2:137); and that would be suicide indeed.

In fact, Lawrence Klein's work among Shaftesbury's private papers has shown that Mandeville's analysis was shrewd, and that Shaftesbury's inner life was frequently in a turmoil requiring the artificer-self to forge the other, allegedly natural self into "One intire & self same Man" (Klein 1994, 83–90). In his memoranda to himself, he struggles to find a self his other self has lost: "Who am I? . . . I [may] indeed be said to be lost, or have lost My Self" (PRO 30/24/27/10, pp. 134, 285; quoted in Klein 1994, 73). For Mandeville, such a confession would amply illustrate his doctrine: "The imaginary Notions that Men may be Virtuous without Self-denial are a vast Inlet to Hypocrisy, which being once made habitual, we must not only deceive others, but likewise become altogether unknown to our selves" (Mandeville 1924, 1:331). The *Fable of the Bees* (1724) is his allegory of such self-alienation on a national scale, describing how a hive of bees, who enjoy every advantage of a sociable commerce, imagine they want the extra virtue of honesty, and by emigrating to a hollow tree where they can practice frugality and candor, lose everything by having their wish granted. Mandeville's reading of Hobbes teaches him that Shaftesbury and the bees have arrived at that disjunction of the natural and the artificial person where all that remains is an idol of virtue representing sheer privation, "for an Idol is nothing" (Hobbes 1968, 220). Mandeville accuses Shaftesbury and the bees of having reached the last stage of hypocrisy, when the art of deception loses its ulterior motive, and their wishing selves disappear into the factitious unity of their wished-for selves, to the ruin of the business of self-preservation (Mandeville 1924, 1:344).

At this extreme of self-deception, according to Mandeville's allegory, the "Paradise" formed from the congregation of substantial pleasures multiplied and intensified by the social duty of hindering and disguising them, is hollowed out into "a vain EUTOPIA seated in the Brain" (1:24, 37). Any report from such a quarter would be a literalization of the *je ne sais quoi* in the sense of conveying absolutely no information, and indeed this is where the fable has to end. Following Shelley Burtt's characterization of Mandeville's insights into the nature of moral virtue as "fundamentally anthropological" (Burtt 1992, 137), it is possible to see in his traversing the poles of nature and artifice a persistent desire to connect cultural forms, such as the politeness recommended by Shaftesbury, with the reason for their invention, namely the natural desire of pleasure. In calling this kind of analysis "the Prospect of concatenated Events" (Mandeville 1924, 1:91), he occupied a vantage point resembling Shaftesbury's "high road of demonstration" (Shaftesbury 1964, 2:283), from which he planned to reduce the obstructions and windings of human behavior to intelligibility, despite his warning in the *Fable* against letting a such a delusional teleology thwart blind but successful practice. On the one hand, he knew that the splitting of the self provides a mode of self-preservation consistent with luxurious enjoyments; on the other, he was aware that to be historically conscious of such a division is to become suicidally nostalgic for a whole self, virtuously entire. But the only way he could make his point was to produce a history of self-deception that rejects its own tendency as utopian and effectually suicidal, and to argue instead for the perpetual ignorance of a middle state. That is to say, he attached Locke's model of biography, favoring a single forensic self, to Hobbes's model of internal government, requiring a represented and a representing self, in order to recommend what neither would endorse and what is in itself unhistorizable: namely, a set of oxymorons such as vicious benevolence, certain hope, and lewd chastity, which, by identifying as "palpable Nonsense of the heterogeneous Compound" (Mandeville 1924, 1:141), he expected somehow to transcend. To write a history at all, Mandeville had to carry his theme toward a clarification of his paradoxical rule of pleasure, either as the example of the perverse self-sacrificing virtue he held up for mockery, or as a theory that renders delusional virtue at least culturally probable, since it is ethically absurd.

But the change that overtakes the wishing self when it desires to be nothing but what it wishes, is extremely difficult to explain. If it is a rupture in the continuum of personal identity, similar to the crises of self-loss Locke discussed, when strange ideas are roused and tumbled out of their dark cells by turbulent and tempestuous passions (Hacking 1995, 219); or if it is like the fantastic intervals of egoistic self-delight that Hobbes called "internal gloriation of the mind" and compared with the madness of Don Quixote (Hobbes 1994, 50), then loss of pleasure is not the issue, since the self seizes a wild alternative existence that amounts to "nothing" only in the sense that the je ne sais quoi introduces nothing as a measure of unprecedented delight. On the other hand, if the self has sacrificed itself to an insubstantial fantasy of virtue, the circumstances under which pleasure was found no longer to be a motive for action need to be specified, together with an explanation of why a plan of self-denial automatically excludes pleasure, since previously (under the system of hypocrisy) it enhanced it.

As a student of culture, Mandeville was exclusively concerned with the latter hypothesis, and he wanted to say that pleasure disappears the moment the means of achieving it are mistaken for ends. To make the case, he had to suppose a radical change from nature plus culture to culture alone. It is a change he found difficult to handle. Hutcheson noted that Mandeville fudged the issue of natural and social acquirements (Hutcheson 1750, 74), and this is nowhere so apparent as in his discussion of honor, where those elements that are "adventitious, and acquir'd by Culture" (Mandeville 1924, 2:89), such as the refusal to exhibit fear, are blended with those that are physiological and natural, such as the symptoms of shame (1:67). Similarly, in his handling of charity, there is a culture of public benefaction and a physiology of compassion (254–55). Mandeville returned again and again to honor and dueling in an attempt to trace the path leading from private interest to self-destruction; but the transition from one to the other defeated him, as it does in the *Fable*, where no reason is given for the bees' change of direction other than the overwhelming of natural desires by acquired ones, an outcome variously presented as caprice and historical necessity. But the lesson of ignorance Mandeville teaches at the expense of a virtuous moral is at odds with the worldly wisdom that enforces it, unless it is able to include a definitive account of how culture extinguishes the desire of pleasure.

Mandeville seems to get close to the issue when talking of impersonated pleasure. If "we are always forc'd to do what we please" (1:349), then his earlier distinction ("I don't call things Pleasures which Men say are best, but such as they seem to be most pleased with" [151]) looks both ways: to pleasure that is well concealed and to pleasure that is nothing but its appearance. But the "excruciating ambivalence" surrounding the discourse of virtue in the early eighteenth century (Pocock 1975, 428) here afflicts enjoyment too, for if seeming pleasures can still be called pleasant by the arch-theorist of luxurious enjoyment, who is to say that a forced pleasure is unpleasurable? Here is the je ne sais quoi in all its glory, complicating a nothing Mandeville wanted to render unequivocal in his concatenation of the phases of self-loss, and rendering unaccountable a process Mandeville always declared to be so, despite his itch to be concatenating causes and justifying the ways of vice to virtue. With a desire for clarity that is unmistakably utopian, he univocalized the pun of Utopia to Eutopia, trying to eliminate the heterogeneous element from the compound in order to reveal it as the empty idol of perfection. He was reluctant to treat it as a fine idea sprung from its opposite, or to conceive of his own analysis of civil society—where events indicative of the simultaneous absence and presence of moral virtue have been concatenated for the amusement of the reader and the benefit of the nation—as the counterpart of this utopian project.

Nevertheless, he conceded, "Tho' many Discoveries have been made in the World of Self-love, there is yet abundance of Terra Incognita left behind" (Mandeville 1924, 1:230), as if admitting that the connections between the inner and outer spheres of self-preservation are more awkward than his allegory implies. The utopia in the brain and the paradisal possibilities of the terra incognita provide political philosophers as well as mariners opportunities for finding more than nothing in a blank space. The metaphor of the psyche as a map of uncharted territory overlaps the metaphor of the voyage as a probe of the secrets of the mind, giving a global scale to the difficulties of the je ne sais quoi. "What is this Earth and Sea of which I have seen so much, when is it produc'd, and what am I?" demands Robinson Crusoe, putting the two conundrums side by side (Defoe 1972, 92). Prior to the extravagant apostrophe to his uncertain self in the *Treatise of Human Nature* ("Where am I, or what? From what causes do I derive my existence, and to what condition shall I return?"), David Hume compares himself to a forlorn navigator, "who having struck on many shoals, and having narrowly escap'd shipwreck . . . has yet the temerity to put out to sea in the same leaky weather-beaten vessel, and even carries his ambition so far as to think of compassing the globe" (Hume 1969, 311). The exclamation and the reflection correspond closely to Shaftesbury's: "Where am I? or what?" he asks, adding to these fundamental questions a maritime gloss, "Where are we? . . . on board what vessel? Whither bound? . . . under whose pilotship, government or protection" (Shaftesbury 1964, 2:254). The answer to these queries is figured as another voyage, not "the unnatural and unhappy excursions, rovings, or expeditions of our ungoverned fancies and opinions over a world of riches, honours, and other ebbing and flowing goods," but an exploration of the desert island of the mind, "the interior regions and recesses . . . the hollow caverns of deep thought, the private seats of fancy, and the wastes and wildernesses, as well as the more fruitful and cultivated tracts of the obscure climate" (284–86). The successful outcome of this voyage is advertised by Shaftesbury as the "passage from *terra incognita* to the visible world" (286), a figurative version of Prospero's and Crusoe's resocializations, performed in obedience to the legend of the fool's cap of the world, *nosce teipsum* (fig. 1). He will be an eyewitness of the discovery of the "genuine, true, and natural self" (1:183). On the other hand, those who have really gone to the ends of the earth, "tale-gathering in those idle deserts," and returned like Othello with tall stories to corrupt innocent ears, have turned their minds into a wilderness, dwelling in "a desert, and . . . the horridest of solitudes even when in the midst of society" (1:225, 335).

Mandeville had relatively little to say about voyaging, but if the terra

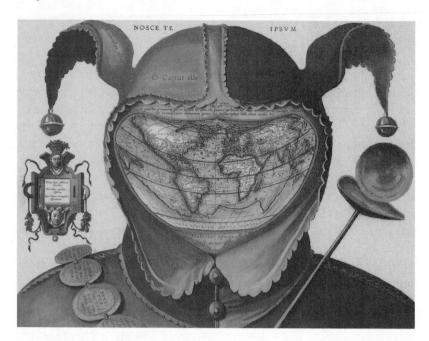

FIGURE I   *The Fool's Cap World Map.* Anonymous painting, circa 1590. © National Maritime Museum, London.

incognita figures as the undiscovered part of self-love, immune (like honor and utopian inclinations) to his analysis of acculturation, then seafaring and discoveries in the New World have a part to play in the enigma. The *Fable* is, after all, a story of migration and colonization, cast in its customary figure of bees swarming to a distant spot. That empty place, like the terra incognita on the maps, or like the vain utopia seated in the brain, is expressive of a plan of virtue too austere for nature, and too difficult for the inquiring mind to compass. On either side of the hollow tree, Mandeville arranges imperial models that stand for virtue (in the manner of the reformed bees) and for sheer pleasure (in that of their previous selves). Of the Spartans, who provide the ancient model of self-denial, he observes, "Certainly there never was a Nation whose greatness was more empty than theirs . . . and though they had been Masters of the World . . . the only thing they could be proud of, was, that they enjoyed nothing" (Mandeville 1924, 1:245). The Spaniards, on the other hand, were proud of enjoying inexhaustible treasure rifled and mined from the Americas, but their voluptuous plan of life is as empty as the Spartan system of virtue. "Thus by too much Money . . . Spain is from a fruitful and well-peopled Country, with all its mighty Titles and Possessions, made a barren and empty Thoroughfare, thro' which Gold and Silver pass from America to the rest of the World" (196). In both cases, the je ne sais quoi is strictly nothing. Between these two coinciding extremes remain the Dutch at Batavia, clinging to their cantonments by pretending to a grandeur and military strength that they do not possess in order to overawe the Javanese, who otherwise could dispatch them when they pleased (163). The Dutch are like those who impersonate virtue for an indirect gain, unable to predict much of the future and bereft of a history from which to draw lessons. But at least their experiment in the terra incognita keeps them from emptiness. Likewise the sailors from the East Indies, whose improvidence Mandeville accuses, and who throw money in the street when they cannot spend enough of it, may be ignorant of the risks they run and the nature of true pleasure, but they are not quite enjoying nothing. For all his acuity, Mandeville can get no further than the ignorance of their middle state, "the Distraction of dissolute Sailors . . . roaring along with Fiddles before them" (118).

No doubt Hume's and Shaftesbury's impatience with the voyage literature that began to dominate the book market by the early part of the eighteenth century, much of it describing the vicinity of the terra incognita, stemmed from the impediments it placed in the way of knowing anything for a truth. In his essay "Of Miracles," Hume compares "the miraculous accounts . . . wonderful adventures, strange men, and uncouth manners" of mariners' narratives with the "monstrous and improbable fictions" of Ariosto (Hume 1903, 528). In a celebrated passage that includes his intemperate reading of Othello's wooing of Desdemona, Shaftesbury condemns "the barbarian customs, savage manners, Indian wars, and wonders of the terra incognita" to be found in travellers' tales: "These are in our present day what books of chivalry were in those of our forefathers . . . written by friars and missionaries, pirates and renegades, sea-captains and trusty travellers . . . [who] dwell with the highest contentment on . . . monstrous accounts of monstrous men and manners" (Shaftesbury 1964, 1:222). It is directly with the problems of novelty and taste that Hume and Shaftesbury engaged, for discoveries of things so wonderful that they have no parallel or precedent are useless for a history of the world or a biography of the self. They leave the unknown spaces of the world and the mind still unknown, and encourage the nonutilitarian propensity to be ignorantly pleased with enchantments of which no one can ever give a full account. And in this respect, a voyage to the terra incognita behaves exactly like a romance.

The debate about romance in the eighteenth century is often conducted in a strictly pedagogical fashion, as in Samuel Johnson's fourth *Rambler* (1750), Charlotte Lennox's *The Female Quixote* (1752), or Jane Austen's *Northanger Abbey* (1818), where the effects of improbable narratives on the unfurnished minds of naïve readers are shown to be boundless credulity, and an expectation of stunning adventures that real life will never afford. The model for this critique of romance is Miguel de Cervantes's *Don Quixote,* the story of a man so deluded by reading tales of chivalry that he takes to the road as a knight at arms, and mistakes everything he meets for an adventure. Don Quixote represents all those individual readers who, like Desdemona, succumb to the allure of improbable narratives, and who, in turn metamorphosed by their pleasure into aesthetic objects, extend the same temptation to subsequent readers. Indeed, Quixote is perfectly aware he is enchanted, and not at all disconcerted to find that he is in print. The spread of his madness, especially the shattering of his self ("I know very well who I am . . . I know that I may not only be the persons I have named, but also the twelve peers of France" [Cervantes 1970, 1:32]), helps to explain why Shaftesbury regarded books of chivalry and voyages as more than simply a nuisance. "Cruel spectacles and barbarities contaminate and corrupt the mind," he declared, turning it via the representation of monstrosity toward monstrosity itself: "Our relish or taste must of necessity grow barbarous, whilst barbarian customs, savage manners, Indian wars, and wonders of the terra incognita, employ our leisure hours" (Shaftesbury 1964, 2:218–22). As good taste is the means of arriving at polite consensus, and as romance is almost always cited as evidence of a bad or barbarous taste, "the Antipodes of Good Breeding" (PRO 30/244/22/4, fols. 153–56; quoted in Klein 1994, 152), it must be understood as a force fundamentally uncivil, appealing to those propensities for mindless pleasure (of which curiosity is chief) that turn readers into monsters: "Now the greatest rarities in the world are monsters. So that the study and relish [of them] becomes at last in reality monstrous" (Shaftesbury 1964, 2:253). He is measuring the interval between Othello's anthropophagi and Iago's beast with two backs. Shaftesbury's anxieties about the state of his self, however, indicate a degree of quixotism on his own part, lodged in a region of his own mind he names the terra incognita, where the libidinal, enchantable ego appears as "this Monster to be subdu'd" (PRO 30/24/24/13; quoted in Klein 1994, 131). It is common, therefore, in readings and rewritings of the story of Don

Quixote to insist upon the hero's or heroine's eventual repudiation of their delusions.

The terra incognita, the unmapped space of the world and mind, is a habitat of monsters that are the vehicles of an extravagant self-assertion whose only narrative form is romance. Hobbes said, "Iron Men, flying Horses, and a thousand other such thinges . . . are easily fayned by them that dare. . . . I can allow a Geographer to make, in the Sea, a fish or a ship, which by the scale of his mappe would be two or three hundred mile long, and thinke it done with out the precincts of his undertaking; but when he paynts an Elephant so, I presently apprehend it as ignorance, and a playne confession of *Terra incognita*" (Hobbes 1971a, XX; quoted in Davenant 1971, 51). But it can be an interested ignorance, the expression of "an irregular Appetite to Riches, to Power, and to sensual Pleasures" (Hobbes 1971b, 57). "Internal gloriation or triumph of the mind" he associated with a company of storytellers, where each individual is keen to outdo the other in a war of words, so "if one relate some wonder, the rest will tell you miracles, if they have them; if not, they will feign them" (Hobbes 1841, 4). Such improbable narratives are comparable with Quixote's adventures, "as when a man imagineth himself to do the actions whereof he readeth in some romant. . . . And the gallant madness of Don Quixote is nothing else but an expression of such height of vain glory as reading of romants may produce in pusillanimous men" (Hobbes 1994, 51, 63).

Pusillanimous they may be, but the interaction of romance and new worlds imparts to the narrators of the one and the discoverers of the other a wild but indisputable place in history. Richard Hurd supposed that what Shaftesbury called monsters, "strange things told and believed in the discovery of the new world," were the originals of "the specious miracles" of romance (Hurd 1911, 98, 110). Contrariwise, Adam Smith suggested that the colonization of the West Indies was the accidental consequence of men actively pursuing absurd fantasies of cities of gold, for "even wise men are not always exempt from such strange delusions" (Smith 1976, 2:563). In his calendar of discoveries, Peter Heylyn lists the terra incognita as a challenge unequalled in romance: "Here we are upon a new and strange Adventure, which no Knight Errant ever undertook before." Not only does he recommend books of chivalry as models that may animate their readers to noble achievements in these unknown lands, "such high conceptions as really may make him fit for great undertaking," he supposes also that in the vast southern continent the actual location of romance is to be found, "such Islands, Provinces, and Kingdoms, in the

Books of Errantry, which have no being in the known part of the World, and therefore must be sought in this" (Heylyn 1667, 1089, 1094).

In recent discussions of the contribution of romance toward the conquest of New Spain, a similar indeterminacy exists regarding the possible cause and effect of exploration. Stephen Greenblatt argues that romance was a repository for the wonders experienced by the conquistadors, a place where they could be stored and appropriated. When, for example, Hernando Cortes and Bernal Diaz del Castillo entered the fabulous city of Mexico and thought they might be dreaming, their knowledge of *Amadis de Gaul* reassured them that what they had before them was a conquerable and alienable marvel, and that what they mistook for a dream was a moment of imperial history (Greenblatt 1991, 129–35). Anthony Pagden identifies in romance a textual model that under extreme conditions, when neither classical history nor Christian Scripture could provide a model for what was happening in the New World, could assimilate wonders and miracles. Romance came to the rescue when "nothing could be made intelligible in terms of an alternative non-scriptural authority" (Pagden 1993, 52). That is to say, it made a story out of the encounter with the terra incognita that was not history or biography, yet did some justice to the passions it aroused.

The bad press received by romance in the work of Shaftesbury and Hume, where the barbarity of the thing attaches to the taste for reading it, is to be explained in the terms proposed by Hobbes as gloriation of the mind, an impudent and uncivil self-assertion, of which nations as well as individuals may be guilty. Essays on the standardization of taste almost always invoke romance as exorbitant to polite consensus because it presents an opportunity for identifying with actions and indulging feelings banned under the social contract of self-preservation. Romance rehearses "that miserable condition of Warre" and "the passionate heats, or boundless extravancy" that supervene when the tyrannizing imagination is unloosed (Hobbes 1968, 223; Locke 1960, 312, 316). Smith suggested that a barbarous existence (from the point of view of young people, at least) offers a compendium of these pleasures: "The life of a savage . . . seems to be a life either of profound indolence, or of great and astonishing adventures; and both these qualities serve to render the description of it agreeable to the imagination" (Smith 1980, 251). Here is the "enchanted" side of the self, its sensations emancipated from historical and social patterns (Cascardi 1992, 32–34). The extravagance of romance, what Henry James called its "fantasy of unrelatedness," reacts with a condition of modernity that Bolingbroke had described as the sense of events being "original, un-prepared, single and un-relative" (Bolingbroke 1752a, 41). If pleasure is the exclusive goal of the wishing self, as Mandeville claimed, then it will be felt with greatest intensity and least emptiness in these dehistorized moments that Locke compared to the emptying of a madhouse, that Hobbes depicted as the onset of pure egoism, and that J. G. A. Pocock has compared to the trances of shamans and pythonesses, "this self-deification of the auto-intoxicated mind" (Pocock 1998, 22). From the point of view of the assertive first person, however, all things under the regime of enchantment acquire the glamour of miracles, free-standing occasions of wonder, of which the only account that can be given is that they are indeed wonderful (Cascardi 1992, 83, 101, 104).

It is clear that what Mandeville was attempting in *The Fable of the Bees* was something like a romance of the enchanted ego, when generic necessity turned it into a utopia. Although he presented this outcome as a contradictory and self-defeating whim of creatures ambushed by a specious moral sense, utopias and romance have much in common. Some early romances include the rediscovery of paradise in India (Grove 1995, 21), and Columbus, the Almiranto Admirans, rose to the challenge by finding paradise in Hispaniola (Daston and Park 1998, 147). Among the romances of the New World, utopias play a real part too. Thomas More lodged his fiction in the fourth of Amerigo Vespucci's voyages, while Vasco de Quiroga founded towns on the model of Utopia near Mexico City and Michoacan that survived for more than fifty years (Zavala 1955, 10–19). Part of the knightly quest often includes a utopian interlude, the visit to a magical castle built of gleaming chrysolites and chalcedony, inhabited by people frozen in time who perform endless and elaborate ceremonies, breathing poignant refrains until the arrival of the hero brings all this artifice to its exquisite consummation. Of Tenochtitlan, Bernal Diaz del Castillo recorded, "It was like the enchantments they tell of in the legend of Amadis, on account of the great towers and cues and buildings rising from the water, and all built of masonry" (Diaz 1996, 190). In *Don Quixote,* the Cave of Montesinos is a hollow space where the hero's desires are fulfilled amidst a formal architectural and ritual unity uncorrupted by time or chance. What is truly utopian in these visions of romance, however, is the imminent disappearance of the vision, the coexistence of absolute perfection with the presentiment of its absence. Eventually Quixote confesses that the Cave of Montesinos was a lie composed while he was lodged in a dark hole in the ground. Diaz adds, "Of all these wonders that I then beheld . . . all is overthrown and lost, nothing left standing" (192). Every place-name used by More's Raphael Hythloday declares the nonexistence of the land he has discovered.

Anthony Pagden suggests that reports from the New World achieved an extratextual intensity that even romance could not entirely comprehend. Intruding into the self-sufficiency of the "found" and "edited" text of chivalry were moments of wonder that look like the je ne sais quoi. "However clearly I may tell all this," said Diaz, "I can never fully explain to one who did not see" (308). This is the voice of the voyaging eyewitness, equally remote from the conventions of true history and the disembodied narrator of romance, one whose presence amidst the wonders and miracles of the terra incognita is without any precedent at all. It is a single, agitated, self-authenticating presence, auto-intoxicated in the company of unheard-of novelties, and the target of readers who despise narrators imparting "information about things of which they were ignorant" (Oviedo 1959, 2:182). From the embarrassments of this voice, the genre of utopia emerges as an autoptic romance, an eyewitness report of a community so improbably beautiful and just that no consensus can vouch for its authenticity, only the first person singular: "If you had been with me in Utopia and had presently seen their fashions and laws, as I did which lived there five years and more, and would never have come thence but only to make that new land known here, then doubtless you would grant that you never saw people well ordered but only there" (More 1910, 53). One of Mandeville's bees might have said the same thing of its hollow tree. The participant eyewitness is, of course, a hypothesis as vain as the je ne sais quoi. As the reader never was or could be with the voyager in his discoveries, and can imagine nothing equal to what he reports, there is nothing to be derived from his narrative but the pleasure of a witty fiction.

Utopias may be further distinguished from romance insofar as this pleasure is not just implicit in the act of writing and reading, but thematized in the very construction of the immortal commonwealth. Strictly speaking, the bees of the *Fable* pursue a libidinal logic to its conclusion, and make a place where enjoyment is so pure it looks like rigor. For all its apparent ordering of life, More's *Utopia* exhibits the means of pleasure perfectly distributed in social space, calculated for the maximum delight of its citizens, as Hythloday is rather surprised to find out:

> But in this point they seem almost too much given and inclined to the opinion of them which defend pleasure, wherein they determine either all

or the chiefest part of man's felicity to rest. And (which is more to be marvelled at) the defence of this so dainty and delicate opinion they fetch even from their grave, sharp, bitter, and rigorous religion . . . . they pronounce no man so foolish which would not do all his diligence and endeavour to obtain pleasure by right or wrong, only avoiding this inconvenience, that the less pleasure should not be a let or hindrance to the bigger. (More 1910, 84–85)

It is precisely when he viewed such a prospect that Diaz fell into the je ne sais quoi, and it is of the remarkable circumstances of Montesinos's cave that Quixote, only this once in his history, delivers himself in the first person. The threat of nullity is countered by a moment of enchanted self-assertion that takes the form of an architecture fit to mediate between propensities and social forms, and to harmonize the difference between the instinct and the law of self-preservation. The enchantments and gloriations of the self are projected as a public space, a theater of dainty and delicate delights.

In the eighteenth century, the utopian option grew stronger not only because of the proliferation of reports from terra incognita but because opportunities for self-assertion were multiplying inside the impenetrable medium dividing private interest from public good, allowing fantasy to short-circuit the narrative of social progress (Cascardi 1992, 54; Koselleck 1988, 170–74; Habermas 1971, 284). The irreconcilable impulses of self-preservation, toward glory and toward social utility, could be harmonized only by imagining a social order founded on passion and pleasure (Ricoeur 1986, 294). The voyage to a strange country is the standard model of the utopian narrative in an age when the market was redoubling the needs of navigation and fantasy. In this respect, the journey taken by Mandeville's bees asks to be understood as a move from the private pleasure of consumption to the formalization of pleasure as an architecture of common enjoyment, and not (as Mandeville indicated) from luxury to mere self-denial. As long as the threat of real emptiness and pure nothing can be averted, the utopian bees conserve the wishes of the natural self more successfully in this most operose of utopian contrivances than by inventing substantial new treats for the senses. The anonymous author of *Hildebrand Bowman* uses the Grass Cove Massacre, when eleven of the *Adventure*'s crew on Cook's second voyage were killed and partly eaten by Maori, as the starting point of a romance of stadial history that terminates in pure hedonism. The inhabitants of Luxo-Volupto report, "We have [the sense] of Touch or Feeling in as exquisite a degree as human nature is capable of supporting without turning pleasure into pain" (*The Travels of Hildebrand Bowman Esq.* 1778, 267).

The terra incognita is where nothing and savagery—the self exempt from law—combine in a wanton and improbable egoism, according to the defenders of civil realism, delivering "Vanity, and Lyes, and Nothing" (Hobbes 1968, 357). Romance, for these critics, is just a larger version of the same thing, and so is autoptic warrant of the distant voyager, for if nothing is to be imagined equal to what a rambling ego witnessed, then nothing, just nothing, is what remains. But what the bees explore, along with Hythloday, Bowman, and other navigators of the terra incognita, is the region Mandeville himself tried to chart between the coordinates of the wishing and wished-for self, a space where social forms and private desires achieve an equilibrium, and fantastic propensities combine with solid principles to build a common habitation. In this respect, the anthropology of virtue is a curious rehearsal of the unprecedented experience of the mariner; it points in the same direction.

The projection of personal pleasure as a public space produces odd overlappings of fact and fancy in the exploration of new worlds in the Western Hemisphere. Peter Heylyn could joke that the terra incognita had yielded "the Isle of Adamants in Sir Huon of Bordeaux; the Firm Island in the History of Amadis de Gaul; the hidden island, and that of the Sage Aliart in Sir Palmerin of England." Furthermore, he could declare that Edmund Spenser's *The Faerie Queene* took place there. He knew for a fact it is where Joseph Hall's *Mundus alter et idem* and More's *Utopia* are situated; the location is undeniable (Heylyn 1667, 1094). But when Diaz started to operate inside the narrative of Amadis, and when de Quiroga built utopian towns in Mexico, the joke is less outrageous because, like the enchantments and gloriations of the individual ego, it finds a real location. Nothing has somewhere to dwell; and this somewhere provides the alibi for other nothings: the nothing of the je ne sais quoi and the nothing to which the traveler's tale claims to be equal.

It is at this point in literary history that it becomes very hard to tell imaginary and real voyages apart (McKeon 1987, 110). Richard Brome wrote *The Antipodes* (1638) about Peregrine, a man whose mind is as addled by voyage literature as Quixote's by books of chivalry; but when Pedro Fernandez de Quirós made his way to the antipodes, he behaved just like Don Quixote. With Alvaro de Mendaña he had gone "to fetch the Queen of Sheba from the Isles of Solomon" (de Quirós 1904, 1:33); and when he arrived at the place he thought was paradise, he set about founding orders of knighthood and holy sodalities of chivalry (Kelly 1966, 1:215–17). Swift's *Gulliver's Travels,* a satire against such enchanted egoism, was presented as a sequel to William Dampier's narratives of landings in New Holland, generically and rhetorically indistinguishable from the original, for each greets the emptiness of the new place with a detailed list of what it lacks, as proof either of its savagery or its amenity. With Gulliver having attested to the solemn truth of what he has narrated of horses by citing Sinon the liar, it is eerie to find David Samwell forty years later in roughly the same place enforcing the same claim for the veracity of his report of Cook's death by quoting Othello as his model of candor (Swift 1902, 368; Cook 1967, 2:1202–2). Louis-Antoine de Bougainville's real narrative of Tahiti provided Denis Diderot with a way to reincorporate the noble savage of Rousseau's second *Discourse* into the ocean of fantasy whence it originated, superimposing the terra incognita of the mind upon the whole Pacific Ocean even while it was being mapped. Bernard's late eighteenth-century watercolor of Bougainville's voyage, *L'evention d'Otaheidi,* celebrates the coincidence of fantasy and exploration with an extraordinary display of mannered medievalisms[3] (fig. 2). Just as Heylyn wittily placed *The Faerie Queene* in the terra incognita, once it was settled, Sir George Grey found he could only give an adequate idea of the revenge cycles of Maori myth by quoting from Spenser's romance (Grey 1869, 362). O. H. K. Spate calls the cycle of Polynesian Hawaiki voyages "a *gesta* greater in range and more marvellous in event than medieval Europe's matters of Troy, of Arthur, or of Charlemagne" (Spate 1988a, 11).

When the antipodal adventure arrives home in the form of a traveler's assertion, delivered in language that confounds the fabulous and the authentic, a whole line of metaphors used to attack the romancing ego falls into abeyance, and cannot be renewed without also aggravating the "excruciating ambivalence" at the heart of civil society's mode of reproducing itself. Although there was a handy argument concerning the degeneration of mariners running from Horace to George-Louis Buffon, and thence to Guillaume Raynal, which held that their minds and bodies decay in proportion to the distance they traveled from home (Pagden 1995b, 60, 161), it was hard to call utopias symptomatically corrupt, since they represented the perfection of the social order in a manner immediately recognized by

---

3 In composition and style it resembles the frontispiece of the *Lettera di Amerigo Vespucci* (1505–6), reprinted by Bernard Quaritch in 1893, which shows three vessels of a similar shape moored off an island dominated by naked figures, houses, and palm trees.

FIGURE 2   S. Bernard, *L'Evention d'Otaheidi.* Watercolor, late eighteenth century.
© Christie's Images, Ltd. 1994.

citizen and rampant egoist alike. James Harrington thought it no idol to
represent a commonwealth as a calculable as well as an immortal organism, arguing that contradictions—including all of those opacities standing between intention and outcome in the history of civil society—are
chief among the causes of political dissolution (Harrington 1992, 218). As
mariners acquired more authority, and still insisted on reporting that they
had seen terrestrial paradises, where men and women went naked without shame and loaves of bread grew "in a manner spontaneously upon
trees" (Cook 1970, 18), Shaftesbury's idea of monstrosity and savagery had
to widen to include evidence of the best aspects of human nature among
the metaphors of the worst. The double nature of self-preservation un-
derlying this confusion was easily transferred to the inhabitants of the
terra incognita, estimated as noble or ignoble depending on the coordinates of the observer's internal geography.

2

THE ROMANCE OF NAVIGATION

It was too fantastic to suppose that the exigencies of commerical exploration would lead to such extremities. . . . We were not in the South Sea Islands; nor were we puppets of romance. We were in Europe.

—Erskine Childers, *The Riddle of the Sands*

He who has not made the experiment . . . will scarcely believe how much a few hours take from the certainty of knowledge, and distinctness of imagery; how the succession of objects will be broken, how separate parts will be confused . . . and conglobated in one gross and general idea. To this dilatory notation must be imputed the false relations of travellers, where there is no imaginable motive to deceive.

—Samuel Johnson, *A Journey to the Western Isles*

In the "Introductory Discourse containing the History of Navigation," which he supplied for Awnsham and John Churchill's *A Collection of Voyages and Travels* (1704), John Locke cites William Dampier's two landfalls in New Holland and exclaims, "The Empire of Europe is now extended to the utmost Bounds of the Earth . . . and the Relation of one traveller is an Incentive to stir up another to imitate him, whilst the rest of Mankind, in their accounts without stirring a foot, compass the Earth and Seas, visit all Countries, and converse with all Nations" (Locke 1704, 1:lxxiii). Thomas Hobbes lists navigation as one of the advantages of civil society (Hobbes 1968, 703). It banishes error: "Our own Navigations make manifest, all men learned in humane Sciences, now acknowledge, there are Antipodes" (703); and its excellence lies in "the division, distinction, and portraying of the face of earth" (1994, 74). Having stated the poor odds for survival at sea, Bernard Mandeville goes on to proclaim the material benefits of seafaring for society: "Promote Navigation, cherish the

Merchant, and encourage Trade in every Branch of it; this will bring Riches, and where they are, Arts and Sciences will soon follow . . . [thus] it is that Politicians can make a people potent, renown'd, and flourishing" (Mandeville 1924, 1:184–85). This vision of expanding wealth and territorial knowledge, accommodating private ambition within a scheme of national glory, resembles Mandeville's beehive before the swarm, where passions such as avarice and greed collaborate with the public interest; it enforces Hobbes's arguments for the social benefits of knowledge; and it gives a global dimension to Locke's advocacy of history. The business of this chapter is to measure the level of fantasy in the metropolitan embrace of the whole world.

The national advantages of antipodal navigation acquired more distinct shape with the formation of the South Sea Company 1711. They were set out in detail in the voyages and pamphlets Robert Harley encouraged into print as part of his publicity for a trading empire in the South Seas. His plan was effectually a revival of Oliver Cromwell's Western Design of 1655, which had established a British presence on Jamaica (Armitage 1992; Spate 1983, 2:133–38). The route into the Pacific from the East Indian side had been effectually blocked by the Dutch since the massacre of British merchants at Amboyna in 1623 (Markley 1998, 1–17). The buccaneers and privateers operating from Jamaica were the first British crews to exploit the isthmus of Panama, known as Darien, as a route from the "North Seas" of the Caribbean to the "South Seas" of the Pacific. Dampier was able to use it to renew the maritime explorations of Australasia begun earlier in the seventeenth century by the Dutch. His reports, supplemented by the accounts of colleagues such as John Welbe, Lionel Wafer, William Funnell, Edward Cooke, and Woodes Rogers, provided the basis of Harley's publicity.

By the terms of the Treaty of Utrecht, which ended the War of Spanish Succession, Britain acquired the right under the Asiento (a contract setting out the terms of the agreement) to transport slaves, and one ship's cargo of goods a year, to the Spanish possessions in the New World. The South Sea Company was established by act of Parliament to exploit this opportunity, and in 1713 it was presented with the Asiento. The company's writ ran "from the river of Aranoca to the southernmost part of the Terra del Fuego; and on the west side thereof, from the said southernmost part of Terra del Fuego, through the South Seas, to the northernmost part of America; and into, unto, and from all countries &c. within the said limits . . . or which shall hereafter be found out or discovered" (Anderson 1801, 3:44). In 1711, Herman Moll published *A View of the Coasts, Coun-*

tries and Islands within the Limits of the South-Sea-Company, explaining, "When the Publick Welfare of these Kingdoms depend so much on the Success of the Company newly Establish'd to carry on a Trade to the South Seas, it cou'd not but excite the Curiosity of all who wish . . . to know what are the Countries, Commerce and Riches which are the Subject of our present Views and Expectations" (Moll 1711, [i]). In 1712, there appeared Woodes Rogers' *A Cruising Voyage round the World*, Edward Cooke's *A Voyage to the South Sea*, the anonymous *Providence Display'd: or a very surprizing Account of one Mr Alexander Selkirk*, Sir Richard Steele's account of Selkirk's marooning in *The Englishman* (issue no. 26), and Daniel Defoe's *Essay on the South-Sea Trade*, all intended to pique public curiosity about the possibility of establishing a trade route in the Pacific. Frequently mentioned was the plan of founding a staging post at the uninhabited island of Juan Fernandez (Selkirk's desert island). Rogers praised the wisdom of the nation's decision "to establish a Trade to the South-Seas, which, with the Blessing of God, may bring vast Riches to Great Britain," adding that "it should be lawful for us and the Dutch to seize by force what Lands and Cities we could of the Spanish Dominions in America, and to possess them as our own" (Rogers 1712, v, viii). Defoe thought it a pity Britain "should so long lye still, and leave unattempted, a Trade which in the Enemies Hand is fatal to us, and which in our Hands might be so fatal to them" (Defoe 1712, 5).

In much of the publicity surrounding the formation of the South Sea Company there was, therefore, an emphasis on the potential value of trade in the Pacific, and on the benefits accruing to Britain from exploiting it. In private memorials to the government, John Welbe, a shipmate of Dampier's, lays out "A Scheme of a Voyage Round the Globe for the Discovery of Terra Australis Incognita" (Welbe 1716, fols. 213–17; Williams 1994, 122; Williams 1997, 183–89). He promises to find mines of gold and silver, "which when explord, will bring in as great a Revenue to the Crown of Great Britain, as Peru dos to the Crown of Spain, if not delayd till other Nations take Possession" (Welbe 1716: fol. 215). More practically, an anonymous author of "An Essay on the Nature and Methods of carrying on a Trade to the South Sea" points out that illicit traffic was already maintained between the French and the Spanish on the Pacific seaboard, "& as Interest has Induc'd the Merchts of Peru & Chili to Trade wth the French contrary to the Antient Constitution of those Kingdoms, so may we not rest assured that the same powerfull motives of Interest & Advantage will induce the Spanish to Trade with Us" ("An Essay" 1707–46, fols. 20–28). In his fictional account of Selkirk's life on a desert island,

The Life and Surprizing Adventures of Robinson Crusoe (1719), Defoe mythologizes the isolated British presence in distant seas not as the acquirement of fabulous personal wealth and treasure, but as an infant colony capable of resupplying British merchant shipping. Although in *Robinson Crusoe* the island is taken out of the Pacific and placed in the Caribbean, in a subsequent impersonation of a privateer's journal, *A New Voyage Round the Globe* (1725), Defoe repositions the axis of trade in the southern ocean. Here he predicts successfully not the commodities but the coordinates of the nineteenth-century trade in *beche de mer* and sandalwood. The author traces Dampier's route to the coast of Australia and finds on the journey eastward tropical islands filled with noble savages possessed of gold; he imagines taking woolens and kerseys to the South Seas, obtaining in exchange the bullion to buy cargoes in China (Williams 1973; Markley 1994). To manage this trade properly, Defoe notes the advantages of Juan Fernandez, and is particularly taken with Patagonia, where, at Port Desire, "we found a post or cross erected by Sir John Narborough, with a plate of copper nailed to it, and an inscription signifying that he had taken possession of that country in the name of King Charles II. Our men raised a shout for joy that they were in their king's own dominions, or, as they said, in their own country; and indeed . . . I never saw a country in the world so like England" (Defoe 1935, 185, 322).

Despite their pitiable lot at the sharp end of navigation, mariners appeared eager to join in the national promotion of the South Seas, to provide sound information concerning real possibilities of trade and settlement, and thus to be eased, as Lionel Wafer put it, "of the Odium of Singularity" (Wafer 1933, lxviii). They and the government aimed to win a consensus in favor of navigation in the region of what was still the terra incognita. Richard Helgerson has pointed out how, in contrast to the epic conception of the Portuguese maritime empire, or the evangelical pretensions of the Spanish, the British never lost sight of the commercial purpose behind exploration, and what the anonymous memorialist of South Seas trade called "the same powerfull motives of Interest & Advantage." Unlike Luis Vaz de Camoens and Fernández de Oviedo, Richard Hakluyt in his great compilation, *Principal Navigations* (1589), unobtrusively unites a pragmatic concern for the economic advantages of newly discovered markets with patriotism and the magnification of England's glory (Helgerson 1992, 166–81). In Hakluyt's view, the merchant is a trader and something of a hero of romance, an individual jousting with the Spanish for the honor of the nation and the increase of its revenues. And in this coalition of private enterprise and patriotism, he anticipates the mutuality of interests shared by the self and the state in the theory of civil society. In *Hakluytus Posthumus; or, Purchas His Pilgrimes* (1625), the sprawling promotional calendar of the globe's attributes and commodities published by Samuel Purchas, the writ of James I is proclaimed coextensive with the achievements of English circumnavigators. This global prerogative nevertheless acknowledges the diversity and importance of private initiatives such as Sir Francis Drake's and Thomas Cavendish's, whose seizures of Spanish treasure gild the author's tempting exordium concerning King Solomon's mines at Ophir (Boon 1982, 157).

As far as the South Seas were concerned, three great voyages linked Hakluyt's and Purchas's compilations to the Churchills': Drake's (1578), Narborough's (1669), and Dampier's (1688). Each commander had entered the Pacific through the Straits of Magellan and while successfully raiding Spanish shipping, had wondered about a surer method of seizing some of the spoils of the region from the Spanish. Drake accepted the sovereignty of northern California on behalf of Queen Elizabeth (Callender 1967, 1:302); Narborough was under secret instructions to seize bases in Chile (Williams 1997, 77); and Dampier emphasized the importance of the Darien isthmus as "the door to the South Seas" (Dampier 1729, 1:180). Lionel Wafer was so persuasive about the advantages of Darien that the Scots invested a great deal of energy and money in an effort to settle it; and like Woodes Rogers and Edward Cooke, Wafer also saw the merits of Juan Fernandez (Wafer 1933, 1, 144). For an enterprise so romantically conceived, there is remarkable unanimity, extending from Hakluyt to Defoe, about how to exploit these discoveries for the good of the nation; for Hakluyt also believed that English commerce in the South Seas required a base (he recommended the Strait of Magellan). Like Defoe, he thought cloth would be the main export; and again like Defoe, he considered the jewel in the crown of such a trading empire to be the China market, hitherto the sink of English bullion because there one could purchase "the most noble merchandise of all the world" only with gold and silver (Helgerson 1992, 164–67).

The emphasis on the personal heroism and enterprise of the navigator, a man whose strengths and resources are both singularly his own and yet typical of a national temperament, is an important element of the vision shared by Hakluyt and Purchas, and later by Defoe and the buccaneers, of joining the expansion of commercial opportunities to a celebration of national glory. Hakluyt credited King Arthur with the origin of England's maritime achievements, and the the Saxon Edgar with the foundation of its navy (Hakluyt 1907, 1:29, 32). Finding in chivalric romance a convenient genre for combining the double attributes of enterprise and patriotism, these chroniclers of English achievements avoided the tight necessities of the epic structure chosen by Camoens, as Helgerson points out. The frame of epic is too closely bound to a destiny and program of national foundation: an epic navigation proceeds to an outcome that is already foretold and collectively acknowledged as necessary, being served and honored as a common cause, and therefore ineluctable, immune to individual initiatives, and lacking in suspense (Bakhtin 1981, 37). The journeys of romance, on the other hand, are more digressive and more exposed to chance; what is more, the honor of what the hero wins belongs to himself as well as to his liege lord. "Spenser, and the same may be said of Ariosto, did not live in an age of planning" (Warton 1807, 1:21); consequently, regulation is at a minimum, and improvisation and initiative at a premium, in narratives dealing with the "epiphenomena of the conflict between individually occupied and socially occupied identity" (Ferguson 1992, 98). The hero of romance evades "the inconvenience of a related, measurable state" (Seltzer 1992, 68), for everything goes from his imagination to his fingertips, his impulse being erotic love, and his law being the strength of his arm, as Don Quixote several times points out (Cervantes 1970, 1:76). Anthony Cascardi says that "romance is motivated by the hero's unsatisfied need for personal love and individual fulfilment," a goal consistent with an enterprise culture and the fashioning of the modern subject (Cascardi 1992, 101). Indeed, Helgerson makes it a point to emphasize that chivalric romance was invented and developed by a commercial people, thriving in the industrial and mercantile centers of Europe, not in feudal courts (Helgerson 1992, 43). It was apt for accommodating and idealizing the egoistic heroism ascribed by Defoe, in his *Essay on Projects* (1702), to the true-bred merchant. Like Columbus, this individual has the wit first to imagine what he may then explore, handle, know, and profit from. Like the chivalric knight, the merchant is at large, "the most intelligent man in the world," because his negotiations bring him, like Ruggiero on the Hippogriff or Don Quixote on the back of Clavileno, a view of the whole world: "Every new voyage the merchant contrives, is a project, and ships are sent from port to port, as markets and merchandises differ, by the help of strange and universal intelligence, wherein some are so exquisite, so swift, and so exact, that a merchant sitting at home in his counting-house at once converses with all parts of the known world" (Defoe 1861, 7). The same "strange and universal intelligence" emanates from the travel narratives introduced by Locke to curious readers, who may immerse themselves in them and "without stirring a foot, compass the Earth and Seas, visit all Countries, and converse with all Nations."

Here, then, is the outline of the resourceful traveler's common cause with the nation, particularly attractive to the British because it anticipated eighteenth-century political philosophy in aligning self-preservation and the appeasement of its associated propensities with the reinforcement of the public good. Instead of events being concatenated in time, as in Locke's pattern of history or biography, voyaging provides a spatial theodicy running from terra incognita to a spectacle of the visible world, a view extending from China to Peru, blocked by nothing and available (as Locke put it) for conversation. The obfuscating medium that blinds the multitude to the future, according to Adam Ferguson, so that they lurch toward "ends which even their imagination could not anticipate" (Ferguson 1980, 122), is dispersed by a map of the world and a system of communication that is answerable to the stretch of imagination and makes intelligence universal. And as maritime exploration begins to incorporate ethnological data, a new form of world history is to emerge, based upon the cultural differences observed in America and the Pacific islands, manifesting the four stages of human development (nomadic, pastoral, agrarian, commercial) in the form of "the great map of mankind," as Edmund Burke was to put it (Meek 1976, 173). Notwithstanding the evident instability of romance as a model of global intelligence, and Peter Heylyn's ironic assessments of its value, it seems to work well in matching social utility ("our present views") to propensities ("curiosity") (Moll 1711, [i]). The leading compilers of voyages wished to make this union quite plain. "I am confident you will meet with nothing that is dictated by any other than a publick Spirit in the Volume which I present," asserts John Harris in the premier collection of travels (subsequently edited and expanded by John Campbell) between the Churchills' and John Hawkesworth's ([Harris] Campbell 1764, 1:iv). Hawkesworth himself picks up the patriot theme: "Nothing can redound to the honour of this nation, as a maritime power, to the dignity of the Crown of Great Britain, and to the advancement of the trade and navigation thereof, than to make discoveries of countries hitherto unknown" (Hawkesworth 1773, 1:i). And in the authoritative retrospect of British activity in the Pacific during the previous century, James Burney calculates the formal requirements of a subject naturally so versatile: "The utility of method and compression, to prevent irregular exuberance in so important a branch of science, is evident beyond contradiction" (Burney 1803–16, 1:iii).

Not all collections were so severely bound to the purpose of national utility, however, suggesting a latitude in editorial practices and readers' tastes consistent with the allure of romance. David Henry was quite frank about the appeal of his collection: "Nothing can excite or gratify curiosity more than relations of marvellous events that happen in succession, and in circumstances equally critical and important" (Henry 1774, 1:vii). The reader who identifies with the romance of a voyage to a new land, lamenting the perils and admiring the improvisational courage of the narrator ("what heart is so callous, as not to sympathize?" [ibid.]), participates in an adventure whose purpose may be conjectured and whose national significance may be supposed, but whose real value is unknown and whose outcome cannot be determined—at least while the suspense lasts. The frisson comes first, the moral later: "When we read in these Voyages of men that eat men, not for hunger, but from savage ferocity, we shudder to think of the depravity of our nature, and are convinced of the necessity of bounding our passions with wholesome laws" (vi). One way or another, propensity maintains a balance with sociability, and curiosity with "our present Views" while the public interest is served by the private pleasure taken in stories of navigators whose otherwise odious singularity is guaranteed a place in the production of a national history.

At least this is how the larger narrative of the exploration of the South Seas is supposed to work. But like the original contract described in chapter 1, the notion of a common interest shared by the individual and the nation originates in a purely speculative idea. Robert Harley was engaged in publicity, not a project of knowledge. His aim was the formation of public opinion in favor of a national adventure. He was no more certain of acquiring wealth for Britain by expanding its interests westward than were the buccaneers who crossed the Darien Isthmus looking for Spanish treasure. Later, his partner in the scheme was forced to admit that the trading advantages proposed by the treaty were "nothing more than Amusements" (Bolingbroke 1727, 2:287). At this early stage, the national advantage of the quest was imaginable rather than measurable, and all the risks were taken by individuals, either the mariners themselves or the owners of the privateering vessels. At all levels in the enterprise, from the formation of crews to the publication of their narratives, goodwill between participants was notably lacking, as was correspondence between individual and corporate perceptions of interest. These disagreements find expression in various attitudes expressive of romance.

The most fundamental form of disagreement among buccaneers and privateers was mutiny, and the early voyages by British crews in the Pacific were a litany of usurpations, in which the victim was prone to dignify his fall by comparing it (like characters in the romances of Sir Walter Scott or Robert Louis Stevenson) to the sufferings of the later Stuarts. After being turned out by his crew at Juan Fernandez, Bartholomew Sharp feelingly commemorated the death of Charles I, drawing a parallel for his own humiliation with an outrage "for which I believe the English both have and will suffer severely" (Ayres 1694, 55). Dampier recalled his own loss of command of the *St. George* in 1704, and how "that Buffoon Toby Thomas by name, said, Poor Dampier, thy Case is like King James, every Body has left thee" (Dampier 1707, 8). After losing command of his crew, again on Juan Fernandez, George Shelvocke began to compare his plight to Dampier's and gave himself up to Jacobite excesses, lighting bonfires, wearing the white cockade, and drinking to the Pretender's health (Betagh 1728, 118). John Avery the pirate went to sea, it was commonly believed, because the patrimony of his ardently Royalist father was embezzled by a crooked lawyer (Johnson 1980, i–ii). The tradition lingered on in the navy. When William Bligh was certain that he and the remnants of a loyal crew had successfully navigated from Tonga to the Australian coast, he remembered it was the birthday of Charles II, "and the name not being inapplicable to our present situation (for we were restored to fresh life and strength), I named this Restoration island" (Bligh 1790, 55). These are interesting examples of Hobbes's "gloriation of the mind," for the identification with the Stuarts' lost cause looks two ways: toward the breakdown of the social order of a ship, and toward the hero's own isolation from the political order of postrevolutionary Britain. They are double announcements of a potentially odious singularity.

At the level of the ship, this tendency toward romance on the part of self-styled heroes was well understood. When Woodes Rogers matched the narratives of his colleagues against "the Wisdom of the Nation [in agreeing] to establish a Trade to the South Seas" (Rogers 1712, v), he lamented "a particular Misfortune which attends Voyages to the South-Sea, that the Buccaneers, to set off their own Knight-Errantry, and make themselves pass for Prodigies of Courage and Conduct, have given such romantick Accounts of their Adventures, and told such strange Stories, as make the Voyages of those who come after . . . to look flat and insipid to unthinking People" (xvi). John Welbe referred to Dampier's *Vindication* (1707) as a "farraginous Compendium, full of Enthusiasms and improbable Stuff," a publication in which Dampier had referred to his colleague William Funnell as a man of "very Productive Brain," one of those "Mighty Bravoes that are fit to set People by the Ears at Home, and make

Scandal as Rife with me as it is with them" (Welbe 1705, 1; Dampier 1707, 1, 5). Of Dampier's and Rogers's accounts of the natural resources of Juan Fernandez, Jacob Roggeveen sarcastically observed that they were "devised and represented after the fashion of romances" (Roggeveen 1970, 81). William Betagh publicly denounced his former commander's narrative of his career in the Pacific as "a wild story full of abominable romance and vain glory" (Betagh 1728, 109). A similar judgment was made by Horace Walpole after reading of George Anson's achievements in the same place, which he compared with *Gulliver's Travels* for improbability, and whose perpetrator he referred to thereafter as "Admiral Amadis" and "Admiral Almanzor" (Walpole 1937–83, 9:55; 37:550; 35:284). After John Byron returned from the Pacific with tales of giants, Walpole reaffirmed what Heylyn had proposed a century earlier, namely that "[w]riters of Romance have a new field opened to them" (Walpole [1766] 1964, 203). Upon receiving these reports into the *Philosophical Transactions,* Dr. Maty protested that he was not "setting up for a knight errant in favour of the giants of Magellan" (Coyer 1767, 26); but his antagonist, the Abbe Gabriel François Coyer, was already sufficiently dubious of British narratives of the South Seas to have suggested fifteen years earlier that the best commodities to trade in these newly discovered territories were books of fiction, "Delicious Romances . . . Operas fraught with melting Love" (Coyer 1752, 44, 19). On James Cook's second voyage, those members of the crew who got themselves tattooed called themselves "Knights of Otaheite," following the example of the antipodal orders of chivalry inaugurated by Pedro Fernandez de Quirós.

Thus the South Seas stood at the confluence of older traditions of chivalric and utopian romance on the one hand, and a new branch of fiction on the other. A compiler of buccaneer biographies spoke in Heylyn's vein of "the unparallel'd, if not inimitable adventures and Heroick exploits of our own Country-men" (Exquemelin 1684, iv), while Defoe opted for a different kind of novelty in presenting to the public *The Strange Surprizing Adventures of Robinson Crusoe* (1719), thereby launching the Robinsonnade, a specialized romance whose theme is the largely problematic relation of the solitaire to society, and of the savage paradise to civilization. Charles Gildon compared this work to *Guy of Warwick* and *Bevis of Southampton* (Gildon 1719, iii). More than a hundred years later, Benjamin Morrell was complaining that reports from the South Seas were "fables more difficult to believe than Gulliver's Travels, or the mythology of ancient Greece" (Morrell 1832, 41).

The threat of improbability, then, loomed large in calculating the utility of these voyages. In an effort to correct the balance, Dampier, Rogers, Cooke, and Shelvocke, the chief navigators of the first two decades, delivered abundant facts in the sober, circumstantial style that Jonathan Swift and Defoe were to exploit in their fictions (McKeon 1987, 352; Rennie 1995, 55–59). Dampier, already defensive about this, remarks in the preface of his *Voyage to New Holland,* "It has been objected against me by some that my Accounts and Descriptions of Things are dry and jejune, not filled with variety of pleasant Matter to divert and gratify the Curious Reader" (Dampier 1729, 3:[i]). He tries to make it clear that his purpose was a public benefit rather than a private obsession with novelties. His determination to avoid the imputation of romance made him lavish with illustrations as well as facts, and he included rough cuts of various birds, fish, and plants, along with some silhouettes of promontories and islands. However, facts without a model of truth, like specimens without a taxonomy, have more rhetorical value than anything else. Although Dampier promises "a Methodic Discourse, ranging the several Particulars under their proper Heads" (2:[i]), he can be ambushed by a trifling accident: "One Time our Captain after he had haled in a good fish, being eager at his Sport, and throwing out his Line too hastily, the Hook hitched in the Palm of his Hand, and the Weight of the Lead that was thrown with a Jerk, and hung about six Foot from the Hook, forced the Beard quite through, that it appeared at the Back of his Hand" (2:20). This is an event without any bearing on another, and without consequence. Dampier wants to describe it for its own sake, and to do it exactly, because it surprises, amuses, or fascinates him. It is like his cousin Gulliver's description of the tumble he took into a cow patty, which he pretends he has included for the benefit of the learned. Both claim public attention and belief by using the language of experimental science as recommended by the members of the Royal Society (of London for the Improvement of Natural Knowledge), but demonstrate that truth-claims in the scientific discourse of the late seventeenth century were by no means simply made. Hobbes, for one, thought them fraught with vainglory (Schaffer and Shapin 1985). Steven Shapin shows how Robert Boyle cultivated the attributes of a sober, scientific eyewitness not because he felt sobriety marked the resemblance between the observer and what is to be observed, but rather the opposite. Boyle was a man of volatile imagination, weaned on romances, and one whose pursuit of truth through experiment was shaped by a strong taste for the marvelous as well as rigorous standards of

evidence. Just as Don Quixote appeals to Sancho to witness his extravagant antics performed naked in the Sierra Morena, marvels of distraction
the world will hardly credit ("Thou shalt be a witness of what I will do . . .
a thousand things that will fill thee with astonishment" [Cervantes 1970,
1:186]), so Nature appeals to Boyle, the Christian Virtuoso, to "see such
things performed by her, as [will] make him think the vulgar catalogue of
impossible or incredible things far greater than it might be" (Shapin 1995,
199). Eyewitnessing therefore is a trial of wonder: "The natural power that
Boyle defined . . . allows mute objects to speak through the intermediary
of loyal and disciplined scientific spokespersons" (Latour 1993, 30).

Voyagers in the South Seas often confronted things—even ordinary
things—as if they were wonders, and catalogued them more in a spirit
of admiration than appraisal. Listing the contents of an Indian canoe
("stones, Macassites, Bones, Calabashes, Baggs of Seal-Oyles, Javelins
Shafts & Heads; Bows, Bowstrings, fflintstones—Sulphur Mineral, In-
dented Daggers cut out of Bone, Seals flesh dryed: A Childs fflesh dryed,
Beads, Braceletts, Slings, some few pieces of old Iron sharpned which
they had taken up from some Shipwreck, Wings, ffeathers, ffurs, Netts"),
the privateer Richard Simson is aware that his catalogue is swelling to the
proportions of romance: "The Author of Garagantua had a good hand at
drawing up such Curious Inventories, for my part, because I would be
concise, I but touch at the particulars, enumerating the various sorts of
things so near as I can remember of wch the odd collection did consist"
(Simson [1689], 16v). In romances such as *Tirante the White,* as Miguel de
Cervantes makes clear, a strong vein of domestic realism was by no means
considered a breach of convention (Cervantes 1970, 1:38). Similarly, the
rhetoric of wonder relied upon an exhaustive particularity, not only to do
justice to the appearance of marvels, but also to satisfy the curiosity it
aroused (Daston and Park 1998, 144). Voyagers found, however, that their
attention to detail was an isolating technique, emphasizing the odious
singularity of the eyewitness who portentously recites the wonder of
things lacking public significance. Far from authenticating their contribution to a national purpose, or setting new things in a context of existing knowledge, their particulars licensed the imaginations and aroused
the irresponsible curiosity of their Desdemona-like readers, whose appetite for pleasure overrode their desire of knowledge. George Forster, a
scientist on Cook's second expedition, adverted to this state of affairs by
remarking, "Facts were collected . . . and yet knowledge was not increased.
[The learned] received a confused heap of disjointed limbs, which no art

could reunite; and the rage of hunting after facts, soon rendered them incapable of forming and resolving a single proposition" (Forster 1777, 1:xi). As a cartographer, Herman Moll expressed exasperation with the carelessness and vainglory of the early reckonings, which included imaginary territories such as Davis Land, named after one of Sharp's colleagues and for a while assumed to be a spur of Terra Australis Incognita: "Sharp, Cowley, and other Voyagers, say little of either side of the Continent, and what they do say is without Order" (Moll 1711, [ii]). A hundred years later, mariners were tracking "those unstable islands in the far Pacific, whose eccentric wanderings are noted in each new edition of the South Sea charts" (Melville 1964, 35).

In any event, the real object of a voyage in the South Seas between 1680 and 1740, as far as the participants were concerned, was not knowledge but plunder. Shelvocke archly observed, "It has generally happen'd that those Gentlemen have had some other design in view, than to make compleat discoveries" (Shelvocke 1726, iii). They had their eyes fixed on gold, specifically the treasure ship that plied once a year between Manila and Acapulco. They gambled with gold they hadn't yet seized, and they died with gold strapped to their backs (Wafer 1729, 274). Rogers, Anson, and (it was generally believed) Shelvocke returned from their cruises laden with booty. The closest treasure got to the public eye was the parade of loot through the city of London after Anson got home; but behind the show a fierce legal battle was being fought by the survivors over who had best title to it (Williams 1967), just as another had been waged over the spoil of Rogers's expedition (Williams 1997, 158–60). Shelvocke avoided this trouble by cleverly hiding what he had taken, contributing in his way to the folklore of buccaneers' buried treasure, apt emblem of the privacy of the privateering enterprise, whose doctrine is preached by Israel Hands to Jim Hawkins: "I never seen good come o' goodness yet" (Stevenson 1947, 127). As there was a very narrow line between legal privateering and piracy, it is not surprising that men such as Sharp and Dampier, who promoted themselves as public benefactors, were tried for piratical acts, and that some, like William Kidd, were hanged for them (Baer 1996; Burney 1803–16, 4:121).

Why, then, was Locke so sure that Dampier's achievements had extended knowledge and commerce "to the utmost Bounds of the Earth"? In his memorial, Welbe emphasizes how little exploration had been done, "He having only 50 Men in his Ship, was not strong enough to search the Country, and consequently it is unknown what those parts abound in"

(Welbe 1716, 3). Dampier's landfall on the coast of New Holland had produced two insignificant encounters with local tribes, of whom he observed, "They are the miserablest People in the World." Their habitat he could record only as privations, such as the want of houses, garments, animals, and fruit. When he turned to the land itself, he could likewise only record its destitute condition. "There is neither Herb, Root, Pulse nor any sort of Grain for them to eat, nor any sort of Bird or Beast that they can catch" (Dampier 1729, 1:464–66). Yet this sum of negative attributes ignited the imagination of a philosopher, a professed enemy of enthusiasm, and tempted a sober trading nation into not only armchair travel, but unparalleled speculative excesses, "extraordinary and romantic projects" (Anderson 1825, 31).

Between 1719 and the middle of 1720, the price of South Sea stock rose from 114 points, fourteen over par, to somewhere between 950 and 1000, roughly ten times its original value. This spectacular rise was engineered solely by means of publicity and the manipulation of the national debt, not in the least by trading profit. Between April and June 1720, the directors made three issues of new stock at successively higher prices, using the cash they raised from previous sales as loans to fund further purchases of stock (Carswell 1960, 132–57; Neal 1990, 77). This was the bubble, a figment made of paper, circulated between people "lost to all sense of our true interest" (Berkeley [1721]1953, 6:69). Stock bred stock in what was supposed to be an endless circuit of transactions, well oiled with heavy bribes. Then public confidence faltered and two-thirds of the national credit was reduced to waste paper (Carswell 1960, 192), leaving such a complicated scene of ruin that even Mandeville was shocked. Of the South Sea Bubble he said, "The Year seventeen hundred and twenty has been as prolifick in deep Villany, and remarkable for selfish Crimes and premeditated Mischief, as can be pick'd out of any Century whatever" (Mandeville 1924, 1:276). The Scots had already suffered as badly by erecting a dream of commercial empire on Wafer's slender text, losing one-third of their national capital between 1698 and 1700, when they finally pulled the survivors out of Darien (McPhail 1994, 131–34). In France, investors could buy shares in the Mississippi Company on the installment plan; prices rose ten points a day for seven consecutive months in 1719, until they collapsed. John Law, the Scottish financier who had pioneered this huge extension of French credit, had to flee for his life.

The Bubble was comparable to the tulip mania in Holland in 1636–37, the canal mania in Britain in 1794, and even the wild pursuit of Internet and biotech stock at the present time, insofar as there ceased to be any probable connection between the price of the paper and its earning potential. What made the crisis national was not simply its scope, but also its brutal and sudden contradiction of the contemporary assumption of public benefit from such propensity for gain. If the ruin of the country were to be explained to the public, either this assumption had to be dismantled, or errant villainy had to be discovered. Either the foundations of civil society were to be understood as an unstable equilibrium of virtue and vice (as Mandeville argued both before and after the event)—or an innocent public was to be vindicated and its enemies shamed by bringing to light "the dark contrivances of those men, who were the cause of all the misfortunes which attended the amazing execution of this scheme" (Toland 1726, 404). The latter was by far the most popular strategy, but Mandeville was not alone in embracing the former. Although the real threat to the nation posed by the South Sea Bubble was not in the end much more substantial than (Prime Minister) Sir Robert Walpole's role as noble preserver of it (Neal 1990, 104–10), the void that yawned beneath an imagined commerce in terra incognita struck contemporaries as real enough. George Berkeley was appalled at the oscillation it exposed between opulence and destitution: "Some men shall from nothing in an instant acquire vast estates . . . while others are as suddenly stripped . . . and left on the parish" (Berkeley [1721] 1953, 6:71). Alexander Pope said of the investors (who included himself), "They have dreamed out their dream, and awakening have found nothing in their hands" (Pope 1956, 2:53–54). Defoe had earlier pointed out that burst bubbles leave "nothing but Cobweb, and a tangled Husk of Emptiness" (*Review* no. 126, *Review of the State of the English Nation* (1706): Defoe 1938, vol. 8; quoted in Nicholson 1994, 101). If all Dampier had discovered for the British in the terra incognita had been specimens of nothing, then nothing was all that was to come of Locke's dream of extended trade. Adam Smith said that the only "real foundation" of such an extravagant speculation was "the idea of the possibility of multiplying paper money to almost any extent" (Smith 1976, 1:317).

As for any commercial advantage, the state of the case was succinctly stated by James Burney: "In the year 1711 was erected . . . a South Sea Company . . . its formation had no relation to any scheme or plan for establishing a commercial intercourse between the British Nation and the Countries bordering on the South Sea, or to any maritime Enterprise then carrying on, or in contemplation" (Burney 1803–16, 4:486). The South Seas part of the enterprise was a speculation based literally on nothing. The Asiento slaves were landed on the Caribbean side and marched over the isthmus as they were needed, and the single British trading ship specified under the treaty was not allowed into the Pacific. Later, when the company was re-formed, it began a whale fishery in the Greenland seas, not in the Pacific (Defoe 1962, 1:252). Bolingbroke, who had in fact been allotted a share in the Asiento venture as a member of the administration responsible for the Treaty of Utrecht, entertained serious doubts about the "nominal commodity" of South Sea stock. "I do not conceive how this imaginary Commerce subsists with solid Traffick," he said, after the fact and clad in the patriotic guise of Caleb d'Anvers (Bolingbroke 1727, 2:20). Although the act instructed the South Sea Company to commence trading in the Pacific as a matter of "the greatest Consequence to the Honour and Welfare of this Kingdom" (2:284), the directors neglected to do anything about it, he noted, and committed themselves to "Chimerical Schemes . . . mischievous and damnable Schemes, which had almost overturned the British Constitution" (2:283, 301). Defoe had argued in 1712 that the South Sea Company was a real and substantial commercial venture, not a pretense of trade (Defoe 1712, 10); but after the crash, he compared the effect on the public imagination to enchantment: "Our late South-Sea Stock . . . run up . . . and gained upon Mankind by a general Infatuation, and may well be called Magick in its very Abstract" (Defoe 1728, 237). He identified the magic as credit, "this invisible *je ne scay quoi*, this non-natural, this emblem of a something, though in itself nothing" (Defoe 1951, 118). John Trenchard gloomily agreed: "Our highest Enjoyment is of that which is not: Our Pleasure is Deceit; and the only real Happiness that we have is derived from Non-Entities" (Trenchard 1725, 2:51).

Aside from the blow to national credit, abstract damage had indeed been sustained. When Berkeley complained, "This poor nation hath sorely smarted of late" (Berkeley [1721] 1953, 6:83), he was not alluding figuratively to the damage sustained by a group of individuals, but to a real blow to the national body. Trenchard believed that a deep wound had been inflicted upon "the being of a Kingdom" (Trenchard 1725, 1:49). "Poor England!" he cried, personifying the Britain as Job. "What a Name art thou become! A Name of Infatuation and Misery" (1:64). Defoe called the emergency a national frenzy: 1720 was the year "when England took leave to act the frantick," and when the nation was in the grip of "that terrible infatuation" (Defoe 1962, 1:159, 336). The infatuation and ruin of a whole country is a crisis of a special kind. Although Shaftesbury and Swift had studied the effects of enthusiasm upon groups of fanatics, there was no precedent (except among Mandeville's bees) for a nation so deluded by passion that it loses touch with reality. Under such extraordinary circumstances, the country and its various synonyms acquire the attributes of an unsteady individual, leaving the alarmed commentator trying to appeal to public opinion in the interests of the state, but with nothing to justify him, only a "People quite distracted" (Trenchard 1725, 1:59). Archibald Hutcheson, having drawn the analogy between "particular Persons" and "Bodies Politick," wondered in this emergency "how to find a Plaister large enough for so great a Sore," and warned that until all debts from the crash were discharged, "we can scarcely said to be a People" (Hutcheson 1721, 109, 117). Everything Hobbes had said about vainglory and romance, and that Locke had said about self-loss, came home to the kingdom, which had so far lost its system of self-representation as plainly to have confessed its obsession with terra incognita. Also, by removing its gaze from the visible world to the phantasms of the South Seas, it had given itself up to, and indeed had become, "an Idol, or meer Figment of the brain" (Hobbes 1968, 220). In short, it had gone mad, and with no "artificiall Person" to represent this distracted nation, something like a state of nature had supervened.

When Knight the South Sea Company cashier fled to France in 1721, he wrote to friends, "Self-preservation has compelled me to withdraw myself" (Carswell 1960, 226). Meanwhile, Trenchard was invoking the same fundamental principle to justify vengeful measures so lurid that they had doubtless contributed to Knight's decampment. The task of finding the people responsible for this national disaster, and punishing them suitably for a crime outside the framework of existing laws, was to do no more, he said, than to act upon "the great Principle of Self-Preservation, which is the first and fundamental Law of Nature" (Trenchard 1725, 1:75). It was also a challenge for the imagination. Trenchard's fantasies of revenge include "a thousand Stock-Jobbers, well trussed up," the invention of "new Tortures, and new Engines of Misery," and a sinister Jack Ketch who will say as he prepares them for their end, "I have a delicate and ready Hand at cutting and tying; so let them take Heart, the Pain is nothing, and will be soon over" (1:8; 134, 144; see Aravamudan 1999, 131). The extravagance of these imagined punishments was as much a symptom of social and national breakdown as was the infatuation of the market. Although he aimed for Mandeville's "prospect of concatenated events" (Mandeville 1924, 1:91), and wished to speak and act as the country's vindicator by restoring some sense of propriety to the law of self-preservation, Trenchard was plunged in passions from which no rational justification could possibly emerge. In the end, he found he could speak for no one but himself. The mysteries of credit and the blindness of collective action remained unchallenged by reason; and under their unabated pressure, self-preservation is only a law of nature, uninfluenced by the political covenant or public spirit. He confronted the directors, therefore, as one of the many individuals undone by their chicanery, not as a representative of the nation.

Trenchard was painfully aware that in the aftermath of national infatuation with fantasies of the South Seas, patriotic avowals of good faith were as undemonstrable as any other posture adopted in this theater of artifice and fraud. "When we call any Man disinterested, we should intend no more by it, than that the Turn of his Mind is towards the Publick, and that he has placed his own personal Glory and Pleasure in serving it. To serve his Country is his private Pleasure. . . . Disinterestedness is any other Sense than this, there is none . . . sometimes the great Difference between an honest Man and a Knave, is no other than . . . a Piece of Chance" (Trenchard 1725, 1:16, 2:52–53). By a chain of paradoxes worthy of Mandeville, Trenchard then declared that "[g]overnment first arose from every Man's taking Care of himself, and Government is never abus'd and perverted, but from the same cause" (2:54), concluding that civil society is nothing "but a Mock-Alliance between Hypocrisy and Credulity" (1:24). His only defense against the unlimited effect of the law of self-preservation was to preserve himself against men such as Knight, fighting like Don Quixote a battle of the enchanted against the enchanters: "Pity and Compassion do not consist of protecting Criminals from Justice, and in suffering the Devourers of a Nation to go off with the Plunder of a Nation . . . nor in engaging a Kingdom in wild and romantick Expences, to serve wild and romantick Purposes" (1:61). But his sole resource was romance: to fancy executions that will never happen and to proclaim a disinterestedness he has no means of authenticating. Thus Britain's first full-scale attempt to combine a capitalist economy with an antipodal trade ruptured the illusion on which this economy was founded, namely the compatibility between private and public interest in a romance of commercial expansion.

Trenchard's is a grim picture of the power of fiction in a commercial market, and a tormented exhibition of the destruction of civic virtue by a privatized law of self-preservation. From inside the whale as it were, Trenchard found out what happens when, in a national romance, the visible world and the original contract are supplanted by a nonentity (Brantlinger 1996, 20–42). Self-loss was everywhere figured as the invasion of metropolitan space by the savagery of the South Seas. "Will not every

Day discover Scenes of the wreck'd Fortunes of those who have adventured into this unhappy Ocean?" asked Archibald Hutcheson (Hutcheson 1721, 90). Swift wrote, "Meantime secure on GARR'WAY'S Clifts / A savage Race by Shipwrecks fed, / Ly waiting for the foundred Skiffs, / And strip the Bodyes of the Dead" (Swift 1958, 1:256). A ruined speculator called Thomas Hudson distractedly patrolled Exchange Alley, "wrapped in a rug, and leaning on a crutch, and without either shoes or stockings," for all the world like Selkirk on Juan Fernandez (Anderson 1825, 18). The metaphor of cannibalism was in wide circulation to express the vulnerability of people like him. "We are in danger of having Common Honesty and Morality entirely abolish'd, and . . . shall fall even below Duke Trincolo's Criterion of good Christian, and become so very bad, as to eat and devour one another" (Hutcheson 1721, 90). William Hogarth's plate *The South-Sea Scheme* (1721) depicts a scene of cannibalism at the left hand, while in the center and on the right, personifications of the moral vir-tues are being tortured to death. Trenchard thought these parallels did not reach the villainy of the directors: "Nay, it gains visible Advantage by the worst Comparisons that you can make: your Terror lessens, when you liken them to crocodiles and Canibals, who feed, for Hunger, on human Bodies" (Trenchard 1725, 1:11). Everybody was confirming the justness of Shaftesbury's critique of antipodal lies, namely that fantasies of the terra incognita generate savagery, not only among cheating directors but among their victims too: "Blood-suckers of the People should . . . make the People some Amends, by restoring the Blood that they have sucked. . . . My teeth particularly water, and my Bowels yearn, at the Name of the Brokers; for God's Sake, let me have the Brokers" (1:144, 152).

The war of the state of nature arises, according to Hobbes, from three privations: the want of exchange value, for "there is no use of commodities"; the want of history, for "there is no account of time"; and the want of charity, for "glory, or internal gloriation or triumph of the mind, is that passion which proceedeth from the imagination or conception of our own power, above the power of him that contendeth us" (Hobbes 1968, 107; 1994, 50). When Trenchard contemplated these privations in the wake of the Bubble—after pretensions and lies broke the tie (or the illusion of one) between the individual and the public, when a crisis in national identity stopped the historical clock, and when self-preservation became an urgent matter for everyone—he did not blind himself to the excruciating ambivalence of what they disclosed. He confronted the world as an eyewitness, and tasted the full paradox of utopia. "The only real Happiness that we have is derived from Non-Entities," he said, admitting that the truest sentiments as well as the most disgraceful figments are based on nothing. In this respect, the happiness of a South Sea Company director is no more substantial or valuable than that of a quixotic patriot, since their dreams are equally insubstantial and never tested—except in the broad sense of never taking place as realities. This leads to Trenchard's equation between rogues and honest folk, on the grounds that their motivations are identical ("The best Things that Men do, as well as the worst, are selfish" [Trenchard 1725, 2:77]); consequently, their fame is a lottery ("Sometimes the great Difference between an honest man and a Knave, is no other than a Piece of Chance" [2:53]). His own fantasy of preserving the nation from its despoilers could never transcend the privative condition and egoistic passion of the war of all against all, or disguise the fantasy—or at least the absence of consensus—in all utopian alternatives to the corruption of the times. He entered fully into the contradictions that combine truth and fiction and war and plenty in utopias, all part of "the palpable Nonsense of the heterogenous Compound," as Mandeville called it when reviewing locutions such as "certain hope." He developed a way of speaking that united commentary on the Bubble with utopian and paradisal projections. When Gonzalo contemplates the possibilities of Prospero's island, or Montaigne studies the cannibals of Brazil, the excellence of their theme is expressed in negatives. The Brazilians have no traffic, no history, and no law (Montaigne 1711, 1:289); likewise, in the island commonwealth Gonzalo promises,

> I would by contraries
> Execute all things, for no kind of traffic
> Would I admit; no name of magistrate;
> Letters should not be known; riches, poverty,
> And use of service, none; contract, succession,
> Bourn, bound of land, tilth, vineyard, none. (*The Tempest* 2.1.145–50)

The emptiness that defines Hobbes's miserable condition of war here defines the limits of sociable happiness too. What proclaims the one announces the other, either as cause and effect (the Spanish incited to ravage the New World "for the Sake of a pleasant Dream" [Trenchard 1725, 3:71]), or as a perpetual oscillation between the best and the worst. Dampier produced his grim picture of New Holland by execution of the very same contraries that permitted Gonzalo, Montaigne, and Swift to fancy utopias in the New World.

The imbrication of utopias with the state of war is no surprise to readers of ideal commonwealths. A war breaks out in Henry Neville's *Isle of Pines* when George Pine's (black) descendants assume the same sexual liberties as their founder (Neville 1668, 17). Thomas More's Utopia is on a perpetual war-footing, just like George Orwell's Oceania; and gold, despite its supposed lack of value, purchases mercenaries whom the Utopians would just as soon see dead, "filthy scum" the world can do without (More 1910, 113). In Rabelais's *tiers livre,* the Utopians (or Amaurots) are in deadly conflict with the Dipsodes, and eventually colonize the land of their enemies. Every year the horses of Gulliver's fourth book debate the option of genocide. No sooner does Robinson Crusoe discover the Arcadian beauties of his island than he plans for mass murder.

Whether a utopia incorporates war as an actual threat to its own perfect organization of production and resources, or makes room for the kind of politics it represses, as More's *Utopia* makes room for Macchiavelli's *The Prince* or as James Harrington's *Oceana* makes room for Mandeville's *The Fable of the Bees,* war is the negative lining of a proposition concerning a state of being to which nothing can be added. Whereas common sociability is the result of trying to add more to what is less, and has its "Origin from [Man's] Wants, his Imperfections, and the Variety of his Appetites" (Mandeville 1924, 1:346), utopian happiness is an idea of complete satisfaction, everything with nothing added. Robinson Crusoe says of his life in a state of nature, "I had nothing to covet, for I had all that I was now capable of enjoying" (Defoe 1972b, 128). Similarly, Tacitus said of the ancient German tribes, "Against the malignity of the Gods, they have accomplished a thing of infinite difficulty, that to them nothing remains even to be wished" (Tacitus 1728–31, 2:349). "All" is expressed by its contrary, nothing ("no ravenous Beast, no furious Wolves or Tygers . . . no venomous Creatures . . . no Savages," "no house to inhabit, no land to cultivate" [Defoe 1983, 132; Tacitus 1728–31, 2:340]), suggesting that the utopian proposition, "Everything plus nothing equals happiness," can just as easily be reformed to read, "Happiness with everything amounts to nothing." According to Hobbes, making a property of our dreams of plenty is just such an empty case: "There is no such thing in this world, no way to it, more than to Utopia" (Hobbes 1994, 44).

Coincidentally with the rise and fall of South Sea stock, there rose and fell the fortunes of the men whose efforts had made possible the dream of treasure below the equator, namely the Jamaica pirates and buccaneers who crewed the privateers raiding the coasts of Panama, Peru, and Chile.

Former privateer Woodes Rogers broke the back of Caribbean piracy in 1718, when, as governor of the Bahamas, he superintended the trial and execution of eight of the most notorious. In 1721 he sailed back to London, the job done. The account of his achievement concludes the second volume of Charles Johnson's *General History of the Pyrates* (1728), generally attributed to Defoe, where the compiler dryly observes, "There were but few (beside the Governor's Adherents) among the Spectators, who had not deserved the same Fate" (Defoe 1972a, 660).[1] Defoe had used his history to make a wider sweep of the activities of pirates and the nature of piracy itself. In his chapter on Captain England, he tells with what relish the captain's crew retired to Porto Bello to enjoy their plunder, adding, "I can't say, but that they had known what was doing in England, at the same Time, by the South-Sea Directors, and their Directors, they would certainly have had this Reflection for their Consolation, viz. That whatever Robberies they had committed, they might be pretty sure they were not the greatest Villains then living in the World" (Defoe 1972a, 134; Novak 1962, 105, 110). It was a popular comparison. Alluding to the same directors, Trenchard exclaimed that "the Wealth of Nations is measured out and divided amongst private Men, not (as by the West-India Pyrates) with Shovels, but by Waggons" (Trenchard 1725, 1:141). The comparison was strengthened by their own request to be ceded the island of St. Christopher, a sugar island once dominated by buccaneers, as part of the remission of the company's debts (Trenchard 1725, 17). But the parallel went deeper; for if the directors exposed a state of war by pursuing utopian dreams, so did the pirates. Defoe published his debunking version of John Avery's utopia in the Indian Ocean, *The King of Pirates*, in the same year that the Bubble burst (Turley 1999, 69).

The most fascinating in Defoe's collection of pirates is a Frenchman, Captain Misson, purely fictional but based on the career of Avery, the Indian Ocean pirate bilked of his inheritance, who seized a vast treasure from a Mughal ship and set up a fort on Madagascar, where he and his companions lived like kings. In his play based on Avery's career, *The Successful Pirate* (1713), Charles Johnson shows a hero, Arviragus, who, Averylike, has "declared War upon Mankind . . . and fixt himself . . . on this fair island, of which he is sole Monarch" (Johnson 1980, 3). Although scornful of Avery, Defoe develops in Misson these qualities of the heroic solitaire that had intrigued Johnson. Both were interested in a man who

---

1   This is a contested attribution, particularly the life of the fictional Captain Misson, but I am happy with it. See Turley 1999, 103–7.

dares to live in a state of war, and whose reward (at least for a time) is utopian happiness. Misson is shown by Defoe being seduced by the arguments of his Machiavellian companion, Caraccioli, who tells him he has only to act in order to "reign Sovereign of the Southern Seas, and lawfully make War on all the World" (Defoe 1972a, 391). Taking his mentor's advice, he founds the commonwealth of Libertalia on Madagascar, a community remarkable for the "Regularity, Tranquillity, and Humanity" of its members, who find no difficulty in reconciling their state of war with the retired conditions perfect peace (Rediker 1996, 125–34; Defoe 1961, iii; Baer 1985, 21–22; Turley 1999, 80). For his part, Arviragus has "leapt the Pale of Custom, and is a Royal Outlaw," ruler of a utopia called Laurentia, where he has "bound and cemented by civil Laws a Race of Vagabonds, the Out-casts of the Earth" (Johnson 1980, 3–4).

Arviragus and Misson exhibit an amphibian quality that fascinated Denis Diderot and Guillaume Raynal. The later editions of the *Histoire des deux Indes* (1772–87) rehearse the stories of the West Indian buccaneers who, impelled by "an energy of soul" and "powers unknown before," set up utopian communities on the islands of Catalina, Providence, Tortuga, and Santo Domingo. "The principle which actuated these extraordinary and romantic men, is not easily discovered," said Raynal, warming to the mystery of this Caribbean romance (Raynal 1783, 5:79–82). Buccaneers lived in same-sex couples (called *matelotage*), and apart from occasional forays at sea, hunted the wild cattle, dressed themselves in hides, and desired no more than a good pack of dogs and a musket that would fire a one-ounce ball. Having expelled or killed all the local inhabitants, they evolved a system of popular government known on privateering vessels as "Jamaica discipline," where all decisions were taken by a vote, and leaders could be voted out of office. "Theft was unknow'n among them, though no precautions were taken against it; and what was wanting at home was freely borrowed from some of the neighbours, without any other restriction than that of a previous intimation . . . a custom, which bears the double character, both of a primitive state, in which every thing was in common, and of times posterior to that, in which the idea of private property was know'n and respected" (Raynal 1783, 5:38). Although addicted to gambling, and so careless of consequences they would frequently bet themselves, they used a primitive scheme of social insurance: "If they had lost a hand, an arm, or a leg, they received two hundred crowns. An eye, or a finger, lost in fight, was valued only at half the above sum. The wounded were allowed three livres a day for two months" (5:53). It is precisely the same scheme of insurance Defoe borrowed for his *Essay on Projects* as the most effectual inducement to sailors to defend their ships against privateers (Defoe 1860, 23). Raynal saluted them as a utopian anomaly in the stream of time, "a people wholly distinct in history; but a people whose duration was so transient, that its glory lasted, as it were, but a moment" (Raynal 1783, 5:81; Hobsbawm 1959, 59; Hill 1986, 3:163–78).

Other commentators on the buccaneers emphasized their warlike aspect. Alexandre Exquemelin gave a horrifying account of the tortures visited by Sir Henry Morgan on the hapless townsfolk of Maracaibo solely to satisfy his lust for gold (Exquemelin 1684, 2:63). Burney talked of their mode of self-dramatization ("a propensity to make things which are extraordinary appear more so"), prompting them to commit lurid cruelties, such as Francois l'Olonnais's tearing out the hearts of his enemies and eating them. The same propensity inclined them to pursue extravagant punctilios, such as Montbar the Exterminator, a Frenchman so outraged by the Spanish oppression of the Indians that he dedicated his life to killing Spaniards (Burney 1803–16, 4:45, 55). Burney mentioned their attempt in 1664 to set up a republic on Santa Catalina, just off the Mosquito Coast, under the leadership of a seaman called Mansvelt; without regret, he recorded how it was put down by Morgan, one of their own subsequently purchased by the governor of Jamaica. As far as he was concerned, the "brethren of the coast" were notable for nothing but "usurpation and barbarity" (4:56, 37). To read Burney alongside Raynal is to hear of radical sons of liberty who tyrannize over local populations, holders of property in common devoted to a career of violent robbery, stoics abandoned to the pursuit of pleasure, lords of contingency addicted to games of chance, torturers who have a welfare system for the maimed—in short, a collection of people inhabiting an isthmus between utopia and the state of nature, everything and nothing, and exhibiting to its maximum Mandeville's heterogeneous compound. Theirs is the ambivalence belonging to all utopians, being neither settlers nor mariners, neither creoles nor savages, neither entirely noble pioneers of a new social order nor altogether ignoble degenerates.

Defoe had no time for pirates—his *General History* was meant to be their swan song. In his *Review* (18 October 1707), he lists sarcastically the variety of pirate trades constituting an anticommonwealth, all enemies to true commercial society: "Clandestine Trade Pyrates, who pyrate upon fair Trade at home; the Custom-stealing Pyrates who pyrate upon the Government, the Owling [illegal wool trade] Pyrates, who rob the Manufacturers, the privateering Pyrates, who rob by Law" (Defoe 1938, 4:425–

26; quoted in Johnson 1980, v). Shaftesbury was of the same opinion. With pirates like Avery in his sights, he said it is "impossible that a pirate, or any villain of less degree, who is false to the society of mankind in general . . . should have any fixed principle at all . . . and thus the more he sets up honour or advances zeal, the worse he renders his nature" (Shaftesbury 1964, 1:307). Hutcheson disagreed, supposing that it might be possible to establish a new society after rejecting the old: "Let us suppose a Band of such Villains cast in upon some desolate Island . . . these Persons are capable of Knowledge and Counsel . . . that they may return to a State of Love, Humanity, Kindness, and become Friends, Citizens, Husbands, Parents . . . and form an honest happy Society" (Hutcheson 1725, 132–33). None of these judgments engaged, however, with the amphibian qualities of pirate and buccaneer communities at the level attempted by Raynal, where he began to appreciate how the best and the worst of all political projects are united in them—just as Trenchard began to understand how his own reaction to the Bubble was bubblelike.

In the same issue of the *Review* quoted in the preceding paragraph, Defoe identifies the nature of piratical heterogeneous compounds, highly social and antisocial at the same time, as a prime reason for destroying them, for they confound the categories that provide the only justification of civil society, mocking the best with the worst, and confounding the worst with the best. In *The Successful Pyrate,* Defoe's views are shared by the traitor De Sale, who explains his attempted overthrow of Arviragus as an attempt to purge the political atmosphere of ambiguity:

> I hate this Renegade, this Scepter'd Rogue:
> And why? Because he is but half himself,
> His Virtues share his Faults; ay therefore 'tis,
> My Eyes abhor him. (Johnson 1980, 26)

In spite of himself, Defoe (like De Sale) was intrigued by what he would like to annihilate, and in his *Captain Singleton* (1721), he takes a second opportunity to investigate the ambivalence of piratical propensities—not so much with regard to utopian settlements, although the hero does spend time on Avery's Madagascar, as to objects, chiefly gold. Singleton is guided toward gold partly by ignorance and partly by his friend William. Gold is what his brethren mightily desire, and he can project no alternative goal, being a blind creature of chance who attaches little significance to the episodes of his life "for want of having a sense of their Tendency and Consequence" (Defoe 1963, 12). Besides, William, his Caraccioli, instructs him, "Your Business is Money," and in the pursuit of it advises him to trust no one, saying, "I would as soon trust a Man whose Interest binds him to be just to me, as a Man whose Principle binds himself" (266, 242). Nevertheless, Singleton is destined to forge such a fast friendship with William that "we neither had nor sought any separate Interest" (329); and in the course of what he calls "a Voyage and no voyage . . . bound *some* where and *no* where" (39), he comes to view money as something more, or less, than a "glittering Commodity" (242).

While making his way across Africa, Singleton discovers that gold has no intrinsic value, and that its conversion from dirt to treasure, or from treasure to trifles, is owing solely to fancy and agreement. The Africans with whom they trade prefer money that is attractive, and the only way the pirates can make their bullion current is to beat iron, gold, and silver into plate, and then cut it into pleasing shapes. "For a little Bit of Silver cut out in the Shape of a Bird, we had two Cows . . . thus, that which when it was coin was not worth six-pence to us, when thus converted into Toys and Trifles, was worth an Hundred Times its real Value" (34). This is Captain Bob's first lesson in the nature of token or fiduciary money, instituted in England in 1694 with the foundation of the Bank of England and the circulation of bank bills worth nothing but what people believed them to be worth. Defoe's understanding of paper credit is supplemented here with descriptions of the fetish gold of the West African coast, which was worked into shapes and entangled with other materials, such as wool and wood, and circulated as a similar token form of money called Kakeraas (Pietz 1988, 110n. 10). Like a fetish, a mixture of wood, metal, fabric, and hair disguised as an idol or an amulet, fetish money emphasizes its materiality in order to hide its intrinsic emptiness. Singleton's artist, a former cutler, goes into overdrive once the aesthetics of these transactions is understood, fashioning "Elephants, Tygers, Civet Cats, Ostriches, Eagles, Cranes, Fowls, Fishes, and indeed whatever he pleased," truly the very coinage of his brain (Defoe 1963, 159). The basis of the resemblance between his art and that of the South Seas directors, with their increasingly elaborate issues of stock, has been noted as "a process of fetishistic misrecognition, whereby debt, absence, and powerlessness are transubstantiated . . . into their opposites—into wealth, a plenitude of laws and institutions, and power" (Brantlinger 1996, 20). Adam Anderson gives a good example of what Swift describes as financiers' witchcraft ("Bankers . . . squeezing Images of Wax" [Swift 1958, 1:240]): "I can well remember one of these named Globe Permits, which came to be currently sold each for sixty guineas and upwards in the alley, which neverthless was only a square bit of a playing card, on which was the impression of a seal in wax, being the sign of the Globe tavern in the neighbourhood, with the motto or inscription of Sail Cloth Permits, without any name signed thereon" (Anderson 1825, 68). Simon Schaffer has pointed to the parallel between Defoe's conception of a credit economy as a je ne sais quoi and his description of the manufacture of fetish money in *Captain Singleton* as one depending on value as the exclusive product of fancy and agreement. He also points out that before the South Sea Bubble, Locke and Isaac Newton made attempts to de-fetishize the economy (the first in 1695, the second in 1717) by establishing a public criterion of intrinsic value in the form of gold coins of a guaranteed weight (Schaffer 1996b, 12–14).

No more than Trenchard could Defoe transcend the antinomies of credit. His impatience with pirates and their utopias could go only so far before he found himself and his commercial principles participating in the same chimerical blend of contraries. He who averred in 1712 that the South Sea Company was a real and solid advantage to the nation, not an "Amusement of Trade," was forced to admit ten years later that it was a terrible infatuation with terra incognita, a scheme of voyages that were no voyages bound to somewhere and nowhere. His own experiments with fiction date from the period of the Bubble, at least four of them concerned more or less directly with the Indian Ocean and the South Seas. They are romances, moreover, whose relation to real history is blurred by the same exhaustiveness of detail that makes Dampier's and Anson's journals indistinguishable (in the opinion of many readers) from Gulliver's. As Misson is to Avery, so is Crusoe to Selkirk, each telling stories of self-preservation and the intense pleasure associated with it that renders the distinction between true and false temporarily meaningless. The question of truth itself is implicated in the chain of impossible conjunctions —nobility and savagery, isolation and community, war and peace, glory and self-loss—imported from the South Seas into the metropole. When Locke talked of narratives bringing home to the hearth "the utmost Bounds of the Earth," stories compassing all countries and nations, the largeness of the claim, like all the others being made with respect to terra incognita, was determined by its emptiness, "the names of Nothing" (Hobbes 1968, 691).

3

SCIENCE AND COLLECTING

Two chronometers the captain had,
One by Arnold that ran like mad,
One by Kendal in a walnut case,
Poor devoted creature with a hangdog face.

All through the night-time, clock talked to clock,
In the captain's cabin, tock-tock-tock,
One ticked fast and one ticked slow,
And Time went over them a hundred years ago.

　　　—Kenneth Slessor, *Five Visions of Captain Cook*

The shop seemed to be full of all manner of curious things—but the oddest part of
it all was that, whenever she looked hard at any shelf, to make out exactly what it had
on it, that particular shelf was always quite empty, though the others round it were
crowded as full as they could hold.

　　　—Lewis Carroll, *Through the Looking-Glass*

It is generally agreed that the business of exploration became a great deal
more deliberate and exact in the era of Philip Carteret, Samuel Wallis,
John Byron, Louis-Antoine de Bougainville, and James Cook, whose exploits inspired another generation of explorers such as Alessandro Mala-
spina; Jean-Francois de Galaup, Comte de La Perouse; William Bligh;
George Vancouver; and Matthew Flinders to complete what they had begun. But of all these feats, Cook's three expeditions remain the most remarkable. As a result of his efforts, William Dampier's crude illustrations
were outstripped by the superb drawings of Sydney Parkinson, the artist
on Cook's first voyage, whose accuracy as a draftsman was equal to the demands for Linnaean distinctions of species made by Joseph Banks and
Daniel Solander, the natural historians on board. The work of William

Hodges and John Webber, on the second and third voyages, provided vivid supplements to the ethnographic observations of the two Forsters, Johann Reinhold and George, and of Cook himself. The haphazard cartography of privateers such as Edward Davis, William Cowley, and Bartholomew Sharp, whose mistakes were preserved (as Lemuel Gulliver complains) in Herman Moll's maps, is superseded by the definitive charts of New Zealand, Tahiti, and Hawaii supplied by Cook and Bligh. Larcum Kendall's and John Arnold's chronometers, carried on the second voyage, contributed, like the astronomical instruments used in measuring the transits of Venus and Mercury, to the discovery of the longitude and the ability of navigators to plot the exact location of themselves and their discoveries. And the uncertain anthropology of the early explorers, who lumped together all the peoples west of America as Indians, benighted in an indistinguishable state of savagery, yields to the theories of cultural difference and historical change propounded first by the Forsters, and then by Adam Ferguson; Henry Home, Lord Kames; John Millar; and Gottfried Herder.

The reason for this improvement in knowledge—again, it is generally agreed—lies in the switch from the contingent desires motivating the privateers (who laid claim to whatever goods and data happened to come to hand) to the more disciplined and disinterested approach of scientific inquiry. Science not only endows the curious observer with a means of uniting disparate facts into a true history, and of gathering specimens into a universal taxonomy, but also dignifies him with a vision of territory as truth, altogether more solid and real than John Locke's and Daniel Defoe's intuitions of how knowledge, trade, and settlement might be managed in the South Seas. The "views of ambition and avarice," as George Keate put it, yielded to "the improvement of science and geography" (Keate 1788, v). The Royal Society stands as the alpha and omega of this project of extending empire jointly with the arts and sciences: Francis Bacon's *New Atlantis,* an academy of the sciences set in the South Seas, is its utopian forerunner; and the Earl of Morton's hints, issued in the name of the Royal Society to regulate Cook's accounts of strange people, stars, and oceans, confirm its authority on the other side of the globe as arbiter of the real and true.

The focus of this empire of science is the human eye, and its limits are the space and the time of the world. Instruments such as telescopes, sextants, and chronometers were improved to increase the accuracy of observations, which were then submitted to new methods of calculation and tabulation in order to determine their significance within the scheme of things (Sobel 1995; Sorrenson 1995). What was to be known was what was to be seen, measured, and understood; and what was understood was then the property of the eye and the "I," not an isolated witness but the agent and recorder of a national history of the globe. The world was seized in images printed on the retina of this punned imperial eye; territory was the object of optical instruments that revealed sites of improvement, "resources to be developed, surpluses to be traded, towns to be built" (Pratt 1992, 61). The ego acting as the fuse between this new world and the nations with interests in it was allegedly very different from the romantic paladin, whose service to commerce and chivalry unraveled as private passion in the course of earlier navigations. This scientific self is the impartial first person of a universal language (Foucault 1970, 147), capable of establishing a cognitive superiority over all other eyes and "I"s, and of commencing the first sentence of a history whose theme is everything everywhere (Foucault 1972, 12; Spivak 1994, 66). Science and this representative ego march hand in hand, celebrating "a physical, topographical, material sublimity . . . coextensive with that of man" (Stafford 1984, 54). The vastness that had power to overwhelm the mind in Edmund Burke's treatment of the sublime now finds its measure, and the mind declares its supremacy. Alexander von Humboldt aligned the end of scientific voyaging to Friedrich von Schelling's union of identity with totality (Dettelbach 1996, 278), supposing a degree of observational competence coextensive with the providence of God.

Success in such an enterprise requires an invincible self and a sturdy platform, superior to the stresses that might distort its measurements of things, or trouble the sense of its own consistency. There can be no mistake about the duty of accurate investigation, or the means by which it is achieved, communicated, and processed. Success, therefore, also depends upon a secure relationship between the self and the public it serves, much more regular and exact than the romances of buccaneering knights errant. The coalition of private and public interests relies upon rational and punctilious attention to detail, not propensities and lies. Facts declare their truth as they are fitted into a global order that renders the purposes of the nation and the self coterminous. In their impartial journalizing and dispassionate notation, Cook and his followers anticipated von Humboldt's magisterial formulation: "In a narrative, the principal end of which is the progress of physical knowledge, every other consideration ought to be subservent to those of instruction and utility" (Humboldt 1907, 1:105).

Guidance in the assembling of such a narrative was explicit. Cook sailed with two sets of instructions and a letter of advice, to leave him in no doubt about what he was to look for and how he was to search for it. He was to find the Great Southern Continent, if it were there, and to map New Zealand, if it were not. He was to arrange "to observe the Passage of the Planet Venus over the Disk of the Sun on the 3rd of June 1769" (Cook 1955, cclxxix). He was told to be attentive to the rights of islanders, and to take pains not to shed their blood. "You are to observe the Genius, Temper, Disposition and Number of the Natives . . . and endeavour by all proper means to cultivate a Friendship and Alliance with them . . . Shewing them every Kind of Civility and Regard" (cclxxxiii). He was taught how to make signs for hunger and thirst, and advised to soothe the savage breast with gentle sounds: "If there are Instruments of Music on board they should be first entertained near the Shore with a soft Air" (515). He was to take careful note of their "Features, Complection, Dress, Habitations, Food, Weapons"; to consider their "Religion, Morals Order, Government, Distinctions of Power, Police"; and to report "Animal, Vegetable and Mineral Systems" of the country. He was also to register carefully "Tides and Currents, Depths and Soundings of the Sea, Shoals, Rocks &c" (517; cclxxxii). Even unprecedented events found a place in this protonarrative, and a proper course of action was formulated to deal with them: "You are in all such Cases, to proceed, as upon advice with your Officers you shall judge most advantageous to the Service on which you are employed" (cclxxxiii). By paying strict attention to all these matters, Cook and his successors were to produce a distinct and full account of the undiscovered moiety of the earth.

In order that the representations of the contents of this region not be mistaken for idols or monsters, a clear and necessary route was demarcated, leading from experimental accuracy to general truths, from facts to Providence. Real knowledge aimed at the status of theodicy: that is, the capacity to justify exploration and discovery as the completion of the grand design inscribed by God in nature and time. Nothing can escape this pattern as anomalous or contingent; therefore, nothing can justify fantasy. In his critique of previous narratives of discovery, George Forster shows how well he understood this: "I have always endeavoured in this narrative to connect the ideas rising from different occurrences, in order, if possible, to throw more light upon the nature of the human mind, and to lift the soul into that exalted station, from when the extensive view must 'justify the ways of God to man'" (Forster 1777, xii). The system of commerce, the honor of the nation, and the plan of empire are satellites of this vaster organization of meaning. Forster hinted at his faith when he talked of "the thread of Ariadne, by the help of which [the traveller]might guide his steps through the labyrinth of human knowledge" (xii).

The thread of Ariadne had been defined by Carolus Linnaeus as classification (Pratt 1992, 25). In botany and in all branches of natural history, classification provided a home, a history, and a relation for all discovered things. Daniel Solander, on Cook's first voyage, and Anders Sparrman on the second, were Linnaeus's students, charged with the task of collecting specimens and field notes and sending them back to their master, the justifying intelligence sitting at the center of his worldwide web (Pratt 1992, 27). After his traveling days were over, Sir Joseph Banks sat at the center of a similar web, his agents spread over the world in order to supply him with plant and animal specimens (Mackay 1996, 38). Given this wide and clear "prospect of concatenated events," in Bernard Mandeville's phrase, it became theoretically possible to rearrange the distribution of flora to the advantage of nations. Linnaeus dreamt of breeding llamas and growing tea and cotton in Sweden (Koerner 1996, 131–39); and Banks saw the Tahitian breadfruit as a cheap source of food for slaves in the West Indies, a transplantation Bligh was trying to put into effect when he was overtaken by a mutiny (Gascoigne 1998, 106). In this theodicean account of knowledge, the disinterested collection of data precedes the interested application of knowledge. The imperial eye must contemplate the world as an object of dispassionate inquiry before it may be appropriated and used. In naming Cook commander for the first scientific expedition to the Pacific, the Admiralty chose someone who, unlike George Anson twenty-five years before, had no personal interest in the trip in the prospective form of prize money. The *Endeavour* was to make no raids on the Peruvian coast, nor to seize the Acapulco treasure ship. As the views of the voyage terminated solely in the public good afforded by knowledge, and as there was no emergency which had not been foreseen, there was no room for any propensity not defined by social utility, nor for any action not guided by instructions.

That, at least, was how it was planned and is often remembered. Part of the reason for assigning such a high degree of experimental accuracy to the later eighteenth-century voyages lies in an assumption that the history of navigation runs parallel with the history of science, and that the history of science in Britain runs parallel with developments in Europe. In this chapter, I want to explore some of the discontinuities in these three lines of development, particularly as they affect the level of public trust reposed in the eighteenth-century navigator to the South Seas. I mean to argue that the voyager could never be sure that his techniques of discovery, and the language in which he framed his discoveries, were thoroughly understood at home, even though they might be enjoyed. I want to suggest that part of the reason for the failure of this understanding was the inherent weakness of truth-claims in voyage narratives which, combined with a heterogeneous scientific community in England by no means unanimously attached to a set of common epistemological principles, rendered the reception of these narratives uncertain. A climate of distrust afflicted communications between scientists at sea and their metropolitan audience, and then damaged the exchange of sentiments among the scientists themselves, leading to a sense of isolation among the discoverers unprecedented in the history of navigation of new worlds.

Recent research has shown how wonders and monsters, traditionally supposed to congregate at the ends of the earth, were reorganized within the protocols of seventeenth-century experimental science to become legitimate objects of metropolitan inquiry. By detaching the marvelous or anomalous thing from a system of legible signs, so that it no longer betokened occult sympathies, divine intentions, or textual archetypes, inquirers endowed it with the singularity of an as yet (in Lord Bolingbroke's phrase) "unrelative event," or of an obdurately unconnected fact, worthy of close observation for its own sake. Commonly defined as divine suspensions of the law of nature constitutive of a special message to mortals, miracles (for example) were undergoing a revision of their evidentiary value, a change Lorraine Daston summarizes as follows: "Evidence *of* miracles became a debate over the evidence *for* miracles" (Daston 1994, 245). Although it was a common method of disparaging testimony of miracles to say it was as improbable as romance, and even to compare the miracle worker to Don Quixote (Woolston 1727, 5:38; Voltaire 1993, 9: 295), this change in status put miracles at the forefront of experimental reasoning, to the extent that the St. Medard miracles of the holy thorn in late seventeenth-century France "are among the best-documented historical facts of the early modern period" (Daston 1994, 271). A bare fact, whether it was associated with a miracle or an experiment in mechanics, was productive of wonder. Robert Boyle the Christian virtuoso, addicted to romance in his early years (Shapin 1995, 138), found romance breeding in the laboratory among events so astonishing (the vacuum, a breach in nature) as to make him "think the vulgar catalogue of impossible or incredible things far greater than it ought to be" (Boyle 1772, 6:679; quoted in Shapin 1995, 199).

To accomplish this change in the status of wonders from a medium of meaning to an object of inquisition, three constant elements in the production of visible truth were slightly rearranged: these were wonder, sociability, and particularity. Early collections of mirabiles could serve the purpose of binding or strengthening a community, such as the treasures of the Abbey of St. Denis superintended by its ambitious archibishop Suger, or the wonders assembled by Philip the Good in order to give credibility to the recently formed Burgundian state (Daston and Park 1998, 77, 103). The prestige of the objects was absorbed by the institution that housed them. When experimental scientists took up the study of wonders, the community of wonder shifted its ground. Instead of being the effect of the power of wonder, sociability became the cause of wonders being gathered and studied. Before exploring the mysteries of the vacuum, Boyle fashioned himself as the urbane participant in an enterprise chartered as the Royal Society, comprising a group of gentlemen virtuosi whose words were their bonds, and whose sociable exchanges were founded on unlimited mutual trust (Shapin 1995, 36–38; Latour 1993, 30). His membership in this society warranted his investigations and the reports he made of them, in which he affirmed the importance of facts as the sum of an experiment, whether it succeeded or failed, not as clues to divine providence. Boyle greeted his cohort with the particulars he witnessed, thus preserving the earlier way of registering (though not of interpreting) wonders, namely by laying great stress on the circumstances of their appearance. "Habits of concentration and meticulous attention" provided both the means of studying marvels as signs (Daston and Park 1998, 147) as well as generating the empirical density of scientific reports. "In Boyle's experimental writing this meant a highly *circumstantial* style, often specifying in excruciating detail when, how, and where experiments were done; who was present; how many times they were reiterated; and with exactly what results" (Shapin 1996, 108). In this respect, the extravagant claims of veridical testimony in romance, for example the reputation for "punctual and impartial historiography" enjoyed by Don Quixote's narrator, Cide Hamet Benengeli (Cervantes 1970, 1:98), are part of this heritage, cousins to the principle of *nullius in verba*, that close, naked, and natural way of speaking recommended by the Royal Society as the language fit for the experimental eyewitness.

When the advent of the eighteenth century saw a sharp rise in the threshold of belief, making the testimony of extraordinary things less current, the function of sociability was once again redefined. Wonder ceased to be either the means or the occasion of a common bond between people, and served instead to exemplify the conflict between social norms and a desire for surprising things. *Nil admirari* became the motto of the gentleman: "Not to Admire, is all the Art I know, / To make men happy, and to keep them so," said Alexander Pope, quoting Thomas Creech's *Horace* (Pope 1963, 630). Shaftesbury denounced as vulgar and barbarous all literary forms trading on popular credulity, including voyages to remote lands. Common sense became the standard of probability, and facts were accounted true if they were already familiar, part of that continuum of cases linking the immemorial to the constitutional, the natural to the social, common law to statute law, propensities to moral sentiments, and so on. Wonders might be amusing on account of their novelty, and writers of romances and novels might well rely on that particularizing style to fasten their grip upon the audience, but they could make no claim to be writing biography or history. There was suddenly no great use for the rhetoric of eyewitnesses, truth being lapidary, and its style sententious. It was an age that "feared the entry of the false more than the exclusion of the true" (Daston and Park 1998, 251–52).

This shift was especially awkward for writers of voyages. They saw the popularity of their genre rise to dizzying heights for the same reason that denied it in public opinion any access to the truth (Spate 1983, 2:157). As Lady Mary Wortley Montagu and William Wales both complained, a traveler who recites familiar things will not be read, but the one who tells of wonders will not be believed. She lamented, "We travellers are in very hard circumstances: If we say nothing but what has been said before us, we are dull, and we have observed nothing. If we tell anything new, we are laughed at as fabulous and romantic" (Montagu 1906, 156). Wales, a scientist and mathematician, equipped with the most potent means of enforcing his veracity, echoed her: "If he tells nothing which is uncommon, he must be a stupid fellow to have gone so far, and brought home so little; and if he does, why—it is hum—aye, a toss of the Chin, and—he's a Traveller" ("Journal" in Cook 1961, 839). Wonders now fed the taste of a single representative figure, often "the curious reader," who stood for a public interested in pleasure, not truth, whose loyalty to authors (whether they pretended to be eyewitnesses or compilers) lasted only as long as the pleasure. Voyagers interested in asserting the singularity as well as the accuracy of their observations were bereft of a means of doing so, for not only was the audience largely indifferent to the distinction between true and false, other than as an index of their pleasure, but also the battery of rhetorical strategies engineered by the discoverers of the New World in order to vouch for the truth of an eyewitness's strange testimony were all in abeyance. Columbus had been able to quote his admiration for the paradises he visited because a body of texts ranging from Pliny to Sir John Mandeville, and from Herodotus to Marco Polo, warranted the wonder and the strangeness of what he saw (Greenblatt 1991, 55, 73). Sir Humphrey Gilbert perished off the coast of Newfoundland quoting from a copy of *Utopia* he was holding in his hand (Armitage 1998, 107), aware that his intended landfall or his death equally abetted the translation from one text into another (Grafton 1992, 147). Blockage itself had been part of this rhetoric, the je ne sais quoi a measure of significant rarity (Greenblatt 1991, 121; Grafton 1992, 79). Even those most tormented by the novelty of what they saw, like Bartolome de Las Casas and Fernández de Oviedo, had scriptural models that allowed them to fashion themselves as lonely sufferers—at a dead lift they could rely on the precedent of romance to give a frame to the unimaginable and incalculable (Pagden 1993, 66–70).

When William Dampier, the first Englishman to land on the coast of New Holland, confronts his reader as an eyewitness, none of this applies. He makes the same complaint as Montagu and Wales: "It has almost always been the Fate of those who have made new Discoveries, to be disesteemed and slightly spoken of, by such as either have no true Relish and Value for the Things themselves that are discovered, or have had some Prejudice aginst the Persons by whom the Discoveries were made" (Dampier 1729, 2:[i]). He means that either the material is found tedious or the narrator is taken for a liar. Knowing he lacks a sociable and trusting readership, Dampier's only resource is to stick doggedly to the particularity of the facts, pretending that credit will be given him at least by the odd "intelligent" (as opposed to "curious") reader: "Choosing to be more particular than might be needful, with respect to the intelligent Reader, rather than to omit what I thought might tend to the Information of Persons no less sensible and inquisitive . . . my chief Care hath been to be as particular as was consistent with my intended brevity, in setting down the Observables I met with" (1:[sig. A3]). When he goes on to assert that his candor has no need of "a Polite and Rhetorical Narrative" (2:[ii]), he sums up the poverty and vulgarity of his demeanor, placing himself in exactly the posture Shaftesbury had assigned retailers of wonders of the terra incognita, barbarous and unsociable (Shaftesbury 1964, 1:221–22). Effectually, he puts himself at a loss for any method of seriously attaching the reader's attention; so that when he is driven to use the je ne sais quoi, it is devoid of rhetorical and social significance: "The Reader may better guess than I can express, the Confusion that we were all in" (Dampier 1729, 1:496). Which reader? The reader who couldn't care less, or the one addressed by his colleague William Funnell as likely to be amused by "the great Variety of Accidents we met with, and the . . . particular Accounts of the manner how our Attempts miscarried" (Funnell 1707, [ii])? When these travelers say that nothing the reader is capable of imagining is equal to what they saw or felt, they are exactly stating the case, removing blockage from the comforting sphere of rhetoric, and binding the je ne sais quoi to the modern, isolated condition of those who talk of the new to a public that will not heed them.

The same isolation from the reader, driving the traveler into a purely private surprise at things that may or may not be intrinsically wonderful, is maintained in imaginary voyages too. Robinson Crusoe declares his baking of bread and his firing of crude pots to be part of "a long series of Miracles" and "a Croud of Wonders" (Defoe 1972b, 132). The footprint he spies in the sand is exemplary of wonders that are as ordinary as they are private, of no significance to a community of readers. Of the kitchen implements in the royal palace of Lorbulgrud, Gulliver exclaims, "But if I should describe the kitchen-grate, the prodigious pots and kettles, the joints of meat turning on the spits, with many other particulars, perhaps I should be hardly believed" (Swift 1948, 131). No longer sure of what constitutes the marvelous, he halts the description of his diet with the Houyhnhmns, fearful of imitating travelers who enlarge upon this matter, "as if the readers were personally concerned whether we fare well or ill" (286). Whenever he takes up a narrative, Gulliver is morbidly aware of the disbelief it will encounter. As he is telling an incredulous horse of equestrianism in Europe, and imagines how the story of such a conversation would be greeted there, Gulliver acknowledges his isolation between two rival forms of disbelief (295–96). With the same grim intuition of double solitude, both on his island and on the page, Crusoe announces his longing for society in a je ne sais quoi that only confirms his lack of it: "I cannot explain by any possible Energy of Words, what a strange longing or hankering of Desires I felt" (187). The combined effect, in real and imaginary travels alike, is to make the singular experience sublime and its representation an object of curiosity or incredulity. Particularity is transposed from the rhetoric of the collector or the word of a gentleman scientist into the sphere of verisimilitude, and even there it threatens to be superfluous. Meanwhile, the relationship of the traveler and reader crystallizes into an unsociable, nonpolite pairing, subsisting in that state of suspended hostility Thomas Hobbes and Walter Shandy called war.

David Hume exclaimed, "With what greediness are the miraculous accounts of travellers received, their descriptions of sea and land monsters, their relation of wonderful adventures, strange men, and uncouth manners?" warning that if the love of wonder ever should ally itself with a mode of authority immune to reason, then "there is an end of common sense" (Hume 1903, 528). With this assertion he also said that Crusoe's je ne sais quoi (specifically his sighting of the inexplicable footprint in the sand [Hume 1955, 153]) menaces the necessary connection of our ideas as much as it does his own, and should be set aside as a private crisis amidst the unimaginable.[1] Hume's and Shaftesbury's critiques of voyage narratives were close to Hobbes's disapproval of Boyle's experiments with the air pump, which he thought distanced the testimony of the eyewitness and the demonstration of first principles to the degree that little difference existed between the sociable words of these civil gentlemen and the vainglorious talk of alehouse braggarts, "as when a man imagineth himself to do the actions whereof he readeth in some romant" (Hobbes 1994, 51; Shapin and Schaffer 1985, 62–68). The difficulty faced by Hume was that there were for him no first principles, only customary associations of ideas. A stark, unrelative, or extraordinary fact had a much greater power to unsettle the mind, therefore, since the textual and rhetorical frameworks that helped the discoveries of the New World toward legibility *secundum scriptura* (Pagden 1993, 52) were no longer operating. When Adam Smith came to consider how wonder could "so entirely disjoint the whole frame of the imagination" as to induce lunacy or frenzy, he tackled the problem of the sheer singularity of impressions that Hume had recognized but failed to regulate in his essay "Of the Standard of Taste." "When something quite new and singular is presented," Smith wrote, "it stands alone and by itself in the imagination, and refuses to be grouped or confounded with any set of objects whatever" (Smith 1795, 5, 11–12).

The South Sea Bubble had already shown how frenzy and infatuation could become a national distemper once extraordinary ideas were generally admitted, and how they could destroy the credit of the state as well as an individual. The strictures against wonderful facts indicate not so much an Enlightenment confidence in reason as a new and alarming susceptibility to unique impressions. The uneven progress of science in Britain during the eighteenth century is partly to be accounted for by its hos-

---

1 No doubt with Crusoe's moment of colossal shock in mind, when he sees the single footprint in the sand and can make nothing of it (Defoe 1972b, 154), Hume said, "The print of a foot in the sand can only prove, when considered alone, that there was some figure adapted to it by which it was produced. But the print of a human foot proves likewise, from our other experience, that there was probably another foot which also left its impression, though effaced by time or other accidents" (Hume 1955, 152).

pitality toward unexpected spillages of wonder. When Richard Boulton undertook to make Boyle's experiments accessible to an audience more interested in utility and profit than the protocols of mutual trust, he swept away a great deal of the prolixity of gentlemanly word keeping, leaving the air pump that Boyle first described an overloaded object, fetishized by metaphors appropriate to desire and pleasure rather than to mechanical precision (Markley 1993 240–56). Here is the beginning of the aestheticized appearance of the air pump and related equipment in later eighteenth-century representations, such as the machines in Joseph Wright of Derby's "A Philosopher giving [a] Lecture on the Orrery" (1766), and especially in his "An Experiment on a Bird in the Air Pump" (1768). These are sublime engines worked by a magus whose gestures disclose a metamorphosis that commands wonder, reverence, horror, not a sober conviction of the truth. Leyden jars, ivory balls, and crystal rods fed "streams of fine purple Fire" that glowed on the lips and fingers of demonstrators whose finesse and timing showed how much natural philosophy was beginning to owe to histrionic skill (Schaffer 1994, 60–69). When Thomas Beddoes and Sir Humphrey Davy used their pneumatic machines to inhale mind-altering gases, they were credited with having "invented a new pleasure for which language has no name" (Southey; quoted in Schaffer 1994, 88). Wonder, pleasure, and vulgarity go together. One of the less consoling things Burke had to say about the sublime concerned the ignorance needed to take delight in it: "It is our ignorance of things that causes all our admiration, and chiefly excites our passions. Knowledge and acquaintance make the most striking causes affect but little. It is thus with the vulgar, and all men are as the vulgar in what they do not understand" (Burke 1987, 61).

Although Shaftesbury and Hume resented the threat of this vulgarization so much that they debarred news of unprecedented things from any claim upon the truth, the Royal Society was not so rigid. In its *Philosophical Transactions* of the mid-eighteenth century, it is not uncommon to find prodigies and marvels, such as a report of "A Monstrous Human Foetus" (December 1766), "An Account of a remarkable Fish" (June 1763), "An Account of a remarkable Darkness at Detroit in America" (March 1763), and "An Account of an uncommon Phaenomenon in Dorsetshire" (April 1761). Not much had changed since a hundred years before, when the journal was receiving reports of monstrous births, bizarre weather, and celestial apparitions (Daston and Park 1998, 247). Developments in microscopy collaborated with the scientific taste for wonder by revealing "the incoherent uniqueness of grotesque or ambivalent entities," smudging the familiar boundaries between species and compromising the language of classification (Stafford 1996, 250). But because the modern culture of wonder no longer had a method of reading marvelous events as legible signs, and because it was held in suspicion by arbiters of taste as imbecile and vulgar, mariners were still embarrassed in their efforts to tell a credible tale. Coleridge's seafarer has to tell his again and again because all he can excite in his audience is wonder, not belief.

With this in mind, I turn again to Cook's instructions, the "pretext" of Cook's account of his voyage. They are in two parts, unsealed and sealed. The former concern the Royal Society's interest in the ethnographic details of native life and the measurement of the transit of Venus, a rare astronomical event whose accurate observation was expected to allow scientists to make a reliable estimate of the earth's distance from the sun. The latter holds orders for Cook's discovery of the Great Southern Continent, with the fallback job of mapping New Zealand. With the exception of this last order, which he fulfilled admirably, the enterprise was not a success. It was while he was actually trying to follow his instructions with regard to indigenous resistance (to subdue rebarbative natives that they might better be convinced of their visitors' good intentions, "a generous Christianlike Plan" [Cook 1955, 170n. 4, 515]) that Cook, aided by Solander and Banks, shot and killed four Maori in a canoe, shortly after their arrival in Poverty Bay. It was an event of such surprising savagery that none of the participants could justify it, other than by the law of self-preservation. The measurement of the transit of Venus was imperfect, a partial failure according to a recent commentator, and totally useless according to J. C. Beaglehole (Orchiston 1998, 59; Banks 1962, 1:29). Even John Harrison's great chronometer, and the copies of it carried during the second voyage, were inaccurate. Twenty-five years later, armed with five of them, all going fast, Vancouver put the coast of Alaska fifteen miles inland (Vancouver 1984, 1:51). The Great Southern Continent was not located, as Cook awkwardly admitted to the Lords of the Admiralty: "I have failed in Discovering the so much talked of Southern Continent which perhaps do not Exsist & which I my self had much at heart yet I am confident that no part of the failure of such discovery Can be laid to my Charge" (Cook 1995, app. 1, p. 501). He wrote this from Batavia, where he lost a third of his crew to an epidemic, having a few months before narrowly managed to avert shipwreck on the Australian Barrier Reef. He was experiencing what Daniel Boorstin has called "the ardours of negative discovery" (Boorstin 1985, 278).

A good part of the explanation for Cook's defensiveness lies in the purely speculative nature of a voyage in which he was commanded to find out what he could in a place of which no one had firsthand knowledge. Since the days when Herman Moll had asserted of the South Seas, "'Tis impossible for any [Person] to have a just Idaea of the Settlements that may be made, the Trades that may be carry'd on, and the Advantages that may arise" (Moll 1711, [ii]), no substantial addition had been made to maritime knowledge. Cook marked part of the coast of New Zealand "No Body Knows What" as if aware he was traversing a general je ne sais quoi (Vancouver 1984, 1:361). There were, however, gradations to this public ignorance and the interests various parties had in it. The Admiralty was interested in trade routes and undiscovered territory; Alexander Dalrymple was interested in the Great Southern Continent; and the Royal Society was interested in reports of Patagonian giants.

Despite the alibi of science, Cook's secret instructions defined a nationalist and mercantilist agenda differing little from the fantastic vision of empire extended to the utmost limits of the earth, which Locke raised on the basis of Dampier's exiguous reports. The expedition was sped and furnished by the same territorial and commercial ambitions that had first carried British ships into this ocean, namely the possibility of a staging post that would allow the British to compete for trade with the Spanish and possibly the Dutch (Spate 1988a, 3:77, 81; Frost 1988, 27; Harlow 1952, 1:37; Baugh 1990, 30–34; Williams 1996, 25). As well as directing him to the careful notation of people, things, coastlines, and landforms, Cook's instructions also bade him "to take possession of Convenient Situations in the Country in the Name of the King of Great Britain" (Cook 1955, cclxxciii). Bougainville had already inscribed an act of possession on an oak plank, and buried another in a firmly corked bottle, before he left Tahiti (Bougainville 1772b, 240). After the Seven Years' War (1757–63), both nations were eager to find a foothold in this part of the world. Such an advantage, wrote Lord Egmont, "will render all our Expeditions to those parts most lucrative to ourselves, most fatal to Spain, & no longer formidable, tedious, or uncertain in a future War" (PRO SP 94/253; quoted in Byron 1964, 161).

The chief territorial objective of Cook's first and second expeditions was the Great Southern Continent, formerly the terra incognita, the vast landmass believed to cover the greater portion of the high latitudes of the South Seas, stretching from the South Atlantic to the Indian Ocean and acting as counterweight to the continents of the Northern Hemisphere. How Peter Heylyn would have laughed, and how Lord Shaftesbury would have agonized, to think that this utopian fantasy was being seriously pursued as an official objective in cartography and foreign policy in the second half of the eighteenth century. Why Cook and successive companies of scientists should have been twice dispatched to search for this nonentity, and sent a third time to look for another—the Northwest Passage—is to be explained partly (like the South Sea Bubble) as the result of successful publicity. Alexander Dalrymple was convinced of the existence of the Great Southern Continent ever since he read Pedro Fernandez de Quirós's account of his discovery of Austrialia del Espiritu Santo, which he believed to be part of it. The more Dalrymple thought about it, the more it grew into "the great Passion of his life" (Dalrymple 1767, vi). Convinced that New Zealand formed the west coast of this continent (102), he had published two collections of South Sea voyages, and various charts, memorials, and letters designed to interest the government in his scheme of discovery and settlement of this huge temperate territory. In 1771, he composed with Benjamin Franklin a scheme for transporting the conveniences of life to New Zealand, the seaboard (as he still imagined) of his favorite continent, "as fowls, hogs, goats, cattle, corn, iron, &c, to those remote regions, which are destitute of them, and to bring from thence such productions, as can be cultivated in this kingdome to the advantage of society, in a ship under the command of Alexander Dalrymple" (Franklin 1806, 2:403). And four years later, having been obliged by the nonappearance of the Great Southern Continent in the Pacific to concentrate instead upon its situation in the South Atlantic, he proposed that a seal and whale fishery be set up on what he assumed now to be its northern coast (namely the Falkland Islands), for which he framed a utopian constitution based on civic humanist principles, apportioning each inhabitant a yeoman's share of land sufficient to supply his own needs (Dalrymple 1775, 10–13). Clearly in the grip of an obsession exacerbated by his exclusion from the first voyage, Dalrymple refused at first to accept the evidence that no continent extended eastward of New Zealand. He quarreled with John Hawkesworth, Cook's compiler, for botching the charts (Dalrymple 1773, 23–25); in return, Hawkesworth impudently wished "that a southern continent may be found, as I am sure nothing else can make him happy" (Hawkesworth 1773 [2d ed.], xxv).

Dalrymple was not alone. In his collection of travels, *Terra Australis Cognita* (1766), John Callender argues that the Dutch were already fully apprised of the extent of the Great Southern Continent, "and by the neglect of other nations, they are at full liberty to take such measures as appear to them best for securing the eventual possession of this country whenever they think fit" (Callender 1967, 1:44). Accordingly, the *Resolution* was ordered to do a further search for this territorial prize, far to the south beneath the fiftieth parallel, causing Johann Reinhold Forster bitterly to exclaim against the inhuman cruelty of Dalrymple's *idée fixe:* "There are people, who are hardened to all feelings, & will give no ear to the dictates of humanity & reason; false ideas of virtue & good conduct are to them, to leave nothing to chance, & future discoverers, by their perseverence; which costs the lives of poor sailors" (Forster 1982, 3:444). By this point in the second voyage, it is plain at least to Forster that scientific method had been usurped by passion and that an idol, a mere figment of Dalrymple's and Callender's brains, had been conveyed to the British government as a plausible imperial venture. From Forster's point of view, confined to a stressed ship growing crank with ice, plunging into seas where any mishap was bound to be fatal, Dalrymple's obsession figured as an all-or-nothing bet on utopia, a gamble with other people's lives for the sake of that internal triumph of the mind that Dalrymple called sublime heroism (doing that "which no one else ever did before, or can do after him" [Dalrymple 1770–71, xvii]), Forster obstinacy, and Hobbes vainglory.

At a later date, George Vancouver joined the debate, defending Cook from "the enthusiasm of *closet philosophy,* eager to revenge itself for the refutation of its former fallacious speculations." Cook was not to be blamed for deciding, on the best empirical evidence, that a passage from the Pacific into the North Atlantic did not exist (Vancouver 1984, 1:275). More articulately than Forster, Vancouver stood up for the navigator as the true experimental scientist, and for Cook as the model of dispassionate observation, exemplary in "judicious opinions founded . . . on the solid principles of experience, and of ocular demonstration, uninfluenced by any prejudice, and unbiassed by any pre-conceived theory or hypothesis" (1:275). In the same spirit, Philibert Commerson declared the fruits of unbiased observation to exceed the categories and systems of closet-bound Linnaeans, "ces sombres speculateurs de cabinet qui passent leur vie à forger de vains systèmes, & dont tous les efforts n'aboutissent qu'à faire des chateaux de cartes" (Commerson 1772, 256). Bougainville knew well enough how he figured in Paris: "Je suis voyageur et marin; c'est à dire un menteur et un imbecille" (Bougainville 1772a, 1:xl). Charges of inaccuracy and fantasy were cross-traded between seamen and land-based experts over a gulf that Denis Diderot tried by bridge with wit. In his *Supplement,* he suggests that Bougainville's discovery of paradise took place in what always was and will remain "an ocean of fantasy," where navigators and closet philosophers alike are enchanted by the desire to transcend desire (Diderot 1992, 66).

Cook himself was not blind to the conflict of interest between the maritime eyewitness and the metropolitan community that was to sit in judgment on his achievements. Like Forster, he showed himself aware of the appalling risks he had to take to test their ideas; and like Commerson, he was conscious of seeing and feeling more than their systems and hopes would allow for. During the perils of navigating his ship through the Great Barrier Reef during the first voyage, Cook wrote, "Was it not for the pleasure which naturly results to a Man from being the first discoverer . . . this service would be insupportable" (Cook 1955, 380). The defensiveness he exhibits in his letter from Batavia indicates how acutely he anticipated the public reaction to his narrative of empty places, and how coolly the emergencies and tumults of frightened sailors would be discounted by people with an interest in putative discoveries. He continues: "The world will hardly admit of an excuse for a man leaving a Coast unexplored he has once discover'd, if dangers are his excuse he is then charged with *Timorousness* . . . if on the other hand he boldly incounters all the dangers and obstacles he meets and is unfortunate enough not to succeed he is then charged with *Temerity* and want of Conduct" (ibid.). When he met the solid wall of Antarctic ice that thwarted his cruise toward the South Pole during his second voyage, and knocked on the head the dream of a continent in the South Seas, Cook's narrative acquires a new kind of vibrancy as he tasted the equivocal triumph of discovering nothing: "I whose ambition leads me not only farther than any other man has been before me, but as far as I think it is possible for man to go, was not sorry at meeting with this interruption as it in some measure relieved us from the dangers and hardships, inseparable with the Navigation of the Southern Polar regions" (Cook 1961, 2:322).

The rising sense of his own importance as an eyewitness, sharpened by the difficulty of exposing the keenness of his own impressions to public incredulity, leads Cook to conduct the weird travesty of a Boylean experiment designed to bring indisputable proof of cannibalism among the Maori. "Desireous of being an eye witness to a fact which many people had their doubts about," he describes how he ordered a portion of human flesh to be taken from the corpse of a warrior, grilled in the *Resolution*'s galley, and given to a Maori bystander, who ate it with great relish in front of the mustered ship's company, "which had such an effect on some of them as to cause them to vomit" (293–94). In fact, the reactions were varied: Oediddee (Hitihiti) burst into tears, some men laughed, others offered to join the feast, and some were very angry (Forster 1777, 1:513). Cook defies the public who would not believe him ("That the New Zealanders are Canibals can now no longer be doubted" [Cook 1961, 294]) by turning scientific eyewitnessing into a macabre scene of connoisseurship. While remaining for the most part grave, economical, and unreflective in his journals, Cook never meets this sort of crux without succumbing to a kind of excitement that has nothing to do with the science of navigation. He interrupts his official self to make a claim for the propensities of another self, whose interests are not necessarily identical with those of the navy and the nation. Cook's ambitious "I" exposes itself to the pains of privation and danger not just in the silent stoicism of duty, nor solely in the disinterested pursuit of knowledge, but also in the act of flushing out a countervailing pleasure intense enough to overbalance the misery of looking for something that is not there.

Interludes of unauthorized self-interest, bordering upon fantasy and sometimes entering into it, interspersed these voyages, and blurred the sharp distinction drawn by Vancouver between the dispassionate navigator and the capricious metropole. They often occurred at the conjuncture of an old South Seas myth and a modern investigation—the terra incognita and the Great Southern Continent, for example—and they were accompanied by an irregular exuberance at odds with the constraints of social duty. For example, Commodore John Byron, leader of the first of the four expeditions mounted by the British in the 1760s to explore the Pacific Ocean, reported that he had sighted in the Southern Atlantic a great stretch of land, on whose shore the surf could plainly be seen beating, only to find that it was a fogbank that "vanished all at once" (Hawkesworth 1773, 1:10). With this sighting, he revisited one of Girolamo Cardano's favorite preternatural phenomena, the blue clouds of the Strait of Magellan (Daston and Park 1998, 166), prefatory to revisiting another. For when he landed at the Rio Gallego, near Cape Fairweather on the southern tip of South America in December 1764, and discovered people of an enormous size, Byron put fresh life into a controversy as old the Magellanic navigation.

Magellan claimed to have found giants on the coast of Patagonia (literally, "The Place of Big Feet"), an achievement sung in prophetic vein in the tenth of Luis Vaz de Camoens' *Lusiads:* "Rather more than halfway from equator to South Pole he will come on a land, Patagonia, where the inhabitants are of almost gigantic stature; then, farther on, he will discover the strait that now bears his name, which leads to another sea and another land, that Terra Incognita" (Camoens 1952, 246). Sir Francis

Drake's experiences in the same place, as reported by John Winter and then published by Richard Hakluyt, failed to authenticate Magellan, being limited to meetings with people "of a mean stature" (Hakluyt 1600, 3:751). But Samuel Purchas restored giants to Patagonia in order (James Boon suggests) to preserve lurid associations of giantism, sodomy, and devil worship with the Spanish imperium (Boon 1982, 37–38). Despite Sir John Narborough's decisive rejection of the evidence for Patagonian giants after his expedition in 1669, there were frequent recurrences to Magellan's opinion. Among the buccaneers, Amédée Frezier, highly respected as a navigator, mentioned a tribe of Indians in southern Chile called Caucabues, said to stand "near four Yards high, that is about nine or ten Foot", who frequently migrate to the east coast (Frezier 1717, 84). William Cowley, an associate of William Dampier's, found giants as far west as the Ladrone Islands, where he came across huge human bones, "the Legg bone being three foote and two Inches long, the Anckle Bones about foure Inches and three-quarters Circumferance" (Cowley 1684, 26v). John Bulkeley, who sailed with Anson, reported seeing Indians in southern Chile "of a gigantick Stature" (Bulkeley 1745, 70).

It was on the same expedition that John Byron sailed as a midshipman on the *Wager*, sharing the hideous privations that descended on her crew when she was wrecked on the southern Chilean coast. He saw no giants then, but the second time he was luckier. Whether it was owing to a reawakening of his former anxieties, or to the bulky cloaks of the inhabitants, or to the fact that they were chiefly seen while sitting down —or, as Bougainville speculated when he saw no Patagonian standing above five feet and ten inches, to their immensely broad shoulders and their large heads, which caused them to appear like Titans (Bougainville 1772b, 146–47)—Byron was convinced that the Indians of Patagonia were of a preternatural size, "of a gigantic stature [that] seemed to realize the tales of monsters in a human shape" (Hawkesworth 1773, 1:28; fig. 3). Thus he revived a story Herman Moll had set aside as romance (Moll 1711, 32) concerning creatures whose origin (it has been suggested recently) actually lay in a chivalric romance called *Primaton of Greece* (1512) (Chatwin 1977, 95–97).

Overcoming what must have been his initial skepticism about these colossi, Hawkesworth set himself to give a spirited paraphrase of Byron's journal (and one rather too free with what remained of its facts, according to Helen Wallis and R. E. Gallagher [Byron 1964, 185–96]). But in his preface, he considers at large the question of monsters in remote places, concluding with a long quotation from the French historiographer

FIGURE 3   Johann Christian Gottfried Fritzsch, *A Representation of the Interview between Commodore Byron and the Patagonians.* Engraving, 1774. By permission of the National Library of Australia.

Charles de Brosses concerning the status of the preternatural in narratives of voyages: "That men have a strange propensity to the marvelous cannot be denied, nor that fear naturally magnifies its object; but . . . it is certain, that all who have affirmed their stature to be gigantic, were not under the influence of fear; and it is very strange, that nations who have an hereditary hatred to each other . . . should agree in asserting an evident falsehood" (Hawkesworth 1773, 1:ix). James Burnett, Lord Monboddo, thought Hawkesworth had fairly stated the evidence for the phenomenon of outsize creatures in human shape (Monboddo 1774, 267–68). James King, responsible for editing and publishing the journal of Cook's final voyage, was equally positive in hoping that the fact of Patagonian giants, "whose stature considerably exceeds that of the bulk of mankind, will no longer be doubted or disbelieved" (Cook and King 1784, 1:lxxi).

Dr. Matthew Maty of the Royal Society credited the accounts, and received reports of giants into the *Philosophical Transactions* in 1767 and 1770, along with reports of monstrous births, climatological anomalies, and a remarkable fish. A brisk debate was carried on between British and French intellectuals concerning this phenomenon, which the resources of scientists could neither authenticate nor explode. Abbe G. F. Coyer sided with Charles-Marie de la Condamine in assuming that the British were circulating the story of giants in order to conceal a valuable mine they had discovered in southern Chile, relying successfully on the perpetual gullibility of the public ("witness those gigantic books of knight-errantry" [Coyer 1767, 7]). The propensity to believe in prodigies overwhelmed the citadel of science with the same importunate energy that the myth of South Seas wealth had subdued the citadel of commerce fifty years before, with no better reasons than those offered by Don Quixote to his squire: "I tell thee they are giants" (Cervantes 1970, 1:46). Charles Clerke's "An Account of the very tall Men, seen near the Streights of Magellan" was published in the *Philosophical Transactions,* wherein he testifies to the intensity of his astonishment not by means of his notes ("I am debarred being so particular as I could wish, from the loss of my journals") but with the same eyewitnessing truculence Cook used to affirm the marvel of cannibalism: "We were near enough and long enough with them to convince our senses so far as not to be caviled out of the very existence of those senses at that time" (Clerke 1767, 78). In this case there is no need of defiance, for scholars were ready to believe his evidence, at the cost of their own reputations, for it was not only the French who thought British scientists were either knaves or fools. "The scale of Being ascends," said the sardonic Horace Walpole: "Naturalists, Politicians, Divines, and

Writers of Romance, have a new field opened to them" (Walpole [1766] 1964, 201). As giants and tall stories go together (Stewart 1993, 96), the currency of Byron's account in the metropole was bound to cause embarrassment. "This is the age," wrote Samuel Johnson with terrific scorn, "in which the giants of antiquated romance have been exhibited as realities" (Johnson 1984, 108).

Because enthusiasm can be excited at the point of observation as well as in the cabinets of the heartland, it is not only between closet philosophers and mariners, but also between mariners themselves, that disagreements occur. The tradition of disputes between South Seas voyagers was well honored in the age of scientific navigation. After Cook's first voyage was ended, Joseph Banks was involved in an unedifying squabble with the brother of Sydney Parkinson over the distribution of his dead brother's effects, including scientific specimens. Banks and Cook publicly dissociated themselves from Hawkesworth's treatment of their journals in his *Account of the Voyages*. And in the wake of the second voyage, the astronomer William Wales disagreed in print with George Forster's account of it, disputing an astonishingly heterogeneous collection of issues. One of them was the waterspout witnessed off Cape Stephens, chosen by William Hodges as a specimen of the sublime, and more recently by Barbara Stafford as an exemplary moment of scientific observation ("when the absorbed beholder deliberately enters into the activity or existence of a phenomenon" [Stafford 1984, 408–10]). But Wales denied it had been possible for the Forsters to see it from their position below decks, where they had chosen to cower (Wales 1778, 23). Another issue in dispute was whether Wales's cat ate Forster's bird; another was whether Arnold's chronometer was stopped, or stopped of its own accord, after the departure from New Zealand; and another was whether Kendall's stopped because it was not wound by the forgetful Wales (40, 47, 20). Ranging between the most trivial things and matters crucial to the conduct of experiments, between occasions for irritation and the grounds of scientific infamy, Wales summarized the difficulties of giving an adequate account of any event, much less the theodicy that Forster promised: "I cannot avoid remarking the unfortunate situation of every man of real knowledge and ingenuity, whose works . . . must pass through so many hands before they can reach the eye of the Public; thereby giving an opportunity to every piratical pretender, either through interest or bribery, to purloin and publish them as his own, sometimes before the real author has been able to do it" (14).

Notwithstanding their "unparallel'd, if not inimitable adventures and

Heroick exploits," Alexandre Exquemelin extolled the buccaneers for "such candour of stile, such ingenuity of mind, such plainness of words, such conciseness of periods, so much divested of Rhetorical Hyperbole, or the least flourishes of Eloquence, so hugely void of Passion or national Reflections," that he declared them impossible to disbelieve (Exquemelin 1684, 1:[iv]). The same vouchers of fidelity were repeated endlessly by the later navigators. Remarked William Wales, "What I have to offer concerning the Place and Inhabitants consists chiefly of little Circumstances" (Wales 1961, 835). "Every little circumstance becomes interesting," suggested George Forster, following the lead of his father, who warned, "It may perhaps look mean to descend to these minutiae, but there is an absolute necessity for it" (Forster 1777, 1: 46; Forster 1982, 2:188). And John Walter observed, "It is by a settled attachment to these seemingly minute particulars, that our ambitious neighbours have established some part of that power with which we are now struggling" (Walter 1776, xv). As if aware that minute details are no longer current as self-evident vouchers of experimental accuracy, and that they are more likely to be recognized as outriders of unacceptable novelties and marvels, eyewitnesses are also ready to apologize for them: "But I fear I am too prolex in this Description" (Dampier n.d., 233v); "It will probably be thought by many Readers, that I have related the nautical events too minutely" (Hawkesworth 1773, 1:vi). Glancing at Gulliver, who was celebrated around Rotherhithe as a man prodigal of circumstances in his testimony, Abbe Coyer indulged some raillery at the uneasy coincidence of little circumstances and large improbabilities when he said of the Patagonian giants, "The circumstantial accounts we have received of them, as well with regard to time and place as to several other particulars, seem to carry with them sufficient marks of veracity, to remove our natural prejudices to the contrary" (Coyer 1767, 13). But Gulliver himself tries to reduce the pressure of circumstances on his narrative, owning, "I blotted out several passages of less moment which were in my first copy, for fear of being censured as tedious and trifling, whereof travellers are often, perhaps not without justice, accused" (Swift 1948, 104).

It was a sign of how little trust was reposed in these narratives that compilers of voyages began to lop and edit them in an effort to present a credible narrative to the public. John Harris stated the problem: "For private Interest is apt to interfere, and get the better of the public Service, [so] that it is very hard to be sure of any thing of this sort." Part of his solution is carefully to select, as leaders of expeditions to distant places, "a Person of Parts and Experience . . . of unspotted Character, who, on his

Return, should be obliged to deliver his Journal upon Oath" (Harris 1744, 1:332). In this way, it might be possible to do as John Campbell promises in a later edition of Harris's compilation, and present the reader "with a complete System of Relations, drawn up by Eye-witnesses of what they deliver, with a proper Account of the Credit due to each" ([Harris] Campbell 1764, 2:iii). Of course, any attempt to stabilize the standard of creditworthiness rested on the unfair assumption that the eyewitness had an interest in lying, while the compiler had no interest but in the truth; and even if such an assumption had been defensible, Boulton's redaction of Boyle's prolixities shows that compilers and editors can produce the opposite of what they intend.

Antoine-Francois Prévost and Charles de Brosses were pioneers in the editing of narratives of discovery so that the outline of a credible report would be disclosed. Prévost, shocked at the xenophobia of Hakluyt and Purchas, wished to present things in their totality, "un système de Géographie moderne, & d'Histoire, autant qu'un corps de Voyages" (Prévost 1746, 1:v). This was to be managed by careful editing ("beaucoup de retranchemens & d'abbréviations") until the various different narratives might combine into a methodical account of everything that is known. That is to say, Prévost treated these reports as Forster planned to treat disjointed facts, articulating them into a theodicy. De Brosses approached his material in the same spirit, one of his chief objects being to reduce superfluous detail: "on retranche, ou l'on abrège une quantité de détails dont la lecture seroit peu supportable" (Brosses 1756, viii). He and Prévost anticipated the methods of James Burney's magisterial history of Pacific exploration, *A Chronological History of the Discoveries in the South Sea* (1803–16), in which, "to prevent irregular exuberance in so important a branch of science," it was necessary to digest the material by placing "each particular of information in its respective class" (1:v, vii). On his own account, Burney seems to anticipate the importance attached to perspective by nineteenth-century students of natural history such as Georges Cuvier, who believed that a station removed from the messiness of actual exploration permitted an efficient interrogation of the facts by a mind whose sense of personal identity was never under threat, and which lay under no temptation to say the thing which was not (Outram 1996a, 262–63). But de Brosses conceded the necessity of keeping a narrative format, especially of important voyages; otherwise too much of their interest would be sacrificed (Brosses 1756, 1:vii). He believed the best technique of sustaining this interest was to maintain the narrative in the first person, aware that method would come dryly to the reader's palate without the immediacy of the eyewitness. Thus all his voyagers speak in their own voices, "à la premier personne, comme s'il y eut ainsi écrit d'un seul fil" (1:viii). This protocol is observed in Dalrymple's *An Historical Collection of Voyages and Discoveries in the South Pacific Ocean* (1770–71) and, most notoriously, in Hawkesworth's *An Account of the Voyages and Discoveries in the South Hemisphere* (1773), where the compiler justifies his impersonation of Cook and Banks as a negotiation of these extremes of authenticity and interest. On the digestive side, Hawkesworth explained, "it was determined that the narrative should be written in the first person, and that I might notwithstanding intersperse such sentiments and observations as my subject should suggest"; and on the side of excitement and pleasure, "it was agreed that a narrative in the first person, would, by bringing the Adventurer and the Reader nearer together without the intervention of a stranger, more strongly excite an interest" (Hawkesworth 1773, 1:v, iv).

In following the system of de Brosses and Prevost, Hawkesworth stood at the hinge of an important development in the production of South Seas narratives. Although the Frenchmen were the first to attempt a systematization of evidence, they were not the first to broker the testimony of eyewitnesses. Gulliver talks of Dampier's text being shaped and finished by a university scholar before publicly resenting the alterations made to his own text by other hands (Swift 1948, 376); and the manifest disparity between buccaneer manuscripts and their appearance in print suggests that this was common practice (Williams 1994, 117; Edwards 1994, 29). Richard Walter wrote up Anson's voyage, and his manuscript was further polished by Benjamin Robins (Williams 1967; 230); later, George Keate ghosted Henry Wilson's account of the wreck of the *Antelope* on the Palau Islands. In the next century, the most popular of the beachcomber biographies were finished by other people: William Mariner's by John Martin, and George Vason's by Solomon Pigott, who used the same justification as de Brosses and Hawkesworth, namely "to render the Narrative more interesting" (Vason 1810, vii). What was interesting? In terms of a system of relations and a narrative void of passion, it had to be whatever was surplus to such an authoritative and socially useful account, the moiety of agitation in first-person reports that had caused the public to call them romance and lies. What was interesting was the matter exorbitant to a process Dorinda Outram describes as "the replacement of the responsive inner space of the roving field naturalist by the controlling eye of the sedentary enquirer" (Outram 1996a, 263). In short, it was whatever approximated to the novelistic without seeming too improbable. Unlike Shaftesbury, these compilers believed that mariners had a part to play in the production of truth that went beyond the supply of bare details. And by making room for emergencies and suspense in true narratives, they contributed directly and indirectly to the early theory of the novel.

Hawkesworth thought the best method of achieving a balance between the eyewitness and the controlling eye, and between the feelings of the voyager and the sympathies of the reader, was to be as circumstantial as was consistent with sententious summaries. In this way, he hoped authenticity and interest might coexist. "The relation of little circumstances requires no apology," he said, "for it is from little circumstances that the relation of great events derives its power over the mind" (Hawkesworth 1773, 1:vii). He derived his authority for this judgment from two disparate quarters. One was the journal of Joseph Banks, a man whose calling was vindicated by his rank ("a Gentleman of station and office"), whose details were therefore not to be impugned: "I found a great variety of incidents which had not come under the notice of Captain Cook . . . much more full and particular than were expected . . . the materials furnished by Mr. Banks were so interesting and copious" (Hawkesworth 1773, 2:xiv). The other was the fiction of Samuel Richardson, whose *Pamela* "is remarkable for the enumeration of particulars in themselves so trifling, that we almost wonder how they could occur to the author's mind" (1:vii). It is evident that Hawkesworth wanted to put something like Boyle's experimental community (people bound by their word to state the truth as they see it) in touch with those who read voyage literature with pleasure because it they believe it is not true. He thought that little circumstances, properly arranged, could be experimentally accurate, interesting enough to arouse curiosity, and morally significant. In some respects, this synthesis that he copied from de Brosses and Prevost modernizes Exquemelin's coalition between candor of style and inimitable adventures; but Hawkesworth put it on a far more ambitious base than anyone had yet attempted, supported by three generic models: the circumstantiality of experimental philosophy, the descriptive prolixity of the novel, and the urbane summarizing style of the periodical essay (Pearson 1972, Lamb 1994). Thus pariah mariners, hitherto only enjoyed for the tallness of their stories, could be welcomed into polite and candid society.

Some years later, Richard Payne Knight made a similar comparison between the circumstantiality of travelers and the particularity of modern fiction, using *Gulliver's Travels* and Samuel Richardson's *Clarissa* as instances: "We have a work . . . in which the most extravagant and improbable fictions are rendered, by the same means [i.e., minute particulars], sufficiently plausible to interest, in a high degree, those readers, who do not perceive the moral or meaning of the stories. I mean the Travels of Gulliver. The author of the novel of Clarissa Harlowe attempted to make his fictions interesting by the same sort of minute precision and exactitude in the detailed relations of all common circumstances" (Payne Knight 1805, 283). Payne Knight knew that the use of copious circumstances to combine interest and moral significance is bounded at one extreme by improbability and at the other by verisimilitude; experimental accuracy has nothing to do with either. He used the model of the voyage because it is associated in his mind with marvelous specificity, not with truth. Perhaps it was Hawkesworth's skeptical approach to scientific method that inclined him to find in voyage literature and in the language of detailed testimony the same inconsistencies observed in Boyle's experiments and in the Royal Society's reception of Byron's reports. Given the Patagonian giants, it was a fair inference to draw, but it blinded him to two related states of affairs: first, that the entrée into polite society enjoyed by voyagers was at a low ebb; second, that polite society was strengthened by the contempt it felt for maritime testimony. Shaftesbury wore his as a badge of civility. As for the minute circumstances of the novel, Richardson demonstrated with what difficulty they are made to exemplify a moral truth, hence the sententious clutter of footnotes, prefaces and postscripts in *Clarissa*.

There was little chance that Hawkesworth's attempt to marry knowledge with interest would succeed, although he tried hard for accuracy. He penciled a notation in Samuel Wallis's log alongside his remarks about the Solomon Islands, "conjectures in wch he appears to have been mistaken, relate these therefore in 3 person" (PRO ADM 55/35, fol. 164). It stands as evidence of Hawkesworth's intention to preserve only the best facts for the first person. Nevertheless, there are occasional impersonations that strike a very false note, as when he writes of compasses, "I do not remember that I have ever found two needles which exactly agreed at the same time and place, though I have often found the same needle agree with itself" (Hawkesworth 1773, 2:248). In terms of his material, he was unlucky too, for among the copious materials furnished by Banks were many erotic scenes that caused him, the impersonator, to be accused of giving "very luscious descriptions" and indulging "sallies of a prurient imagination" ("An Epistle" 1774, 11 n). Because his narrative and charts did not in all respects agree, he attracted criticism, and gave color to Dalrymple's assertion that the cardinal point of the voyage, the Great Southern Continent, had been lost by Hawkesworth and Cook between them.

As for his sententiousness, it seldom reduced a particular event to the dimensions of a polite truth. Rather like Samuel Johnson's massive apothegms, Hawkesworth's summary statements let in more exceptions than they expel, leaving what is harsh and unconsoling in them salient and unmollified. In the matter of cannibalism, for example, he makes no concessions to the motives among the public for disbelieving Cook's first accounts of it; instead, he concludes a short disquisition on the relativity of tastes merely by observing, "Among those who are accustomed to eat the dead, death must have lost much of its horror; and where there is little horror at the sight of death, there will not be much repugnance to kill" (Hawkesworth 1773, 3:448). The question he raises by the libertinism of the *arioi* sect in Tahiti, who performed a public copulation for Cook's benefit, is like Mandeville's anthropology, too speculative to escape the humbug of his enemies: "Whether the shame attending certain actions, which are allowed on all sides to be in themselves innocent, is implanted in Nature, or superinduced by custom?" (2:128). Regarding the slaughter of four Maori by Cook and his scientists at Poverty Bay, he says simply, "In such situations, when the command to fire has been given, no man can restrain its excess, or prescribe its effect" (2:290). The best he can offer in palliation of the inevitable loss of life in maritime exploration is the observation that there is no department of productive labor "in which life is not in some degree sacrificed to the artificial necessities of civil society," and that such deaths may be "among the partial evils that terminate in general good."[2] The public did not like to be reminded again that good springs up and pullulates from evil.

Owing to a relish for the imbecility of human reason, Hawkesworth enjoyed affirming, like Ferguson and Smith, the invisibility of causes and the unpredictability of ends; and it led him into his greatest mistake, which was to dispense with Providence as the final category of facts. Of the lucky drop in the wind the night the *Endeavour* stuck on the Great Barrier Reef, Hawkesworth has no more than this to say: "We can with no more propriety say that providentially wind ceased, than that providentially the sun rose in the morning" (1:xxi). His public was scandalized by this repudiation of divine management. "You are *lawful Game*," a correspondent of the *Public Advertiser* tells him, "and ought to be *hunted* by every Friend of Virtue" (2 July 1773). Elizabeth Carter wrote to Elizabeth Montagu, "It gives one pleasure to find that this nation has still virtue

---

2 Compare Mandeville: "should we take a View of the manifold Mischiefs and Variety of Evils, moral as well as natural, that befal Nations on the Score of Seafaring and their Commerce with Strangers, the Project would seem very frightful" (Mandeville 1924, 1:360).

enough left to be shocked and disgusted by an attack upon religion, and an outrage against decency" (Carter 1817, 2:209). Hawkesworth's death some months later was blamed by Fanny Burney on "the invidious, calumniating and most unjust aspersions which had been so cruelly and wantonly cast on him" (Burney 1907, 1:273; Lamb 1994). In effect, he had ventured little more than Ferguson when he said, "Like the winds, that come we know not whence, and blow whithersoever they list . . . every step and every movement . . . are made with equal blindness to the future" (Ferguson 1980, 122). His error was to specify and illustrate these sentiments, and to do so in the person of a sailor.

In the course of the *Endeavour*'s grounding on the reef, for example, Hawkesworth tries rousing the reader's interest in the scene by exploring the implications of human blindness. Using Banks's gloomy estimate of the chances of bringing the ship off the coral ("We well know that our boats were not capable of carrying us all ashore, so that some, probably most of us, must be drownd" [Banks 1962, 2:79]), he works up the emergency by adding details for which he had no authority at all, although the inference on which they rested was plausible enough: "We well knew that our boats were not capable of carrying us all on shore, and that when the dreadful crisis should arrive, as all command and subordination would be at an end, a contest would probably ensue, that would increase the horrors even of shipwreck, and terminate in the destruction of us all by the hands of each other" (Hawkesworth 1773, 3:548). The wreck of the *Wager* twenty years earlier had produced behavior worse than this. Like his cool estimate of the inevitability of death in the process of voyages of exploration, Hawkesworth was saying what no one could seriously deny. They preferred not to discuss it, however, because it brought home the harsh business of self-preservation to civil society, via Banks the gentleman, and via the language of polite periodical wisdom. Hawkesworth's synthesized first person was spurned as doubly impolite, therefore, for passing off the details of maritime violence as a sociable truth. The accuracy with which he delineated the embattled egoism of Cook, delivered in an easy universalizing tone, ensured its failure as an acceptable message. Of no acknowledgeable moral or scientific significance, it inspired an interest only in this negative sense of provoking intensely unfriendly feelings. Hawkesworth was not, as has recently been claimed, the Joseph Surface of the South Seas (Edwards 1994, 92); he was its Mandeville. Although he did not live long enough to be fully aware of it, he sacrificed himself to Cook's reputation, for all the odium of voyagers fell to his share, leaving the navigator free to enjoy an unclouded and unparalleled public success, notwithstanding Cook's own reservations about the standards and motives of public approbation.

If Hawkesworth's synthesis of first persons was peculiarly faithful to the propensity for self-preservation, it was no less attentive to moments of aesthetic pleasure. He enters willingly into the je ne sais quoi, remarking that the dissolute sensuality of the Tahitians is of a scale "no imagination could possibly conceive" (Hawkesworth 1773, 2:207), and that the gestures of the Timorodee dance are "beyond imagination wanton" (2:206). Moreover, the west coast of New Zealand "has the most desolate and inhospitable appearance that can be imagined" (2:380). He alludes to the "frightful singularity" of Maori tattooing and facial ornament; and for a sense of the peculiarity of their carving, he can only refer the reader to Parkinson's copies, as it is "of a singular kind, and not in the likeness of any thing that is known on our side of the ocean" (3:463). Hawkesworth is trying as hard as he can to follow Banks's appreciation of the uniqueness of the things he met: a Tahitian dress "so extraordinary that I question whether words can give a tolerable Idea of it" (Banks 1962, 1:378), and a Maori carving of such a wild taste, "I may truly say [it] was like nothing but itself" (2:24).

In his hospitality to singular phenomena encountered by his gentlemen, and in his readiness to preserve these wonders as the private delight of the first discoverers of them, Hawkesworth was magnifying the connoisseurship of his borrowed "I"s. In the widely reproduced portrait by Benjamin West (1772), Banks gazes at the viewer bedizened in the trophies of his voyage, as if undecided whether to present them as specimens or curiosities. Nicholas Thomas has argued recently that the image is an icon of the practice of taste among South Seas collectors, who operated outside any model of theodicy or classification, even though they gestured at principles of order: "There was in this period nothing like Linnean classification that could be applied to artificial curiosities: they were not drawn into any comparative study of technology or craft; they played no significant part in the ethnographic project of discriminating and assessing the advancement of the various peoples encountered . . . they were specimens because they were treated as such, and their display in the space of the specimen . . . was part of an expressive work that evoked the science of men like Banks and licensed their curiosity" (Thomas 1997, 113). Similarly, Banks's enthusiasm for the breadfruit went beyond the pale of a naturalist's description when he identified not only the limitless applications of the tree (canoe timber, cloth, gum, birdlime) but also the mysterious link between erotic love and the fruit of paradise (Banks 1962, 2:330;

Spate 1988a, 3:35). The same excitement that led Cook to defy his public, and vouch for a private and largely incommunicable passion, induced Banks to dramatize his pleasures, to stage them with maximum eclat, just like the impresarios of electricity and gas. His real audience consisted of men of special taste, the Society of Dilettanti for whose amusement he collected many of his curios, and clad himself in them. Their relish for the *virtu* of an artificial curiosity allowed him to challenge metropolitan norms as defiantly as Cook when, in the company of more vulgar dilettanti, he arranged and witnessed the cannibal feast.

Finding pleasure in novelty, and collecting things that had never been seen before, took up much of Cook's first voyage; in emphasizing this, Hawkesworth thought he was establishing a second major focus of interest, for as he points out in his fourth *Adventurer* paper, it is curiosity as well as passion that a good narrative ought to excite (Hawkesworth 1752–4, no. 4). As self-preservation is the strongest propensity in human nature, it is also a "natural propensity of mankind to assume importance, by pretending to have seen wonderful things," gratifying readers of voyages, who evince "a strange propensity to the marvellous" (Hawkesworth 1773, ix, xviii). Although everyone agreed that Hawkesworth had missed or distorted the social end of these propensities, he was careful to frame each instance of the curious, and in doing so emphasized an aspect of Cook's voyages that was of absorbing interest to the participants, if not the public.

Observing an almost mathematical precision in the variations played upon the volute in Maori *kowhaiwhai* patterns, Parkinson said, "Their fancy, indeed, is very wild and extravagant, and I have seen no imitations of nature in any of their performances" (98). His pictures of tattooed Maori heads exhibit the same supererogatory attention to extraneous detail found in Giuseppe Arcimboldo's allegories of the seasons, themselves prime objects within the collections of Austro-Hungarian royalty, where faces are picked out of arrangements of disparate things. In fact, it is possible that in his most stunning profile (fig. 4), Parkinson transposed a *puhoro* design, reserved for the thighs and buttocks, to the face in order to emphasize the startling incongruity between the lines of a countenance and the flow of the pattern (fig. 5; Gell 1993). So much specimen drawing exhibits how the sensibilities of South Seas voyagers "penetrated the aesthetic realm," and made reportage more a matter of sentiment than information (Smith 1992, 59). "Isn't there something cruel about its exquisite lingering over every detail," Paul Carter has asked recently of

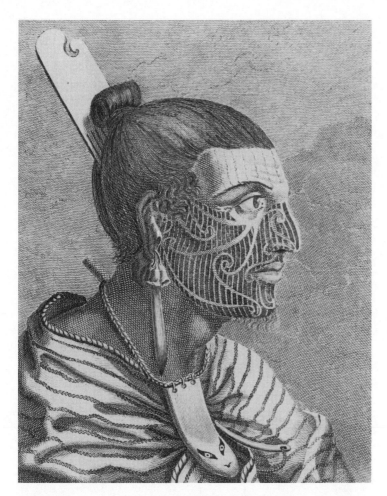

FIGURE 4 Sydney Parkinson, *Tattooed Head.* Engraving, 1773. From John Hawkesworth, James Cook, and Joseph Banks, *A New Voyage, round the World . . .* (New York: James Rivington, 1774). By permission of Princeton University Library.

Ferdinand Bauer's illustrations of birds, "something deeply voluptuous about the blood-red pigments congealing into the wing of *Trichoglossus haematodus moluccanus?*" (Carter 1998, 20). In these contexts, the little circumstances of voyages to the South Seas are the alibis of passion, not the rhetoric of objectivity they are sometimes alleged to be (Beer 1996a, 322–24). They produce wonders, not a sober inventory of the resources of

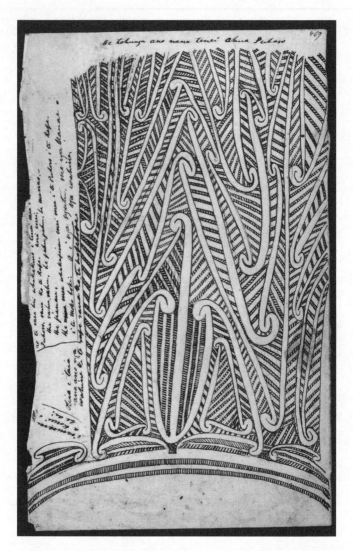

FIGURE 5   *Puhoro* thigh tattoo. Anonymous drawing, circa 1840.
Courtesy Special Collections, Auckland City Libraries NZ.

a new territory (Parker 1987, 143–47). They are vouchers of taste, licenses of a curiosity not necessarily ambitious of a meaning beyond the satisfaction of "a Lust of the Mind that . . . exceedeth the short vehemence of any carnall Pleasure" (Hobbes 1968, 124). For curiosity "cannot stay for Satisfaction. . . . Hunger and Thirst are not Appetites more vehement and more hard and difficult to be repress'd. . . . Nothing but the *present Now* is able to allay it" (Defoe 1720, 148).

In their illustrations of the finest curiosities of the British Museum, John and Andrew van Rymsdyk promise something besides information about the world, "a luxurious Banquet . . . the most voluptuous Entertainment" (Rymsdyk 1791, iii; quoted in Thomas 1997, 115). And on the beach, the same sort of entertainment was demanded. Nicholas Thomas has drawn attention to the rage for curiosities that overtook Cook's expeditions, a periodic frenzy that involved the entire crew in the pursuit of artifacts, and raged beyond all reasonable bounds. He cites Cook's entry in the journal of the second voyage: "It is astonishing to see with what eagerness everyone catched at every thing they saw, it even went so far as to become the ridicule of the Natives by offering sticks stones and what not to exchange, one waggish Boy took a piece of human excrement on a stick and hild it out to every one of our people he met with" (Cook 1961, 255). The natives were equally importunate. In Queen Charlotte's Sound, the Maori were "giving the clothes from of their backs for the merest trifles, things that were neither usefull nor curious, such was the prevailing passion for curiosities and caused me to dismiss these strangers sooner than I would have done" (171). When his own men became indiscriminate, bartering their clothes for "Cloth and other curiosities, things which I did not come here for" (255, 249), Cook tried to shut down the trade, as if there were more important matters to be attended to, such as the Great Southern Continent and the transit of Venus.

The fear of emptiness at the heart of the adventure, like the anxiety that taste is arbitrary, and that the je ne sais quoi is simply a way of disguising the nothing which is all that it amounts to, prevented the voyagers from acquiring the self-consciousness that would have allowed them to stabilize and justify their delight. Distrust and incredulity at home combined with insecurity about their own love of rarities, and guilt about the pleasure of being first, prevented them from boldly avowing their fancies, and even from experiencing an unalloyed delight. This is the reason that Banks, not usually inclined to equivocal gestures, clothes his curiosity in the licensed garb of science in West's portrait. They were more alert than Hawkesworth to the odium of singularity. Shaftesbury found curiosities as contemptible as miracles and monsters; and of collectors he said, "In seeking so earnestly for rarities they fall in love with rarity for rareness's sake," furnishing cabinets so reflective of "the real pattern of [their] minds, replete with the same trash and trumpery of correspondent empty notions and chimerical conceits . . . their whole delight is found to consist in selecting and contemplating whatever is most monstrous, disagreeing, out of the way, and to the least purpose of anything in Nature" (Shaftesbury 1964, 253). The same depravity was mourned by Adam Ferguson, "when men . . . bestow their attention on trifles; and . . . have recourse to affectation, in order to enhance the pretended demands of a sickly fancy, and an enfeebled mind" (Ferguson 1996, 256). The ego that takes pleasure in such things is not authoritative or representative, not the "genuine, true, and natural self" Shaftesbury admired (Shaftesbury 1964, 182–83); nor is it the artificial person who keeps Hobbes's storytellers from retailing wonders and miracles (Hobbes 1841, 4). It behaves in the same way as Mr. Periwinkle in Susanna Centlivre's play *A Bold Stroke for a Wife*, who is promiscuously tempted by curiosities from "the utmost limits of the globular world" (Rogers 1994, 215).

Igor Kopytoff argues that the singularity of things is proportionate to their removal from indices of cultural intelligibility. Thus the designs that Parkinson and Banks thought so extraordinary measure out the distance at which these artifacts stand from any European standard of beauty or utility; and when they are collected and put in a cabinet or museum, then this isolation and their extraordinariness is confirmed (Kopytoff 1986, 70). A thing that is like nothing but itself carries no information; nor does agree with any standard of judgment. It materializes the romantic fantasy of unrelatedness and exhibits, as Nicholas Thomas points out, "a puzzling lack of content" (Thomas 1997, 100). The negativity that lingers in early ethnography, notably in the habit of identifying things by the absence of European attributes (Hodgen 1964, 197), haunts collectors too, who run the risk of becoming so addicted to collecting for the sake of collecting that they empty their cabinets of any principle of difference, and of any value other than curiosity or nicety. Stephen Bann cites Arthur Pinion's collection, deemed by a court of law to consist in "absolutely worthless pictures" (Bann 1994, 79), and Kryzstof Pomian instances Teodoro Correr's accumulation of pointless objects, undistinguished by any public standard of taste (Pomian 1990, 256). Erasmus Darwin mentioned a Sicilian garden with six hundred statues of imaginary monsters, all of such surpassing and pointless ugliness that the state made plans for destroying them (Darwin 1789, 50). For the period of their predominance over the mind of the collector, curiosities supplant treasures, commodities, and evidence, for no one pursuing them has the power to estimate value comparatively. Indeed, Blackstone argued that it was no felony to destroy or detain curiosities, "because their value is not intrinsic, but depending solely on the caprice of the owner" (Blackstone 1770, 2:393). Whether subsequently they reenter an economic or taxonomic system of value as "semiophores" (Pomian 1990, 31), intelligible signs whose meaning can be divulged for the benefit of science, is by no means an ineluctable next step. The interest in collections of species and artifacts from the Pacific shown by "overlapping communities of curiosi, virtuosi, and savants" afforded, as Simon Schaffer and Adrienne Kaeppler both point out, no definite account of the principles upon which they were put together and presented (Schaffer 1996a, 337; Kaeppler 1978, xiii; 39–40). Cook's artificial curiosities in the British Museum were numbered randomly and poorly catalogued, besides being badly conserved and negligently dispersed (Kaeppler 1978, 46; King 1981, appendix 1, p. 97).

In a fascinating history of ethnography, tracing its rise from cabinets of curiosities and *Wunderkammer* to institutes of customs and fashions, Margaret Hodgen has suggested that the difference between a mere collection like Pinion's or Correr's and a nascent system of manners like Johann Boemus's *The Fardle of Facions* (1555) is the addition of a set of concepts capable of distinguishing among the collected items, without which any survey of human behavior would be meaningless. In short, ethnography is collecting plus culture (Hodgen 1964, 114, 165). The conceptual emptiness of the pure collection lingers, however, in the rhetoric of cultural knowledge. Hodgen notes the frequency of the figure of litotes in, for example, Montaigne's essay "Of Cannibals," where he lists the absence of acquirements among the Topinamba ("no kind of traffike, no knowledge of Letters . . . no use of service, or riches . . . no contracts, no successions, no dividends"); and similarly in Boemus, when he numbers up instances of frugality as testimonies of virtue: "Ther is no glittering apparell, no ratteling in sylkes, no rusteling in velvettes . . . no face painted, no skinne slicked" (197, 201). In *The Tempest*, Gonzalo builds a New World commonwealth out of contraries: "No use of metal, corn, or wine, or oil; / No occupation, all men idle, all" (2.1.15–16). Hodgen enables us to see in the negative formulations of the connoisseur (the je ne sais quoi) and the eyewitness ("Nothing you can imagine is equal to what I saw") the same blend of nullity and multifariousness indicative of a transitional mode of testimony between wonder and knowledge. More specifically with respect to eighteenth-century travelers, it is a discourse that is particular, interesting, and self-denying all at the same time.

Dampier's account of his two arrivals on the coast of New Holland is a collection of absent things. He produces a litany of that which is not: "no Houses, and skin Garments, Sheep, Poultry, and Fruits of the Earth, Ostrich-Eggs . . . no Instruments to catch great Fish . . . there is neither

Herb, Root, Pulse nor any sort of Grain for them to eat . . . nor any Bird or Beast that they can catch. . . . Neither did they seem to admire any thing that we had" (Dampier 1729, 1:464–68). Ten years later, he was still struck by what was not to be found. "There were no Trees, Shrubs, or Grass to be seen . . . I saw there was no Harbour here . . . a place where there was no shelter . . . we searched for Water but could find none, nor any Houses, nor People, for they were all gone" (3:102). When Dampier's cousin Lemuel Gulliver lands on a coast in the same vicinity, he encounters a parallel want of familiar things, which he lists the same way: "No dungeons, axes, gibbets, whipping posts, or pillories. . . . No fops, bullies, drunkards, strolling whores, or poxes. No ranting lewd, expensive Wives: No stupid, proud Pedants: No importunate, over-bearing, quarrelsome, noisy, roaring, empty, conceited, searing Companions: No Scoundrels raised from the Dust upon the Merit of their Vices" (Swift [1902] 1948, 347). There are some obvious differences between these two descriptions. One concerns a real place; the other, a satirical fantasy. Dampier was a historical figure who really landed in Shark Bay and saw what he saw, or rather what he didn't see; whereas Gulliver is a creature of Swift's brain who never went to the land of the Houyhnhmns. Dampier's account registers disappointments with the state of nature, while Gulliver's attacks the superfluities of civil society. But the resemblances between the two are more intriguing. Their attempts to describe the coast of terra incognita exhibit the same quality of ghostly specificity. The appearance of nothing is tackled as if it were a complex phenomenon, introducing such a peculiarity of wants (ostrich eggs and the versatility of absent importunate companions) that emptiness is filled up with its own particularization, and curiosity resolves itself into pleasure or disgust. There is no difference here except in the taste that decrees such scenes delightful or disagreeable. Johnson was not pleased to find in Scotland "no meat, no milk, no bread, no eggs, no wine" (Johnson 1984, 43). But Herman Melville was delighted to find in the Marquesas "no love-sick maidens, no sour old bachelors, no inattentive husbands, no melancholy young men, no squalling brats" (Melville 1964, 146).

It seems as if an alien shore demands from those who explore it a passionate absorption, coupled with this negative mode of expression, whether they travel there in reality or in imagination. The kind of close attention that might be applied to a prodigy or an experiment is given instead to a landscape so bare of details that it beggars language fully to state the number and qualities of absent things. To this extent, both the historical and fictive accounts are effectually imagined rather than witnessed, and the measure of plenitude and privation alike is in effect a je ne sais quoi. In the language of Gulliver's horses, the eyewitness is forced to reveal the thing that is not, but in this curiously manifold way, as if handling with a mariner's exactitude an exotic something. Whether this enumeration of the qualities of nothing serves to state a case or promulgate a lie, its elaborate form deneutralizes it. The language of specification becomes the language of passion, and the cool scrutiny of the object is invaded by a mood.

The circumstances of such a mood are easily mistaken for an imperial eyeful, an entry in a Domesday book of world resources (Dettelbach 1996a, 301), or an exercise in undecidability (Rennie 1995, 28, 73). It is a mistake that obscures the voluptuousness and infatuation accompanying the encounter with a particulate nothing. At their first advent, these little circumstances, whether narrative or material, are not tokens of anything: they act neither as information nor booty, neither as a gift nor as a commodity. Orphaned from their contexts, they are Hobbes's idols, or Trenchard's nonentities, alibis for the self's fantastic assertion of its independence. When things are thus egoized, they mark the boundary enclosing not a particularized universality, which is how the Enlightenment is usually supposed to have shaped the truth-claims of travelers, but an extravagant and utopian singularity. Hawkesworth was punished by the public for having a strong intuition of this unique delectation.

4

SCURVY

His bones were black with many a crack,
All black and bare, I ween;
Jet-black and bare, save where with rust
Of mouldy damps and charnel crust
They're patch'd with purple and green.

—Samuel Taylor Coleridge, *Rime of the Ancient Mariner*

Anthony Pagden has pointed out that the damage caused to the self by its own mobility is a topos of Western literature. Horace and Claudian thought those who put to sea and left the enclosure of the polis soon lost the faculty of civic virtue (Pagden 1995b, 18, 61). In the eighteenth century, seamen were commonly believed to be less than civil. *"Like Beasts,"* exclaimed Johann Reinhold Forster, after his second experience of Christmas on board the *Resolution,* "for the little sense they have, was soon lost in Liquor: & clamour & fighting was all over the Ship seen & heard" (Forster 1982, 4:697). Philibert Commerson, along with Jean-Jacques Rousseau, wondered if sailors had souls (Taillemite 1977, 2:508). For his part, Henry Fielding demanded to know why sailors should "think themselves entirely discharged from the common bands of humanity, and should seem to glory in the language and behaviour of savages" (Fielding 1996a, 36). The Black Legend of Spanish cruelties in the New World, darkened by the eighteenth-century boom in slave trading across the Atlantic, led Guillaume Raynal to address this enigma of the maritime self in the successive editions (thirty published between 1772 and 1787) of the *Histoire des deux Indes.* Raynal's earlier vision of *douce commerce* was heavily qualified, as his collaborators, principally Denis Diderot, tried in vain to account for the events of the last three hundred years. "Is it possible that civilised men . . . who were brought up in the midst of polished cities . . . is it possible that all such men, without exception, should pursue a line of conduct equally contrary to the principles of humanity, to their interest, to their safety and to the first dawnings of reason; and that they should continue to become more barbarous than the savage? . . . This change of character in the European who quits his country, is a phenomenon of so extraordinary a nature, the imagination is so deeply affected with it, that while it attends to it with astonishment, reflection tortures itself in endeavouring to find out the principle of it, whether it exist in human nature in general, or in the peculiarities of navigators, or in the circumstances preceding or posterior to the event" (Raynal 1783, 5:2).

Diderot's urgent inquiries lent an air of authenticity to Shaftesbury's earlier complaints against the barbarities of voyagers; and likewise to John Trenchard's warnings against the self-extrusion caused by the terra incognita: "People are like Wire: the more they are extended, the weaker they become" (Trenchard 1725, 3:70). By midcentury, travel was widely pursued but frequently reviled, either as a failure in pedagogy ("All Classic learning lost on Classic ground" [Pope 1963, 782]), or as an unpleasant necessity arising from infirmity. Adam and Eve were the first people compelled to move from one spot to another, Henry Fielding sourly remarked as he set out for Lisbon (Fielding 1996a, 26); while Tristram Shandy, heading rapidly for France with Death close behind him, thinks the verse in the Book of Psalms ("Make them like unto a wheel") "a bitter sarcasm, as all the learned know, against the *grand tour*" (Sterne 1983, 395). If they believed journeying was the effect of corruption, John Brown was certain it was the cause. His widely read *Estimate of the Manners of the Times* (1757) traces an unmistakable link between travel and the onset of corruption: "No Circumstance in Education can more surely tend to strengthen Effeminacy and Ignorance than the present premature, and indigested *Travel*" (Brown 1757, 34). The self spoiled by enlargement produces not only tall stories of monsters and prodigies, but also misshapen political entities. Samuel von Pufendorf thought empires "shapeless, huge and horrifying," incapable of preserving a decent outline (Pagden 1995b, 107).

Degenerationist thinking about Europeans in the New World went in two directions. Either there was some deficiency in the soil or climate of America that caused indigenes and settlers alike to lose the excellence of their natural faculties; or the passage itself from one world to another occasioned a deficit in the animal and moral economy that could not be made up. In adopting the latter view, Diderot and Raynal supported the opinions of Joseph-Francois Lafitau and Pierre-Francois-Xavier de Charlevoix, who understood the stoicism and simplicity of Native Americans to be the virtues of the noble savage. But George-Louis Buffon, improving an idea of Jose de Acosta's, thought that the New World itself was to blame for the decay of Europeans, since all species on the continent were below their natural size, and the tribes that had originally migrated there, as well as more recent settlers, "grew barbarous and uncivill" (Pagden 1995b, XX; Meek 1976, 47). Robert Boyle received a report from Virginia that stated, "People do not look so well here as in England wch may proceed from the nature of the food, their salt meats and unwholsom drinkes as much as from ye Climate" (Papers 39:182). This anonymous correspondent offers a simple but potent explanation for the decay of the travelling self, that extraordinary phenomenon that astonished Diderot and Raynal, when he says it may lie in a salt diet.

Self-preservation at sea in its most literal sense means the preservation of health. Many books were published on the topic, such as William Cockburn's *Sea Diseases* (1706), Charles Fletcher's *A Maritime State Considered* (1786), and Leonard Gillespie's *Advice on the Preservation of the Health of Seamen* (1798). They supply good reasons for Bernard Mandeville's hunch that ships would be viewed with horror and detestation were the real figures of mortality at sea available. On top of the many factors that made the odds of survival for a sailor so poor—wounds, worms, fevers, constipation, hernia, and all the afflictions incident to overwork, overcrowding, poor ventilation, extremes of temperature, and contaminated water—there was a rottenness that caused the bodies of the mariners to grow "foul and degenerate" (Addington 1753, 9). It was called scurvy, and resulted from a lack of vitamin C in the diet at sea, particularly on long voyages, where the best source of ascorbic acid—fresh fruit and vegetables—was not available. It was a disease capable of sweeping away whole crews, particularly those crossing the Pacific, where landfalls were so few and so uncertain. In his *Voyage to the South Sea,* Sir Richard Hawkins calls scurvy "the plague of the Sea, and the spoyle of Mariners" (Hawkins 1905, 17:77; Lind 1757, iii).

Scurvy is seldom mentioned in voyages of discovery to the New World; Columbus, for one, lost only one man to disease on his voyage of 1492. It does not become a problem until navigators probe the Indian and Pacific

Oceans, and then it takes a terrible toll. In 1499, Vasco da Gama lost 116 of his crew of 170; In 1520, Magellan lost 208 out of 230; and in 1742, George Anson lost more than 1,300 of his complement of almost 2,000 — all mainly to scurvy (Watt 1991, 22–27; Gordon 1984: 155-66). In locating his New Atlantis in the Pacific, Francis Bacon took account of this factor, for when they arrive, seventeen out of a crew of fifty-one are sick with scurvy. They are cured by means of scarlet oranges and "a box of small gray or whitish pills" (Bacon 1968, 106, 108). In the "melancholy accounts of a dreadful and alarming mortality" that emerged from Pacific voyages (Forster 1996, 358), Samuel Taylor Coleridge finds the nightmare of a ghost ship, with the crew dead on the deck (Lamb 2000). Pedro Fernandez de Quirós tells of the prostration of Alvaro de Mendaña's men during the second voyage to the Solomons, with only six fit to stand and the rest rolling in their own filth, and dying at the rate of three and four a day (Quirós 1904 1:104). It was no better during his own expedition when, moored off Vanuatu, "the Ships were like a town hospital with the plague, and none could stand on their feet" (2:447). Two hundred died on Anson's flagship as he was trying to reach Juan Fernandez, with only eight people fit to work the vessel (Walter 1776, 105).

Scurvy came to public notice in England from the well-documented accounts of its terrible effects on the crews of Anson's squadron; thereafter, medical experts often cited Richard Walter's narrative of its effects, "the lively and elegant picture there exhibited of the distress occasioned by this disease" (Lind 1757, vii). Three aspects of this malady came to the fore in public discussion: first, its dramatic symptoms of physical corruption; second, its puzzling etiology; and third, its effect on the mind. All three tended to confirm Raynal and Diderot's judgment that the phenomenon of degeneration at sea, whether it affected the body or the mind, was in all respects extraordinary.

In its later stages, the symptoms of scurvy were peculiarly gruesome, for the body seemed to rot while it was still alive. John Woodall said it "oft offendeth the mouth and gummes of the diseased, and causeth the flesh thereof to rot and stink . . . [and] the issuing of much filthy bloud and other stinking corruption thence" (Woodall 1617, 161–62). Richard Walter, the chaplain on Anson's voyage, reported that the legs of the victims "were subject to ulcers of the worst kind, attended with rotten bones, and such a luxuriancy of fungous flesh, as yielded to no remedy" (Walter 1776, 102). "A person so affected," said James Rymer at the end of the century, "is really in a state of actual dissolution and decomposition" (Rymer 1793,

36). Eventually, the legs would stiffen, as if in the rigor of death, and edematous blisters, black as ink, would discolor the skin, as if it were putrefying (Cockburn 1696, 1:9; Lind 1757, 255). Of the grotesque swelling of the gum tissue, which da Gama's men cut off with their knives, Luis Vaz de Camoens reported, "'Twas handling of a dead man's wound, / The rawest novice with his Instrument / might cut, and never hurt the Patient" (Camoens 1940, 167). Richard Addington concluded, "Corruption seems to be the Essence of this Disorder" (Addington 1753, 3). In his "Rime of the Ancient Mariner," Coleridge produces the figure of Death as a montage of scorbutic symptoms. The awful countenance, the blackness of his bones, edged with purple and green, and his stertorous breathing ("half whistles, and half groans"), are typical of the disfigured face, the bruising of the skin, the greenish scum of the urine, and the asthmatic working of the lungs incident to the disease (Beddoes 1793; Trotter 1792, 91, 122, 128). More macabre yet, Henry Ettrick, surgeon on the *Centurion,* opened the corpses of scurvy victims and found that "their Bones, after the Flesh was scraped off, appeared quite black" (Williams 1999, 60).

It was widely assumed that this mysterious putridity corrupted everything, animate and inanimate alike: human flesh, the sea, even the planks of ships. If it were not for the motion of the sea, "it would corrupt all the world," Hawkins believed. Certainly, its "loathesome sloathfulnesse" could infect the ocean: "The experience I saw in Anno 1590 lying with a Fleete . . . about the Islands of the Azores almost six moneths, the greatest part of the time we were becalmed: with which all the Sea became replenished with several sorts of gellys, and formes of Serpents, Adders, and Snakes, as seemed wonderfull: some greene, some blacke, some yellow, some white, some of divers colours, and many of them had life" (Hawkins 1905, 17:76). William Wales and Johann Reinhold Forster made similar observations during James Cook's second voyage, suggesting that phosphorescence owes its beauty to the state of high putrescence in an ocean growing stale after a long period of calm weather (Forster 1778, 66–67; Smith 1956, 144). Those familiar with the slave trade, especially the horrors of the middle passage, where scurvy was rife, were aware that a slaver's decks would not last more than ten voyages, for "the heat and stench arising from diseased bodies rot the very planks" (Coleridge 1796, 138). At the end of Mendaña's expedition, the corruption of bodies ("ulcers coming out on feet and legs") was matched by the parlous state of the vessel: "The ship was so open in the dead wood that the water ran in and out . . . when we sailed on a bowline" (Quirós 1904, 1:105–7). Coleridge's interest in this sort of decay culminated in the skeletal bark of his poem, "a plankless Thing / A rare Anatomy! / A plankless Spectre," (Coleridge 1993, 31) floating over a rotting deep whose viscous surface is crossed by slimy creatures. Simply by traversing the South Seas, a mysterious and dreadful change afflicted every material thing, including the flesh, fluids, and organs of a crew, reducing them to "their original singularity" (Smeeks 1995, 15).

While everyone was aware that fresh fruit and green vegetables would quickly restore the victim to health once on shore, the task of preventing scurvy at sea, or containing it once it had broken out, demanded more than empirical observations of what James Lind called "casual predisposing causes" (Lind 1757, 64). Various theories were proposed to account for its origin and progress: thickening of the blood and sclerosis (Smeeks 1995, 12; Willis 1684, 170); loss of oxygen from the organism (Beddoes 1793, 45; Rymer 1793, 41; Trotter 1792, 140); restriction of the animal spirits (Cockburn 1696, 1:13). Forster thought the corruption arose from eating rotten food (Forster 1996, 363); Tobias Smollett put it down to salt, but wondered why salt should consume flesh as well as preserve it (Smollett 1979b, 194). Erasmus Darwin explained that salt exhausts the tissues (Darwin 1803, 2:60). But no one had a means of demonstrating the truth of these conjectures. Lind was convinced he was dealing with "a simple identical malady," not "a hodge-podge or complication of various different diseases" (Lind 1757, 351); but as soon as he tried to define it, he was driven to confess the versatility its symptoms: "The disease would often, from various circumstances, take a favourable turn, which cannot be ascribed to any diet, medicine, or regimen whatever" (Lind 1774, 537; quoted in Carpenter 1986, 70). After many years studying its effects, he could say no more than "There are frequent occurrences in this disease, which I think very difficult to account for" (537, 540; quoted in Carpenter 1986, 70). Pascoe Thomas, aboard Anson's flagship, the *Centurion*, observed the embarrassment of the surgeon, Henry Ettrick: in the face of the disease's multiform and confusing appearances, he had to jettison a theory in favor of coagulant food and admit "that though some of the concurrent helps of this disease were plain enough, yet that the grand centre was certainly the long continuance at sea, or an entire secret; and that no cure but the shore would ever take place" (Williams 1967, 86–87). Diagnosis was not made any easier by scurvy's mimicry of other diseases, such as leprosy, asthma, and rheumatism (Crosfield 1797, 2; Spilsbury, n.d.). Walter called the disease "the most singular and unaccountable . . . its symptoms inconstant and innumerable . . . its progress and effects extremely irregular . . . and is therefore not to be described by any exclusive and infallible criterions" (Walter 1776, 143).

The enigma provoked language closer to the terms of connoisseurship than of medicine. Lind talked of the propensity it excites, stimulating "the curiosity of many to enquire into the nature of a malady accompanied with such extraordinary appearances" (Lind 1757, vii). Walter himself became enthusiastic, exclaiming, "The effects of this disease were in almost every instance wonderful" (Walter 1776, 102). "The debility of Scurvy," Thomas Trotter noted with awe, "is of so singular a nature, that nothing seems analogous to it: certain it is, that no disease is related to it . . . [it] is attended by a train of symptoms peculiar to itself, and which the genius of the distemper has rendered extremely difficult to explain" (Trotter 1792, 106). John Woodall talked of scurvy as a marvel, "infinite and unsearchable" (Woodall 1617, 161); and Benjamin Morrell declared, "It surpasses the wonderful,—indeed it is miraculous" (Morell 1832, 94). In attempting to speak of it at all, Trotter found himself using the rhetoric of the eyewitness: "Throughout the whole symptoms of this disease, there is something so peculiar to itself, that no description, however accurate it may be, can convey to the reader a proper idea of its nature" (Trotter 1792, 71). For his part, Philip Saumarez, an officer on the *Centurion,* went straight to the language of aesthetics to give some faint idea of scurvy's "scarcely credible" effects: "'Tis not my province to account for what the most learned only perplex, but I could plainly observe that there is a Je ne sais quois in the frame of the human system that cannot be renewed, cannot be preserved, without the assistance of certain earthly particles" (Williams 1967, 166).

Owing to the lack of any clear cause of scurvy, and to the circumstances of horror in which it generally supervened, it was frequently associated with nonphysiological factors, such as mood or temperament. Sorrow was placed high on the list of causes (Spilsbury 1785, 26), or what R. T. Crosfield called "a falling down of the whole soul" (Crosfield 1797, 177). John Clark maintained that dejection, and whatever might cause lowness of spirits, such as harsh discipline or bullying, were to blame for outbreaks of scurvy. He recommended that "[o]fficers should therefore carefully prevent every kind of oppression on board of ships" (Clark 1792, 531). According to Francis Milman, "It attacks the discontented, the repining; whilst persons of more chearful dispositions escape" (Milman 1782, 14). Thomas Trotter invoked misery as the cause of the terrible losses to scurvy on slave-ships, where the people are so extremely afflicted by homesickness and exasperation that they succumb very rapidly (Trotter 1792, 63). But besides these incidental factors precipitating the affliction, its specialists noticed in the victims an extraordinary susceptibility to sensation as they came to the crisis of the disease. Richard Walter had observed that there develops "a disposition to be seized with the most dreadful terrors on the slightest accident" (Walter 1776, 101).

Joseph Banks adverted to its milder effects when, off the coast of New Guinea toward the end of their cruise of the South Seas, the crew of the *Endeavour* "were pretty far gone with the longing for home which the Physicians . . . esteem a disease under the name of Nostalgia." He was identifying that "unconquerable desire of returning to one's native country frequent in long voyages" discussed by Erasmus Darwin, and experienced by Darwin's grandson Charles while cruising the Pacific in the *Beagle* (Banks 1962, 2:145; Darwin 1803, 4:82; Beer 1996a, 22–23). Thomas Trotter related the intense longing for land associated with the disease to a state of mind he called "scorbutic Nostalgia": "I consider these longings as the first symptom and the constant attendants of the disease in all its stages. The cravings of appetite, not only amuse their waking hours, with thoughts on green fields, and streams of pure water; but in dreams they are tantalized by the favourite idea; and on waking, the mortifying disappointment is expressed with the utmost regret, with groans, and weeping, altogether childish" (Trotter 1792, 44). In *The Farther Adventures of Robinson Crusoe* (1719), Daniel Defoe records a first-person account of starvation aboard ship that includes this scorbutic yearning. His female informant remembers "a kind of earnest Wishing or Longing for Food; something like, as I suppose, the Longing of a Woman with Child"; and then she recalls having dreams of eating followed by the intense disappointment of waking: "I was exceedingly sunk in my Spirits, to find my self in the extremity of Famine . . . I fell into a violent Passion of Crying" (Defoe 1927, 3:66–67). This fierce longing is commemorated on a dinner service presented to Anson at Canton, after his voyage was over, where scenes of Juan Fernandez and Tinian are mixed with domestic images of dogs, sheep, the Eddystone Light, and Plymouth Sound, "betraying the nostalgia which commonly accompanied vitamin deficiency" (Watt 1998, 577).

The longing for home resolves itself under pressure into the simple and irresistible longing for land. That topos of literature, the calenture of the sailor who fancies "Green Fields and floury Meadows on the Ocean, / Till leaping in, the Wretch is lost for ever" (Rowe 1720, 41),[1] commences with the story of Juan Francisco, a sailor on de Quirós's voyage, who made himself a life raft, settled his affairs, plunged into the ocean ten miles from the shore, and was never seen again—an extraordinary thing, exclaims Martin de Munilla, "filling us with wonder and amazement, for it is quite a singular and strange affair" (Kelly 1966, 1:261). Jonathan Swift updates this topos in his satire on the South Sea Bubble, where the deluded bankrupt is compared with the febrile mariner who sees "On the smooth Ocean's azure Bed / Enamell'd Fields, and verdant Trees" (Swift 1958, 1:251).

As infatuation is the only explanation for the Bubble, so it is often the only term adequate for some of the wilder effects of scurvy. After the *Wager*, a ship in Anson's expedition, was wrecked on the Patagonian coast, the survivors suffered hideous privations. The commander, David Cheap, was doubtless suffering from a combination of pelagra (owing to a shortage of vitamin B) and hypervitaminosis A (a surplus of vitamin A) from eating seals' liver (Watt 1991, 27), when he was described by John Byron as follows: "I could compare his body to nothing but an ant-hill, with thousands of those insects [lice] crawling over it; for he was now past attempting to rid himself in the least from this torment, as he had quite lost himself, not recollecting our names . . . or even his own" (Byron 1768, 166). Before he reached this crisis, Cheap had shot and killed one of his own midshipmen, Henry Cozens, for reasons he could not make plain. John Bulkeley wrote, "Captain Cheap . . . was certainly a brave and intrepid Commander; but from his Behaviour one would imagine he was infatuated" (Bulkeley 1745, 25). Byron extended the diagnosis to everyone: "a strange infatuation seemed to prevail in the whole conduct of the embarkation" (Byron 1768, 2).

Infatuation is a word serving not to explain but to collocate certain gestures and actions belonging to the mental state induced by scurvy in the South Seas. In his third voyage there, Cook's strange behavior supports Sir James Watt's suggestion that he was suffering from a lack of vitamin B, and evincing the personality changes typical of pelagra (Watt 1979, 155). He burned houses and canoes in retaliation for the theft of a goat, and cut off the ears of a man who stole a sextant (Cook 1967, 2:1068,

---

1   See, for example, John Dryden's *Conquest of Granada*, where Almahide tells Almanzor,

Like the distracted Passager you stand,
And see, in Seas, imaginary Land,
Cool Groves, and Flow'ry Meads, and while you think
To walk, plunge in, and wonder that you sink. (Dryden 1978, II:133)

1071). James Trevenen called Cook's fits of temper *heiva*, "the name of the dances of the Souther Islanders, which bore so great a resemblance to the violent motions and stampings on the Deck of Capt Cooke in the paroxysms of passion, into which he often threw himself upon the slightest occasion" (1:cliii). His crew summed up his last days, when he threw off his clothes and allowed himself to be worshipped as Lono, as infatuation: "a degree of infatuation . . . which rendered him deaf to everything," "an infatuation altogether unaccountable" (Harvey in Cook 1967, 1:537n. 2; Ellis 1969, 108).

The calentures of seamen were not altogether unpleasant. Sailing with Samuel Wallis toward the discovery of Tahiti, George Robertson reported that men down with scurvy were longing for "wild Game, gold, Silver, Diamonds Pearls & some for Girls" (Robertson 1948, 113). When they arrived at the island, their dreams came true. Then, as Trotter had noted, "the spirits are exhilarated, by the taste itself, and the juice [of fruits] is swallowed, with emotions of the most voluptuous luxury" (Trotter 1792, 141–42). Sometimes, however, the pleasure of the shore crossed the threshold into pain. Herman Melville reported a sailor so scorbutic that the very smell of flowers wafting from the shore caused him to cry out in agony, and, as it were, to die of a rose in aromatic pain (Melville 1968, 64). On the other hand, the touch of earth itself was all that was needed to effect a cure. Anson told Richard Mead of one of his men at Juan Fernandez, almost dead of scurvy: "When landed the poor man desired his mates, that would cut a piece of turf out of the soft ground, and put his mouth to the hole: upon doing this, he came to himself, and grew afterwards quite well" (Mead 1794, 119). Burying the sick up the neck in soil was reckoned a sovereign remedy among seamen, a weird literalization of nostalgia, the *maladie de pais* (Watt 1991, 25).

The slide from loneliness and disgust to an intense pleasure taken in textures, shapes, and colors is typical of scorbutic nostalgia. It is the theme of Coleridge's poem, as the mariner's morbid sense of rotting on a putrescent ocean yields to a spring of love as he watches the colors successively thrown off the backs of the iridescent creatures, whom he blesses for their beauty (Lamb 2000, 157–77). All navigators touched by scurvy experience the same cycle of disgust and wonder. Hawkins and Forster were at first repelled ("loathesome" "stinking and putrid") and then fascinated by the rotting sea. De Quirós nearly died of famine and plague in the paradise he called the New Jerusalem, and again in another he named Graciosa (Quirós 1904, 1:95). In the first Pacific voyage of 1520, Magellan found himself alternately loathing and loving what he found there, making way for that celebrated division between the good and bad of the South Pacific, the Wallace Line (Boon 1985). Walter tried to describe the crossing from dismay to voluptuous delight that occurred when the *Centurion* reached Juan Fernandez. On the boat, everyone was awash in their own filth and in the grip of scorbutic nostalgia: "In our distressed situation, languishing as we were for the land and its vegetable productions (an inclination constantly attending every stage of the sea-scurvy), it is scarcely credible with what eagerness and transport we viewed the shore" (Walter 1776, 111). When they landed, it was like Satan's removal from Hell to Eden: "some particular spots occurred in these valleys, where the shade and fragrance of the contiguous woods, the loftiness of the overhanging rocks, and the transparency and frequent falls of the neighbouring streams, presented scenes of such elegance and dignity, as would with difficulty be rivalled in any other part of the globe. It is in this place, perhaps, that the simple productions of unassisted nature may be said to excel all the fictitious descriptions of the most animated imagination. . . . I despair of conveying an adequate idea of its beauty" (120). The morbid sensitivity among victims of the disease no doubt contributed to Louis-Antoine de Bougainville's belief that he had found Cythera, and to his colleague Commerson's conviction that he had arrived at Utopia, when they made landfall at Tahiti and saw an apparition of Venus rise upon the deck. Irresistible voluptuous sensations were the only explanation William Bligh could offer for the mutiny on the *Bounty,* having refused to admit to scurvy: his men were prepared to risk death, he said, for the prospect of "allurements of dissipation beyond any thing that can be conceived" (Bligh 1790, 10).[2]

There is no doubt that these intensities were experienced and that they stemmed partly from the nervous irritability belonging to scurvy; but as the cause and tendency of the disease were unknown, and the sensations associated with it impossible to convey in all their richness, it is hard to extract a historic or moral significance from the moments of sheer sensa-

2 In his journal, James Morrison noted that on the run from the Cape to Tahiti, scurvy appeared on the *Bounty:* "several of the seamen particularly the oldest began to complain of Pains in their limbs and some simptoms of the Scurvy began to make its appearance, and weakness and debility began to be observed through the Ships Company, for which Essence of Malt was given to those who appear'd worst with portable soup & rice from the Surgeons Chest, the salt provisions were also stopd & flour given in lieu" (Morrison 1935, 27). After reading this, Bligh flatly denied that it was the case: "Captain Bligh never had a symptom of Scurvy in any Ship he commanded" (Bligh 1937, 153). It was important to naval self-esteem not to have the disease on board. Vancouver could not conceal his dismay when he found it on his ship: "To my utter astonishment and surprize, I was given to understand from Mr Menzies that the sea scurvy had made its appearance amongst some of the crew" (Vancouver 1984, 4:1470).

tion that interspersed Pacific navigations. The reason that the terra incognita was so often represented as a utopia or a paradise owed less to the long literary tradition that had located immortal commonwealths in the New World and the South Seas, on which Columbus and Sir Humphrey Gilbert had relied for scriptural authorization of their discoveries, than to this pathological state of the nerves, keyed up to overreact to any stimulus after long voyages. Any land was paradise; all earth showed fair. Colors and birds loom large as the objects of these unreasonably acute sensations. As he succumbed to scurvy, Forster became fascinated by the colors of the ice and the Southern Lights, just as Hawkins had reacted to the green, black, yellow, and white of the serpents in the scorbutic sea. The icebergs were "as blue as Ultramarine, the shades were all blueish, even to the very sumits [sic]; the sea when washing it looked as a tincture of verdigrease" (Forster 1982, 2:227). His son's painting *Ice islands with ice-blink* (1772–73) gives full range to this palette, where vibrant blues lighten into sulphur yellows, and thicken into bruised purples and greens, all framing the surreal shapes of the ice (see Smith 1992, 152). Retinopathy, or the night-blindness associated with vitamin A deficiency, is responsible for the missing red end of the spectrum. The image glows so strangely because it is copied from a scurvied retina.

Sick and starving, de Quirós listened with "marvellous pleasure and contentation" to the birdsong in Vanuatu, and Walter saw a bird on Juan Fernandez, surpassing "all Description, Imitation, or even Imagination" (Lowes 1927, 316). In Indonesia, Antonio Pigafetta discovered a bird more brightly colored than he had ever seen before, perpetually on the wing, and he called it the bird of paradise. Locating a parallel for the slaying of the albatross in Coleridge's "Rime" by citing a portion of Anders Sparrman's narrative of the landing at Dusky Bay, Bernard Smith provides a fine example not of moral evil but of scorbutic pleasure. The lengthy spell in New Zealand was taken to recover from the scurvy caused by fierce exposure to the ice. It was during this period that Sparrman remembered shooting ducks, and how "the blood from these warm birds which were dying in my hands, running over my fingers, excited me to a degree I had never previously experienced. . . . This filled me with amazement, but the next moment I felt frightened" (Smith 1956, 138). Who is to say that on these unregulated moments of pure sensation, verging equally on terror and enchantment, the great divisions between ignoble and noble savagery were not fantastically reared, so that ever since, the orderly divisions of a universal taxonomy have obscured the pathological "chinks of excitement" they originally served to fringe? (Boon 1985, 42). These strange scenes of passion, ranging from mild curiosity to violent frenzy, are congenial to the most incongruous pairings, of good and evil, desire and loathing, dismay and delight. Nostalgia, the leading emotion triggered by scurvy, combines the strong twin intuitions of possessing everything and finding nothing of what you need. This feeling suffused so many moments in the South Seas, magnificent and trivial alike, from the recognition of Tahiti as a terrestrial paradise to Cook's frantic search for naval property in the hours before his death. When Richard Walter described the scene on board the *Centurion* as its crew struggled to bring her up at Juan Fernandez, with the sick dying amidst their own waste, while others gaze passionately at the shore "to feast themselves with this reviving prospect" (Walter 1748, 156), despair and joy were blended in a moment of suspense in which privation and pleasure were dilated to fantastic extremes. Not to reach the shore is to release, as Hawkesworth remarked of a parallel situation, "the power which fancy is perpetually exerting to aggravate the calamities of life" (Hawkesworth 1773, 1:93); while to reach it is to do what Bougainville did on Tahiti, and let fancy carry a sensation beyond its natural limit. In either case, nostalgia is capable of renewing the intimate relation of pain ("cravings of appetite") to delight ("emotions of the most voluptuous luxury" [Trotter 1792; 44, 142]), for from "the lurking seeds of the scurvy . . . none of us were totally exempt" (Walter 1748, 165).

It has been noticeable that the alternation between horror and pleasure among the victims of scurvy extended to students of the disease, who were so curious in tracing its puzzling variety that they could not help calling its most gruesome effects wonderful, or referring to the mysterious agency of the disease as its genius. Scurvy is an affliction that suspends its observers amidst its variegations, incapable of making a judgment, just as Coleridge's mariner is suspended in his own story, unsure what to make of it. It prompts one to wonder how many of its students were also victims. Thomas Trotter, who wrote so vividly about it, had probably suffered from it too. But even among the chiefly shore-based experts such as Lind, there was a kind of contagion caught merely from meditating on an ailment that is an engine of the unique, capable of making all discourse about its symptoms itself symptomatic: peculiar, singular, extraordinary, distinct, and beyond the power of words to describe. When Philip Saumarez, invokes the je ne sais quoi in his account of scurvy, he invades the language of medicine with the language of taste. He establishes a link not only between the undemonstrable causes of the disease and the equally undemonstrable nature of sensual pleasure, but also, as Howard Caygill has shown, with all the other mysterious connections between the private appetite and the public good that dogged discussions of commerce and patriotism as well as of taste in the eighteenth century, and were always signaled with the je ne sais quoi. When George Vancouver discovered scurvy on his ship, despite all the precautions learned from Cook, he follows the sequence precisely, being astonished and surprised at a malady made "the more inexplicable" by its appearance among a crew in good plight, and causing him a degree of solicitude that is "more easy to imagine than describe" (Vancouver 1984, 4:1471).

In other words, the connection between the symptoms of scurvy and the South Seas voyage narratives is extensive and exact; at all points, it provides a literal and physiological accompaniment to the degenerationist and utopian drifts of self-preservation, no matter how subtle or fantastic they might be. It is the starkest example of the interaction of material effects and psychological impulses; and out of the mutuality of these processes, each equally irreducible to a cause, emerge the most dramatic examples of perceptions and concepts infiltrated by sensations. These sensations are such vivid blends of pain and pleasure that scorbutic nostalgia seems to form the sensational core of all those descriptions where fullness is defined by negatives, whether it is de Quirós's Graciosa and New Jerusalem, John Milton's Eden, William Dampier's New Holland, Gulliver's Houyhmhmnland, Bougainville's Tahiti, or Cook's Dusky Bay. Alongside these mixed feelings is a predominant sense of the singularity of things that culminates in an almost infantile egoism, which, when it speaks, inevitably chooses the rhetoric of the je ne sais quoi. Whether a victim or an observer, everyone undertaking to describe scurvy becomes in effect an eyewitness, reporting marvels: "A wonder which fills the mind with greater astonishment and reverential awe, than it is in my power justly and properly to describe" (Forster 1996, 59); "No description, however accurate it may be, can convey to the reader a proper idea of its nature" (Trotter 1792, 71); "It surpasses the wonderful,—it is indeed miraculous" (Morrell 1832, 94).

Scurvy set a formidable challenge to which Cook quite consciously rose. He believed the disease could only be overcome by "the authority and example of the commander" (Cook 1961, 2:1188). The seaman dedicated to the conquest of the Pacific had to triumph over scurvy first, since it was the greatest impediment to extensive sea travel, both with respect to the management of ships and the conduct of the self. This explains why Bligh refused to admit the least trace of it on the *Bounty,* and why Vancouver felt so astonished and surprised when it appeared on the *Discovery.*

It is impossible to say how frequently, or to what degree, scurvy conspired with other causes to provoke a mutiny, or to feed those feelings of self-importance that tempted Cook to talk of his achievements in the first person, and which John Byron confessed to as outright egotism (Byron 1768, i). But considering how often in the annals of the South Seas a paradisal island stimulates and focuses rebellion ("They imagined it was in their power to fix themselves in the midst of plenty, on the finest island in the world, where they need not labour, and where the allurements of dissipation are beyond any thing that can be conceived" [Bligh 1790,10]) and how islands appear most beguiling to scorbutically nostalgic sailors ("it is scarcely credible with what eagerness and transport we viewed the shore" [Walter 1776, 111), it seems likely that incipient scurvy played a part. As for the self, upon whose punctual responses to stimuli the accurate perception and connection of phenomena depends, the more extraordinary its sensations, the more probable that they are morbid. With scurvy rampant, discipline, cartography, measurement—and the dreams of commercial and scientific progress depending on them—all suffer because the eye, and the "I," can no longer be trusted. Indeed, the scorbutic observer seems capable only of garnering outward signs of his own inner rottenness. Like the scurvied ocean in Coleridge's poem, which paints a ship out of the palette of witches' oils pouring from its own putrid bosom, diseased mariners are fascinated by the extraordinary outward tokens of what is wrong with them.

It is precisely on account of Cook's exemption from the seeds of scurvy that his circumnavigations have traditionally been praised. O. H. K. Spate says, "Few myths about James Cook have been so enduring or so widespread as that which claims that he 'conquered' scurvy" (Spate 1988a, 191). Most recently, Christopher Lawrence has renewed the celebration of Cook as a practitioner of prophylaxis and hygiene, a navigator as magnificently competent in empirical medicine as he was in the science of exploration and mapping. Fully aware of the connection between the preservation of health and the preservation of distinctions—the hierarchies on which all orders of rank and species rely—Cook's first battle was with the disease that menaced the order of a ship by interfering with the capacity to think clearly (Lawrence 1996, 82). By liberal use of dietary supplements—especially malt and portable soup—combined with regular airings of the ship, prompt attention to the supply of good water and dry clothes, and a plentiful distribution of fresh vegetables, fruit, and fish whenever they became available, Cook did better than any other commander sailing the Pacific, reputed not to have lost a man to the distemper in those notorious seas, even during the long run down the Antarctic in the second voyage. His regimen became known as the Cook model, which functioned, Lawrence points out, as "a representation and an endorsement of eighteenth-century social order" (90). It was deeply admired and closely followed by Vancouver in his voyage to the northwest coast—for whom it failed to work.

Even in the contemporary accounts of Cook's triumph over scurvy, this is far from the whole story. Thomas Beddoes reckoned Cook's efforts to keep his ships well aired was the crucial factor, but that his reliance on malt-wort was mistaken, as its antiscorbutic effect was very weak (Beddoes 1793, 53, 91). Gilbert Blane wondered if malt had any effect at all (Blane 1785, 464). Yet Cook's devotion to it was so decided that he said he was risking mutiny shortly before he made landfall at Kealakekua Bay, on his last voyage, in his determination to make his crew drink it in the form of spruce beer. As for portable soup (made from gelatin and stock [Stead 1993, 95n. 59]) and sauerkraut, both widely touted at the time as the secret of Cook's success, Thomas Trotter derided their efficacy as either "very trifling" or "mere placebo" (Trotter 1792, 183). Cook had a high opinion of the antiscorbutic virtues of sugar (Forster 1996, 368), but Crosfield thought the high-sugar diet of the English made them especially prone to scurvy (Crosfield 1797, 212). Francis Milman set out to explain Cook's success on the basis of his decision to keep three watches instead of two, drying out the ship regularly, distributing Magellan jackets for the cold, taking excess fat out of the ship's diet, and distributing fresh water as frequently as possible. Thus, he said, "Captain Cook's seamen lived with impunity on their salt provisions" (Milman 1782, 40). In venturing this many-sided explanation, Milman flies in the face of James Lind's fundamental caveat with respect to the disease, which is that " the scurvy is not a hodge-podge or complication of various different diseases, but is itself a simple identicial malady" (Lind 1757, 432)—not to be cured, that is, by a variety of remedies unless they attack a simple identical cause. Against these scattergun theories of prevention, Trotter opted for the psychological explanation for Cook's relative success with scurvy, pointing out the huge difference between the *esprit de corps* of a ship bound on a voyage of discovery and that of a vessel engaged in station duty; that besides being more frequently near land, and carrying more water (which he did regard as important), everyone is in a state of expectation that arms them against lethargy, fear, and melancholy, harbingers of the sickness (Trotter 1792, 174).

These more measured estimates of Cook's success against scurvy are echoed in a recent assessment, which cites the broad spectrum of symptoms in the *Resolution* during Cook's second voyage, the one generally celebrated as decisive in Cook's conquest of the disease (Watt 1979, 134). That it was tactless to mention the disease, especially on this expedition, is evident in William Wales's querulous self-diagnosis when, having mentioned that a number of the crew are down with scorbutic complaints, he added, "I suppose I shall be believed when I say that I am unhappy in being one of them" (Cook 1961, 64n. 3). It is interesting to trace the changes wrought by scurvy on the mind of the elder Forster, since, like Cook, he still enjoyed the reputation as an observer more authoritative than most during the course of the second voyage. As the *Resolution* commenced its journey from the Cape of Good Hope to New Zealand, he praised the management of British naval vessels, particularly "their many preparations against the Scurvy," in contrast with the French, and "the distresses to which the poor Sailors under Bougainville were reduced" (Forster 1982, 2:188). Contrariwise, the "steady, settled mind" required to view remarkable novelties of nature with composure is ensured by a regime of health consistent with "the honour of . . . the British Nation, & to the skill, perseverence, & good Conduct of their Seamen." Warming to his patriot theme, Forster declared, "It is reserved to the free-spirited sons of Britannia, to navigate the Ocean wherever it spreads its briny waves" (2:196, 216). After two months at sea, however, Forster's identification with naval patriots began to wear thin, and had become (as Trenchard said all patriot effusions were bound to) a pretence: "I put on a good face, & wanted to shew a mind superior to all these inconveniences . . . but had my Shipmates had a Sight of my most private thoughts they would have me [sic] found widely different, from want I wanted to appear" (2:234). Three days later, Forster reported that several crewmen fell sick with scurvy; and although he still praised the wort, he acknowledged that "scurvy is gone pretty far" by the time they reached Dusky Bay (2:235).

When the quest for the Great Southern Continent resumed toward the end of 1773, Forster's commitment to national glory had become heavily qualified with fretful egoism as he contemplated the waste of waters: "We have seen nothing which has not been seen before" (Forster 1982, 3:439). By Christmas Day, he confessed that he was scorbutic: "[M]y case is very much the same with a great many people in the Ship, who are all very ill" (3:440). From this point, his obsessive interest in his own preservation overrode any broader affiliation to Britain and the annals of science. He had begun to attack the pointlessness of the enterprise, and accused experts such as Alexander Dalrymple and the powerful men at the Admiralty of a pitiless and pointless curiosity. Here scurvy marks very exactly the disjuncture of self-preservation and the interests of civil society. Complaining of toothache and pains in his joints, Forster wrote, "All things look gloomy and dismall. I do not live, not even vegetate, I wither, I dwindle away" (2:447). Afraid that they were all about to die of scurvy, and now contemptuous of Cook's antiscorbutic diet, Forster quoted Juvenal's eighth satire to the effect that they were engaged in the destruction of the point of living for the sake of an idea, *propter vitam vivendi perdere causas* (3:448). In this state of mind, Forster could not assign disinterested motives to anyone, least of all Cook, whom he accused of lengthening the cruise amidst the icebergs "in order to satisfy interest & vanity" (3:447). In these scorbutic crises, passion and ego close the horizon of everyone's observations, as everyone is to a greater or lesser extent rapt in the infatuated contemplation of their dwindling selves.

5

THE POLYNESIAN PERSON AND
THE SPREAD OF LEPROSY

"I" does not exist.
I am not
My self belongs not to me because "I" does not exist.
"I" is always "we,"
is a part of 'ainga
a part of the Au a teine,
a part of the Aufaipese,
a part of the Autalavou,
a part of the Aoga Asa Sa,
a part of the Church,
a part of nu'u,
a part of Samoa.

　　　—Sia Figiel, *Where* we *once belonged*

The emotional sensitivity of the native is kept on the surface of his skin like an open sore which flinches from the caustic agent; and the psyche shrinks back, obliterates itself and finds outlet in muscular demonstrations which have caused certain very wise men to say that the native is the hysterical type. . . . The circle of the dance is a permissive circle: it protects and permits. At certain times on certain days, men and women come together at a certain place, and there, under the solemn eye of the tribe, fling themselves into a seemingly unorganised pantomime, which is in reality extremely systematic, in which by various means—shakes of the head, bending of the spinal column, throwing of the whole body backward—may be deciphered as in an open book the huge effort of a community to exorcise itself, to liberate itself, to explain itself.

　　　—Frantz Fanon, *The Wretched of the Earth*

The alteration or depletion of the civil self caused by crossing the sea was not fully visible until a beach was landed on and crossed as well. This crossing was a constitutive event, for at once it materialized the fantasies of dwindled maritime egos, and (if the beach was populated) it affected the indigenes on the other side. Willy-nilly, they participated in a series of exchanges that tested and in various degrees transformed their relations to artifacts and to each other. In this chapter, I want to suggest that these encounters provoked in native populations some of the same excitements that their visitors knew as infatuation. Just as Europeans acquired an egoistic passion for singular things, blended with those mixed feelings I described in chapter 4, so local populations reoriented their attitudes toward things, collecting them with an unprecedented avidity that forbade their circulation. And just as a passion for the extraordinary coincided with a loss of civility among the visitors, so the turbulent engagement with novelties transformed the nature and politics of tribal identity. If the upshot of one sort of excitement was the collecting of curiosities and visions of utopia and paradise, so the result of the other was the establishment of great storehouses and a widespread belief in millenarian prophecies and cargo cults. Finally, I will argue that just as scurvy is a disease that infiltrates and advertises infatuation, so leprosy concentrates a century of contact into a gruesome pantomime.

To make the case that natives' encounters with Europeans changed their attitudes toward objects and others, I must trespass upon a discussion of identity in Polynesia and Melanesia that has been conducted largely by anthropologists. No doubt some damage will be done to the finer discriminations of their debates, for which I apologize in advance. In comparing developments on one side of the beach with those on the other is to blend two events that are, no matter how physically proximate and materially entangled, utterly different in their historical profiles and cultural valences. With this caveat in mind, I shall consider how changes in attitudes toward things on the landward side of the beach, particularly their arrangement in space, indicate changes in the self symptomatic of a shift in cultural and social priorities—a shift that is literally as well as figuratively expressed by disease.

In one of the most penetrating studies of identity in the Pacific region, Marilyn Strathern mounts in effect a critique of the original contract. She says, "Society and individual are an intriguing pair of terms because they invite us to imagine that sociality is a question of collectivity . . . society as an ordering . . . unifying force that gathers persons who present themselves as otherwise irreducibly unique . . . individuals conceptually distinct from the relations that bring them together" (Strathern 1988, 12). The fiction of a contract between the self and the state upon which Western notions of identity rely is preposterous in exactly this way. It has to suppose a presocial self possessed of attributes that can be acquired only in society, and then to imagine that the self is only fully in charge of its interests when it plies between its natural and artificial forms; that is, when it considers itself as operating simultaneously in and out of society.

Such a divided notion of social being requires considerable ingenuity on the part of political philosophers who wish to sustain it. John Locke defined the primary form of self-preservation as the ownership of property, which is preserved in turn by a social contract guaranteeing a right obtained in a state of nature—that is, the right to pick something up and call it your own because you need it to subsist. That you might be hanged in civil society for trying to preserve yourself by natural right is a paradox owing to an evolution in the form of the property right which disguises the difference between the natural and social selves, between what is given and what is made. Thomas Hobbes's Leviathan emerges as both the result and the efficient cause of the social contract by investing sovereign authority with the same illusory antecedence that Locke allowed the property right. It is specifically with respect to property that Strathern pursues her critique. She notes how, in the culture of the West, the identity of persons and of things is assured on the basis that persons are like things, unique and self-identical, whereas in the gift culture of Melanesia, things behave like persons, socially: "That in a commodity economy things and persons take the form of things is encompassed in the proposition that objects (of whatever kind) are reified as things-in-themselves. Concomitantly, in a gift economy, objects act as persons in relation to one another. . . . For the one makes an explicit practice out of apprehending the nature or character (convention) of objects, the other their capabilities or animate powers (invention)" (Strathern 1988, 176).

It is worth pausing on this issue of convention before tackling invention. In the system of property developed by Locke, two distinct eras are separated by the contract, one in which value is determined by use, the other in which it is determined by exchange. By use—that is, by the labor of finding and preparing a natural thing so that it will contribute to the subsistence of the laborer—property is acquired. "Whatsoever then he removes out of the State that Nature hath provided, and left it in, he hath mixed his Labour with, and joyned to it something that is his own, and thereby makes it his Property" (Locke 1960, 329). This addition to the thing of an element of the identity of the person who transforms it is an abstract quality, imparted not by any single material act (neither in boiling, eating, digesting, nor, as Walter Shandy rudely adds in his commentary on this passage, shitting [Sterne 1983, 176]), but transfused, like a spirit. Once this transfusion has taken place, the owner and the property are inseparably and inalienably combined. Indeed, it was generally in metaphors of consumption and incorporation that Locke resolved property and identity into the same material form: "The Fruit, or Venison, which nourishes the wild Indian, who knows no Inclosure, and is still a Tenant in common, must be his, and so his, i.e. a part of him, that another can no longer have any right to it" (Locke 1960, 328). Similarly, the self that attaches property to itself is a thing that owns its own actions and is in turn owned by the "person" who legally represents it (Locke 1961, 1:287).

With the advent of the means of preserving property, which before would spoil if not used, exchange becomes possible; and with exchange, money. Once production has become a social rather than a purely self-preservative act, property changes its nature once again, for it no longer comprises what a single laborer can incorporate, but a great deal more than anyone can consume. And when its exchange value is distilled into the money form, the labor of self-preservation is stored up, instead of dissipated from day to day. This refinement of property is owing to two conventions. The first is the agreement that so much of one commodity is worth so much of another, thus identifying a quality common to both but intrinsic to neither, namely an agreed price. The second is the agreement that this price can be represented in money, which "has its value only from the consent of Men" (Locke 1960, 344). Convention replaces invention.

Disposing of property in a money economy constantly reproduces the terms of the original contract, when individuals exchanged their self-evident right to all things in common—that is, the successive incarnation of their identity in things—in return for an assurance from the state of the preservation of their property, lives, and liberties. Property preserved under this agreement loses its immediate link with identity, a link already weakened by the system of exchange, where it has become alienable by contract. Contract mends the breach it makes between preserved selves and preserved things, repairing by an inaugural act of exchange the damage suffered by identity in all subsequent ones, where self-preservation is no longer dependent upon "the sole strength of good contrivance" (Hobbes 1963, 49), but upon a series of conditional engagements that leave its relation to property mediate and reliant upon good faith. This is the difference Blackstone noted between "a choice in possession" and "a choice in action" (Blackstone 1770, 2:397). Any invasion of the right to property therefore touches the self, now without the right to procure its own subsistence by incorporation. "[T]he great and chief end therefore, of Men's uniting into Commonwealths, and putting themselves under Government, is the Preservation of their Property" (Locke 1960, 395). Without preserving that, self-preservation is impossible. Under such a regime, there is a close analogy between an ownable thing and a person, as Hobbes pointed out: "The value, or WORTH of a man, is of all other things, his Price; that is to say, so much as would be given for the use of his Power" (Hobbes 1968, 151).

In the Polynesian and Melanesian cultures discussed by Strathern, an artifact is not "a thing-in-itself." It does not acquire identity from those who make or use it, nor transfuse identity to those who obtain it. A thing is part of a chain of obligations and desires that is strengthened by means of circulation, things passing from hand to hand as gifts, not commodities, confirming sets of social relations and eliciting new ones through further acts of giving and receiving. Not only is a thing inseparable from these relations to other things, it behaves like the people who wield them, for whom social life consists in perpetual movement, "constant and repeated" actions and performances that evolve new sets of relations which "never come to completion" (Strathern 1988, 103). This is invention as opposed to convention. Thus, "[i]f in a commodity economy things and persons assume the social form of things, then in a gift economy they assume the social form of persons" (135). Such persons are not identities in any Western sense of individuals, with a property in themselves, or an interest separable from the business that absorbs them, or a value others can conventionally assess; but rather what she calls "dividuals" or "partible persons," the product of innumerable acts of social reproduction whose "enchainment" allows for no division between a person socially and individually conceived (162). She says that "a plurality of individuals as individuals ('many') is equal to their unity ('one')" (14); each person embodies the social labor that made him or her "a complete, multiple entity, constituted by the acts of others . . . identity is really a shorthand for all the actions that others took to establish the marriage, give birth and nurture the clan person" (Strathern 1992, 178–79).

It is clear that Strathern, in distinguishing between invention and convention, has in mind Marx's notion of commodity fetishism, that metamorphosis instigated by the market causing things to usurp the social being of their owners. What she proposes is the reverse. In order to draw out these implications of Strathern's term *enchainment* and its importance for understanding identity in the Pacific, it is necessary to outline the features of the gift economy on which it depends. The abstract quality that makes a thing behave socially is, according Marcel Mauss and Marshall Sahlins, the *hau* of the gift. In the system of Pacific prestation, there is no external constraint upon the donor of a gift to part with it. Things circulate because of the *hau* of the gift, and the *hau* of those who handle it impel things into circulation. *Hau* commands a variety of meanings, not all congenial to each other; but to keep within the terms of Strathern's argument, it is probably safe to translate it as the instinct of the thing to be mobile, its inclination to preserve the social form of personhood. *Hau* ensures that ownership is a fluid and common affair, a constitutive system of obligations that never inheres in a person or a thing. Any attempt to keep the gift to oneself would be equal to enslaving or cannibalizing the *taonga,* or treasure, of the whole group, digesting the *hau* in a sacrilege called *whaangai hau* or *kai hau,* feasting on the spirit of the gift (Sahlins 1972, 161). Such a transgression would be mortally dangerous to the *hau* of the eater, who, although culturally incapable of absolutely incorporating and owning a gift, can pervert or delay its social movements *(hau whitia),* a misdeed likely to be visited with terrible consequences. So gifts are treated with a great deal of awe, as responsibilities best quickly shed, since their immobility threatens the destruction of the person who handles them (Mauss 1990, 10; Parry 1989, 64–93). *Hau* is really an abstraction of the unbreachable nature of enchainment, a name for that aspect of tribal sociality that makes it impossible for a thing to be stationary or self-identical. *Hau* is the inconceivability of property as purely personal.

In an extraordinarily subtle commentary on *The Gift,* Sahlins compares Mauss's treatment of prestation in Polynesia to the conditions governing not Locke's but Hobbes's original contract. The overt scheme of *The Gift,* he suggests, is Hobbes's state of nature, where everyone has a right to everything; as a result, everyone exists in a virtual state of war. This remains virtual because no one exercises his or her right, and keeps to a tacit covenant of giving. Just as the sword bespeaks this general surrender of rights in the government of Leviathan, so the *hau* bespeaks the necessity of giving and receiving. It is the unspoken general will in its abstract or spiritual form. It causes what otherwise would be a restless desire for power and possessions to move in a reverse cycle, fulfilling itself not in aggressive acts of possession but in endless acts of reciprocation. Mauss outlines "a social contract for the primitives" (Sahlins 1972, 169), where the result of a common desire for peace is the activity of a force that transcends any political decision to release it, and operates without any need of a political definition. There is always already a *hau* of the gift, the menace of the *taonga,* and the horror that would attend not doing what is socially pleasing, just as there is always already the sword of the covenant, poised to implement what everyone has agreed on. The state of war could only become actual if the golden age of property described by Locke were to take place, where everyone has a right to everything, and the self is preserved by incorporating things into proper (i.e., nonpartible) persons.

Corresponding to Strathern's notion of enchainment, where things circulate perpetually in a social motion, just like people, a notion of encompassment explains how the *mana* of a chief spreads out to cover all contingencies, and to naturalize them as elements of tribal unity. The chief is peculiarly fit for such a job, being the synthesis of opposite principles—outsider and autochton, heir and usurper, human and divine—a powerful mixture of contrary qualities expressed in the widespread cognomen, the shark who travels by land (Kaplan 1995, 27; Sahlins 1985b, 79, 98; Dening 1982). The Makahiki festival (stumbled upon by James Cook when he landed in Kealakekua Bay in 1779) was a ritual usurpation called *kali'i* (a pun embracing the meanings "to mar a chief" and "to make a chief" [Sahlins 1985b, 118]), performed annually. This mingled deed of removing and investing a king takes place when Lono, the weaker resident god, accepts the challenge to fight made by Ku the arriviste, only to lose and be banished. Contempt for heritable right, accompanied by admiration for the violent or cunning seizure of power, are celebrated too in the Promethean feats of 'Umi and Maui, the founding heroes of Hawai'i and New Zealand. 'Umi is a bastard son who makes his way to the throne by killing his half-brother, a usurpation whose success is confirmed when, in a confrontation on which the *kali'i* is based, he dodges a spear hurled by Oma'okamau and dispatches him (Valeri 1985a, 79–103). Usurpation is to power what giving is to property: it prevents its becoming personal, dynastic, a monopoly. Sahlins traces the remarkable capacity for self-renewal in Polynesian polities to the tolerance of sacrilege and treachery, committed not in the interests of self but on behalf of the principles of mobility and interchange. The blasphemous Maori prayer, "Be thou god undermost / While I am uppermost," is fulfilled in the cannibal feast, where a chief's triumph is celebrated as people eat the food only gods should eat (Sahlins 1985a, 195, 215; Best 1982, 335). "Rather than a normal succession, usurpation itself is the principle of legitimacy" (Sahlins 1985b, 80).

When a chief talks in the first person, therefore, he exhibits remarkable powers of projection and assimilation, speaking as the fuse through which the most subversive conflicts have been stabilized, not as an enlarged ego.

He is the heroic version of Strathern's partible person, comprising a "oneness in many-ness" that permits enormous latitude to the first person singular, "the kinship 'I,'" as it reverberates the voice of the tribe and its ancestors (Sahlins 1985a, 215; Schrempp 1992, xii; Johansen 1954, 37). J. Prytz Johansen tells an often retold story of Te Rauparaha, the formidable chief active in New Zealand during the Musket Wars, who ordered the silencing of an infant whose cries were threatening to give away the position of his war party. To the father he said, "My friend, you must strangle your child, for this child is I" (Johansen 1954, 37). Similarly, when the Ngapuhi chiefs looked across at the canoes of the Ngati Wakawe they intended to seize in battle, each incarnated the chosen vessel in a variation of cannibalism called *tapa,* where the first person is animated with such zeal that it can speak for what it wants: "That canoe is my backbone . . . my skull shall be the baler to bale it out . . . those two canoes are my thighs" (Maning 1863, 162). "This throws a certain light on the relationship between kinship I and individual I," Johansen concludes. "The latter may, indeed, exist apart, but then certainly it is a being of very little life" (Johansen 1954, 55). Sahlins points out that "any member of the independent Maori *hapu* could use the first person singular 'I' to refer to the whole group" (Sahlins 1985a, 215): "'You will kill me,' says the embattled warrior to his enemies, 'My tribe will kill you and the land will be mine'" (Sahlins 1981, 13–14). Without *mana,* the "surfeit of being" that authorizes the "I" to speak as many (Sahlins 1985a, 207), it is impossible to complete the transformation between "intelligent acts of individuals" and the "fatal outcomes for the society." The "I" without *mana* refers to nothing but a diminished singular being; and what it tells of other people and events is an untruth, for "an action that fails for want of *mana* is a lie" (Sahlins 1985b, 41, 38). Such a failure has no place in any history of the tribe: narratively speaking, it makes no sense. Encompassment means that the speech and actions of the successful first person comprehend the horizon of all that is known and believed within the *hapu* (sept) or the *iwi* (clan).

The inventiveness of encompassment conspires with the illimitable sociability of enchained things to prevent any leakage from the cultural system: there is no shock it cannot absorb, no thing it cannot circulate, and no true event it cannot narrate. The point Sahlins is at pains to make about Cook's entry into the Makahiki is precisely that his appearance on the beach was recognized for what it was—he was a shark come ashore whose usurpation could be legitimized by his induction into the ritual. He could do no damage to such an elastic structure, which easily stretched to enfold him, but this encompassment strained his own more brittle conventions, and caused them to shatter. And they shattered (as they always did with Cook) over the issue of property—the missing cutter, cask lid, tongs, and midshipman's cap (Cook 1967, 2:1191–94). The majority of cases of violence against Polynesians committed by Cook and his crews, ranging from hostage taking and mutilation to attacks with swords and firearms, were in response to theft, either in the form of dishonored bargains or pilfering. The increasing violence with which he reacted in defense of property suggests that he felt directly threatened by its loss, which he regarded as an increasingly intolerable breach of trust. There were other reasons contributing to his infatuated efforts to secure restitution, but the system of property outlined by Locke helps to explain the rising agitation felt by Cook as the signs of his identity were inventively removed. He was fetishizing commodities because he did not want them turned into gifts. To see things moving by other means than contracts of exchange was a scandal that disturbed his own sense of himself, and he began to behave out of character in defense of the propriety of things.

If scandal from the seaward side of the beach arises from the neglect of convention, it follows that from the landward side, it must arise from the neglect of invention, from the desire to eat the *hau* of the gift. Locke's golden age of property is just such a scandal, where the individual takes an unenchained interest in property, immobilizing and ingesting whatever comes his way: "The Fruit, or Venison, which nourishes the wild Indian . . . must be his, and so his, i.e. a part of him, that another can no longer have any right to it" (Locke 1960, 328). Although *whaangai hau* or *kai hau,* the eating of the spirit of the gift, may have been inconceivable before the arrival of Europeans, the multifarious artifacts littering the beach afterwards ensured that it could not only be conceived, but also committed. Perhaps the most spectacular examples of sclerosis in the movement of things occurred among the great chiefs. Kamehameha I was the inheritor of Cook's death. The *mana* of it flowed to him, and with that he controlled the terms of trade with Europeans, generating in his court a frenzy of consumption that was still too weak to waste the vast argosies unloaded in Honolulu (Kirch and Sahlins 1992, 1:41–42, 57–58). Silks and muslins rotted in Kamehameha's storehouses in an orgy of what was effectually gluttony: "The accumulation of deluxe items outran any possibility of personal consumption . . . [so] trade goods functioned as glorious artificial extensions of sacred chiefly bodies that were already stretched to their organic limits" (1:80). It is the gargantuan version of Locke's Indian, where the consumer's body distends to enclose the *hau* of what are no longer enchained gifts, but stationary personal possessions. It is no longer a culture of giving but a problem of storage.

Kamehameha set an example that was followed throughout the Pacific. In Tahiti, Queen Pomare; in Fiji, Cakobau; in the Marquesas, Iotete; and even on the little island of Apemama in the Gilberts, Tembinoka— all amassed power and goods to a degree never seen before (Melville 1968, 309; Kaplan 1995, 22; Thomas 1990, 145–57; Stevenson 1986, 28). At Queen Pomare's court, Herman Melville was struck by incongruous juxtapositions of tools with things whose value appeared to lie in their uselessness: "Superb writing-desks of rose-wood, inlaid with silver and mother-of-pearl; decanters, gilded candelabra; sets of globes and mathematical instruments; the finest porcelain; richly mounted sabres and fowling pieces; laced hats and sumptuous garments of all sorts . . . were strewn among greasy calabashes half-filled with 'poee,' rolls of old tappa and matting, paddles and fish-spears, and the ordinary furniture of a Tahitian dwelling" (Melville 1968, 310). On Apemama, Robert Louis Stevenson was equally amazed by the collections of Tembinoka, the grandson of the usurper Tenkoruti, whose taste for the exotic knew no limit: "House after house, chest after chest, in the palace precinct, is already crammed with clocks, musical boxes, blue spectacles, umbrellas, knitted waistcoats, bolts of stuff, tools, rifles, fowling pieces, medicines, European foods, sewing machines, and, what is more extraordinary, stoves: all that ever caught his eye, tickled his fancy . . . and still his lust is unabated" (Stevenson 1986, 281).

This lust looks like curiosity, and the collections of goods look like cabinets of wonders; but how could such private tastes for singular artifacts develop from a structure of enchainment, where persons are partible and where things circulate sociably because they are held in common? Part of the answer lies in the rapid transformations of things in the course of contact between a commodity economy and a gift economy. Cook and Bougainville noticed that there were two levels of exchange: one a simple bartering for necessary things, such as food and iron; the other a more variable trade in articles both sides esteemed as aesthetically pleasing rather than useful. The axes, hatchets, and knives traded for food were different from "what is merely Ornament," such as blue beads, red cloth, and looking glasses. The former retained their value over the whole course of trading, whereas the latter "may be highly valuable at one time and not so at a nother" (Cook 1967, 161). Bougainville started with barter, pigs, and bananas in return for caps and handkerchiefs (Bougainville 1772b, 216). From there new branches of commerce opened up, involving more subtle estimations of value: "They brought with them several instruments for fishing; stone chisels, strange kinds of cloth, shells, etc." (218); and in exchange they demanded earrings.

It did not take long before things of significant ritualistic or genealogical value, such as greenstone weapons and preserved heads, began to be produced as commodities for exchange. William Yate reported that it was well known in New Zealand for agents of the Sydney market in heads to "give property to a Chief for the purpose of getting them to kill their slaves, that they might have some heads to take to New South Wales" (Dalton 1990, 82n. 103). In a bastardization of an important ritual, these heads were posthumously tattooed to resemble those of *ariki* (chiefs) in order to lift their price as curiosities. George Vancouver noticed the deleterious effect on neolithic manufacturing skills: "The knowledge they have now acquired . . . of the more useful implements, have rendered these, and other European commodities, not only essentially necessary to their common comforts, but have made them regardless of their former tools and manufactures . . . in the few of their bone, or stone tools, or utensils, that were seen amongst them, those offered for sale were of rude workmanship, and of an inferior kind, solely intended for our market, to be purchased by way of curiosity" (Vancouver 1801, 332; quoted in Oliver 1974, 3:1285). Vancouver's remarks make it plain that entry into such a trade required two adjustments to be made by those previously handling things in a system of enchainment: they had to make the conceptual shift from gift to commodity, and then from commodity to curiosity.

There is no doubt that in this complex passage of goods that Nicholas Thomas has discussed as "entanglement" (Thomas 1991), the shifts were more rapid and reversible than this sequence implies. Although an interest in curiosities derived from an understanding of the market, wonder was experienced (on both sides of the beach) from the first moments of contact. No doubt the man who leapt from the deck of the *Resolution* clutching a copy of *Tom Jones* was acting under the influence of an "immediate propensity which operates . . . independent of all ideas of obligation, and of all views either to public or private utility" (Wales in Cook 1961, app. 5, p. 789; Hume 1987, 466). Bougainville was sure Tahitians were provoked to steal by the sheer novelty of what they saw: "Doubtless their curiosity for new objects excited violent desires in them" (Bougainville 1772b, 229). On their own account, they describe the strong effect of these new things upon their minds: "When I saw how white men lived my head went around. . . . I was amazed at the things in [their houses]"

(Lacey 1990, 194), and "When the people saw what great things the papalagi had in their ship—the axes, the fish-hooks, the soft cloth—they were crazy to get them" (Lupo 1923, 240; quoted in Thomas 1991, 89). Abraham Fornander said, "It was an era of wonder, delight . . . to their chiefs it was an El Dorado" (Fornander 1878, 2:321).

James Burney's observations among the Maori at Grass Cove on his second visit there, after it became plain there was to be no reprisal against the chief Kahura for instigating the slaughter and consumption of the crew of the *Adventure*'s cutter, give an extra dimension to this marveling appetite for things-in-themselves. He said, "They often appeared to have a great deal of friendship for us, speaking sometimes in the most tender, compassionate tone of voice imaginable; but it not a little disgusted one to find all this show of fondness interested and that it constantly ended in begging. If gratified with their first demand, they would immediately fancy something else, their expectations and importunities increasing in proportion as they had been indulged" (McNab 1914, 2:198–99; quoted in Salmond 1997, 127). Because they were doing nothing to recover the *hau* of their cannibalized friends, the British and their possessions appeared to the Maori equally consumable, with no peril—nor any limit—attached to eating either (Salmond 1997, 104). Thus a European curiosity had from the first moment the glamour of *taonga*, but none of its menace, because it was stranded and could not be returned.

The incident at Grass Cove specifies the scandalous temptation presented by all things in a ship to those on the shore. They promise to supplant the constitutive social acts that produce the partible person or the heroic tribal "I" with things that are nothing but things, beguiling potential owners into personal pleasures of the gluttonous sort that finally spill over into the stockpiled curiosities of Kamehameha and Queen Pomare. With Kamehameha, as with Kahura at Grass Cove, this new relationship to things and to power is fostered by a new relation to edible flesh, for in both cases the accumulation of goods is mediated by the jointed and (some said) partly consumed corpse of a *haole* or *pakeha* (European) that is ingested, just like the venison of Locke's Indian (Cook 1967, 1:542n. 3; Fornander 1878, 2:195; Melville 1964, 261), giving a wholly new meaning to partibility and narrowing considerably the social range of the first person.

But the route to these growing hoards of things, identified by Melville and Stevenson as museums (Melville 1968, 309; Stevenson 1986, 336), is not straightforward. The metamorphosis of food, a gift, a tool, or a ritual object into a commodity, then from a commodity into a curiosity, is interspersed with reimplications of the thing into the system of enchainment and fresh intuitions of what chiefly encompassment might involve. The case of Iotete the Marquesan chief is exemplary, not least because the European things he found most amazing are muskets. Of course, they were intended to be so, in the same manner that tattoos, from the other side, were meant to stun those who looked at them. In the hints of the Royal Society, the Earl of Morton instructs Cook in the irenic management of a firearm: "Shewing them that a Bird upon the wing may be brought down by a Shot.—Such an appearance would strike them with amazement and awe" (Cook 1955, 514 [appendix 2]). Consequently, guns were immediately valued as prestige objects by Maori, Fijians, and Marquesans, and considerably enhanced the power of a chief not only as instruments of war, but also as gifts that would command respect. After his visit to England, the Maori chief Hongi exchanged everything he had been given for muskets (Wilson 1973, 245). Frederick Maning said that when he arrived in the Hokianga harbor in New Zealand in the 1830s, a white trader was "of a value, say about twenty times his own weight in muskets" (Maning 1863, 21). There were no trade goods in which Iotete had a deeper interest, for "[g]uns and gunpowder had taken sole possession of his mind" (Thomas 1990, 145).

Thus far, the novelty of firearms was encompassed, and they circulated as gifts in the way of enchainment. But there were two contradictions inherent in the treatment of guns as *taonga* of the tribe. The first was that the power they gained through war destroyed the balance between warring chiefs in favor of him who possessed the greater number of weapons and the means of firing them longer. The second was that the recipient of such a gift received something so much out of his power to reciprocate that they confirmed the growing power of the donor as absolute, at the same time that they became immobile, operating less as a gift than as a physical incarnation of power—just as money in a commodity economy incarnates labor (Thomas 1990, 154–57). Convention was replacing invention, and the abstract quality of *hau* was being materialized as property. Then, when the immobility of the muskets coincided with the hegemony of a chief like Iotete, whose open-ended pursuit of power had left him unassailable, the musket became something else again; for when Titiutu, Iotete's wife, died, her embalmed body was surrounded with muskets, "all most sacred, and cannot be touched" (151). These muskets advanced from commodities to gifts, then from gifts into tokens of tribal power, then from tokens into sacred objects, or fetishes. However, it was as curiosities that they survived. Melville remembered old flintlocks hung up for monuments in the valley of the Typee, battered and mostly useless but held in high esteem: "From their great age and the peculiarities they exhibited, [they] were well worthy a place in any antiquarian's armory" (Melville 1964, 209).

Whether muskets were mainly the object of accumulation, as in the Marquesas, or whether it was the appeal of exotic trade goods, as in the Gilberts and Tahiti, chiefly power soon exceeded all previous limits, and chiefly lines proclaimed themselves royal dynasties, indisputably in control of islands and archipelagos, putting an end to usurpation. When Tembinoka said to Stevenson, "*I* got *power*," pointing out, "Here in my island, *I* 'peak'" (Stevenson 1986, 336, 286), it is a question what sort of first person makes this announcement: a kinship or partible "I" whose oneness is in many, or an ego more singular than that, in keeping with the chief's taste for owning singular things? One might pose the same question of Pomare, Kamehameha, Cakobau, and Iotete; and what Stevenson says about Tembinoka might equally well apply to all these ambitious kings: "To feel, to use his power, to embellish his island and the picture of island life after a private ideal, to . . . extend his singular museum—these employ delightfully the sum of his abilities" (336).

At this point, it is useful to consider fetishism once again, not exactly Marx's commodity fetishism or Freud's supplement of the missing maternal penis, but that class of objects observed by Dutch and English traders on the Guinea coast when, during the seventeenth and early eighteenth centuries, they noted transformations of things resembling these in the Pacific. On the long borderline of traffic running from Senegal to Angola, European commodities passed into the African hinterland, and African gold entered the European markets as minted coin—guineas, the surest incarnation of value. The pidgin word *fetish* derived from the Portuguese name for artifact, *feitiço*, and referred either to things having no part to play in this trade or those that disturbed or impeded it. The local name for fetishes was *kakeraas, krakra, grogories,* or *grigri* (Pietz 1988, 110; Boyle Papers 39:90; Barbot 1746, 5:104, 247) and referred both to things looking like human heads, made of feathers, clay, or leather, set up in trees or in little huts; and also to gold that had been worked with other materials, such as wool, wood, silver, or copper. They were used in local and apparently improvisational acts of worship. "When they have a mind to make any offerings to their idols, or desire to know anything of them, they cry, let us make feitisso" (Barbot 1746, 5:372). But fetish gold was also exquisite, "buttons plain, or in filigree; rings plain, or in chains; toothpickers; curious hatbands, and sword-hilts; besides many other sorts of curiosities" (5:57); and in some cases it was meant to deceive, being cleverly disguised as false nuggets and factitious gold dust (5:230). To some observers, fetishes seemed to be the result of an arbitrary decision to set value on things outside the ambit of trade, "a bird's Feather, a Pebble, a Bit of Rag, a Dog's Leg; or, in short, any thing they fancy" (Smith 1744, 26; quoted in Pietz 1987, 41); to others it seemed a calculated attempt to cheat Europeans by giving false measure.

In the discussion of *Captain Singleton* in chapter 2, it was evident that Daniel Defoe knew enough about fetishes to describe them ("they set up a long Pole between them and us, with a great Tossel of Hair hanging, not on the Top, but something above the Middle of it, adorn'd with little Chains, Shells, Bits of Brass, and the like" [Defoe 1963, 33]); and enough about fetish gold to imagine Europeans coming out of the hinterland skilled at making it. In the course of this narrative, Defoe evacuates all concepts of value—use, exchange, fiduciary, intrinsic—until he is left with nothing but the aesthetic value of a curiosity, a piece of metal shaped like a bird or an animal, the coinage of the maker's brain: "an Idol, I suppose, of their own making" (245). In the *Farther Adventures,* Crusoe comes across another such fetish, "a frightful Nothing, a meer imaginary Object dressed up by themselves, and made terrible to themselves by their own Contrivance" (Defoe 1927, 3:181). And in Exchange Alley, Defoe in his own person encounters another in the form of credit, "this invisible *je ne scay quoi,* this . . . emblem of a something, though in itself nothing" (Defoe 1951, 118).

Locke called bullion and precious stones "things, that Fancy and Agreement hath put the Value on, more than real Use" (Locke 1960, 342). They are fetishized when fancy alone, without the aid of agreement, assigns them importance, and when the pleasure (or terror) they afford the senses or the imagination is all they need accomplish. "Fetishes are diverse, according to the diverse fantasy of each" (Loyer 1714, 43; quoted in Pietz 1988, 111). Pietz emphasizes that this liberated fancy is not a defense of local norms; rather, it is the creolization of taste typical of intercultural spaces. And Simon Schaffer suggests that it embraces both sides. Europeans, whose entry into a credit economy made them homesick for a world of intrinsic values, began to fetishize pure gold and silver; and Africans, whose system of values having been disturbed by intruders eager to buy what they esteem as mere earth, started turning dross into gods (Schaffer 1996, XX). Meanwhile, in Exchange Alley, fetishes were available in many forms, including Sail Cloth Permits, or Globe Permits, "which came to be currently sold each for sixty guineas and upwards in the alley, which nevertheless was only a square bit of a playing card, on which was the impression of a seal in wax, being the sign of the Globe tavern in the neighbourhood, with the motto or inscription on of Sail Cloth Permits, without any name signed thereon" (Anderson 1825, 68).

Laurence Sterne went to the Guinea coast for a metaphor suitable for this world of whims and hobbyhorses, where connoisseurs try to naturalize their taste for curiosities: "The whole set of 'em are so hung around and befetish'd with the bobs and trinkets of criticism . . . and have that eternal propensity to apply them upon all occasions" (Sterne 1983, 143). Charles de Brosses, the foremost compiler of travel narratives in France, wrote a book on this transformation of arbitrarily chosen and indecipherable "objets terrestres et materiels," calling it a primitive polytheism. He understood it to be a habit observable "chez tous les peuples grossiers de l'univers" (Brosses 1760, 10, 185). Fetishes—bobs and trinkets, *kakeraas* and *grigri*—are unlike commodities, then, for they lack the abstract quality of a common price; and they are unlike gifts because they lack the abstract quality of *hau;* and they are unlike icons or totems because they lack the abstract quality of a represented godhead. Like Hobbes's and Defoe's idols, fetishes represent nothing but themselves; and even when designed to deceive the spectator as false nuggets and gold dust, still they represent nothing but what they are—earth, sheer matter. Immanuel Kant called fetishism "an idolatry that sinks as deeply into the trifling as appears to be possible in human nature" (Kant 1960, 111). Fetishes are artifacts that cannot be consumed, trafficked, or understood as signs: they add nothing to the person, and nothing to the community. They may be beautiful, but they do not have to be. They are experienced as untranscended materiality by a self that is excited and singularized, but certainly not preserved, by its taste for them. This is how Iotete regarded the muskets placed around the corpse of his wife, and how Cook regarded the cask lid, cutter, tongs, and hat for which he risked and lost his life.

If the period of England's crisis over the purity of its coinage (lasting roughly from 1695 to 1717) shaped its interest in the fetish coast of Africa, then its crisis with credit (acute from 1720 onward) defined its interest in the South Seas beach, and the artificial curiosities that landed on it. Both were driven by the contradiction in the contract (securing what is alienable, making a property of what is invisible) that forces the self to be involved so deeply in its own preservation that eventually it reaches the state of infatuation. If the parallel between the seaward and landward sides of the beach runs, as I have suggested, between lines of disintegrating identities, then the same sort of contradiction found in convention must also be evident in invention. In the debate over the death of Cook, Marshall Sahlins argues that the changes on the beach caused no traumatic interruption in the lives of Hawai'ians, and certainly none of the cultural amnesia that Gananath Obeyesekere blames on Cook's invasion of the island, so severe it makes it impossible for us ever to recollect how pre-European Hawai'ian sociality worked. Between these two points of view another is possible: namely, that substantial changes did take place (manifestly there was a serious interruption in the passage of gifts and power, both there and elsewhere) that could not have happened unless the system of invention, with its encompassed first persons and enchained social processes, were not as watertight as Strathern and Sahlins maintain. This is to suppose there were historical tensions and contradictions in Hawai'an society that were destined to encourage the monopolization of power and goods once trade with Europeans was under way; and necessarily this supposition introduces another, which is that the Hobbesian state of war was not just a virtuality based on an equilibrium formed by prestation and usurpation, but that a real struggle existed between rival beliefs about how power and personhood were to be preserved and handed on. Were this the case, the European presence didn't inaugurate an absolute change from a gift economy to crippled dependency on the world market, so much as magnify differences and oppositions already thriving outside the envelope of the *hau,* and the sequence of usurpations it legitimized.

In the history of eastern Oceania, Nicholas Thomas has detected "a very broad counterpoint or conflict between a variety of forms of inspirational or shamanic agency and the centralising force of chieftainship or kingship, which, as an encompassing ideology, "tends to assimilate and incorporate all forms of important capacity" (Thomas 1994c, 15). He suggests that shamans (*kaula* in Hawai'i, *taura* in Tahiti) and the prophetic movements they instigate are the rims of politico-cultural black holes left by the collapse of a whole structure of ancient privilege, of which all that remained by the time of Cook was sporadic anti-chiefly outbreaks (Thomas 1990, 119). There seems to be good evidence showing that cultic activity in Melanesia predated Europeans, and involved a radically different approach to goods from those Strathern regards as typical (Lindstrom 1993, 65–66). The Polynesian *kaula* or shaman would own Lono for his tutelar divinity, and speak strangely in the voice of the god while performing equally strange gestures ("numberless strange and mad pranks" [Burney in Cook 1967, 620n. 2]), all aimed at the death of the king and dissolution of the encompassing hierarchy of royalty (Thomas 1990, 127; Wilson 1973, 218; Gunson 1962, 217; Freeman and Geddes 1959, 193).

Thus there is room to suspect that Cook's last act at Kealakekua Bay, and perhaps the whole of his induction into the Lono cult, was orchestrated by the priesthood not as an accompaniment to ritual *kali'i* but as the overture to a real shamanic challenge, something Kalani'opu'u realized almost too late, and which Cook never understood at all. What was the meaning of that mysterious coconut, which the priest Keali'ikea was thrusting so importunately into Cook's unwilling hands shortly before his death; and why was food supplied so generously by the priests of Lono to his ships and to the astronomers camped onshore, even after he was killed (Sahlins 1985b, 124)? The challenge was not issued by an exotic culture embodied in an Englishman mad with pride, as Obeyesekere suggests; nor was it a usurpation assimilable to the legitimizing phases of the Makahiki, as Sahlins maintains. It was more like "an explosive, arbitrary incident" (Thomas 1990, 117) provoked by the ghost of a rival idea of politics and social relations, and its failure caused a consolidation of chiefly power on an unprecedented scale.

What alternative political system, and what ancient privileges, were the servants of Lono—priests and *kaula* alike—defending? Consistent with Lono's responsibility for fertility, his cult supports stories and practices linked exclusively to the land, and to an autochtonous myth that has humans growing out of the earth, like the sweet potato that sustains them (Sahlins 1995, 166; Kaplan 1995, 28). As opposed to chiefs, who are from the sea, and who occupy the land by driving Lono offshore, the cultic desire is to repatriate Lono, to bring him home from the sea to the earth that is his own. It was in that pseudoindigenous role (the spokesman of the land god forced to travel on the sea) that Cook was hailed by the priests of Hawai'i, sensing a great opportunity (Sahlins 1981, 11). The prophetic movements in New Zealand have found untiring hospitality and protection among the Tuhoe people of the Urewera ranges, *tangata whenua,* people sprung from the land who are, unlike the other major *iwi* of those three islands, without a canoe myth. As for enjoying what the land affords, it is not a privilege reserved to a few, according to the prophets, but extends to everyone. According to Valerio Valeri, "the *kaula* represents a totality directly accessible to the individual" (Valeri 1985b, 139; quoted in Thomas 1994, 27). If this totality is of the earth, earthy, and promised to *tangata whenua,* who claim it as individuals, not partible persons, then the prophets outline an economy very different from gift culture. Certainly the *kaula* talks in a first person quite unlike a chief's. It is not a tribal but a divine voice that speaks. William Mariner recalled that in Tonga, the prophet "sp[oke] in the first person as if he were the god" (Mariner and Martin 1817, 1:108), and Te Ua Haumene used the decollated head of a militia officer called Lloyd as a speaking tube for the first person voice of the angel Gabriel (Wilson 1973, 218). As these speeches foretold, in a kind of fatidic syllogism, the death of kings and the distribution of good things ("fine Islands, uninhabited, with all Kinds of food in great plenty" [Robarts 1974: 62])—"rich viands and delicious fruits were supposed to be furnished in abundance . . . handsome youths and women, *purotu anae,* all perfection, thronged the place" [Ellis 1829: 1.327])—it seems probable that the "I" who talked did not encompass other "I"s in order to reproduce quotidian sociality, but greeted them as appetent individuals with a taste for pleasure who were poised on the edge of a new epoch.

Certainly the *arioi,* the cult that was flourishing in Tahiti when Cook arrived in 1769, and still very active during William Ellis's period there as missionary forty years later, conforms closely to this model of shamanic practice. Their god was Roma-tane, son of 'Oro (Lono). The famous *maro'ura,* the red feather girdle incorporating the pennant of Samuel Wallis's ship together with the hair of Richard Skinner, one the *Bounty* mutineers, which subsequently became an icon of critical importance in Pomare I's bid for preeminence, was known as "'Oro in the feather body" and derived from a Lono cult active in the early eighteenth century (Oliver 1974, 2:915, 3:1213–15; Dening 1996, 133). Because it was an item over which conflict between cultic and chiefly interests had occurred, one of the many varieties of antichiefly mockery used by the *arioi* was to sport a red girdle, burlesquing its ritual function as a claim to kinship title and power; occasionally they sacrificed a pig tied with a similar girdle (Oliver 1974, 2:921, 2:934). Although it was identified by George Forster as a company of aristocrats, the *arioi* opened their company to anyone capable of putting on a good performance, a system of self-election constituting a club of individuals who developed their own talents for giving and taking pleasure (2:937). The ego stood well to the fore in their shows, and seems to have articulated a veiled threat to the power of chiefs: "It is I," the leading *arioi* would intone, "I stand comedian of the wind that vibrates to the sound of a gun." They would lay their claim to things, saying, "I am come to the king's house; I want food, give me that pig; I want apparel, give me that piece of cloth" (2:916, 958). Everyone was agreed that it was a movement that pushed epicureanism to its limits. They were capable of mounting stunning displays, "their streamers floating in the wind, their drums and flutes sounding, . . . with their wild distortions of person, antic gestures, painted bodies, and vociferated songs, mingling with the . . . dashing of the sea, and the rolling and breaking of the surf, on the adjacent reef" (Ellis 1829, 1:319).

The *arioi* knew of a place in Raiatea called Temehaui unauna, "lovely and enchanting in appearance, adorned with flowers of every form and hue, and perfumed with odours of every fragrance" (1:327). William Bligh gave this paradise a local habitation, the island of Teturoah, where the *arioi* resorted to enjoy "peculiar dainties." He reported, "They have luxuriant and fine situations where they have their Meetings, and live with all the dissipation imaginable, and they vary the enjoyments of their lives with the Seasons of the Year" (Bligh 1975, 298). The phrasing suggests a resemblance between the *arioi* paradise and the one meditated by his own mutineers, who "imagined it was in their power to fix themselves in the midst of plenty, on the finest island in the world, where they need not labour, and where the allurements of dissipation are beyond any thing that can be conceived" (Bligh 1790, 10). The same island was purchased by the latter-day Fletcher Christian, actor Marlon Brando, who still owns it.

With the extension of chiefs into dynasts and their household goods into museums of curiosities, it might be expected that the role of prophets, shamans, and *arioi* was at an end, their pleasures dwarfed by royal splendor, their first-person voices silenced by the tremendous egoism of the new collectors, and their jokes about an autochtonous independence losing all point. On Hawai'i, this was certainly the intention of the chiefs when in 1819 they attempted to obliterate all local religion in "the spectacular abrogation of the old tabus" (Kirch and Sahlins 1992, 1:57). But the concentration of chiefly power did not result in the extinction of shamanic practices. Cults in general and the *arioi* in particular appear to have taken two directions in the aftermath of chiefly consolidation, the one actively subversive of chiefly power, the other complicit with it. On Fiji, the *tuka* movement preached the expulsion of the Bau chiefs, and in response its leading shamans were persecuted and put to death by Cakobau (Kaplan 1995, 3, 44, 117). Likewise the Mamaia sect in Tahiti, whose prophets had *arioi* connections, was vigorously suppressed, its adherents made to walk barefoot to their place of exile over coral reefs, and two of its leaders hanged (Gunson 1962, 209, 226). The Hauhau, Papahurihia, Whiowhio, and Ringatu prophets in New Zealand were harried by settler governments, and Te Kooti, the most famous, was hunted by an armed constabulary and native levies and only with great difficulty evaded capture (Binney 1995). These sects were millenarian, preaching imminent salvation on earth for all true believers and a restoration of the land. Land was to be redistributed according to principles of primordial justice, and goods such as cloth, wine, and cows were expected to fall from heaven (Gunson 1962, 226; Ralston 1985, 311). Although these prophecies might have had a parabolic rather than a material significance, and have been distinguished from full-scale Melanesian cargo cults by the title of "adjustment" cults (Ralston 1985, 308), there seems no reason to doubt their appeal to needy people who warmed to promises of comfort and pleasure.

But there were others sects, to some extent less visionary and certainly more voluptuous. The Hulumanu cult, which flourished between 1826 and 1840 in Hawai'i jettisoned doctrine in favor of pure hedonism, doing without prophets, visions, and promises of redemption, cultivating instead traditional sports and sporting ornamental feather capes (Ralston 1985, 316, 321). If that sounds like an importation of the exhibitionist pleasures of the *arioi*, the possibility of such cultural borrowing existed by the early nineteenth century. The importance of voyaging—homecoming—was evident in the later cultic emphasis on shiplike structures and the arrival of trade goods. The Hauhau conducted their ceremonies around a flagpole, or *niu*, rigged to look like a ship's mast (Cowan 1911, 24–25). Cult leaders such as the Samoan Siovili, or Joe Gimlet, and Nacirikaumoli and Nakausabaria of the *tuka*, had traveled in ships or were scheduled to arrive in them (Thomas 1991, 109; Freeman and Geddes 1959, 187; Kaplan 1995, 56). In fact, Siovili had been in Tahiti, and perhaps it was owing to *arioi* influence that he became fascinated by European manufactures such as timepieces and necklaces, and preached (according to George Pratt) consumerism, "a religion pleasing to flesh and sense" (Freeman and Geddes 1959, 156). Indeed, the period of dynastic establishment on Tahiti appears to have coincided with a growing lavishness of *arioi* performances. The picture Ellis reluctantly paints of their stunning arrival at the beach in the early nineteenth century is much more impressive than surgeon Ellis's description of the same thing from Cook's third voyage (Oliver 1974, 2:918). In part, this stemmed from Queen Pomare's active sponsorship of *arioi* customs, such as ceremonial gift exchanges followed by night dancing (Gunson 1962, 230). Her court was notorious for dissolute behavior, which it indulged like a traveling *arioi* company: "[The queen] spent the greater portion of her time sailing about from one island to another, attended by a licentious court; and wherever she went, all manner of games and festivities celebrated her arrival" (Melville 1968, 303).

Such an alliance between a queen and the *arioi* is not easy to explain, given the long history of their conflict over the feather god. But that this bond is sealed specifically over the issue of pleasure suggests that she turned to the cult for some hint about how to make the insignia of absolute power satisfying to herself and, by acquiring the art of exquisite sensations, to know when she had had enough of them. It was for her a problem of taste, and she wanted a result she could define as "wonderful and personally enthralling" (Lacey 1990, 215); so she called in the experts who would teach her how to consummate a process that otherwise was open ended and incremental. Her perplexity can be read in Iotete's collection of muskets, which he was unable at first to fetishize: "Iotete did not have a drive towards a greater accumulation of European objects for their own sake, or a simple desire to control more territory; rather he was attempting to re-create an imagined transformation which he saw as generationally staged" (Thomas 1990, 152). To this dynastic end, he used the court of Pomare I as a mythic form, just as Queen Pomare IV exploited *arioi* displays, as a way of making the signs of power present to the senses. Between autochtony and the sacred, the "*enata* and the *atua*," he sat with his muskets, waiting for something great to happen. Stevenson's Tembinoka was not yet at this stage of reflexive subtlety with regard to fetish objects, and was vainly distending himself with curiosities in the hope that the next acquisition would make sense of all the rest: "He is possessed by the seven devils of the collector" (Stevenson 1986, 281). Stevenson's short story of "The Bottle Imp" explores the agony of someone whose power to acquire things is limitless.

Sovereigns with vast magazines of heterogeneous things are like Pedro Fernandez de Quirós coming to Vanuatu, or Bougainville or Cook landing at Tahiti. They found that tales told of millenarian excess or paradise on earth lay within the realm of actuality, and the discovery confounded them. The most outrageous promises of the cargo cults were already realized in these collections, yet their failure to satisfy their owners had no effect on the currency of visions of an endless supply of European goods, which circulated then as now in Melanesia. The most common reason given for the persistence of the cargo myth is ignorance—a yearning for things whose production is a mystery, "desire without the skill and knowledge of attaining the desired" (Gunson 1962, 210; Freeman and Geddes 1959, 194). The example of the *arioi* and their widespread influence indicates that desire was more subtle than this. This cult had already understood the difference between mere accumulation of artifacts—consumption in its most primitive form—and an aesthetics of display and performance that invested things with a glamour neither purely sacred nor purely political. The cultic approach to things adjusted the relationship between artifacts, pleasure, and power, rather than assimilating unfamiliar technology.

When Europeans fell into frenzies of collecting on the beach, so avid and promiscuous that a Tongan boy asked Cook's men if they would bargain for a turd (Cook 1961, 255), they were in a condition much like Tembinoka's. In order to fetishize an artificial curiosity, it was necessary to convert its singularity into an aesthetic pleasure without assigning it cultural significance or a market value. Sydney Parkinson managed this conversion with tattooed heads ("Their fancy indeed is very wild and extravagant, and I have seen no imitation of nature in any of their performances" [Parkinson 1773, 98]), and so did Sir Joseph Banks when he distinguished a style of spiral designs of "a much wilder taste and I may truly say like nothing but itself" (Banks 1962, 2:24). The uniqueness of the thing provokes the je ne sais quoi, and on that account alone, it finds a place in the inventory of marvels. For this reason, Kimble Bent wanted a full facial tattoo: "What a curiosity I would have been . . . like the bearded lady in the circus" (Cowan 1911, 90).

Margaret Hodgen suggests that ethnography comes about when collections of things can be sorted into different types and kinds by means of conceptual distinctions: "As long as the owners of such collections remained content with the simple joys of accumulation, as long as they remained content merely to look at the treasures [as objects alone] . . . there was no need for classification, conceptualisation or an appeal to the verbal devices of description" (Hodgen 1964, 164). In his discussion of cabinets of curiosities, Horst Bredekamp points out that it is the very suppression of this "criterion of importance" that preserves the link between the arrangement of curiosities and the organization of utopias, for each depends on a sense of wonder not limited or constrained by categorical distinctions (Bredekamp 1995, 58–61).[1] The status of gold in Thomas More's *Utopia*, where it affords pleasure but has no economic value, is an example of this valorization of fancy at the expense of agreement or convention. The weakness of convention likewise reduces the importance of language as a system of signs. Words may be understood as events but not as contracts of meaning and intention; thus the Utopians make no treaties that rely on good faith, only those that instantly can be carried into effect (More 1910, 105). Michel de Certeau has observed that when linguistic

---

1   This is the reason that there is still a place for monsters (giants and midgets who have been exhibited at fairs) at the very center of Sarah Scott's eighteenth-century utopia, *Millennium Hall* (1762) (Scott 1986, 20).

conventions are breaking down, and familiar customs and practices are deteriorating under the influence of time or novelty, words become delinquent in a specifically utopian way. Vocality retreats from meaning into the delight of sheer sound, a glossolalia that releases "the potentialities of the vocal palette" (Certeau 1996, 32). Alexander Selkirk was exploring its range, perhaps, when he started to speak his words by halves.

These three characteristics—erased distinctions, susceptibility to pleasure, and verbal delinquency—are strongly marked in adjustment and cargo cults. If the core distinction in the ethnography of the South Pacific is between the noble and ignoble savage, in cultic lore it is between black and white. Te Ua Haumene taught that history had disturbed a primitive balance, and promised a return to the original color: "It was time that begat the black and the white. . . . Therefore the white must not bait the black nor the black the white . . . what is it to be—the beauty of Mt Egmont or the white of paper written upon so that the bold signs are one with the universe?" (Clark 1975, 123; Meul 1992, 41). The Jonfrum movement insisted that property be marked in black and white, as if to emphasize its imperfect state (Wilson 1973, 325). In New Britain, the cargo cult tells a history of theft by white from black that will end with a general whiteness, "for the desire to escape from the black self is very strong" (Lattas 1992b, 36). On Viti Levu, it seems to have been black, not white, that was the primary color of the cult, for followers of *tuka* were seen drilling with their faces blackened (Kaplan 1995, 63).

It is already clear that pleasure from things is intensified in cultic practice by the *mise en scène,* a technique exploited to its fullest extent by the *arioi* in their performances. Papahurihia preached a millennium where "everything is found in plenty, flour, sugar, guns, ships; there too murder and sensual pleasure reign"—better by far, he said, than the European heaven, where there is "nothing but books to eat" (Binney 1990, 1:328–31)—and he enlivened his doctrine with feats of prestidigitation and ventriloquism, "sleight of Hand tricks" (Binney 1966, 323). Verbal delinquency was common to all cults, but demonstrated by the Hauhau with especial panache. Round the *niu* they chanted what seemed to be a liturgical Maori ("Hai, kamu te ti, oro te mene, rauna te niu") that was in fact transliterated English ("Hey, come to tea, all the men round the *niu*"). It signified nothing, but evidently had a powerful effect as a "vocal event." In this cult, the *hau* of things and of people, the abstract force of an extended sociality, is caught and materialized as sound within the mouth of the initiate, who is endowed with the power of a spell or a curse. "That which is to kill us," wrote John White, a settler during the Land

Wars, "is the noise 'Hau,' 'Hau' which is like the noise of a dog" (Clark 1975, 85).

There is a further resemblance between European utopias and Polynesian/Melanesian cargo cults. The dream of future good coincides inevitably with a sense of past loss. No longer at one with the land, whether as authochton or inhabitant of paradise, the individual can recover birthright only by dreaming of what has been lost, or by appropriating the things that loom in its place. No longer sovereign among the sounds of his island, Caliban must dream,

> and then in dreaming
> The clouds methought would open and show riches
> Ready to drop upon me, that when I waked
> I cried to dream again. (*The Tempest* 3.2.138–41)

Under Queen Pomare's rule, Tahitians exhibited "a constitutional voluptuousness," said Melville, "susceptible to no impressions, except from things palpable, or novel and striking." But he added that it was "a morbid feeling, engendered by the sense of severe physical wants, preying on minds excessively prone to superstition" (Melville 1968, 174–75). In a recent article that considerably modifies her earlier position on enchainment and the social life of things in Melanesian cultures, Marilyn Strathern has identified as nostalgia the coexistence of voluptuousness and loss noticed by Melville. Using as her occasion the yam-growing cult among Trobriand Islanders of Port Moresby, who bring a kinship activity into a situation in which normally they can operate only as individual workers, she considers the difference between synthetic and substantive nostalgia as the difference between simply mourning what is gone, and understanding how an active view of the past can change the present. Of the latter case, a nostalgic practice fully analogous to the millenarian attitude to time in cargo cults, she says, "It is not just that feelings are aroused, but that they must be aroused" (Strathern 1995, 111).

After European contact, shamans found a useful source of exotic additions to their chants. James Cowan calls the Hauhau prophecies in New Zealand "a blend of ancient faith in spells and incantations . . . with English phrases and perverted fragments of church services (Cowan 1922, 2:3). By the intervention of such vocal events, the past is recovered as a promise, and mourning blends with anticipation, or pain with pleasure. After some years resident in Samoa, Stevenson (who had singled out from among all Tembinoka's powers the power to feel [Stevenson 1986, 336]) had a remarkable intuition of such a feeling as he was weeding a plant called, appropriately, sensitive from his garden at Vailima: "This business fascinates me like a tune or a passion; yet all the while I thrill with a strong distaste. The horror of the thing, objective and subjective, is always present to my mind; the horror of creeping things, a superstitious horror of the void and the powers about me, the horror of my own devastation" (Stevenson 1911, 3:246). For cargo cultists, it is the substantively nostalgic feeling of being black when white represents a belief in the original and final transcendence of such distinctions. For scurvy victims, it is the exquisite cusp between feelings of most intense privation and anticipations of scarcely credible delight.

Perhaps because nostalgia is a highly contagious emotion, or because cargo cults menaced chiefly and colonial authority alike, it attracted the metaphor of disease. The cult always spread like an epidemic or an outbreak, and was contained by means of deportation and exile that the authorities termed quarantine (Kaplan 1995, 90, 117). In the late 1880s, twelve prophets of *tuka* together with a whole village of believers were sent to Rotuma, exactly as lepers were being sent to Molokai. Stevenson drew the same parallel between leprosy and cargo when he considered Tembinoka's very strict rules for entry into and departure from Apemana, remarking somewhat equivocally, "this social quarantine, a curiosity in itself, has been the preservation of others" (Stevenson 1986, 285).

Among the prophecies hurled by shamans against the Polynesian dynasts, there was one for Kamehameha that foretold, "He would conquer all the Islands; and rule over them but a brief time; that his own posterity would die out; and that finally all his race would be gathered together on Molokai; and that this small island would be large enough to hold them all" (Nordhoff 1987, 106). Although Johann Reinhold Forster saw several cases of what he thought was leprosy during his voyage (Forster 1982, 3:413–14), the disease was not officially identified until the 1840s, allegedly having been introduced into Hawai'i from China by two albino laborers "white as snow" (Nordhoff 1987, 103). But the *kaula* connected the epidemic to come with a political ambition deriving from Kamehameha's ownership of the Cook cult, by whose means he made museums and impoverished the people. The relation of material excess to human destitution was held forth as cause and effect, the collecting of things culminating in a museum of reduced Hawai'ians, where leprosy would transfer the sickness of singularity from artifacts to people. If this were a prophecy defending the ancient social form of things and people against Kamehameha's gluttonous incorporation and immobilization of the *hau* of gifts, then it would be merely synthetically nostalgic, setting sheer loss against an irrecoverable plenitude. But because it is a shamanic challenge, in which nostalgia is expected to be substantively engaged with the present and the future, disease must be supposed to have a more equivocal place in a vision that is millenarian, not simply apocalyptic. Like shamanism itself, which combines precontact practices with postcontact influences, leprosy comprises elements of the ancient and modern, and of regeneration as well as corruption.

From the time of de Quirós, the disease was associated with utopian dreams. Martin de Munilla recorded that the discovery of Aoba, an island in the New Hebrides group also called Leper's Island, ushered in the discovery of the New Jerusalem (Munilla 1966, 1:196). Bougainville's discovery of paradise on Tahiti preserved the same association between materialized fantasies and leprosy. In a strange abbreviated account of Bougainville's passage from Tahiti to Mauritius, Bernardin de St. Pierre, who met the navigator there, reports that several islands unknown to Europeans had been landed by his crew and that they were keeping it a great secret. These included "une isle des lepreux ou les hommes, les fruits et les arbres sont contrefaits et couverts d'une éspèce de lèpre" (Cook 1994, 851). The lepers' island sounds a little like the island of mimics and pantomimes in Gabriel François Coyer's mock-utopian supplement to George Anson's voyage, a world of strange, factitious, and skin-deep phenomena, glinting with false lights (Coyer 1752). Similar effects were caused by drinking a beverage containing the herb kava, which resulted in "a frightful scaly appearance" of the skin that, combined with the greenish hue of old tattooing, made the bodies of the drinkers resemble "dusty specimens of verd antique" (Melville 1964, 111). The lepers' island also anticipates the weird paradise Molokai was to become, where every face was filled with mirth and laughter, Charles Nordhoff reported, but the disfigurements caused by the disease made it seem as if they were all wearing masks, absorbed in an elaborate and gruesome performance (Nordhoff 1987, 103).

Like scurvy, leprosy was a mystery to those who treated it. It was known to be "feebly contagious" but otherwise no one could tell where the disease came from, how it was contracted, or how it might progress (Daws 1973, 131; Nordhoff 1987, 104; London n.d., 112). It was, therefore, wide open for interpretation. That it was the genocidal outcome of an outrageous desire for wealth and power was the theme of the *kaula*'s challenge to Kamehameha and also of Stevenson's "The Bottle Imp," where the hero's first temptation to have unlimited access to all the things he fancies coincides with the first signs of leprosy. It was a type of all the diseases, from venereal infection to influenza, which followed the routes of discovery and trade, and wasted the populations of all the islands. It stood as emblem of the terrible vulnerability of innocence to the corruption of the West. But by an unpleasant irony, corruption could be turned the other way around, and leprosy be regarded as a physical sign of "an abysmal depth of heathen degradation," as Charles E. Hyde fulsomely stated, "unutterable in its loathesomeness" (Daws 1973, 135). When Father Damien caught the disease while ministering to the lepers of Mokokai, Hyde could only assume that this betokened an inner rottenness that had bloomed into a beastly sexual familiarity between the pastor and his flock, now legible in Damien's skin (Edmond 1997, 196).

From the point of view of healthy Europeans, leprosy fells easily into the categories of noble and ignoble savagery, since it afflicted either those who did not deserve such a hideous fate, or those whose benighted condition maked them prone to infection, physical and moral. Quarantine is the triumph of the distinction between the sick and the well, the corrupt and the innocent (Edmond 1997, 202). There is a notable exception to this orderly division in Stevenson's strangely passionate rebuke to Hyde, *Father Damien: An Open Letter to the Reverend Hyde of Honolulu* (1890). It is a piece in which emotion is as much the theme as the vehicle of his indignation (Smith 1998, 223), and what excites it is an unnegotiable abyss between the comfort of colonial normality, "your pleasant parlour on Beretania St," and the shapeless mass of suffering on Molokai, "the stairs crowded with abominable deformations of our common manhood . . . every fourth face a blot upon the landscape . . . the butt-ends of human beings lying there almost unrecognisable, but still breathing, still thinking, still remembering" (Stevenson 1890, 15). Stevenson is overwhelmed by the contrast between the easiness of Hyde's false explanation and the accumulation of horror it pretends to summarize, for "in such a matter, every fresh case, like every inch of length in the pipe of an organ, deepens the note of the impression; for what daunts the onlooker, is that monstrous sum of human suffering" (17). He reacts to Molokai as a collection of unique miseries, similar in its way to Tembinoka's quarantined curiosities, with an emphasis on the *impression* to which each additional item contributes. When Attwater shows Herrick his collection of maritime wreckage in *The Ebb-Tide,* he asks him if he sees a parable in it. " 'I find at least a strong impression,' replied Herrick" (Stevenson 1894, 146).

Trying to imagine what Damien's impression might have been, Stevenson thinks of him "in that pigstye of his under the cliffs at Kalawao" as someone *hors de categorie,* not unlike the sacrificial *arioi* pig clad in the lineaments of sovereignty, "crowned with glories and horrors" (Stevenson

1890, 11). To arrive at such an impression is to shed all discriminations of degeneration in favor of a powerful mixed feeling very like nostalgia. James Boon calls it the junction of lyrical divinity and bestial triumph, a prismatic union of opposite sensations emerging from the chinks between established categories (Boon 1985, 27). Guy de Cars wrote a love story called *The Unclean* (1953) about Chantal, the beautiful leper banished to "Makogai" who was formerly a mannequin called Nostalgia. As Damien was situated between God and swine, so Stevenson was driven by equivocal impulses the to situate his passion between the Hyde of Beretania Street and some ghostly Jekyll, fascinated by his own rage while thrilling with a strong distaste, vindicating a life while laboring under horrible intimations of his own devastation—in short, experiencing nostalgia in its most extreme form.

For the Hawaiians themselves, Molokai broke up their relation to all certainties in a way that left them, like scurvied sailors, extraordinarily susceptible to sensation, their "savage passions . . . seized and inflamed by that mysterious and lingering disease" (Johnstone 1905, 82). The Board of Health reported in 1870 a complete breakdown of order, with "great irregularities" taking place between the male and female lepers, the supervisor in fear of his life, and the storehouse being looted at will. The board was forced to realize that it had created a state of nature, for it could not fine people who had no money; and without breaching quarantine, it could not imprison people who were already imprisoned (Board of Health 1870, 6–7). When Damien arrived on the island, he saw, amidst appalling squalor, desperation expressed as a cultic renaissance: "The Hawaiian 'hula' was organised after the pagan fashion, under the protection of the old deity Laka . . . the people had reached the climax of despair . . . [acting] as if they were totally mad" (Johnstone 1905, 324). The old deity is companion to Lono, his "sister wife" or his canoe builder (Sahlins 1985b, 116; Cook 1967, 1159n. 3). And hula dancing, along with traditional games and surfing, had played an important part in the political opposition to Kamehameha's dynasty (Kirch and Sahlins 1992, 1:73), bringing full circle the shamanic prophecy of Molokai as the residue of nonroyal Hawai'i bidding defiance to the dynasts. It establishes a continuity of politicized aesthetics that dates to the ornate dancing of the Hulumanu sect, and the extravagant displays of the *arioi* from which they derived (Ralston 1985, 316). Such a performance in masks is not just the pitiable resource of disfigured sentient beings looking for a little fun, but a triumphant nostalgia that resurrects the ancient privileges of the *kaula* and the golden future of autochthons, under the authority and protection of Lono.

This millennial side of leprosy was preserved by quarantine. The exclusion of lepers from the society of the other islands was absolute, for under the terms of the Act of 1865, they were accounted civilly dead. Their spouses were free to remarry, they no longer owned property, and they had no remedies in court (Board of Health 1870, 1; Nordhoff 1987, 100). Reduced to conditions similar to Jonathan Swift's Struldbrugs, their desperation might have been expected to deepen; but in being denied the social form of people (as Tembinoka and Kamehameha denied their possessions the social form of gifts), they were liberated into the enjoyment and the passions of nostalgic individuality. Molokai, consisting of sixteen thousand fertile acres beneath the vast cliff of Kalawao, was a natural paradise, and soon became a utopia. Nordhoff said the ocean there was "bluer and lovelier than ever I saw it . . . the soft trade-wind blowing . . . eternal sunshine; a mild air"; and after Damien's reforms, each of the eight hundred lepers was allowed clothing, a house, and a horse, together with generous rations of beef and salt salmon provided by the Board of Health (Nordhoff 1987, 102–3). What is more, "[t]hey [had] . . . a race-track, baseball grounds, shooting ranges, an athletic club, numerous glee clubs, and two brass bands" (London n.d., 106). All the good things promised by cargo cults came about on Molokai, even though it was prophesied (and at first experienced) as a curse. Those adjudged no longer sick, or misdiagnosed, often refused to leave the island, preferring its artificial amenities ("contrefaits et couverts d'une éspèce de lèpre"), where everything was under the mark of leprosy, to anything the mainland could offer. The leprous mark included not only the effect of a mask, but also of a blanching of the skin, dissolving blackness into whiteness in a manner expressive of millenarian consummations of historical time preached by the *kaula.*

The blurring of such radical differences as black and white, noble and ignoble, autochthon and god, evacuates criteria of difference and encourages nostalgia and infatuation. The collection of wonders that provides (according to Hodgen) the conceptual divisions of early ethnography is here reversed to produce first of all the bulging storehouses of Polynesian kings, and then the utopia of quarantined enthusiasts, where the fetish supplants the curiosity and black equates with white. That this was a hideous as well as a beautiful paradise serves to emphasize the ambiguity of all paradises in the South Seas, which are recognized with a certain thrilling of the mind as hospitals for sick persons, upon whose beaches the scurvied and the leprous alike made their landings burdened with profound feelings of loss, as well as intimations of voluptuous satisfaction.

part two

FROM JUAN FERNANDEZ
TO NEW ZEALAND

6

Void Contracts
and Subtle Islands

Oh! Cast me, Fortune, on the winning shore.
Now let me gain what I have lost before.
— Susannah Centlivre, *The Basset Table*

The first part of the argument presented in this book has maintained that voyagers to the South Seas operated in a contested and uncertain environment. In a long and dangerous conflict with the Spaniards for trade and plunder that required movements over immense distances with very few landfalls, the self became a doubtful point of reference in any effort to define the exotic or the marvelous, and reports of its experiences fell in a generic gray area between romance and true report. There was very little mariners could rely upon. They had no base, no longitude, no system of cognitive mapping, and no loyal home audience. The islands they made for were themselves mobile. The Portuguese in the Pacific called the coordinates of their dead reckoning the *punto de fantasia* (Munilla 1966, 1:51).

These difficulties were compounded by another, which affected each in different ways: namely the two-sided law of self-preservation. Their unstable circumstances forced sailors to invoke the law of self-preservation as both the bond and solvent of the social microcosm of a ship, depending on whether it was operating as a principle of obedience or a mutinous propensity. Apart from external emergencies that placed the necessity of self-defense above the code of behavior, such as attacks by natives ("I was not to stand still and suffer either my self or those that were with me to be knocked on the head" [Cook 1955, 171]) and shipwreck ("They fell into the most violent Outrage and Disorder" [Bulkeley 1745, 34]), there was plenty of room for a self to define its interests as no longer consistent with the contract of the voyage. From Pedro Fernandez de Quirós to William Dampier, and from Woodes Rogers to Captain William Bligh, there are many examples of mutiny. Woodes Rogers's men mutinied for "storm money" to cover extra fighting, "which they alledg'd was a risque more than they were ship'd for" (Rogers 1712, 154). Once a voyage was viewed as a potentially fatal gamble, the reaction of sailors was identical with what Bernard Mandeville had also observed among condemned felons in New-gate, namely a heightened aversion "to the Dissolution of their Being" (Mandeville 1725, 30). This could result in usurpation and piracy, or in a milder modification of the terms of service; but in any event, efforts to preserve the self involved a transition from one form of social organization to another via an interlude of anarchy.

The first English navigators of the Pacific sailed under sets of articles that outlined the mutual obligations of the shipowners and the crew in considerable detail; and even when repudiated, they provided the model for a new set drawn up by the usurpers of the previous command, and were in turn vulnerable to mutinous abrogation. In the person of Captain John Gow, Daniel Defoe confides, "I once knew a buccaneering pirate vessel, whose crew were upwards of seventy men, who, in one voyage, had so often changed, set up, and pulled down their captains and other officers, that about seven-and-forty of the ship's company had, at several times, been in offices of one kind of another; and among the rest they had, in particular, had thirteen captains" (Defoe 1935, 279–80).

The maritime see-saw between the principle and the propensity of self-preservation dramatized a paradox at the heart of all contractarian theories of society, succinctly stated by John Trenchard as follows: "Government first arose from every Man's taking Care of himself; and Government is never abused and perverted, but from the same reason" (Trenchard 1722, 54). These sailors were testing at its limit (in every sense) the consequence of a shift in the nature of corporate allegiance. Ships' articles and charter parties were miniatures of the original contract and subject to the same strains of adjustment between the need for authority and the claims of self-interest. In the privateering and buccaneering enterprises proliferating in the Caribbean between the period of the Commonwealth and the Glorious Revolution, the common good was easily monitored by the amount of loot in hand, and the system of ship's government was forced to be responsive to the anxieties of the majority. An uncanny parallel was developing between nefarious and postrevolutionary theories of contract, as each was modified to accommodate the good of the greatest number as the guiding principle of social organization, a fact of which some buccaneers seemed to be perfectly conscious (Defoe 1972, 383–418, Hill 1986, 3:164: Pocock 1975, 423; Pagden 1995b, 157; Cascardi 1992, 208).

In the South Seas, treaties, constitutions, laws, contracts, and even papal decrees were regarded variously as the means, screens, and impediments to making a profit: "For tis morally certain, that as Interest induced ye Spaniards to Trade in English Manufactures from Cadiz, & to pay for them in Gold & Silver contrary to the Laws of Spain, & as Interest brought ye W. Indians to Trade with our selves from Jamaica, notwithstanding all ye Laws & Prohibitions of ye Indies, & as Interest has induc'd yet Merchts of Peru & Chili to Trade wth ye French, contrary to ye Antient Constitution of those Kingdoms, so may we not rest assured that ye same powerful motives of Interest & advantage will induce ye Spaniards to Trade wth us" (*An Essay* 1707–40, 17). One of the earliest narratives of the Jamaican privateers in the Pacific begins, "Wee resolve now to cruise these Seas for wealth" (Jameson 1923, 101). Any scheme dedicated to taking advantage of the prevailing influence of interest was vulnerable to the same weakness of laws and contracts that it was exploiting. Any contract drawn up under these conditions was attempting to remove the difficulties that make contracts necessary, a sort of self-abolishing efficiency that John Locke outlined in his theory of property, where the alienability of property under the system of exchange is compensated by the contractual assurance of the right to part with it. It is so much yours that it can become someone else's.

Thus privateers who were seizing ships and raiding settlements, distinguishable from pirates solely by virtue of their letters of marque and reprisal (Starkey 1990, 20), were extremely fussy about the procedures and percentages that would constitute a fair division of the plunder. Nor were they shy of invoking the public good as their standard. William Betagh accounted for the difference between George Shelvocke's crew and John Clipperton's in this way: "[Shelvocke's] was a private interest, and [Clipperton's] a public one" (Betagh 1728, 190). But it will shortly become clear that the technical detail of privateering contracts was necessary because honor, loyalty, and charity had no place in the business of self-preservation, as Mandeville called it, and that is why they afforded no insurance in the end against their failure to serve the interests of all its parties adequately. In the most extreme instances of this failure, the self was driven back upon its own resources, with some surprising results.

I have indicated in chapter 2 that the labile circumstances of a privateering cruise transformed a contract from a legal instrument into a formal wager, similar to the system of indemnities of the Jamaica discipline

(Rediker 1987, 264–65), bearing the amphibian mark of the institutions it supported, where welfare and violence, property and theft, forethought and impulsiveness were adjacent and sometimes mutually inclusive concerns. The agreement following each mutiny was one in a series of deals struck to order the relationship between chance and desire on terms agreed by all parties as giving the strongest likelihood of satisfaction. But these agreements lasted no longer than the mood of interesting suspense they aroused, and were revoked as soon as boredom, fear, or (in many cases) success made them redundant. It was Thomas Hobbes's original contract without sovereign power to enforce it, and cohered only as an unstable aggregate of single bets. Indeed, gambling pure and simple was endemic among buccaneers and privateers, indicating that all contracts from their point of view, from the ship's articles down to a casual flutter, were considered as aleatory and short term. Given the highly speculative nature of such voyages, where it was impossible to calculate risk reasonably, and where outcomes could be assigned no degree of probability, it is perhaps no surprise that this should be the case; but it threw all contracting parties into a situation in which the practice of risk excluded the theory of risk—where in effect a blind gamble would answer one's desires with everything or nothing, simply because there was no probable medium between the extremes. In the early eighteenth century, as Gerd Gigerenzer points out, "parties to aleatory contracts like gambling, annuities and maritime insurance had agreed upon the price of a future contingency on the basis of intuitions that ran directly counter to those of the probabilists" (Gigerenzer et al. 1989, 25). That is to say, actuaries didn't alter the mortality curve to include factors such as mishap, disease, or age in calculating the length of a life; nor did marine insurers disturb the general ratio of success and failure to take into account weather and enemy action in predicting the security of a bottom; and until the advent of the Parisian gambler Dangeau, it was uncommon to study the fall of the cards in betting on who was holding a winning hand (Kavanagh 1993, 63–64).

Before the emergence of probability as a model for the representation of exemplary experience—as it was to be in the novel—the party to a contract was individualized, "not subject to a common sum" (Kavanagh 1993, 63; Hacking 1975, 73). The social contract, by analogy, had to be figured as a congeries of selves committed to their own interests; "for social life to be possible, individuals must represent themselves as persons" (Caygill 1989, 27). Although honor, or some other prior social motive for gaining the approval of one's peers, might affect the composure or conduct of someone entering an aleatory contract, desire alone—ultimately the desire for self-preservation—influenced the placing of the bet. But as the outcome was governed by chance, the gambler embarked on a curious adventure with nothing, for in his article on providence for the *Encyclopedie,* Voltaire defines it thus: "Chance is nothing. It is a fiction, a chimera bereft of possibility and existence" (Kavanagh 1993, 163). In this respect, chance was like credit, "this emblem of a something, though in itself nothing" (Defoe 1951, 118 [*Review* 6:31, June 1709]). A privateering cruise was a version of Blaise Pascal's wager, poised between everything (the treasure galleon) and nothing (its failure to appear) (Hacking 1975, 67).

The lack of affinity between the private and public sides of the original contract was magnified by the improbable basis on which many contracts were actually made. This had numerous unsettling after-effects, of which the failure to demonstrate a necessary sociable result from an interested bargain was perhaps the most fundamental and long lasting. This is what Howard Caygill calls the je ne sais quoi in the theory of civil society (Caygill 1989, 37), and what A. O. Hirschman has presented as a web of interests so intricate that it cannot be made to disclose an ultimate principle of connection (Hirschman 1986, 42, 108). The likelihood that in such a state of affairs good might, as Mandeville put it, spring up and pullulate from evil, or vice versa, was simply to render in the starkest way the formal incoherence of any system of contracts based on the law of self-preservation. By the end of the century, this had been reduced by Thomas Malthus to an ineluctable contradiction, demographically verifiable, between the individual impulse to extend one's being, and the disastrous social consequences of acting upon it; for when a state of plenty urges happy parents to reproduce, then "the mighty law of self-preservation," triggered by the immediate prospect of insufficient food for all new mouths, renews its most savage aspect, "and lords it triumphant over the world" (Malthus 1970, 138).

Out of the same puzzling imbrication of the sociable and savage tendencies of the law of self-preservation emerges the antinomy of all interested behavior—"The best Things that Men do, as well as the worst, are selfish" (Trenchard 1725, 2:77)—a truth of which commerce is exemplary. For on the one hand, it is proposed as an aggressive and destructive activity whose adjunct is war (Pocock 1975, 425); and on the other, it is saluted as an irenic, civilizing agency, softening and polishing the manners of all who are touched by it (Hirschman 1986, 107). The individual operating in such a regime could make contracts and bets, and "could identify and pursue the goals proposed to him by his passions and fantasies," as J. G. A. Pocock phrases it, "but he could not explain himself by locating himself

as a real and rational being within it" (Pocock 1975, 466). The ethical confusion is complete when Trenchard stopped in the midst of denunciation
of England's enemies to concede that "sometimes the great Difference
between an honest Man and a Knave, is no other than . . . a Piece of
Chance" (Trenchard 1725, 2:53). Individuals may think they have come to
rational conclusions and acted honestly on the direction they give; but as
they cannot account either for the provenance of the thought or the ultimate tendency of the deed, they might as well be gambling. It is simply "a
Turn of the Mind," as Trenchard said, intended to gratify a "personal
Glory" and a "private Pleasure." Under these circumstances, encountered
most frequently and experienced most intensely on ships in the Pacific
Ocean, the most solid prospects evaporate into nothing and the most
heartfelt professions are indistinguishable from pretenses.

It is a symptom of this indigestible paradox that so many privateers and
pirates sailed under articles forbidding gambling. De Quirós had none on
his ship (Munilla 1966, 1:141), nor did Captain Roberts (Defoe 1972b, 211).
In *Captain Singleton,* the rule of the company is as follows: "If any one of
us, by any Play, Bett, Game or Wager, win any Money or Gold, or the
Value of any from another—he should be oblig'd by us all to restore it
again on the Penalty of being . . . turn'd out of the Company" (Defoe 1963,
115). Like Locke's theory of property, these are contracts that deny what
contracts have accomplished, namely the alienation of what is one's own.
There are two cases of contracts contractually denied that illustrate very
neatly the parallels between the aleatory conditions of privateering and
the fantastic objectives of commercial speculation, already partly examined in chapter 2.

Woodes Rogers sailed with a set of instructions that concluded with
the pious exhortation to use "the most probable method & means not only
to prevent all Animosities, Quarrells & Mischiefs att Sea; but to preserve
a most agreeable Concord & Harmony during the whole Course of the
Voyage on wch mightily depends our good Success" (PRO C104/36 pt. 2,
p. 12). To strengthen the probable means of sociability, the owners supplied his two ships, the *Duke* and *Dutchess,* with a constitution that nom-
inated a ship's council, to which all unresolved matters were to be referred:
"We farther Require & Direct, that all Attempts and Attacks & Designes
upon the Enemy either by Sea or Land, be first consulted & Debated. . . .
And as ye Majority thereof shall Conclude, how or when to act or do, Itt
shall be indispensably & without unnecessary Delay putt chearfully in
Execution" (8). This was a social contract enjoining self-government on
democratic principles: "According to that Determination of ye Major-

ity . . . you are to proceed & govern your selves" (11). It was a recipe for disaster. Carleton Vanbrugh, the owners' agent; Stephen Courtney, captain of the *Dutchess;* and Thomas Dover, a senior officer, used the council to commence a series of machinations against Rogers that at first irked and eventually seriously embarrassed him. Dover put it bluntly, declaring Rogers "a person of different Intrest to ours" (PRO C104/60; cited in Williams 1997, 155). As these disagreements were aired in public as well as before the council, factions were formed among the crew, resulting in mutinous refusals of orders. The mood of the gun room can be gauged from an informant's deposition:

> Newman cam into ye Gun Rom & caryd good newes . . . ye Captains has all fell out and Just parted and . . . Capt Roggars went forward upon ye Duchesses Fourcastell and told thare men that they was all fell out and hee was goin to leave them—hee told them his ship was his owne and if they would goe with him he did not doubt butt to make them brave fellows . . . the Gunnar and his Crewe say that they are shure they will goe with Capt Roggars for they are as true as flooks [flukes] . . . they Swore God dam them thare should bee noe more Committey, nor Councell nor preseden [president] nor agettents [adjutants] for God dam them they had noe accasion for them. Capt Roggars was Comador and hee that had ye Longest sword should carray it and his woard should bee ye Law. (PRO C104/161 pt. 1 [2])

Despite the loyalty of these professions, they were a symptom of everything Rogers considered wrong with Jamaica discipline, from which he understood the constitution to be derived. It led to a state of affairs where chance ruled, and the crew abandoned themselves to excess. He summed up the manners of the buccaneers by way of adverting to the conditions prevailing on his own ship: "They liv'd without Government; so that when they met with Purchase, they immediately squandered it away, and when they got Mony and Liquor, they drank and gam'd till they spent it all; and during those Revels there was no distinction between the Captain and Crew; for the Officers having no Commission but what the Majority gave them, they were chang'd at every Caprice" (Rogers 1712, xvii).

On the *Duke* and *Dutchess,* mutinies ran parallel with a craze for gambling. Carleton Vanbrugh won five guineas from Robert Fry, chief mate of the *Duke,* betting that there were more than two thousand parishes in England and Wales (PRO C104/160; quoted in Williams 1997, 151). Things got so bad that the ship's council placed a ban on gambling with IOUs to control the risks arising from the temper of men who had lost their prize money in advance and were desperate to repair their fortunes at any cost. It prohibited "all sorts of Notes of Hand, Contracts, Bills, or Obligations of any kind whatsoever, that shall any ways pass . . . provided the Sum in Each Note be for Gaming, Wagering, or Abetting" (Rogers 1712, 283). To end gambling by voiding contracts was, of course, to disable the very contractual maneuver by which this reformation was to be achieved, already far too weak to have much effect.

The South Sea Bubble reproduced many of the wonders of the South Sea, such as shipwrecks, castaways, and cannibals,[1] along with the obsession with gambling. Trenchard called the infatuation "our publick Gaming" (Trenchard 1725, 1:18), and Bolingbroke said investors were "in reality a sort of Wild Gamesters" (Bolingbroke 1727, 2:20). Archibald Hutcheson agreed that in the absence of calculable profits from trade, speculators were proceeding "purely on the Foot of Gaming . . . carrying Gaming to so extravagant a Heighth" that their contracts fell, in his opinion, "within the Equity of the Gaming Act" (Hutcheson 1721, 80, 90, 139). The only remedy Hutcheson could suggest was the same proposed by the ship's council aboard the *Duke,* and that was to break "in upon the Laws of Property [by] avoiding Contracts and Agreements which have been actually executed" (139). Once again, the only way to deal with the anarchic play of desire within the realm of chance defined by free enterprise was to reaffirm the conditions of anarchy by disavowing the only legitimate channel between self-interest and social obligation, namely the "original" contract. Hutcheson outlined a futile secondary contract designed to restore a degree of credit to transactions that had already deserted every standard of probability.

It is from within this paradox, where the pursuit of self-preservation is unsusceptible to explanation or contractual limitation, that Rogers and Trenchard made naked pleas for self-preservation. Rogers had lost his brother and suffered two serious wounds in the course of winning his owners a handsome profit with the seizure of the treasure ship *Nuestra Senora de la Incarnacion;* yet he was held on board his ship, first in the Netherlands and then on the Thames, while lengthy inquiries were made into his conduct. In his frustration, he wrote to the owners, "for Christs Sake dont lett me be torn to peices at home after I have been so rackt

1 A ruined speculator called Thomas Hudson distractedly patrolled the city of London looking like a castaway, "wrapped in a rug, and leaning on a crutch, and without either shoes or stockings" (Anderson 1825, 18). Defoe called stockjobbers "man-eating Discounters . . . Cannibals who prey upon the Necessitous and Indigent People" (Defoe 1712, 19). Trenchard called them "Crocodiles and Canibals, who feed, for Hunger, on human Bodies" (Trenchard 1725, 1:11).

abroad" (PRO C104/60; quoted in Williams 1997, 157). He spoke as someone bereft of a place in a social system, incapable of finding any logic in his treatment. In his anger at the damage done to Britain by the directors of the South Sea Company, Trenchard invoked "the great Principle of Self-Preservation" to justify public revenge against them, arguing that unprecedented evil should receive no benefit from existing laws (Trenchard 1725, 1.75). Although he tried to found this claim on the authority of the majority ("the Publick are the best Judges, whether Things go ill or well with the Publick" [1:87]), he knew as well as Rogers that once a rule is proposed at the expense of rules, or a contract deployed against a contract, there is no longer a platform from which to mount a principled appeal, for every maxim of bad conduct proved by your enemies recoils upon you: "We are governed by our Interest, and rail at them that are" (3:262).

The insuperable barrier to a candid declaration of the truth, of which Trenchard's most poignant instance is the impossibility of credibly stating patriotic disinterest, is the ethical side of the failure to find a justifying providence of civil society. By having to rely instead on an imputed relation between interested actions and the public good, rather than a clear demonstration of how one leads to the other, the most chaste mind is drawn to gambling and to the other great evil of South Seas speculation, pretense. Just as gambling sports with the incalculable distance between the moment of desire and the fantasy of satisfaction by supposing chance might unite them, so pretense bridges the same gap by claiming or inventing a spuriously transparent and intelligible link between intentions and deeds. So pervasive is the wish to declare as true and necessary a connection between ideas conjoined merely by custom, interest, or accident, the word *pretence* is forced to straddle both extremes of such declarations: the protestation of the case and the perpetration of an untruth, as in Trenchard's allusion to "the Pretences of the South-Sea Company for getting the Two Millions remitted to them, which Pretences they are pleased to call Reasons" (Trenchard 1725, 3:223), or in Defoe's narrative of the piracies of Bartholomew Roberts: "In this Company there was but one that pretended to any Skill in Navigation . . . and he proved a Pretender only" (Defoe 1972, 208).

All discussions of the South Seas travel in the same circle of pretense, from assertion to imposture. The papal authority cited by the Spanish as their right for being there was an "antient Pretence" challenged by Sir John Narborough's claims on behalf of the Crown to Patagonia, justified "as far as those Pretences may be grounded upon Possession" (Defoe 1726, 293). The fiction of a Great Southern Continent was a "bold pretension"

(Cook and King 1784, 1:xiii). The setting up of the South Sea Company to pay off the national debt was "only colourable Pretence" (Trenchard 1725, 1:46); while the "Pretensions of trading in the South seas" (Bolingbroke 1727, 2:285) were believed to be "an Amusement of Trade," with "other Aims couch'd under this Pretence" (Defoe 1712, 10, 36). This arrangement of "specious Pretences" (Toland 1726, 425) was later assumed to be a plot of the Pretender himself (Bolingbroke 1727, 2:270). Meanwhile, "When Men seek Credit . . . in order to betray, and make use of their Grimace as a Trap to deceive; when they turn their Admirers into Followers, and their Followers into Money, then appearing Wisdom becomes real Villainy, and these Pretenders grow dangerous Impostors" (Trenchard 1725, 2:92).

Finally, since there is no means of telling the difference, "Impostors, Cheats and ignorant Pretenders" rail against impostors, cheats, and ignorant pretenders (Bolingbroke 1727, 1:22). And who better than Bolingbroke to make the claim, since his assault on the craft and imposture of the directors artfully omitted his having been assigned a substantial share of the profits of the Asiento ship by Queen Anne, an entitlement that became what he called "a losing Contract" (2:287) only with his defection to the Pretender's court at St. Germain in 1715 (Anderson 1801, 3:55)! Everything is pretense. Our most serious engagements, as Trenchard bitterly emphasized, are with nonentities, and "our highest Enjoyment is of that which is not" (Trenchard 1725, 2:51). These critics of the South Sea Company experience the joint efflorescence of commercialism and imposture, foretold by Hobbes when he summarized the cause of the Civil War as combined effects of the pretenses of divines, political economists, merchants, and civic humanists, who made "God stand idle, and to be a mere spectator of the games of fortune." Such pretenses were immune to embarrassment, for "hypocrisy hath this great prerogative above other sins, that it cannot be accused" (Hobbes 1963, 4–24, 62). His solution was to frame a contract that could not be spoiled by other contracts. The obsession with evidentiary techniques in the earlier part of the century was likewise a reaction to this culture of pretense, a fear of being deceived and a "deep-seated anxiety about imposture" (Daston 1995, 268).

In the "real" South Seas, the larger of the two islands of Juan Fernandez provided the focus not only of an imagined staging post for British expeditions, but also of a site for mutinies and utopian gambles, where void contracts and pretenses combine to expand the minds of individuals, and fill them with dreams of power and plenty (fig. 6). It was notorious among buccaneers as the place where bets were called off. It was there that

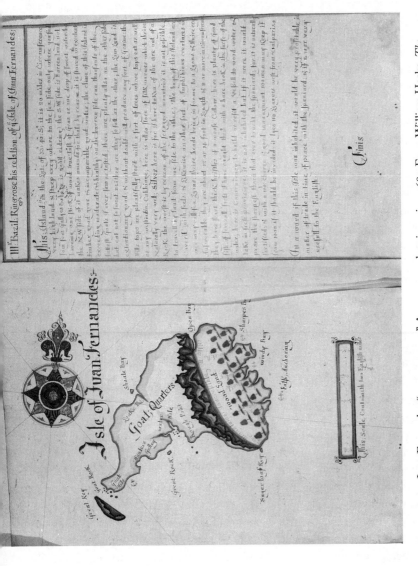

FIGURE 6 Juan Fernandez "goat quarters." Anonymous drawing, circa 1681. From William Hacke, *The Great South Seas Waggoner*, copied and privately circulated by Hacke circa 1683–87. © National Maritime Museum, London.

Bartholomew Sharp was voted out of his command in 1681 in the same mutiny that exposed Edmund Cooke to an accusation of sodomy from his cabin boy. Thomas Stradling briefly lost control of his crew there in 1704; and it was in the same place a few months later that Alexander Selkirk, master of the *Cinque Ports,* refused Stradling's orders and was marooned. In the same vicinity, Dampier was deserted in 1704 by the majority of his crew, and his privateering commission was taken from him by John Clipperton. George Shelvocke was abandoned by his men after his ship was wrecked there in 1720. The island was also renowned as the place where Selkirk commenced a four-year, solitary sojourn that ended when he was picked up in 1709 by Woodes Rogers, who said, perhaps mindful of the fraught conditions aboard the *Duke,* "By this one may see that Solitude and Retirement from the World is not such an unsufferable State of Life as most Men imagine" (Rogers 1712, 130).

Selkirk's story belongs with other tales of mariners stranded there. "Our Pilott saith," recorded Basil Ringrose at Juan Fernandez, "that many yeares agoe a shipp was cast away on this Iseland and onely one man saved who lived alone there 5 years before any shipp came this way" (Ringrose [1680], 77). This anonymous first guest of the island originated a myth, widely circulated among sailors before it became popular with the gambling public and French philosophes, of the single castaway who loses the trappings of civilization and, clothed in skins, finds happiness amidst natural abundance. In 1681, a Mosquito Indian called William was left behind by Captain John Watling, Sharp's successor, and rescued three years later by Dampier and William Cowley. Cowley, perhaps reminded of the noble hunter-gatherers on Tortuga and Santo Domingo, recollected that William had survived very nicely with "nothing but Goates Skins to cover himselfe when wee came there" (Cowley 1683, fol. 6v). An amphibian figure caught between the civilized and primitive worlds, William commanded the same admiration from his spectators as the buccaneers commanded from Guillaume Raynal, Selkirk from Rogers, and Gulliver from the Portuguese sailors who find him clothed in skins. A moment widely celebrated for its poignancy was William's reunion with his cousin Robin. Said Dampier of this widely cited scene, "We stood with pleasure to behold "the surprize, and tenderness, and solemnity of this Interview, which was exceedingly affectionate on both sides" (Dampier 1729, 1:81; fig. 7). When Adam Ferguson contemplated this scene, he clearly regarded William's recurrence to a commodityless existence as a happy restoration of those qualities Raynal located in the primitive simplicity and loving partnerships of the buccaneer hunters. "If we would know what is the religion

Within the engraving:
C. Afecting interview of two MOSKITO-MEN, *one of whom had been left* Three Years *on the Island of Juan Fernandez, by Capt. Dampier.*

FIGURE 7 "Affecting interview of two Moskito-Men, one of whom had been left three years on the Island of Juan Fernandez by Capt. Dampier." Anonymous engraving, circa 1750.

of the wild American," he observed, after quoting Dampier's description, "it is the ardent affection with which he selects and embraces his friend" (Ferguson 1767, 26). When Defoe reworks Selkirk's story in *Robinson Crusoe* (1719), he puts this myth of natural reconstitution through its paces in order to determine the stages necessary to be passed before a solitary individual can be said to have left, or to have rejoined, society. In either case, the regeneration of the single self is envisioned and (I shall suggest) experienced as an encounter with its double: William and Robin, Crusoe and Friday, Selkirk and the huge goat he grapples with and kills.

Juan Fernandez is a sort of laboratory that leaves the experimental challenge of self-preservation quite uncluttered. A single castaway can purge the corruptions of social life without having to remodel society or rely on anyone else. The scenario of Jean-Jacques Rousseau's *Second Discourse*, already derided by Shaftesbury as "this pretended state of nature" (Shaftesbury 1964, 2:80), is transposed from fantasy to an eyewitness narrative, something "I know to be true," as Rogers said of Selkirk's story (Rogers 1712, 130). The publicity Selkirk's sojourn was given subsequently confirmed that his life on the island, after an initial period of melancholy, had produced a physical and spiritual renovation that was (according to Sir Richard Steele) as unique as it was delicious, "his Life one continual Feast, and his Being much more joyful than it had before been irksome" (Steele 1955, 106). Apart from the early "eager Longings for seeing again the Face of Man" (Steele 1955, 107), Selkirk seems to have graduated from a painful state of privation to a life of unself-conscious and uncomplicated ease. However, there are some features of the tale that are worth attending to because they suggest that this isthmus between a social and a savage existence redefines the self in a more complex and more truly utopian role vis-à-vis its own pleasures.

Selkirk was put ashore at his own request because he did not believe the *Cinque Ports* was seaworthy. He gambled that marooning was a better fate than drowning, and he turned out to be right, since Stradling and the ship were lost soon afterwards. But he was not to know that, and at the last moment he repented of his bet and pleaded to be taken aboard again. It seems likely that the sense of sheer loss that overwhelmed him as the *Cinque Ports* put to sea introduced him to an intensity that was to characterize all his moods on the island. Selkirk watched everything he called life ("his Comrades and all Human Society at once" [Steele 1955, 107]) sink below the horizon, and he sat down before a prospect of emptiness that was to be transformed gradually and unaccountably into the experience of limitless joy. Why he should be there and why this should happen were questions he could not hope to answer. Thus he was forced to experience a state of mind Lorraine Daston ascribes to people such as gamblers, operating outside the sphere of probability, bereft not only of the means of calculation and calculability, "but of all that made these possible: the indissoluble bonds between cause and effect, between interest and action, between past and future" (Daston 1988, 163).

To leap from everything to nothing and back again is, of course, the fate of all gamblers, particularly those—like Raynal's buccaneers, Rogers's crew, and Pascal's wagerer—who are ready to stake everything, their freedom or their lives, on the bet. When the terms of the wager include a spell on a desert island, however, the moment of suspense is drawn out, the nerves are taut, and all impressions strike the mind as wonderfully distinct or terribly singular; and the question has to be proposed whether this is a nonsocial condition, a state of nature; a social pause in which social principles are refurbished; or something else altogether. Crusoe insists that life on the island was "a whole Collection of Wonders," "a Chain of Wonders" (Defoe 1983, 258, 273). Although this highly charged reaction to his self-preservation may indicate a return to the primitive sensitivity of the "meer State of Nature," as Crusoe claims (118), it may equally bespeak the purgation of the social self, a refitting and careening of its fundamental values prior to its return to civic duty. But should these vivid experiences amount to a pretended link between two allegedly significant phases of the self's history—its degeneration from a social norm or its recovery of a genuine social impulse via nature—how can its energy be explained or its pleasures be characterized? The analogy between the ignorance of life on a desert island and the condition of people in civil society who cannot explain their position in the chain of causes, suggests that they enjoy severally those private pleasures resulting from the "turn of the mind" Trenchard mentioned. They try to justify their pretenses to a higher destiny, and disguise their ignorance as an intimacy with the machinery of Providence; but that leaves them pretenders only. On an island, however, there is nothing to contradict pretense except the evidence of the senses, and if they report nothing but delight, then the self can expand amidst its own fantasy: "Life grew so exquisitely pleasant, that he never had a Moment heavy upon his Hands" (Steele 1955, 109). Rogers seems to point to consciousness of pleasurable self-enlargement when he remarked that the degradation of Selkirk's language, his speaking his words by halves, had by no means diminished his sense of personal identity, for he "diverted himself sometimes by cutting his Name on the Trees" (Rogers 1712, 128).

These are details carefully laid up by Defoe for a purpose I wish to approach somewhat obliquely through some other stories of stranding. The first took place on one of the Galapagos Islands; the second is a report of the circumstances of a corpse found on Ascension Island; and the third has a claim to be to be the first utopian experiment on Juan Fernandez. Each involves a specifically maritime form of repentance—one sufficiently peculiar to suggest that it was a distinct branch of spiritual autobiography—that can be mistaken (as it is by Steele, for example) for the spontaneous temper of a soul in a state of nature. In fact, the marooned self is reduced to a nonsociable condition that is nevertheless not yet natural, leaving it capable of reflecting upon itself, and even projecting itself in a spectral way. Here is the buccaneer William Cowley writing of being beached on a desert coast and tormented by thirst:

> Wee having killed a large Turtle which could not weigh lesse than between three and four hundred pounds weight, the rest of our men being gone some way from us to see for water, or see for a shipp . . . I being alone dressing of the Turtle and having made a great fire to Roast him neare the sea side, and having within my selfe some serious thoughts thinking with my selfe that I had not long to live without water, and seeing that great fire I had made, and thinking, if I were burning within that fire how terrible it would be, and thinking of my loose life I had lived how dreadfull the fire of Hell would be should I att last goe thither, which would be aggravated with the fearefull sight of those deformed ffiends that were there. Whilst I had those melancholy thoughts in mind, I espyed a great hollow plaice in the Earth within one yard of the fire or against where I stood, there ranne out of the mouth of this Cave a large Sea Dogg, or Boare as he may be termed, much like a Boare Roaring against me, I was for the present surprized with the sudden sight and noyse of him, I having a long pole in my hand, I began to lay on with violence upon the supposed Devill which made him run away as fast as he could and I after him until I had chased him into the sea. (Cowley, 1683, fols. 12r–12v)

Cowley senses the connection between thirst, the fire, and eternal punishment, and by embodying the threat of death and damnation in the sea lion, he performs, as it were, the allegory of his self-preservation by thinking within himself how to act on behalf of himself.

The second is a lurid story of a Dutchman, subjected to the water torture then marooned by his shipmates in 1725 as punishment for homosexual acts. His journal was allegedly found next to his skeleton, giving an account of his slow death from starvation and thirst. "It may perhaps by some be deemed fabulous," says the editor, "on account of the frequent Apparitions mentioned" (*The Just Vengeance* [1730], ii), but his claim for its authenticity seems justifiable to the extent that the story originates in a real Dutch voyage (Davis 1999, 81–90). These apparitions are chiefly auditory hallucinations, or rather the victim's externalizing his own condition as demon, like Cowley's devil-boar that roars against him. He writes that "[a]n uncommon Noise surrounded me, of bitter Cursing and Swearing, mix'd with the most blasphemous and libidinous Expressions I ever heard. . . . I heard a Voice, saying, *Bouger, Bouger:* I cannot afford Paper sufficient to set down every Particular of this unhappy Day" (*The Just Vengeance* [1730], 9–10). Eventually, the voice acquires a form, first of his lover at Batavia and finally of "a ghastly Skeleton," itself indistinguishable from the "moving Skeleton" to which starvation has reduced him (11, 14, 20).

The third narrative is given by Richard Simson, surgeon aboard the *Welfare,* which, in 1690, picked up some men from Juan Fernandez who had been left there at their own request three years before by Captain Edward Davis. In a state of self-disgust consequent upon losing all their money at gambling, they had asked to be put ashore (Woodward 1969, 30). Each had been supplied with equipment and a black servant, and it seems that they set about to build a utopia not unlike the model adopted one hundred years later by the *Bounty* mutineers on Pitcairn. They carved up the island into equal districts that each man was to inhabit separately, with no company but his servant. After a period of melancholy, they decided on a reformation, and "being sencible that their swearing and blaspheming which they still kept up, was provoking to Almighty God . . . they made an agreement in order to begin & perfect a thorough reformation and particulerly of that crime, to live severally and part every Man in a several Cave for some Months, or till they should deposite so bad a habite, which purpose and resolution of theirs being put in practice, had the desired Effect, so far that after that time, they could converse with one another, with all the moderation and gravity imaginable" (Simson 1689, fol. 42r). It appears that this program of moral renewal was hindered by a plot hatched by their servants to cut their throats in revenge for some severe beatings. On being discovered, the plotters ran to the hills, where they were deceived with promises of fair treatment and returned to their masters only to be tortured with the strappado. "They were then tyed a part and disciplin'd with fasting till some sattisfactory degree of reformation was read in their ffaces" (fol. 57v). Thus the enterprise of reformation is transferred to from the individual to his double, in whose countenance the image of his own repentant heart can be discerned—or something like it.

There is a pattern linking these three stories to Selkirk's. Each experience is governed by a strong sense of self—a self accusing itself or reforming itself or, as Cowley said, capable of "having within my selfe some serious thoughts thinking with my selfe." The result of an oppressive degree of isolation and horror, these self-reflections coincide with disturbing sounds and a confrontation with another creature or figure which in some way incarnates the threat of torment and annihilation, as well as functioning as a shadow of the self. Selkirk mentioned the "Monsters of the Deep . . . the[ir] dreadful Howlings and Voices [which] seemed too terrible to be made for human Ears" (Steele 1955, 108), but his fear diminished as he learned how to kill the sea lions, and how to catch goats on the hoof, although he was nearly killed when he wrestled a large billy goat over a precipice. Cowley was terrified by the sea lion and "the sudden noyse of him," but retained the presence of mind to confront him and beat him off. The Dutchman was tormented by the various personifications of his desire and remorse, advancing from the hideous volubility of the one to the silence of the other. Simson's privateers beheld their own guilt and reformation in their revolted slaves.

It is clear from the Dutchman's journal that a failure to match and conquer the spectral threat will be fatal. But success confirms the self in a position that is both pleasant and powerful. Of Selkirk, who attached his name to trees in sheer wantonness of heart, Steele said that his repose after hunting was "equal to the most sensual Pleasures" (Steele 1955, 108); and Rogers, after calling him governor of the island, added, "we might as well have named him the Absolute Monarch" (Rogers 1712, 131). Simson said of the utopian torturers, "They subtilly pretended that they lived as Kings in the Islands having no Law, or Superior to Controule them, that they wanted for Nothing . . . they made show as if they had been of all the Men in the world, the most Content with their Condition" (Simson 1689, fol. 39v). Although there is a show of social life in these arrangements, where the sinning self contracts to mend its ways and its tongue, and enters into agreements with others, or with itself, to accomplish this, it is only a pretense—a pretended contract guaranteeing a pretended sociability. Selkirk's dancing with his animals is a pleasant mockery of family life, just as the privateers' division of the island is an unpleasant mockery of kingship. The pretense has no other purpose than to define the interests of the self and to heighten its pleasures, chiefly by reflecting its weaknesses as strengths.

It is consistent with this solipsism that language should undergo a sea change, being multiplied, halved, or pared until it is absorbed into the murmur of the island, its communicative function at an end and its instrumental function advancing. Like the pretense of social forms, words in such a place have no other task than to embody the desires and sensations of the self, standing in the same relation to their potency that Ariel's songs and masques stand to Prospero's will once his spells have made the island his own. Such a change dramatizes the difference pointed out by Humpty Dumpty in *Through the Looking-Glass* between saying what you mean, and meaning what you say (Carroll 1971, 190). The limitless pretense that makes the sound of words—the vocal event—the reality of a place lies at the heart of all utopias, arising as they do from the fantastic sociality printed by egoistic hedonism on a distant island. The year he was composing his *Utopia,* Thomas More dreamt he was a king in his own fiction, telling Erasmus, "I feel so expanded . . . I can see myself now marching along, crowned with a diadem" (Greenblatt 1980, 55). The ban on gambling in Utopia, and Utopia's refusal to enter into leagues with other states (More 1910, 196), show how remotely a realized pretense stands (at least in its own terms) from chance and the meager protections from risk provided by a contract. Swearing and gambling were forsworn by Simson's privateers because each saw himself as did More and Selkirk, an absolute monarch, whose utterances are no longer futile or expectant, but performative and real.

This pattern is so carefully and ingeniously elaborated by Defoe that the production of an island self out of a shattered social self dominates the plot of *Robinson Crusoe.* At the beginning of his life as a castaway, Crusoe remembers how "the Anguish of my Soul at my Condition would break out upon me on a sudden, and my very Heart would die within me" (Defoe 1972, 113). In that passionate mood he cannot explain, "by any possible Energy of Words, what a strange longing or hankering of Desires I felt in my Soul" (187). Eventually, he renders this intensity of feeling as an alternation between assertions of absolutism and servitude, governance and naturalism, bliss and misery, exalting the simple double-entry arithmetic of good and evil ("I am divided from Mankind . . . But I am not starved" etc. [66]) to a dramatic sense of contradictions. Thus he is "Majesty and Lord of the whole Island . . . the lives of all my Subjects at my absolute Command" (148); "absolute Lord and Lawgiver" (241); and the unheard inhabitant of a "Scene of silent Life" (63), prey to anxieties he can never resolve or narrate (176). He dwells on The Island of Despair (70), which he apostrophizes "O happy Desert," and names the most pleasant place in the world (139). He is obliged, like many utopians, to represent his island life by contraries: "my Reign or my Captivity, which you please" (137). His island reflects the two opposite moods of self-preservation, the constraint and the reach of an individual who is thrown alone into an empty place but finds the means to set a table in the wilderness. The two sides of self-preservation, need and supply, proliferate as various outward shapes that by turns threaten and cherish the self. They represent the improbability and the triumph of survival, the antagonist of the solitaire and his mirror image. *Robinson Crusoe* is a novel demonstrating how, at the beginning of the modern period, "the categories characterising rational discourse were mapped onto haunted ground" (Armstrong and Tennenhouse 1992, 112).

The identification of these phantoms begins with animals which, like the sea lion for Cowley or the goat for Selkirk, incarnate and objectify the afflictions of the solitary self. The dying billy goat in the cave at first terrifies Crusoe, and at last transpires as his counterpart: "I could have been content to have capitulated for spending the rest of my Time there, even to the last Moment, till I had laid me down and dy'd, like the old Goat in the Cave" (Defoe 1983, 180). When he returns to his country estate after the desperate sea adventure, where he risked being swept away into the ocean, Crusoe is awakened from his first sleep by a familiar complaint: "Poor Robin Crusoe, Where are you? Where have you been? How come you here?" (143). He realizes after a moment of shock that he is hearing his own voice echoed by his parrot. In these more intimate transactions with his tame creatures, he not only sees himself in them, but hears half of his voice in theirs. His discovery of the cannibals who visit his island is much more fraught, causing his imagination to veer between terror and vengeance, until he recovers a sense of contraries and dreams the dream that produces for him not only an image of the self preserved but also a real and substantial companion, Friday (198–201). Such a dream cancels the difference between the world he fancies and the one he moves in. He wants to call it possession or inspiration ("secret Hints and Notices . . . [the reader] may think there is no Possibility of . . . being real"), but it is the enthusiasm of self-preservation, what Shaftesbury called "the evidence of the senses lost, as in a dream" (Shaftesbury 1964, 1:31).

Crusoe reinforces the intensity of his relation to himself by a constant use of reflexive propositions, particularly the ethical dative, as in phrases such as these: "I made me a cave" (Defoe 1983, 60); "I made me a large tent" (59); "I made me a spade" (119). He always has himself in his eye: "I frequently stood still to look at myself" (167); "What to do with my self, I was now to consider" (34); "I never so much troubled my self to consider what I should do with my self" (197); "My thoughts were now wholly employ'd about securing my self" (59); and "I argued with my self, That this really was not the way to deliver my self, but entirely to ruin and destroy my self" (172). A tendency strong from the beginning of his adventures is to glimpse himself in action: "I found my Head and Hands shoot out above the Surface of the Water" [45]), as if he were in the two positions at once of observing subject and observed object. Charles Gildon drew attention to this feature of the narrative in the same year it was published: "I can't omit one Observation of his, which is, that the Waves buried him twenty or thirty Foot in their own Body; I would fain know by what Art Robinson could distinguish between five Foot, and twenty five or thirty" (Gildon 1719, 14). This sort of art can develop into a full-scale self-rescue: "It was self-preservation in the highest degree, to deliver my self from this Death of a Life" (Defoe 1983, 199). Crusoe's labor on behalf of himself includes dialogue: "Sometimes I would expostulate with my self" (62), demanding of himself, "Where are the rest of you?" and "What am I?" (92). He puts to himself the impossible question, "I shall die and then what will become of me?" (90). Mindfulness of self ceases to have any social or spiritual drift, for he confesses, "I would ask my self whether thus conversing mutually with my own Thoughts . . . was not better than the utmost Enjoyment of humane Society in the World" (136).

It is evident, therefore, that the reflexive quality of Crusoe's speech, and the division of his perceptions between a self who is subject and a self who is object, organize all his relationships with things, animals, and finally people (see Armstrong and Tennenhouse 1992, 180). As objects of care, they are the reproductions of his first responsibility, the preservation of himself; as objects of terror, such as the mysterious footprint and the cannibals, they are specters of his worst feelings, arising from his ignorance and violence. Finally, when something like a population moves on to his island, he sees himself reflected in them. After he is assured that Friday has no desire to leave him, he says, "He made me at last entirely his own again" (Defoe 1983, 224), a mutuality of feeling Crusoe is not shy of calling love (213). When the three prisoners of the mutineers come ashore, he beholds in them his former desolation, and relishes all the more his power of preserving them, as he preserved himself (252). When he emerges from his thicket, they greet his "staring Spectre-like Figure" as an angel ("You must be sent directly from Heaven"), and he responds with

FIGURE 8   Augustus Earle, *Robinson Crusoe*. Pen and ink drawing, circa 1820. Rex Nan Kivell Collection. By permission of the National Library of Australia.

a spectral echo, "I told him, I looked upon him as a Man sent from Heaven" (254, 273; fig. 8).

These encounters are generally understood to represent Crusoe's progression from the stage of use value, to which life on the island has reduced him, toward civil society; for as well as giving each of them the story of his life, he draws up contracts with all his human counterparts: Friday (Defoe 1983, 226), the Spaniard (245), and the master of the British ship (256) (see McKeon 1987, 326; Rees 1996, 81). It is his humor, however, to make a joke out of these arrangements: "How we were to have this done, when I knew they had neither Pen or Ink; that indeed was a Question which we never asked" (Defoe 1983, 248). The mutual confidence a contract is meant to impart already belongs to Crusoe by virtue of his throbbing brain, whose power to invent a reality "better than sociable" (135) is frequently the theme of his self-reflections. His fear of the savages provokes a surge of fantastic ideas that shape the next stage of his life: "Contrivances I hatch'd, or rather brooded upon in my Thought."

These eventually take shape as the dream of Friday's actual arrival, driven through the roaring thoroughfare of his brain by "Impetuosity of Desire" and "the extraordinary Fervour of my Mind" (168, 198). This activity taking place between his imagination and his island instructs him that there is a "secret Converse of Spirits" (250), an idea he returns to in the *Farther Adventures:* "I am satisfied our Spirits embodied have a Converse with Spirits unembodied" (Defoe 1927, 2:166). Rather than a redemptive acknowledgment of Providence or even an idolatrous familiarity with the genius of the place, these sentiments celebrate the means of his self-preservation—the improvement of his luck beyond a doubt—and a vindication of his habit of holding dialogues with himself. He objectifies the fertility of his mind as a company of invisible messengers capable of shifting the odds entirely in his favor and translating his dreams into realities. This is his pretense.

Whether this is no more than the utopian fantasy that Mandeville said results from a wishing self entering too far into the realization of its wishes, or that gloriation of mind Hobbes detected in authors overidentified with their own fictions, it establishes at the end of Crusoe's story a close resemblance between his contrivances and Prospero's rough magic. His visitors come into "an inchanted Island . . . there were Devils and Spirits in it" (Defoe 1983, 266), a place governed by a specter who refuses at first fully to reveal himself, and whose agents are conversible spirits. When Friday misleads the mutineers with noises, drawing them deep into the island by "hollowing and answering, from on Hill to another" (265), he replays Ariel's tricks upon Stephano, Trinculo and Caliban, charming their ears "that calf-like they my lowing followed through / Toothed briars, sharp furzes, pricking gorse, and thorns" (*The Tempest* 4.1.178–80). This is part of a larger structure of pretenses designed to keep blurred the difference between what is and what isn't. Prospero calls them "subtleties o'th'isle, that will not let you believe things certain" (5.1). Crusoe calls them "reasons of state" (Defoe 1983, 268), not because he is refining his role as absolute prince of the island, but because he holds it important to keep things subtle and obscure, "that they might not see what Kind of a Governour they had" (269). "This more perfectly amus'd them," he adds, commending the success of a ruse that is "all a Fiction."

In the history of Captain Misson, Defoe defines reason of state as "a Term of Art which means Self-Interest" (Defoe 1972, 384), and it is fair to say that none of Defoe's heroes and heroines neglect it. However, in *Robinson Crusoe* and the *Farther Adventures,* reason of state betokens a delight in pretense beyond the bare need for it, a relish of imposture for its own sake which, like Prospero's masque in *The Tempest,* evinces the exuberance of a mind fully conscious of its power to variegate its circumstances and its own incarnations. At the ultimate stage of his art, Crusoe, like Prospero, is addicted to surrogacy. If the goat, the parrot, and the footprint were formerly his family, his wraiths and messengers, now in this latter stage of his history he happily distributes himself among human agents whose relation to himself is no different. They stand in for himself, castaways to his castaway, angels to his angel, just as he stands in for them too, showing himself to the two hostages as his own viceroy, "the Person the Governor had ordered to look after them" (Defoe 1983, 271).

If Prospero finds it hard to abjure his rough magic, and to declare everything his mind has made of the island to be an insubstantial pageant, so it is for Crusoe, whose hankerings for his island create the sequel of the *Farther Adventures* and are commemorated in it: "My Imagination run upon it all Day; it was uppermost in all my Thoughts, and my Fancy work'd so steadily and strongly upon it, that I talk'd of it in my Sleep; in short, nothing could remove it out of my Mind; it even broke so violently into all my Discourses, that it made my Conversation tiresome; for I could talk of nothing else, all my Discourse run into it, even to Impertinence, and I saw it my self" (Defoe 1927, 2:112). The degree of obsession suggests that the gift Crusoe makes of his story to the people who land upon his island ("I gave them every Part of my own Story" [277]) is not the prologue to a treaty or a contract, but an enthusiastic memorandum to himself. It is fitting, therefore, that one of them happens to be called Robinson.

When Simson said of his privateer-utopians, "They subtilly pretended that they lived as Kings in the Islands having no Law . . . but they pulld off this Vizard before we sayled from thence, and declared themselves glad to have the opportunity of seeing their owne Country once more" (Simson 1690, fol. 39v), he outlines a difference between extravagant pretense and bare truth that detects the emptiness of a utopia, and the irresistible attraction of civil society. It points a moral that the Lockean reading of *Robinson Crusoe* likewise underscores, which requires the reader to believe that the hero is never so moved by his own imaginings as to palter with what he secretly knows to be the case, and to spoil his chance of going home. He is assumed always to be in charge of his fantasies, just as Simson assumed the privateers were hypocrites, not fools, when they reformed their speech and their slaves, never really meaning that either should improve. But the fantasy of absolute power, so common in the stories of Juan Fernandez, seems to be less an index of an impostor's subtlety than the island's itself, whose noises cause the evidence of the senses to be lost in a dream. This is the theme of one of Robert Louis Stevenson's most enigmatic fantasies, *The Isle of Noises*. To beat off his roaring sea lion, Cowley had to fantasize it by lodging it in his own dream of hellfire. If they were to have deceived their rescuers successfully, Simson's privateers would first have had to make their exit from their own dream and undeceived themselves. Thoroughly to have amused the mutineers, Crusoe would have had to know why the story that necessitates his apparition before them as a specter was only a fiction. In order to manipulate the pretense, they all would have had to lose faith in their own autobiographies as wonderful narratives of their self-preservation, and to deny the efficacy of the furious work of their own brains. To this extent, their pretense is involuntary, and they are part of what is pretended. When Crusoe says he can employ no energy of words suitable to explain his hankerings (Defoe 1983, 187), and when civil subjects are left incapable of explaining their place as real and rational beings within the fantastic world constructed by their desires (Pocock 1975, 466), they rehearse the same difficulty as Trenchard when he said that the law of self-preservation had carried him to a pitch where he could no longer justify his feelings as anything but the desire of private pleasure (Trenchard 1725, 2:52). And when he added that chance alone would determine whether the difficulty could be overcome, he emphasized the impossibility of emerging from it in any condition that would not be improbable and delusive. In this bet, there is no limit to the transitive relations that the self can enter into with itself—self-terror, self-sympathy, self-concealment, self-assurance, or self-amusement—all travesties of social gestures, and all impossible to explain in ways that are not fantastic and egoistic. These are the subtleties of the isle.

With this in mind, I want to examine one of the most remarkable maritime pretenses. Its axis was Juan Fernandez; its precedents were lodged in Dampier's, Rogers's, and Selkirk's narratives of the island; and its significant dates coincide with those of *Robinson Crusoe* and the South Sea Bubble. George Shelvocke was an out-of-work naval officer employed in 1718 by a former shipmate, Edward Hughes, to lead a privateering cruise into the South Seas. He and John Clipperton (Dampier's former colleague), commanders of the *Speedwell* and the *Success* respectively, sailed from Plymouth in 1719 under a British flag, taking advantage of the recent outbreak of hostilities between England and Spain to raid the coast of South America and, if possible, to seize the treasure galleon that plied between Lima and Panama. The enterprise was dogged by misunderstandings, drunkenness, scurvy, and (some said) piracy, and in 1722 Clipperton returned to Galway in the last stages of alcoholism, so overcome by the tribulations of his voyage that he died soon afterwards of a broken heart, or a ruined liver. For his part, Shelvocke hitched a ride home in an East Indiaman, after selling the leaky prize he had sailed to Canton; and when he got to London, he was placed in the Wood Street Compter by the owners of the ship he had lost long since, for they were convinced that he had defrauded them of substantial sums of money. Shortly afterwards, Shelvocke disappeared, and nothing more was heard of him except three versions of a narrative of his voyage, and a letter.[2] In all four documents, Shelvocke presents himself as an ingenuous and patriotic sailor ("An Author's chief motive in works of this kind ought to be the desire of serving his Country" [Shelvocke 1726, vi]). In his published narratives, he documents the afflictions by which he was beset—mutinies, shipwreck, and the loss of his men—and he repudiates indignantly the scandalous aspersions of a cabal of enemies, against whom he levels in turn a series of charges.

It is to William Betagh that the public was indebted for an entirely different account of this voyage. In his *A Voyage round the World* (1728), he disputes every aspect of Shelvocke's vindication, calling it "a wild story full of abominable romance . . . his stupid incoherent romance" (Betagh 1728, 109, 215). He says the failure to rendezvous with Clipperton at any of three agreed points was owing to Shelvocke's determination to keep to himself the *Success*'s supply of liquor, and to cruise without any interference from his colleague. He goes on to affirm that Shelvocke covertly organized two mutinies against himself, first at St. Catherine's on the Brazilian coast, and then on Juan Fernandez, in order that the subsequent revisions of the ship's articles governing the division of prize money, from which Shelvocke benefited, could not be charged to him as his initiative or responsibility. Furthermore, Betagh alleges that the mutiny at Juan Fernandez was prefaced by the deliberate wrecking of the *Speedwell*, which Shelvocke, whom everyone agrees was a skilled seaman, contrived to make look like an accident, although every phase of the disaster unfolded on a serene day. His purpose, according to Betagh, was to void the contract between himself and the owners. Betagh goes on to accuse his captain of thinning his crew by sending them on dangerous errands, or by leaving

2 The letter is dated 26 May 1726, and addressed to the lords of the Admiralty. In it he strongly recommends the advantages of the island of Chiloe as a British base (BL Add MS 19,134, fols. 84–86). The narratives consist of a manuscript journal, Admiralty Library (MS 18); an expanded version of the journal, published as *A Voyage round the World by way of the Great South Sea* in 1726; and another edition of the same narrative, corrected to deal with Betagh's book and published by his son in 1757.

them on Juan Fernandez, where eleven of his crew finally remained. Betagh's last accusation concerns the capture of the *Concepcion de Recova* near Sansonate. Notwithstanding the stiff resistance made by this vessel, it contained (according to Shelvocke) nothing but "flour, loaves of sugar, boxes of marmelade, jars of preserved peaches, grapes, limes, etc" (Shelvocke 1726, 371). Betagh claims that the "etc." included more than one hundred thousand pieces of eight, plunder Shelvocke secretly divided among his cronies and fraudulently concealed from the owners. This deception is at the center of a web of pretense—the "pretence of watering" at Juan Fernandez, his "pretended natural history of California," his "pretended narrative" (Betagh 1728, 170, 217, [ii]). Betagh associates these pretenses with Shelvocke's Jacobitism, his raising frequent glasses to the health of the Pretender, and his organizing a feast in his honor on Juan Fernandez. Altogether, they form a vast and intricate plot.

The fact that Betagh wrote his account to deny two serious accusations against himself, and that more than half of the events he mentions he was unable to witness, relying for his details on the journals of George Taylor and Thomas Dodd, somewhat dents the probability of his narrative. Nevertheless, the shortage of other corroborative material causes most commentators on the dispute to give Betagh some credit.[3] In the eighteenth century, John Campbell scrutinized the evidence more carefully than anyone else, and he was relied upon by John Callender and James Burney when making their judgments of the affair. It was Campbell's opinion that three aspects of Betagh's story deserve close attention: first, Clipperton's refusal to cruise with Shelvocke after their accidental reunion in the Pacific, once it was clear Shelvocke was not going to honor the original contract with the owners; second, the loss of ten men, six on the coast at Sansonate and four on board *The Holy Sacrament*, because Shelvocke believed, or said he believed, that peace might have been concluded between the Spanish and the British, and just wanted to make sure; third, the lading of the *Conception de Recova*, which, he said, "explains Abundance of dark Things in the preceding and in the subsequent Part of this Expedition" ([Harris] Campbell 1764, 1:230).

However, there is one charge leveled by Betagh against his captain that no one seemed willing to entertain, and that is the allegedly deliberate wrecking of the *Speedwell* on Juan Fernandez. In their accounts, Camp-

---

3   W. G. Perrin, in his edition of 1928, thinks his account of the St. Catherine's mutiny is basically correct (Perrin 1928, xv), and so does Philip Edwards in his recent discussion of the *Speedwell*'s voyage (Edwards 1994, 50).

bell and Burney both agree that maritime law would not have excused Shelvocke from compliance with the owners' contract once he was afloat again. As Campbell points out, "In a Bark built out of the Remains of the Speedwell, they were as much in an Owners Bottom, as in the Ship herself; and, if they could imagine this be obviated by taking and cruising in another Ship, then he might as well have quitted the Speedwel . . . and gone to Sea in a Prize, without the hazardous Experiment of the Shipwreck" (1:214). Neither he nor anyone else bothers to comment on Betagh's tales of Jacobite toasts and white cockades, although O. H. K. Spate says, "one may discount Betagh's more atrocious charges" (Spate 1983, 213).

The two prominent threads in Shelvocke's narrative, the voiding of contracts without seeming to be able to help it, and the ability to present in a highly finished form "such Parts of the Picture as are likely to strike the Reader most, and to give him strong Impressions in the Captain's Favour" ([Harris] Campbell 1764, 1:238), become apparent to Campbell first in Shelvocke's treatment of Clipperton. Because Clipperton was still sailing with the original contract, and invited Shelvocke to resume its terms, he is exhibited by Shelvocke as being guilty of the very crimes of which he himself might have stood accused: drunkenness, piracy, bloody-mindedness. Thus Clipperton is abused for throwing away the lives of his men, chiefly Mitchell, his second in command, whom Shelvocke says was dispatched in a prize to a nonexistent island and never seen again (Shelvocke 1726, 308). Clipperton is supposed to have said "with an inhuman sneer," to Shelvocke himself, "What could it signify if [Shelvocke] should, through want, be obliged to surrender, [he] should only undergo the same fate, that, perhaps, some others had before [him]"—by which he appears to have meant William Dampier, whose privateering commission had been taken by Clipperton in 1704, a theft that nearly cost him his life at Batavia (326). Although Shelvocke twice got rid of his own ships to avoid trouble with the owners, he adduces Clipperton's decision to sell his ship in Lisbon as clear evidence of a sinister move (445), just as earlier he projects what may have been his own piratical instincts and Jacobite tendencies as the renegade behavior of Betagh, whom he accuses of deliberately going over to the Spaniards on the expectation that his Catholicism would win him favor. That Hendrie, the owners' agent, should have seized the opportunity of getting out of Shelvocke's ship when they met the *Success,* and that Shelvocke should dispute Clipperton's reasons for separating when his own narrative bears them out ("Does not Captain Shelvocke's own account speak it?" [(Harris) Campbell 1764, 1:225]) convinces Campbell that he was hiding his own acts and motives under what seems to be a set of tu quoques, whereby his adversary is made to bear the guilt of the chicanery and the inhumanity he had himself practiced.

Thus, when he gets to the story of the loss of the men at Sansonate, who were sent ashore to confirm news of an Anglo-Hispanic truce, only to be taken prisoner, Campbell pauses to mark this as "the most important and remarkable Part of Captain Betagh's Book" (1:225). Likewise, he introduces the story of the *Concepcion de Recova* as "a Matter which gives us the greatest Light into the true Scheme of, at least, the latter Part of the Voyage . . . a very extraordinary Piece of secret History" (1:230). But what exactly this history might be, he leaves the reader to judge, simply citing the shocking survival rate for the voyage (33 of the *Speedwell*'s original 106), and pointing to the moments of pathos in Shelvocke's narrative as being the signs of hidden intention: "Such are the Mutinies that fell out in the Beginning of the Voyage; the tedious, troublesome, and melancholy Sojournment in the Island of Juan Fernandez, the Diligence, Skill and Care, he shewed in getting a Bark framed out of the Wreck, and carrying off in it such a Body of People, almost against their Consent" (1:238).

Is there any more to "the true Scheme of the Voyage" than these fits of intemperance, cruelty, avarice, and fraud, varnished over with sly appeals to his reader's better feelings? Did Shelvocke have an overarching plan comprising the destruction of his vessel and crew, and the breaking of his contract? And if so, what had the wrecking of his vessel to do with it; and why should he labor so hard over the moving details of his "melancholy sojournment" at Juan Fernandez?

Shelvocke's talent for self-pity and rebounded accusation displays, in common with other characteristics of castaways on Juan Fernandez, a facility for self-projection that combines fantasies of impregnability with an extraordinary sense of isolation. In fact, Shelvocke's descriptions of the island are superb, especially the sounds: "Nothing can be conceiv'd more dismally solemn," he writes, "than to hear the silence of the still night destroy'd by the surf of the sea beating on the shore, together with the violence roaring of the sea-lions repeated all around by the ecchoes of deep vallies, the incessant howling of the seas . . . so that in this confused medley, a man might imagine that he heard the different tones of all the species of animals upon earth mix'd together" (Shelvocke 1726, 258). The breadth of this Noachic observation makes way for an identification like Selkirk's and Crusoe's with the goats, and Cowley's with the sea lion, by which Shelvocke seems to allude to his own formidable vigilance and power as leader of the group: "There is always an old [sea] lyon, of the largest size, which is incessantly on the watch, and at the approach of any one makes a hideous roaring, and threatens certain danger to any who should be so hardy as to molest them" [255]).

Shelvocke's skill at recognizing his own reflections extends to other people's narratives. Betagh claimed to have heard him aver on several occasions, "It was not difficult living at Fernandes, if a man should accidentally be thrown there, since Mr Selkirk had continu'd upon it four years by himself" (Betagh 1728, 172). Setting sail the year *Robinson Crusoe* was published, and heading directly for what Burney called "the land of Robinson Crusoes" (Burney 1803–16, 4:465), Shelvocke seems preternaturally aware of himself as someone voyaging between the lines of other seamen's yarns. He cites Amédée Frezier, William Dampier, William Funnell, and Woodes Rogers frequently; indeed, Campbell tells us, "The last thing the Propietors did, was, to present each of the Captains with Mr Rogers's Voyage, that they might never be at a Loss for proper Precedents throughout the Expedition" ([Harris] Campbell 1764, 1:186). Shelvocke says of the period on Juan Fernandez, "I, on my part, never fail'd to encourage [the people] by adding to such stories of things, or actions, that I had known or heard of, to have been done by the like number of men in distresses of this kind" (Shelvocke 1726, 216). Although Betagh sourly observes, "But our captain was above confining himself to any precedent" (Betagh 1728, 11), I think he was wrong.

Shelvocke cites the mutiny against Dampier as a way of blackening Clipperton's character, but he is interested in it for other reasons too. Surviving depositions in Chancery, including one of Selkirk's, suggest that scuttlebutt had Dampier rated as a far from innocent victim of mutiny: a drunkard, a coward, a cheat, probably a pirate, and given to fits of bad language (Baer 1996; Williams 1997, 141). Dampier was Shelvocke turned inside out, without pretense, with every fault on show. The loss of his commission was as much a sign of his carelessness about important things as it was of Clipperton's cunning; and Shelvocke's elaborate precautions are attempts to avoid the public odium of Dampier while pursuing private interests identical with Dampier's. His elaborate precautions advertise the pathos of the parallel, not its knavery: "In the midst of these troublesome confusions I order'd my son to secure my Commission in some dry place of the woods or rocks, if such could be found, for I well remember'd how Dampier had been serv'd in these seas" (Shelvocke 1726, 218). When his men insist on his signing new articles at Juan Fernandez, their reason is that "they would not trust themselves under my conduct, because they should always be apprehensive that I had sinister intentions upon them, and should serve them as C———n serv'd some of his men, who (they heard) happening to be taken separately, he denied them, and suffer'd eight of them to be hang'd as pyrates, before his face" (224). The infamy of Clipperton is the melody Shelvocke plucks from the story of Dampier's voyage in the *St. George,* but the leitmotif is the vulnerability of contracts, a hint he is determined to improve.

He reads Woodes Rogers's *A Cruising Voyage* in the same way, and not at all as the owners had expected when they offered him the book as a guide. Rogers's sad catalogue of mutinies, plots, wild gambling, detentions, late payouts, and failed contracts, together with the story of Selkirk's stranding, seems perversely to have been revolved by Shelvocke as a pattern of bad luck rich in possibilities. No sooner were copies of Rogers's *Voyage* given to Shelvocke and Clipperton, than (as Campbell records), "All things fell into Confusion, and Factions were formed . . . so that in this, as well as in many other cases, private Views proved the Cause of public Ruin" ([Harris] Campbell 1764, 2:187). Shelvocke makes himself the monument of this public ruin, a helpless victim of the insolence of his men and the black designs of his officers, who "divested [him] of the authority of their captain, having regulated themselves according to the discipline of Jamaica" (Shelvocke 1757, 227). He complains, as Rogers had done before, "I was at a loss, not knowing what to do in this dilemma, and was distracted at the thoughts of subjecting myself to the caprices of a giddy mutinous gang of obstinate fellows who were dead to reason, and in a fair way of being harden'd to all kinds of wickedness" (224). As the anarchy grows worse on Juan Fernandez, Shelvocke adopts the language of the eyewitness, saying, "It is not in the power of words, to express the wretched condition we were now reduced to, or the surprise we were under . . . or the dread that came upon us of starving on the uninhabited isle we were thrown upon" (212). And then he falls prey to the despair of the castaway: "I became extremely melancholy and pensive" (Shelvocke 1726, 229), drawing the parallel with Selkirk prior to making his transit from terror ("Nothing presented itself to our sight but rocky precipices, inhospitable woods, lofty mountains . . . and a tempestuous sea, which had reduced us to the low state we were now in" [208]), to physical delight ("I became one of the strongest and most active men on the Island; from being very corpulent, and almost crippled with the Gout, I walk'd much, and work'd hard every day" [248]).

Why would Shelvocke want to imitate the worst parts of Dampier's and Rogers's voyages and the worst moments of Selkirk's solitude? The answer is that they are all in different ways stories vividly depicting the ex-

citements and pleasures arising from the dissolution of contracts and social ties. And despite Shelvocke's skill at improving the pathos of a commander subject to the whims of "a little republick" (Shelvocke 1712, 265),
forsaken by those who owed him loyalty, he derives immense satisfaction from beholding the embarrassments of those who expect that a broken contract can be mended by another: "It was beyond their cunning or
skill either to retrieve their own credit, or do any thing that might be effectual towards establishing me again in my Command" (ibid.). Cunning
and skill can improve confusion, Shelvocke seems to have learned, if self-
preservation exploits the improbable moment between contracts, where
it is not certain "whether this be, or be not" (*The Tempest* 5.1). He hur-
ries his crew into this condition, watching contemptuously as they try
to reform the contract of the voyage, while he goes about to secure the
governorship and absolute monarchy of the island that descends to him
through Selkirk and the other rulers of Juan Fernandez. Viewed as a
gamble, Shelvocke monopolizes ill luck, ensuring himself the worst possible outcomes of a privateering cruise. This is the purpose served by
Rogers and Dampier. They lead from disaster after disaster to Selkirk,
and such a thudding accentuation of the negative that Shelvocke is to all
intents and purposes a solitaire left with nothing. This is what he pretends, and from that pretense he can pretend to authority by usurping
the power of a self-imagined wraith, the monstrous sea lion, and then
expanding his ego to fill the spaces that broken contracts and poor risks
have emptied. Thus the desolation of a castaway ("without any thing to
support us, but the uncertain produce of a desolate, uncultivated island,
situated [I may justly say] in the uttermost parts of the earth" [Shelvocke
1757, 218]) is transformed into the je ne sais quoi: "This place is perfectly
romantick; the very structure of the Island, in all its parts, has a certain
savage irregular beauty, which is not to be expressed" (257). And in these
limited circumstances the forlorn commander thrives, like Selkirk before
him, growing lithe and active.

Here is Shelvocke's reason for wrecking his ship: not to rewrite a contract he had no faith in, but rather to feel a gambler's zest in turning a loss
into a win, and a poet's exhilaration in making an empty space romantic.
This is the sovereignty he and Crusoe lay claim to, a sort of awe at their
own inventiveness. If he did indeed put a white cockade in his hat to toast
the Pretender, it is to be suspected it was out the association of the two
ideas, sovereignty and pretense. And his contempt for the leveling instincts of his crew is boundless, not because he is an enemy of anarchy, but
because he thinks it laughable that they should imagine that their project

of self-preservation might compete with his, and their pretenses outshine his own. "They all imagined themselves to be most nearly concerned in their lives, liberties, and fortunes," he declares ironically, before giving the true scale of his own sea-leonine ego: "The meanest of them were taught they were as good as I. . . . I really believe for the pleasure of thinking themselves equal to me, they would contentedly have lived in this desart, at least as long as I had lived" (Shelvocke 1757, 124, 234, 236). Here is the authentic voice of the ego as eyewitness and the isolated enthusiast, pre-served from nothing by the power to digest the improbable and the unimaginable, superb amidst reasons of state, contrivances, and fancies (including the confusions of his crew) that are exclusively its own work. Such a voice is heard in the South Seas from Gulliver to Captain James Cook, from Henry Neville's patriarch in the Isle of Pines to Stevenson's Tembinoka, the sole ruler of his triple kingdom of Apemama. With the exception of Betagh, who tried to speak for the truth by charging Shel-vocke with a secret knowledge of the falseness of all his pretenses, the mu-tineers are stuck inside the envelope of Shelvocke's enthusiasm, a species of controlled lunacy of which typically he accuses Dodd and Hendrie. Such mastery appears to have been fully appreciated only by a Chilean cacique, "that idle story," as Betagh called it, "of the king of the Indians delivering him his sceptre" (Betagh 1728, 215).

In enthralling others by appearing to lose all command, Shelvocke wins a bet that he could never have lost, since it was founded on nothing but the certainty of loss. The game was a scandalous version of Pascal's wager, where you bet on a simple alternative—*infini-rien;* God is, or he is not—in which one expectation is dominant because should it prove correct, it offers the gambler a great deal more than the other. For Shel-vocke, the dominant expectation fell to the side of nothing at the expense of calculable advantages, and if the worst things did not happen, then he staged them. By betting on that outcome, he did infinitely better than Rogers and Dampier, who lost a great deal by hoping for the best (Hack-ing 1975, 65–66). As an insurance scheme, it was a secret tontine, in which the last survivor scoops the pool (Daston 1988, 167). Shelvocke's careless-ness toward the lives of his men suggests that after the shipwreck, he acted as if his self-preservation was the only business he had in hand. But to read anything more into his plan than that—to assume that he had cal-culated on taking a treasure galleon, and had figured out how best to se-crete his fortune—is to credit him with a clairvoyance and a faculty for probable calculations he could not have possessed. Like the South Seas investors, Shelvocke was sporting with nonentities, and when real plunder turned up, it was an unpredictable bonus, a supererogatory testimony to the power of the preserved self to squeeze something out of nothing. There is a peculiar trace of candor in Shelvocke's imitations of the pretenses of others. By a species of double obliquity, he ends up saying exactly what he is doing. His whole plot is presented in the following summary: "I was to consider that the next appointed place of rendezvous was at the island of Juan Fernandes, in the South Seas . . . a navigation I was apprehensive our ship was in no condition to cope with . . . . the prospect being so full of danger, it was necessary to employ all our thoughts how best to prepare ourselves for so perilous and undertaking. . . . I resolved not to look back, but to proceed in such a manner as might prevent the evils I could foresee, taking especial care to betray nothing in myself that might daunt or dismay my ship's company." As Campbell says, "Does not Captain Shelvocke's own account speak it?" ([Harris] Campbell 1764, 4:225). His tu quoques are the same, a careful register of the things he did reflected from men he regarded solely as his creatures, equivalent to cats, goats, and parrots: I did not sacrifice my men, Clipperton did; I did not betray my colleagues, Clipperton did; I didn't lose my commission or my command, Dampier did; I did not drink toasts to the Pretender, Betagh did; I did not feign melancholy madness, it was Lieutenant Dodd who "had a mind to act the mad-man" (Shelvocke 1726, 218). Himself the old sea lion, he makes these human adversaries reflect nothing but himself, transforming their weakness into his strength.

To pretend is not simply to lie, as Shelvocke did when he said a sudden storm from the north drove the *Speedwell* onto the shore of Juan Fernandez, when no less an authority than Selkirk said that in four years he never knew the wind to blow off the sea there (Rogers 1712, 134). A pretender's attitude toward the social world is too arrogant and too uncertain to make systematic mendacity worthwhile. Pretense is the result of a perpetual interest taken in the self, and a fascination with the sheer variety of its amusements. As the reflective Robinson Crusoe says, "All reflection is carried home, and our dear self is, in one respect, the end of living . . . all that the reflections which he makes are to himself; all that is pleasant he embraces for himself; all that is irksome and grievous is tasted but by his own palate" ("Serious Reflections of Robinson Crusoe," Defoe 1860, 7). Out of that protean resource Shelvocke's utopia is constructed. By cultivating disaster in order to ensure his self-preservation, he turned everything surrounding him into a mirror of himself, whether admirable or opprobrious, funny or sinister. He populated the enchanted island of Juan Fernandez with his reflections in a perverse act of universal sympathy; and as long as no one could prove that these extrinsic selves were figments of his brain, an elaborate structure built out of the wreckage of other privateers' hopes, there was nothing to interrupt his pleasure in himself. "Who can think that a person in command, would not exert his power to the utmost, to maintain himself in it, when both his honour and fortune were, in a manner, at stake?" demands Shelvocke, consumed with self-delight at the picture he paints of his own vulnerability. The answer to his question is, of course, "No-one," the same person who, along with all the other nullities that define the gambler's and the eyewitness's world as the opposite of the familiar one, stands guarantor of the selves that are preserved on the other side of what is scarcely imaginable.

7

PATRIOTS IN PARADISE

Who were to dispose themselves within the ha-ha, and who without? To this the unthinking will give an off-hand answer, as they will to every ponderous question. Oh, the bishop and such like within the ha-ha; and Farmer Greenacre and such like without. True, my unthinking friend; but who shall define these such-likes? It is in such definitions that the whole difficulty of society consists.

—Anthony Trollope, *Barchester Towers*

In earlier chapters, I have argued that the domestic crisis caused by the South Sea Bubble called urgently into question the degree of compatibility between private and public interest. If speculation, whose only motive was personal gain, could ruin national credit, how was it possible to guarantee, verify, or even plausibly assert that the pursuit of self-interest secured the good of the public? After the event, Alexander Pope defined a "Bubble-Scheme" as the employment of public office "to no other purpose than to serve private Ambition" (Pope 1956, 4:142), in plain defiance of his earlier proposition that self-love and social good were the same ("Ev'n mean Self-love becomes, for force divine, / The scale to measure others wants by thine" [Pope 1963, 525; *Essay on Man* 3.291–94]). In *The Beggar's Opera* (1726), one of the many great Scriblerian satires to be written after Britain's desperate brush with the South Seas, Lockit sings a song about this paradox of civil society, a social organization brought about by the unique coexistence in the human animal of the instincts to herd and to prey.

John Trenchard and Viscount Bolingbroke took to journalism in the wake of this national humiliation. Trenchard wrote *Cato's Letters: or Essays on Civil Liberty* (1725), probably with help from Thomas Gordon; while Bolingbroke, under the pseudonym of Caleb D'Anvers, produced

The Craftsman: being a Critique of the Times (1727). Each tried to analyze what had happened to the nation during the fatal year of 1720, and to find out who was to blame. But they were destined to discover that faction, corruption, and jobbery persisted under Sir Robert Walpole's administration not as contingent evils but as the very tools of government. In casting about for clarity in such a dense climate of corruption, it was hard for anyone to make a candid profession of political faith, since Tories (like Bolingbroke) found themselves impersonating classic Whig positions, and leaders of discontented Whigs (like Prince Frederick) found it convenient on occasion to act like Jacobites. In the wake of a landmark essay by Quentin Skinner, it has generally been agreed a pointless exercise to establish the degree of sincerity in patriot ideology (Skinner 1974). However, in their various prescriptions of an antidote to this disease in the constitution, they evolved a distinct style of political commentary that was to dominate journalism and the tone of politics for the rest of the century. Somewhere between the genres of satire and occasional essay, it was heavily inflected with the pessimism of a voice attempting to make general statements on the basis of private particulars, constrained to tackle the broad stream of corruption by means of fallible and sometimes ridiculous self-exemptions (Lamb 1995).

Notwithstanding Trenchard's skepticism about the public validity of any patriotic sentiment, or Bolingbroke's complaint that the warmest patriot is fashioned out of a "Principle of Self-Preservation" (D'Anvers 1727, 1:181; 2:325 [nos. 21, 75]), the attitude of embattled disinterestedness they struck in their appeals for the preservation of the nation—appeals made to a public both seriously and mockingly addressed as "my loving countrymen" (D'Anvers 1727, 1:286 [no. 31]) by authors who professed their honesty while in disguise—colored all opposition rhetoric after 1720. It was prone to a fundamental and self-acknowledged inconsistency, placarded by patriots themselves as "the plausible pretext of patriotism," and "the pretenses of serving a man's country and of public good," as Horatio Walpole, Horace's uncle, put it (Colley 1982, 262n. 84; Temple 1963, 2), best exemplified in Pitt the Elder's talent for what became known as his *versatility* (Godwin 1783, 150; Lamb 1995, 97–109). Walpole said of Pitt's eloquence, "Where he chiefly shone, was in exposing his own conduct: having waded through the most notorious apostasy in politics, he treated it with an impudent confidence, that made all reflections upon him poor and spiritless, when worded by any other man" (Walpole 1985, 1:64)

Versatility is the result of three problems patriots are trying to solve at once: generic, political, and rhetorical. In attacking the corruptions in the constitution, the lover of his country takes up the position of satirist, and adapts the monitory and particularizing techniques of Juvenal or Horace. "I design," said Caleb D'Anvers, "to lay open the frauds, abuses, and secret iniquities of all professions. . . . My papers . . . consist of general satire against wicked men" (D'Anvers 1727, 1:9, 290 [nos. 1, 31]). On the other hand, in the role of defender and encomiast of a rather indistinct political entity called the public, the people, the country, the patria, or the nation, he needs constantly to bear in mind where satire must end and panegyric ought to begin; two extremes not easily reconciled in the one address. This requires that the patriot be able to distinguish between what is essential and what is superfluous to the idea of the state, despite his hazy terminology for it. In accomplishing this delicate negotiation, he must also be aware that his audience is not homogeneous, being divided between his enemies and his dearest friends; thus "the gentle reader" and "my loving countrymen" are ironically and frankly greeted by turns, as the effects of allegory and innuendo serve alternately to immunize the patriot from what is wicked in the public, and to identify with what is good in it. In this respect, the potential conflict between the patriot and his reader resembles that between a voyager and his. Each is concerned about publicizing the truth of a unique and private impression of things, an awkward coalition of the je ne sais quoi and a common cause leading to a combative way of winning friends, and a self-deprecating form of candor.

Bolingbroke, for example, mentions Lemuel Gulliver as the travesty of a patriot, a man who published falsehoods and contradictions "in a grave and serious manner, with the same solemn Grimace and repeated professions of truth and simplicity" (D'Anvers 1727, 1:116 [no. 14]). Yet he was aware that the second book of *Gulliver's Travels* (1726) had been widely understood as a dramatization of patriot kingship and that Gulliver's removal from Lilliput to Blefescu in the first book had been interpreted as a defense of his own flight to France (Kramnick 1968, 209; Dickinson 1970, 213). Pitt appears to have dealt with this problem not by avoiding it but by brandishing and ornamenting his own inconsistencies in front of an audience either too shocked or too pleased to reproach him, rather as William Dampier loudly justified his attachment to dry and jejune facts in spite of the objections of "the Curious Reader," turning instead to "the intelligent Reader" to excuse his deficiencies (Dampier 1729, 1:sig. A3, 2:[i]).

The drama of patriotism, then, is one of national peril averted by singular, atypical individuals who are destined to rescue the public from the public, and to save, as Mrs. Slipslop might say, some folks from other folks. In words that anticipate Alexander Dalrymple's praise of the sublime voyager, Bolingbroke declares, "We shall find that none but great Souls are capable of so sublime a virtue, and that only men, of the most elevated understanding, can soar so high" (D'Anvers 1727, 2:88 [no. 54]). The sense of patriotic community shrinks proportionately as the menace justifying the patriot ideal grows, leaving the patriot looking quixotic as well as sublime. The "nation" he serves is correspondingly exiguous, imagined, ideal. In this respect, patriotism is different from satire, although it borrows many of its techniques from it; for if satire attacks corruption as the sin of modernity committed against ancient and immutable values, patriotism both defends and deplores the consequences of recent history by invoking a set of values that is much more labile. The satirist grows more pungent and confident as he particularizes his target, but the patriot becomes more embarrassed as he tries to specify the common practice of a nation. He tries to find refuge in abstract language ("to love the public, to study universal good, and to promote the interest of the whole world" [Shaftesbury 1964, 1:27]) of the sort Jonathan Swift had mordantly impersonated in his antimodernist satire the *Tale of a Tub* (1704); or he gets enmeshed in particulars (such as Trenchard's vivid fantasies of revenge against the South Sea Company directors, or Bolingbroke's compromised relation to the narrative style of Gulliver) that feed a private passion or a personal anxiety not easily communicated and not necessarily public spirited. Satire is impatient of ungoverned passions. All the major satirists of the first half of the eighteenth century treat enthusiasm as the source of corruption. But patriots cannot deny the affective side of their commitment. On this account, Pope was advised by his friends in the opposition to give up writing satire ("Patriots there are who wish you'd jest no more" [Pope 1963, 689]).

Hovering between the substantial historical experience of a nation and a bodiless or singular attempt at identifying with it, patriots run straight into the charge of hyprocrisy, of saying the thing that is not, and, like their opponents, uttering "blackest deceits covered with the fairest pretences" [D'Anvers 1727, 1:291 (no. 32)]. Trenchard had pointed out besides that the constant and stoic refusal of pleasure demanded by the patriot is impossible, and that disinterestedness itself is no more than a turn of the mind toward the public, a private pleasure taken in a chimera, and the enjoyment of a nonentity (Trenchard 1725, 2:51–53). Patriotism is, therefore, always twinned with its opposite. Henry Fielding's parallel definitions of patriotism as "the Love of one's Country carried into Action" and as the dereliction of those who have "falsely pretended to that glorious Incentive" (Fielding 1987, 116, 210) look the same way as Bernard Mandeville's estimate of patriotism as "First, the real love Men have for their Country, abstracted from Selfishness. Second the Ambition they have, of being thought to act from that Love, tho' they feel none" (Mandeville 1924, 2:345). The most glorious emanation of the human spirit ends up in Samuel Johnson's *Dictionary* as the last refuge of a scoundrel. Confounded at the strong evidence in Pitt's career of ingenuousness and pretense, William Godwin confessed, "It is difficult to bring the scattered features of such a character into one point of view" (Godwin 1783, 286). Pope told Viscount Polwarth that he admired the great spirit of patriots, but at the same time wished he knew what it was (Pope 1956, 4:217).

The question whether a patriot's concern for country overrides that of self-preservation, teaching him to keep his last breath to wish, "O save my country, Heav'n!" (Pope 1963, 689), or whether it is simply a refined form of indulgence in which "Self takes equal Possession of the Soul" (Brown 1757, 159), runs alongside the question concerning the accuracy of a patriot account of nationhood. Is the picture of national decline an analysis or a mood? Alternatively, is the prospect of national enlargement a program or a sentiment? Are patriot accounts of the state of the country a productive encounter with the stubborn facts of history or merely utopian velleities? Or are they both? As the same enigma is proposed to the audience by the traveler to the South Seas, it seems right to ask also whether terra incognita might provide congenial ground for patriotic inconsistencies.

These questions are aptly posed of Bolingbroke, since his impressive engagement with the concept of patriotism and the duties of national preservation begins and ends in the South Seas. His essays in *The Craftsman,* designed to staunch the flow of corruption from the Bubble by animadversions defining and exemplifying an ideal of public spirit, were in fact strongly to influence George III and to direct, among other things, his patronage of the Pacific explorations of the 1760s; a period when, as George Keate put it, "the views of ambition and avarice" were replaced by disinterested plans for "the improvement of science and geography" (Gerrard 1994, 45; Keate 1788, v). I want to suggest it is no coincidence that Bolingbroke's evolving ideas of patriotism have an origin and terminus in the dreams and data supplied by the Pacific Ocean. The same arc between the real and the fancied, the historical and the utopian, implicit in the formulation of a disinterested lover of one's country, affects narratives of exploration too. The navigation of the South Seas veers between identical extremes of public duty and private exigency, historical veracity and fantastic nullity, no less in the period of scientific inquiry than in that of privateering and bubbling. Thus patriotism not only proffers an idiom in which the achievements of heroic sailors and scientists might be assessed and praised, but also mirrors the vexing equivocality of certain experiences—of solitude, of savagery, of landscape—so salient in maritime exploration, and equally evident in the rhetoric of the singular defender of his country. The sailor and the patriot stand in equally liminal relations to the metropoles; and just as the circumstantial narrative of mariners specifies a case to the point where it becomes meaningless and unimaginable for anyone but an eyewitness, so the patriot's discourse of nation can evaporate into the same self-addressed particularity, the language of the private and ideal world of the je ne sais quoi.

Bolingbroke set out his theory of patriotism in two letters whose titles, *The Spirit of Patriotism* (1752) and *The Idea of a Patriot King* (1749), emphasize the purely hypothetical and imaginary nature of his project. In the former, it is plain that while he is rehearsing familiar topics of political virtue, drawn largely from civic humanist sources, Bolingbroke is mainly excited by the intellectual challenge of inventing a coherent zone of ac-tion for the patriot; and that patriotism in its fullest extent is pure ideation, the heroic feat of conceiving the possibility of a perfect political life: "When . . . a man forms a political scheme, and adjusts various and seemingly independent parts of it to one great and good design, he is transported by imagination, or absorbed in meditation" (Bolingbroke 1752a, 29). If political action is to be thoroughly coherent, then it must be heralded by the contemplation of such coherence. Bolingbroke appears to owe this side of his patriotism to Shaftesbury's neoplatonism, where virtue needs neither to be prompted nor rewarded in the sphere of action because it is suffused with an intuition of unity. Therefore, in *The Idea of a Patriot King*, retirement from the world is recommended as providing the conditions of peace and solitude in which these ideas might best be arranged. But it is here, in the imagined state of contemplative retirement, that Bolingbroke touches the paradox at the core of idea: the patriot must make his exit from the world in order to qualify fully to enter into it: "I have renounced the world, not in show, but in reality, and more by my way of thinking, than by my way of living, as retired as that may seem. But I have not renounced my country" (78). As Pope was to put it when he parted company with the patriots, "If merely to come in, Sir, they go out, / The way they take is strangely round about" (Pope 1963, 699). In framing the patriot ideology of what was known as "The Country Party," Bolingbroke renders the word *country* deeply equivocal. It is the name of the place the patriot occupies between the world (corrupt) and the nation (indefinable), denoting the centrality of a rural backwater, the privacy of a region of public commitments, a space rather like Uncle Toby's bowling green in *Tristram Shandy,* where the heroic ends of creation can be answered in miniature and in a game. It forms likewise an isthmus between the activity of the mind and the daily business of life. The equivocal possibilities of this situation were brilliantly canvassed by writers belonging to the patriot opposition to Walpole, but for Bolingbroke the transcendental option grows more appealing as the chance of political action becomes more remote, acquiring a notional symmetry no different from the lonely fantasy of a man who, in spite of all the evidence of his own career in politics, believes that power and virtue might under the right conditions merge in a common cause.

He maintains such a strict correlation between the perfection of his own contemplations and the wonderful behavior of his imagined patriot king that there is insufficient historical medium between the two to render their connection probable. He gives to it none of John "Estimate" Brown's plangency, or Pitt's impudence, or Viscount Cobham's and Lord Lyttelton's taste, expressed in the variety of horticultural vouchers of political disinterestedness to be found in their gardens. The particularizing satirico-journalistic style used in *The Craftsman* is thinned into sheer conjecture. The reader is informed that the patriot king will not multiply taxes, sustain a national debt, or oppress the people; also, he will exhibit manners void of all affectation, thus the incidents of his private life will be as admirable as his public appearances. Above all he will be guided by the rule of reason in securing "the common rights and interests of mankind" (Bolingbroke 1752a, 210, 221, 81). But as for the actual experience of such perfection, Bolingbroke leaves it in the sphere of the unimaginable, and like Raphael Hythloday adverts to a state so far from the usual that only a visionary eyewitness could vouch for it: "A Patriot King is the most powerful of all reformers, for he is himself a sort of standing miracle, so rarely seen and so little understood, that the sure effects of his appearance will be admiration and love in every honest breast. . . . Innumerable metamorphoses, like those which poets feign, will happen in every deed; and while men are conscious that they are the same individuals, the difference of their sentiments will almost persuade them that they are changed into different beings" (147). From inside a similar miracle, Don Quixote has an intuition of the same metamorphosis when he asks, "For what mortal in the world . . . will imagine and believe us to be the same persons which in reality we are?" (Cervantes 1970, 1:314).

Although *The Craftsman* is generally regarded as the first deliberate attempt to appeal to public opinion, and thus to acknowledge and manipulate a source of power outside the court and the Houses of Parliament, Bolingbroke found it impossible to appeal to opinion as such, for he associated it with self-interest and faction. "Reason has small effect on numbers," he declares. "A turn of imagination, often as violent and sudden as a gust of wind, determines their conduct: and passion is taken, by others, and by themselves too . . . for principle" (Bolingbroke 1752a, 190). In order to broach a manifesto supported by miracles and metamorphoses ("the same individuals . . . changed into different beings"), he appeals instead to the *taste* of the public. People will be struck by the propriety, decorum, and *bienseance* of the patriot king. Just as there is "a last hand as we commonly say, to be given to all works of art," so there will be in this prince a je ne sais quoi, "a certain *species liberalis,* more easily understood than explained, and felt than defined' (220).

The hollowness at the center of this "messianic vision" (Gerrard 1994, 45) reverberates in all bare instances of the je ne sais quoi; and were it not that Bolingbroke's allies had already been fleshing out the bare bones of his patriotic ideal with more vivid scenarios, it is likely that the patriot king would have disappeared into his own inexpressible perfection. The real work of publicity was undertaken by poets such as James Thomson, David Mallet, and Richard Glover; historians such as Thomas Gordon; landowners such as Lord Cobham and Lord Lyttelton; designers such as William Kent; orators such as Pitt; and aspiring princes such as Frederick and the future George III. By substantiating patriotism in stories, earth, statues, pageantry, passionate flights of eloquence, and voyages of discovery, they succeeded in winning public attention to the four chief facets of the patriot aesthetic: the attractiveness of a retired and private life; the importance of a largely immemorial "Gothic" constitution (deriving from what survived of Celtic and Saxon history); the amenity of a landscape garden as the setting of patriotic retirement; and the sentimentalization of reason as an instrument of universal knowledge and peace. These themes could be developed and harmonized in different ways, and were sufficiently pliant to accommodate the novelties of a new world in the Pacific; but no matter how ingeniously presented, they could not escape in the end the allure of pleasure, that turn of the mind toward a delicious nonentity, which Trenchard had affirmed to be the weakness of patriotism, and Shaftesbury the corruption of voyaging.

Prince Frederick provides a good example of how these four patriot themes could be improved and blended. He was, for example, a brilliant publicist of his own private life, dining with open windows at Greenwich, and being visibly pleased with music as he floated down the Thames in an elaborate barge designed by William Kent (Gerrard 1994, 196). His talent for ornamenting and displaying his personal amusements extended to gardening. In 1731, Frederick acquired the lease of Kew House, a mile from Queen Caroline's garden at Richmond Lodge, where there had been developed the prototypical patriot garden that Cobham and Lyttelton were to perfect, the one at Stowe and the other at Hagley Park. At Richmond, Charles Bridgeman had experimented with dense plantations of trees interspersed with extended lawns and serpentine walks; and William Kent had designed and built two Gothic structures, the Hermitage and Merlin's Cave. Although he did not live long enough to transform Kew, in 1735 Frederick took the Gothic hint to his gardens at Pall Mall in 1735, where he celebrated the Saxon and Norman lines of his heritage with statues of King Alfred and the Black Prince (Dawson 1993, 47–50; Desmond 1995, 23). But under the direction of his widow, Princess Augusta, Sir William Chambers built an Alhambra, a pagoda, a mosque, and a ruined arch; and Johann Muntz produced a Gothic cathedral, all raised between 1758 and 1761 (Desmond 1995, 47–57). Their fascination with the Orient yielded, among other things, the Saracen ramlet among the many branches of the Gothic ideal.

Conscious of the strongly georgic emphasis of patriotic landscape poetry such as *Windsor Forest* and *The Seasons*, Frederick did not neglect the principle of utility in gardening, and began to restock the Old Botanic Garden that surrounded the Temple of the Sun (Carter 1988, 282). When George III inherited the garden, he made great strides in improving this portion of Kew, known as the Physick or Exotic Garden. It was ably directed by his mentor Lord John Stuart, third earl of Bute, who had studied botany with Carolus Linnaeus and who was to write a book on the subject, *Botanical Tables* (1784). Bute employed William Aiton and Philip Miller of the Chelsea Physick Garden, and the three rendered Kew fit to receive the vast tribute of specimens that were to arrive after Sir Joseph Banks began, on his return from the Pacific in 1773, to run it as the Royal Botanical Garden (Banks 1963, 1:98). The vast dimension of this enterprise ("all curious productions are collected from every part of the globe" [Chambers 1763, 3]) publicized the new monarch as a friend to the world, to reason, and to science, but in a manner that was aesthetically satisfying. Collecting "fossils, plants, seeds and animals" from around the earth was the duty, according to Johann Reinhold Forster, of "every true patriot" (Bougainville 1772b, xvii). Alluding, among other enterprises, to the voyage that allowed him to make his own contribution to this thesaurus, George Forster observed in faultless patriotic language, "History does not offer an example of such disinterested efforts, towards the enlargement of human knowledge, as have been made by the British nation, since the accession of his present Majesty to the Throne" (Forster 1777, 1:[i]). The Royal Botanical Gardens were the junction between the patriotic voyage of discovery and the public-spirited collection of specimens. They vindicated the pastimes of prince-gardeners whose taste for retirement had prepared the ground, and whose zeal for the public good had dispatched collectors to the ends of the earth in order to stock it.

Patriot kingship has, therefore, been assumed by some historians of colonial expansion to have been the great engine of empire, involving a coherent system of national propaganda, scientific tabulation, species acclimatization, and settlement. But this is to credit it with an efficacy that is always the desideratum of patriot discourse. For one thing, it was an idiom nurtured in opposition, where performances were never needed to authenticate professions. Bolingbroke, the ardent exponent of "the old incomprehensible principle of mere instinctive loyalty," had, after all, deserted his country and decamped to France in 1715 to serve as the Pretender's Secretary of State, and he was impeached for it (Cooke 1836, 1:132, 374, 408). When his pupil George III tried to locate patriotism's key terms—history, nation, virtue, and reason—in a system of national practice, he marginalized himself for reasons cogently set out in Edmund Burke's *Thoughts on the Causes of the Present Discontents* (1770); namely, that he was acting in contempt of public opinion. Never having settled the relation of the private to the public sphere, no patriot (not even the miracle of a patriot king) could speak for the nation, or undertake an imperial enterprise in its name, as Lord Bute was to find to his cost. Pitt, who did more than any single individual to acquire Britain's second empire, prior to George III's losing the largest portion of the first, was unable to offer a coherent statement of national ambition. When driven to locate his founding principles, he harked back to an immemorial moment that had never existed: "He would not recur for precedents to the diabolic divans of the second Charles and James—he did not date his principles of the liberty of this country from the Revolution: they are eternal rights; and when God said, *let justice be justice,* he made it independent" (Walpole 1985, 2:39). Indeed, the Tacitean, Arthurian, and Spenserian strains in patriotic genealogies were distinctly anti-imperial in the Roman sense, favoring instead a *patrocinium* based on tribal identities and affiliations that stemmed from Geoffrey of Monmouth's account of Brutus's settlement and uniting of the British Isles (Armitage 1998, 107–15). But even this was only an idea, the utopian extension of the spirit of patriotism, a versatile grouping of neo-Galfridian sentiments, not an articulate doctrine or even a probable history.

Patriot solitude has two South Seas aspects, sometimes superimposed. The first is formed by the career of the singular first person, isolated from society, perhaps by seclusion on a ship, perhaps by being cast away upon a desert island. The second traces the pleasures of the dweller in a garden, voluptuously alone in a paradise. Patriots proudly brandish the insignia of exclusion and neglect. Pitt was fond of doing this in the most crowded venues: "I stand up in this place single and unconnected," he would intone in the House of Commons (Almon 1797, 1:480). Jonathan Swift cultivated the reputation of a patriot in Ireland, a land where he considered himself an exile and a solitaire ("But, why obscurely here alone? / Where I am neither lov'd nor known" [Swift 1958, 1:203]). With rather more urbanity, Pope flirted with patriotism while idealizing his retirement at Twickenham, anticipating Lord Cobham's quickened taste for gardening after he had been expelled into the political wilderness by Walpole, his punishment for asking inconvenient questions about the sequestration of the estates of South Sea Company directors. In his play *Agamemnon* (1738), Thomson takes as his theme the loneliness of the patriot; and by having his hero Melisander marooned on a barren shore, he is able to marry the patriot condition of political exclusion to the popular narratives of desert islands. Stunned at first, like Selkirk, with his objectless existence, Melisander remembers, "There Desolation reign'd; and there, cut off / From social Life, I felt a constant Death" (Thomson 1738, 34). But astonishment gives way to rapture as he attunes himself to the Edenic symphony of the elements:

In Streams, in Groves, in sunny Hill and Shade;
In all that blooms with vegetable Life,
Or joys with kindred animal Sensation;
In the full-peopled Rounds of azure Heaven;
Where I, studious, look'd, I found Companions. (34)

Melisander's desert island expands, much like Selkirk's and Robinson Crusoe's, to yield tokens of a sympathetic natural whole that is presented as the true basis of political and social choices. "By this one may see," as Woodes Rogers had observed of his rescued castaway, "that Solitude and

Retirement from the World is not such an unsufferable state of Life as
most Men imagine" (Rogers 1712, 130). Sir Richard Steele gave the story
a patriot moral: "He is happiest who confines his Wants to natural Necessities; and he that goes further in his desires, increases his wants in Proportion to his Acquisitions" (Steele 1955:109). Adam Ferguson later made
explicit the link between the restrictions of a desert island and the nobility of primitive sentiments (Ferguson 1995, 18). George Anson's experiences on Juan Fernandez and Tinian found their way into Jean-Jacques
Rousseau's *La nouvelle Héloïse* (1761), where St. Preux recalls that the first
was "an asylum to innocence" and the second a paradise, "more delightful
still than the first" (Rousseau [1803] 1989, 3:29).

Under these terms, the question posed by Guillaume Raynal and Denis Diderot ("Hath the individual, who passes his whole life in voyages,
any idea of the spirit of patriotism?" [Raynal 1783, 8:367]) is not as decisive as it seems. Jacques Delille is only one of many panegyrists who
hails James Cook as "l'ami du monde" because he had sailed alone over
so much of it (Delille 1844, 275). Another Frenchman praised him as the
man who had measured "la ceinture orientale de la Nouvelle Hollande,"
and who therefore deserved the title of "le héros de tous les ages et tous
les hommes" (Lemontey 1792, 30). Cook himself was conscious of the dimensions these elogiums were spanning, between the known and unknown worlds, between the loneliness of the South Seas and the national
attributes of daring and curiosity that are proved there—extremes analogous in their way to Bolingbroke's split idea of "country" as both world
and nonworld. Before his second voyage, Cook had written to his friend
John Walker, "I should hardly have troubled you with a letter was it
not customary for men to take leave of their friends before they go out
of the World, for I can hardly think my self in it so long as I am de-
prived from having any connection with the civilized part of it" (Cook
1961, 689). But only a year before, he had been talking of the South Seas
islands as "Terrestrial Paridises" where people go naked without shame,
and loaves of bread grow "in a manner spontaneously upon trees" (Cook
1970, 20, 18), as if recognizing in the nonworld the same qualities of openness and uniqueness his encomiasts were to recognize in him. Being out
of the world, therefore, represents more than invisibility and absence. It
is a chance to prove in solitude what a *country* (though perhaps not a
world) esteems as the highest proof of public spirit.

Certainly the qualities evinced by Cook and the indigenes he encountered acquired the name of patriotism. Lemontey began by saying, "l'éloge
de Cook doit paraître un hommage vraiment national" (Lemontey 1792,

2–3). Anna Seward elegized him as the global agent of Britannic public spirit (Seward 1810, 34). J. R. Forster had already identified himself as a patriot when en route to the Pacific with Cook (one of the cohort of "free-spirited sons of Britannia" devoted to "the honour of the British Nation" [Forster 1982, 196, 216]); so he was pleased to find the inhabitants of Tahiti of a similar temper, a people "capable of that noble and disinterested desire to work for the common weal as much as lies in their power, which we call *public spirit* or *true patriotism*" (Forster 1778, 1:376). Using the evidence of Cook's first voyage, Henry Home, Lord Kames noted that the resemblance between British patriotism and the savagery of the New Zealanders lay in the fierce resistance of an island people to invasion (Kames 1774, 1:371). Both Kames and Forster drew on the great ethnographers of North America, such as Pierre Lafitau and Pierre-Francois-Xavier de Charlevoix, who made similar claims for the tribes surrounding the Great Lakes; but their observations are more pointed. Instead of supposing a parity of manners between Native Americans and the ancient world of Jews, Greeks, or Romans (Lafitau 1724, 2:283–87), they noticed in the tribes of Polynesia the same virtues they prized most highly in themselves. Although there were patriot views of the South Seas more presumptuous and interested, such as John Dyer's prospect of settlements on terra incognita (Dyer 1761, 182), or Richard Savage's allegory *Of Public Spirit* (1737), where Discovery is sent out at the behest of Public Spirit to find space for Population, Cook and Forster were concerned about not only nobly delineating the nobility of savages, but also (in a typically patriotic straddle) preserving these aborigines from the contaminations of contact with Europeans.

The same troubling adjacency of corruption and virtue that characterized Bolingbroke's and Trenchard's discourse of patriotism here complicates the identification of the patriot with the savage, imparting to their first meetings the poignancy of the Fall. Sexually transmitted diseases, the allure of private property, and the pollution of commercial exchange despoils the voyager of a suitably representative culture as surely as it destroys the "smiling Eden of the southern wave" (Seward 1810, 44). Cook and the Forsters were well aware of the consequences of introducing the "world" to its unknown moiety. George Forster thought the loss of local lives a trifling injury compared with "the irretrievable harm entailed upon them by corrupting their morals" (Forster 1777, 1:212); and after making a similar observation, Cook remarked, "If any one denies the truth of this assertion let him tell me what the Natives of the whole extent of America have gained by the commerce they have had with Europeans" (Cook

1961, 175). The world he bade farewell in his letter to Walker has less consistency in this context, where virtue becomes the property of a marginal, not a national community, answerable to the uncertain definition of "country," perhaps, but certainly to no larger entity. Bolingbroke's dictum, "The antient Britons are to us the Aborigines of our Island" (Bolingbroke 1735, 141) provides the historical coordinate of Cook's discoveries in space. At the beginning of time and at the ends of the earth, corruption destroys aboriginality, opposed only by the patriot, who recognizes and preserves it, even if it is only in himself.

The voyager who finds in Pacific natives the virtues of his own primitive ancestors may simply be using navigation as time travel, looking at the past with an amused sense of his own superiority—as Dyer and Savage when they expected discovery to be followed by the diffusion of trade and civility. Theorists of stadial history, for example, could imagine no real improvement of manners that did not arise solely from parallel improvements in the modes of production and exchange, no matter how picturesque savage life might have appeared to a cultivated eye (Meek 1976). Contrariwise, Roussovian idealizers of a state of nature could conceive of no common basis of primitivism and civility, as the one is inevitably driven out by the other. But if the preservation of aboriginal virtue is the only way to preserve civil society, as the nostalgia of the patriots and the sentiments of Forster, Kames, and Cook seem to indicate, then the culture of savages asks to be consulted as a present remedy for the visitor, as well his responsibility. Only in aboriginality is there any hope. Presumably it was some such hint that the Dutch were acting on when they decided to name their foothold in the East Indies Batavia, in honor of their tribal forebears (Schama 1987, 181).

In 1728, Thomas Gordon, a close associate of John Trenchard's, began publishing his translation of Tacitus, aimed at addressing this problem. He dedicated the first volume, consisting of the *Annals*, to Sir Robert Walpole. This was a history of the Roman emperors representing, according to its translator, "a great tablature of the ugliness and horrors of Tyranny" (Gordon 1728–31, 1:15). Whether Gordon felt that he had missed his mark, and been denouncing tyranny to a tyrant, he switched allegiance three years later, dedicating the second volume to Prince Frederick and prefacing it with an essay that sounds remarkably like an advertisement for *The Idea of a Patriot King,* insofar as it deals with the unstable relation of a prince to his people, and lays down some guidelines for regulating it. Like Bolingbroke, Gordon tries to erase the medium between the people and the prince, opting for a shared "passion for the public Weal" that ensures a spontaneous mutuality of "the interest of a Prince . . . and the interest of his people" (Gordon 1728–31, 2:III, [iv]). The text of Tacitus most apt for illustrating this proposition is his *Treatise upon the Situation, Customs, and People of Germany*, where the historian describes "a people pure, and independent, and resembling none but themselves"; nations where "the Princes fight for victory; [and] for the Prince his followers fight" (2:323, 329). As these aboriginal patriots immediately exhibit "the most secret motions and purposes of their hearts," they do not find the exposure of vice amusing, and they do not palliate corruption as "the custom of the age" (2:335, 332). However, Tacitus and Trenchard found it no easier than Bolingbroke to fill up the sphere of such political probity with plausible details. The virtues of the Germans are founded in negations. The people of the Cattan tribe, for example, "have no house to inhabit, no land to cultivate, nor any domestic charge or care." As for the Chancians, "they provoke no wars, they ravage no countries, they pursue no plunder" (2:340). Meanwhile, the Fennians subsist in "wonderful Savageness . . . destitute of arms, of horses, and of homes; their food the common herb; their apparel, skins; their bed, the earth; their only hope in their arrows, which for want of iron they point with bones . . . secure against the designs of men, secure against the malignity of the Gods, they have accomplished a thing of infinite difficulty, that to them nothing remains even to be wished" (2:349). Tacitus's Germans are displayed with all the negative attributes of the aborigines Dampier met in New Holland, except that he commends in the former a destitution Dampier found quite repugnant in the latter.

Despite the negative picture of aboriginality drawn by Tacitus, his contrast between the corruption of the Romans and the honor of the German tribes was intensely attractive to Walpole's enemies. Frederick himself was attaching the aboriginal stamp to his publicity by allusions to Arthur, Alfred, and the Black Prince, not to mention the Scottish clans, for in 1750 he was spotted at the Middlesex elections dressed in a plaid (Gerrard 1994, 195). In his *Order of the Garter* (1742), a masque designed as a showcase of Frederickian sentiments, Gilbert West has Prince Edward assure his consort,

And rather wou'd I see my Britons roam
Untutor'd Savages, among their Woods,
As once they did, in naked Innocence,
Than polish'd like the vile degenerate Race
Of modern Italy's corrupted sons. (West 1742, 36)

William Giffard's revival of Dryden's *King Arthur* (1735), and Thomson and Mallet's *Alfred* (1740) were Opposition set pieces, presenting primitive virtue in the same embattled posture as modern patriotism, locked in combat with the customs of the age (Gerrard 1994, 113, 139). They commemorated and resurrected the terms of the Gothic or Ancient Constitution, that cluster of immemorial rights and liberties still dimly visible in common law, the birthright of everyone claiming a descent from Cambro-British and Saxon originals (Pocock 1987, 36). In acquiring the title "Gothic," these coincident principles of ancient and modern virtue overrode the injurious meanings the word had acquired among advocates of politeness such as Shaftesbury, who associated Gothic manners and a Gothic taste with corruption, of which he considered travel books a horrible symptom (Shaftesbury 1964, 1:179, 222).

Suitably to this revival of interest in Britain's vernacular politics, patriots followed Frederick's example by placing Gothic icons and structures among the ornaments of their landscape gardens. In "the fair majestic paradise of Stowe" (Thomson 1972, 117), Lord Cobham began by having William Kent, Frederick's designer, build a Temple of British Worthies, an exhedra celebrating the deeds of Gothic heroes such as Alfred and the Black Prince, and explorers such as Sir Walter Raleigh and Sir Francis Drake. In 1741, he commissioned James Gibbs to start on the Gothic Temple of Liberty, a structure whose crenellated front, crocketed spires, and quatrefoil lights rendered it eloquently expressive of aboriginal virtue. But in order to underline the self-evidently Gothic qualities of the temple, it was bounded on the eastern side by the statues of seven Saxon gods. Sanderson Miller built the first Gothic ruin at Hagley Park in 1747 (Thacker 1979, 191), and his colleague Batty Langley published a pattern book of ruins (Desmond 1995, 54), starting a fashion so widely imitated it was mocked twenty years later in George Colman and David Garrick's comedy, *The Clandestine Marriage* (1766).

There was a built ruin at Stowe too, the Temple of Modern Virtue (long since vanished), garnished with a headless statue of Walpole, and placed opposite the Temple of Ancient Virtue. It attracted Horace Walpole's disapproval—not, it would seem, out of shocked filial piety, but out of aesthetic outrage at its clumsy architectural polemic. He found the Gothic Temple "adorable," but added, "I have no patience at building and planting Satire" (Walpole 1937, 34:75). Here was another index of patriotism's antagonism to satire. As far as Walpole was concerned, aesthetic pleasure was not to be interrupted by an allegory. The Temple of Liberty succeeded in pleasing the eye, but the factitious ruin was an arrangement of signs demanding to be spelled into a narrative; and as this narrative depended on seeing "ruin" as the factitious mark of corruption, it brought all other contrived images of age into the purview of satire instead of taste, including the Gothic Temple and Sanderson Miller's ruin at Hagley. Walpole understood just how vulnerably a patriot statement is made, whether in words or stone. It cannot claim to signify aboriginal or ancient virtue without also signifying modernity and corruption. He was amused, for instance, at the depredations made by time upon Cobham's Temple of Friendship, "in which, among twenty memorandums of quarrels, is the bust of Mr Pitt: Mr James Grenville is now in the house, whom his uncle disinherited for his attachment to that very Pylades Mr Pitt" (34:75−76).

Walpole anticipates a point later critics of Gothic architecture were at pains to emphasize, namely that it was a modern portmanteau for a mere idea of ancientness, derived from copies of copies with no authentic original, "ayant l'air délabré sans avoir l'air antique" (Delille 1844, 161). It was uncertain whether Saxon architects had been following Greek, Roman, or Saracen styles, and it was generally assumed that their models were degenerate specimens of the type, provoking even worse imitations. According to William Warburton, this was responsible for "the contrary qualities" of Gothic architecture, which wrapped decadence in a bogus primitive dress, exposing "the artifice and contingency which lurk behind supposedly primordial and natural identities," and inducing in its admirers a taste for aboriginality by means of examples quite depraved (Warton 1800, 74, 108, 120−22n. *n;* Kidd 1999, 284).

Patriot Gothic is quite thwarted if it wishes to proclaim itself genuine and univocal. Its best effects are derived, therefore, from exploiting the variety of its possibilities, "a multiplicity of whimsical shapes . . . an exuberance of decoration . . . a multiplicity of delicate ornaments highly finished" (Warton 1800, 4,8). In the reckless profusion of its buildings and ornaments—its shell temples, fanes, pavilions, cupolas, and obelisks, "ces bâtiments romains, grècs, arabes, chinois" (Delille 1844, 145)—Richmond, Kew, and Stowe were properly Gothic, at least according to Walpole and Warton. Each exhibited a collection of wonders and a feast of sensations loosely tied to the idea of public spirit, not a satire where "every emblem ought to be . . . expressive of its meaning" (Kames 1851, 464), nor a coded message delivered to a political elite (de Bolla 1994, 93). Pitt's exploitation of the inconsistencies of his own political character was self-gothicization, a versatility immune to satire, as Walpole understood all truly Gothic effects to be. He took to its limit the adaptability of Gothic language to "various demands in various spheres" (Kidd 1999, 256), without being troubled by contradictions. Mandeville had identified this language as pure medium some years before Cobham retired to Stowe, arguing that "the beautiful shining Qualities" commemorated in public monuments have no more substance than the sheer surface of the stone upon which they are inscribed: "Where would you look for the Excellency of a Statue, but in that part which you see of it?" (Mandeville 1924, 1:168). When Jemima Grey visited Stowe, she looked no further, observing of its attractions, "They are all small and trifling or clumsy, and are all dirty and decaying already" (Clarke 1990, 182).

There is, however, another level on which a patriot garden such as Stowe operates, besides the display of its heterogeneous wonders. That is when it incorporates a structure or texture that alludes to the equivocality and "contrary qualities" of patriot Gothic, and tries to dramatize what Trenchard, Bolingbroke, and Cook in their different ways described as the traverse between something and nothing, between a real world and an ideal country. At Stowe, the Temple of British Worthies looks across the Styx (a long pond made out of the dammed Alder River) toward the Elysian Fields, and when it was first built, it was surmounted with a bust of Mercury, the god who leads heroes out of this world to the next. As a panegyrical statement it seems clear enough, even if it recklessly blends classical and Gothic motifs (a Roman god taking a Saxon king to a Greek underworld). To give the effect of Stygian gloom, the Elysian Fields were (and still are) densely planted with shrubs and trees, making the spot forestlike and of a texture quite different from the rest of the garden, which is arranged around prospects and views. This retreat is close and still, "l'asile du silence" hidden from the day (Delille 1844, 156). In 1778, a year before his death in Hawai'i, a monument to Cook was placed on the path that crosses the Styx, just above the cascade. On a plinth, his profile in relief confronts a thickset hedge, and behind it lies the dark pool (fig. 9). Originally the plinth supported a globe, as if to emphasize (as Cook did in his letter to Walker) the contrast between the world at large and this other one. Cook is placed—deliberately, it would seem—on an equivocal margin between them, not a hero in the exedra about to be conducted across the liquid boundary to the Cimmerian shades, but a negotiator between the viewer and the "terrestrial Paridise" he told Walker he had found in the South Seas. Under these terms, Elysium is re-registered as an exotic and nonclassical spot; and like Banks's botanic garden at Kew, a wooded enclosure called the Exotic Ground and containing a "prodigious variety of curious plants" drawn from the remotest parts of globe (Carter 1988, 282; Desmond 1995, 59), it proposes itself as a space quite

FIGURE 9   Cook monument raised by Richard
Grenville-Temple, earl of Temple, at Stowe Garden,
Buckinghamshire, England. Anonymous sculpture, 1778.

alien to the known world, being a transplantation of Eden. This is a botanical achievement directly in service neither of commerce nor empire.
Culling and propagating tropical specimens from heavily wooded shores
of Polynesian islands, or letting a garden recover a portion of that original wildness, was considered paradisal work, a deliberate restoration of
the aboriginal cover lost in the course of exploration and settlement
(Grove 1990, 18). The memorial takes the spectator to the edge of the experience Cook called being dead to the world.

There is an interesting parallel between the plinth at Stowe and the
memorial to Cook raised by Jean-Joseph de Laborde in his garden at
Méréville, near Étampes in France. A Doric temple dedicated to the nav-

igator was placed on a small island within a pond, at the edge of an elysium garden (fig. 10). His son, Alexandre Laborde, described it thus:

> The spot in which it is placed is retired and tranquil, the river gently flows
> by it, some natural rocks hang over it, and a variety of trees almost en-
> tirely cover it. Every thing around it inspires recollection and thought.
> A great number of foreign trees seem to reproduce the savage and re-
> mote country which contains the real tomb of that illustrious voyager.
> (Laborde 1808, 109)

Laborde went on to say that this woody oasis in the desert of the Beauce
inspires "a sensation inexpressibly pleasing," inducing "forgetfulness of
the whole world" (98, 111). The reproduction of a savage paradise, in other
words, obliterates the difference between the "world" and the "country"
even while it insists upon it. The whole arrangement has the effect of a
ha-ha, one of those sunken walls that conceals the bounds between the
cultivated and uncultivated parts of a garden. Stephen Bann says that the
original placement of the monument at Mereville (now completely altered) combines a suggestion of limitlessness with the actual limit of the
garden, confounding the sense of what it is like to be inside an enclosure
with an intuition of what lies outside it. He declares, "Cook's monument
is therefore at the extreme edge of the garden at Mereville; here, where
the garden ends, and adjoining hamlets would otherwise occupy the visual
field, the imagination is captured by a kind of rhetorical demonstration of
the breaking of limits" (Bann 1990, 218). Laborde succeeded in reproducing on a smaller scale Cook's own confusing encounter with the end
of the world, not just in the savage islands of Polynesia but also in the
icepack of the Southern Ocean, where he saw the Gothic outlines of the
last frontier ("a variety of Shapes such as old Churches [and] Castles") as
both the end of his task and the gateway to an unknown and feature-
less immensity (Cook 1961, 322–23; Pickersgill 1984, 61). Laborde also
managed to make Cook's experience exemplary of the attempt to map a
terrestrial paradise, "a place on earth but not of earth . . . a barrier and
a portal" (Scafi 1999, 55–56), an equivoke advertised in the bittersweet
flavor of the Elysium garden, where "the Earthly Paradise . . . is always
on the point of reversing itself into the Garden of Eden from which . . .
we have always already been expelled." It combines the senses of being
well in and well out of the enclosure (Bann 1990, 219), delineating that
strangely roundabout way of finding a way in that Pope identified as characteristic of patriots.

Figure 10   Cook monument raised by Jean-Joseph de Laborde in his garden at
Méréville, near Étampes, France. Anonymous engraving, 1808. From Alexandre
Laborde, *Description des nouveaux jardins de France* (Paris: Delance, 1808). Courtesy
Marquand Library, Princeton University.

Balder attempts at bringing up these points have been made. The Mortier map of the Pacific Ocean (Amsterdam, 1780) is bordered at the top with the story of Adam and Eve, while at the bottom a broad expanse represents the extent of the terra incognita, as if to circle the hypothetical place of paradise with the history of it. Cook's memorial in the garden at Chalfont St. Giles is adorned with a quotation from Job, saluting his discovery of the nonexistence of a Great Southern Continent as a feat akin to the divine plan of poising the created world over a void ("He stretcheth out the North over the empty place and hangeth the earth upon nothing" [Job 26:7]). The map and the monument make the same statement as James King when he greeted Cook's nondiscovery of the Great Southern Continent as the magic of Prospero: "It has sunk into the bosom of the ocean, and like the baseless fabric of a vision, left not a rack behind" (Cook and King 1784, 1:xxi). But these examples miss the perplexed mood in which, by the same identical gesture, paradise is gained and lost, and an elysium is discovered only by acknowledging the chimeras that constitute it (Lemontey 1792, 51, 31). Thus Bougainville's Garden of Eden is lodged in Diderot's "great ocean of fantasy," and innocence is no sooner identified than it is corrupted (Bougainville 1772b, 231, 277; Diderot 1992, 66, 42). Ranulf Higden's world map *Polychronicon* expresses this paradox cartographically by leaving an empty space where paradise ought to be (Delumeau 1995, 63). As if aware of what is lost in the act of finding, Lemontey compared Cook's landfall in New Holland with the fiend's in paradise, a dubious achievement made via "les profondeurs du chaos" (Lemontey 1792, 30).

In his response to the English garden, and the arrangement of the Laborde Cook memorial in particular, as an equivocal space, combining like the ha-ha the positions of being well in and well out of an enclosure, Bann provides a corrective to received ideas concerning landscape gardens and how they are recruited for nationalist purposes. The unbounded prospect shared and understood by Pope and Bolingbroke in the opening lines of *The Essay on Man* (1733), where the landscape represents the world as the object of rational diversions, an estate over which they mean to expatiate as free inquirers and sportsmen ("Together let us beat this ample field, / Try what the open, what the covert yield; / The latent tracts, the giddy heights explore" [Pope 1963, 504]), has been construed by John Barrell as the archetypal self-image of a landed elite whose domain is "the ideal, panoramic prospect, the analogue of the social and the universal, which is surveyed, organised, and understood by disinterested public men, who regard objects in the landscape always as representative ideas"

(Barrell 1990, 33). This analysis of landscape as a stimulus to reason, knowledge, and power has been pursued by Peter de Bolla and Ann Bermingham (de Bolla 1994; Bermingham 1994; Lamb 1997), and recently has been further advanced by Dorinda Outram as a model of the extensive view needed to make a remote habitat in the New World legible to "the controlling eye" of the metropolitan spectator (Outram 1996a, 262–63).

In these arguments, the resemblance is drawn very close between the viewpoint of the prospective garden as a trope of political power on the one hand, and the botanic garden as the focus of the benefits of empire on the other; for each is the field of vision of an omnicompetent eye, positioned to understand what it sees as measurable and exploitable data. Certainly this is how the landscape of the South Seas would have presented itself to Cook's eye, supposing he had a vantage from which to observe his passage between the world and the nonworld, civilization and paradise, and had been able to make a surveyor's assessment of the relation between the two. And perhaps it is how Britain would have appeared to Bolingbroke if the universalizing idiom of patriotism had not been a vision of his private hours, but rather the reality of British politics; his world as well as his country. Each would have understood the connections between self-love and public utility, and solved the great problem of the age. Bann shows that gardeners did not mistake Cook's achievement as the consummation of this grand design, but preserved the ambiguities and mixed feelings of his voyages by situating his monument between the long prospect and a wooded enclosure.

Designers were helped in this regard by the situation of an Elysium garden within the structure of the larger estate. Undoubtedly, prospective gardens such as those perfected by Capability Brown at Petworth (and later at Kew), for instance, were exceedingly popular, designed to endow the eye with a property (intellectual and aesthetic as well as economic) in the wider view. But Elysium gardens, evolving into the picturesque designs of William Shenstone and Uvedale Price and owing much to the many botanic gardens situated at the heart and the fringes of the empire (the Chelsea Physic Garden, Kew and the Jardin du Roi, for example, and the VOC garden at the Cape of Good Hope, Pierre Poivre's on Mauritius, and Thomas Dancer's in Jamaica), had a much more intimate design upon the sensibility (Grove 1995, 177). In his *Elegy on the Death of Prince Frederick* (1751), Thomas Warton gestures at it when he locates the prince in a frame of wood and water, "Led by calm thought to paths of eglantine, / And rural walks on Isis' tufted side" (Warton 1802,

26). This is Strabo's paradise, "locus ferax palmis abundans . . . totus irriguus" (Temple 1963, 11). These retreats nestling within a grander design, their pools and greenery leading the eye on a wanton chase to an equivocal border, are the inside-out Edens expressive of the patriot's and the explorer's perplexed relation to the world, well in and well out. They are no more a coherent account of national purpose or of the perfection of rational faculties than the Gothic Temple at Stowe is an account of history. They acted as "a symbolic location for the re-creation of Paradise . . . a Utopian vision" (Grove 1995, 22, 201), analogous to the patriot's idealization of a time and space of aboriginal virtue.

To a significant degree, this was true of botanic gardens too. At Kew, the Elysian went hand in hand with the botanic; and despite the recent heavy emphasis on the scientific and imperial purposes botany was supposed to serve (Miller and Reill 1996), it seems an impoverishment of the work of conservation to suppose that the furthest reach of the botanist's imagination was toward import substitution or the commercial exploitation of exotic species. Banks's plans for Tahitian breadfruit, New Zealand flax, Melanesian sago, and Arabian date palms (Gascoigne 1998, 137) were the georgic side of his passion for collecting. Utility was important, but it was neither an exclusive nor an achievable aim. He announced, for example, that his second tour of the South Seas would be "a Voyage of mere Curiosity" (Carter 1988, 87). Of the 800 potted plants from the Pacific that came back with Bligh in the *Providence* in 1793, many did not survive and only 147 were listed in the *Hortus Kewensis* (Desmond 1995, 97). Besides, the accumulation of specimens at Kew was as anarchic as the collections at the British Museum, for it was not until 1797 that efforts were made to record and tabulate the multitudes of plants that were massing there (Carter 1988, 282; Rigby 1998, 81–100). Although Banks made improvements to his own estate at Revesby Abbey (Brown 1996, 169) and was fond of expatiating over the landscape with a gun (Carter 1988, 49), the Benjamin West portrait of 1771 shows how little taxonomic order meant to him at that time in his life. Surrounded by the impedimenta of islands acknowledged as paradises, he exhibits in that picture an enjoyment of things for their own sakes that is licensed by science, but which is not in itself scientific (Thomas 1997, 113). Whether collecting plants or artificial curiosities, Banks was impelled like Philibert Commerson, the French botanist, by "les mouvements de sa propre curiosité" and responded similarly as "un amateur du merveilleux" (Commerson 1772, 254, 265). He was capable of yielding to that Gothic mood Laborde called expressible pleasure; Bougainville, voluptuousness; and Commerson, delight "de sorte que le bon Utopien jouit sans cesse" (Bann 1990, 217; Taillemite 1977, 1:318, 2:506).

On his passage from Tahiti to Mauritius, then Mauritius to Madagascar, Commerson exulted in the uncataloged profusion disclosed by island paradises to scientists, and poured scorn on those who wished to limit it: "Quelle présomption, de prononcer sur le nombre & la qualité des plantes que peut produire la nature, malgré toutes les découvertes qui restent à faire. Linneus ne propose guère que sept à huit mille éspèces de plantes" (Commerson 1772, 257). For his own part, Commerson estimated that in different "théâtres de vegetation," twenty-five thousand species had been discovered, with four or five times as many awaiting discovery. Far from admiring backseat scientists such as Linnaeus and Georges Cuvier, who, as Dorinda Outram remarks, kept their distance on the same principle as the viewer of a landscape garden, opting for the universal truths warranted by such a long perspective rather than "broken and fleeting" impressions (Outram 1996a, 260–62), Commerson pitied "ces sombres spéculateurs de cabinet qui passent leur vie à forger de vains systèmes, & dont tous les efforts n'aboutissent qu'à faire des chateaux de cartes. . . . Tous leurs caractères classiques, génériques, &c sont précaires . . . tous les lignes de démarcations qu'ils ont tracée s'evanouissent" (Commerson 1772, 256).

Commerson's enthusiasm for the variety and flux of the South Seas is echoed by succeeding generations of travelers and commentators. In his *Botanical Tables* (1784), which Queen Charlotte playfully proclaimed "the produce of Lord Bute's studies," Bute relies on his own horticultural experience of the Western Isles to dispute Linnaeus's system of classification (Desmond 1995, 32). After visiting the same islands, Samuel Johnson was disagreeably impressed by a landscape subject to so little discriminating judgment being "quickened with one sullen power of useless vegetation" (Johnson 1984, 126). Diderot's Orou talks of the impossibility of entering into matrimonial contracts "under a sky that doesn't remain fixed for an instant, beneath caverns poised on the edge of collapse, under a cliff crumbling into dust, at the foot of a tree shedding its bark, beneath a quivering stone" (Diderot 1992, 51). In his Mauritian romance, *Paul et Virginie*, Bernardin St. Pierre enjoys crowding together the names of the varieties of plants, such as calbassia, tamarind, agathis, teminalia, alligator pear, and eugenia (St. Pierre 1820, 46–53). Georges-Louis Buffon himself declared species and classes to be human inventions, having nothing to do with nature (Buffon 1797, 3:326); while Alfred Wallace, having explored the natural diversity of the Malay Archipelago, denounced the Linnaean system as superficial, and ignorant of the creative force that is perpetually changing the face of nature (Wallace 1895, 451, 457).

William Warburton considered the purest form of Gothic to be the representation in stone "of a sylvan place of worship," an atavistic memory of primordial Scandinavian forest (Warton 1800, 122n. *n*). "En Germanie," wrote Charles de Brosses, "les anciens Saxons avoient pour Fétiches de gros arbres touffus" (Brosses 1760, 168). When Columbus found paradise on Haiti, and subsequent voyagers located it in Brazil, they talked enthusiastically of the trees, "the thickest forests, always green and laden with fruits" (Delumeau 1995, 111), well aware that paradise was, as Commerson put it, a theater of vegetation. John Milton described it as "a Silvan Scene, and as the ranks ascend / Shade above shade, a woodie Theatre / Of stateliest View," sealed from the world by an unbroken swathe of foliage, "the verdurous wall of Paradise" (*Paradise Lost* 4.142, 146). When Francesco Colonna invented the island of Cythera in his *Hypnerotomachia Poliphili* (1467), he set its orchards, gardens and copses within "a hedge so thickly leaved one cannot see through it" (Delumeau 1995, 129). Consequently, Bougainville's recognition of Tahiti as Cythera and Eden comprehends the thickness of the foliage as integral to the aboriginal hedonism of the inhabitants. He reported that the landscape of Tahiti is "elevated like an amphitheatre" and that even the steepest parts are clad in green: "We hardly believed our eyes, when we saw a peak covered with trees, up to its solitary summit" (Bougainville 1772b, 217). St. Pierre described his Mauritian paradise as "a verdant amphitheatre" (St. Pierre 1820, 46), a metaphor reemployed by Herman Melville when he arrived in the Marquesas to find "the appearance of a vast natural amphitheatre" whose precipitous sides are "covered with the brightest verdure . . . universal verdure" (Melville 1964, 34, 56, 65). Crusoe's first settlement is contrived as "a thick Grove . . . growing so monstrous thick and strong, that it was indeed perfectly impassable," while his country estate is similarly arranged, with trees planted "that they might spread and grow thick and wild, and make the more agreeable Shade" (Defoe 1972b, 161, 132). On Madagascar, John Avery's pirate commonwealth was similarly constructed: "They made Choice of a place overgrown with a Wood, and situate near a Water; they raised a Rampart or high Ditch around it, so strait and high, that it was impossible to climb into it" (Defoe 1972a, 60). On Tahiti, Fletcher Christian built a fort with the same crude ha-ha—an eighteen-foot ditch facing the beach (Morrison 1935, 57).

Botanic and Elysium gardens conserved the canopy of Eden, "whose hairie sides / With thicket overgrown, grottesque and wilde, / Access deni'd" (*Paradise Lost* 4.136), saving a portion of paradise from the deforestation that inevitably accompanied landing and settling on islands in the Caribbean and the Pacific. The very density of the plantation was an appeal to a past impossible to recover, and of a shore "hérissés de forêts [qui] plaît par sa vigueur sauvage et ses sites pittoresque" (Lemontey 1792, 20). This explains why islands were favorite locations for exotic botanic gardens; why artificial islands in the ponds of Elysium gardens such as those at Méréville and Stowe were surrounded by the enclosed and dense vegetation suggestive both of savage wildernesses and a botanist's care; and why the Elysian Fields at Stowe and the Exotic Ground at Kew stood themselves as islands of denser vegetation within the peeled prospective vistas of landscape gardens.

The connection between landscape gardens, paradises, and desert islands was carefully reviewed by Horace Walpole in his essay *On Modern Gardening*. He begins by celebrating the enclosed and miniature gardens that have always been a source of rapture, such as the garden of Alcinous in the *Odyssey* or Pliny's retreat, consisting of no more than "a small orchard and vineyard, with some beds of herbs and two fountains . . . enclosed within a quickset hedge" (Walpole 1931, 4). Their modest scale stands in contrast with the vast formality of Versailles, which Frenchmen are foolish enough to imagine would have been the plan of Eden (3). In approaching the larger modern gardens of Stourhead and Hagley, Walpole keeps paradise well to the fore, showing that their best effects are derived from Milton's description of Eden, which offers "a warmer and more just picture of the present style than Claud Lorrain could have painted" (24). He particularly admires the relation of thicket to water as a prime source of their "simple enchantment" (43). At Stourhead the river, and at Hagley the fountain, are glimpsed within the sort of dense boscage described by Milton and Commerson as "a woodie Theatre." Walpole credits William Kent and his invention of the ha-ha with the mingled appearance of an inside-outside world, which invites the spectator, in imitation of Kent, to leap the fence and find all nature is a garden, thus "allowing the rudest waste to add its foil to the richest theatre" (47). In maintaining a heightened sense of this equivocal boundary, Walpole is faithful to the Miltonic model of green enclosures bounded by rugged woodland, of which Hagley is, in his opinion, the very picture (24). Any garden arranged on Alcinous's or Milton's model provides "a scene of delights more picturesque than the landscapes of Tinian or Juan Fernandez" (4).

In making this slighting reference to the Pacific Islands, Walpole has two issues in mind. The first is his disapproval of their prominence in the descriptions and illustrations of Anson's voyage, an enterprise for which he had scant respect.[1] Second, he is concerned to quell the enthusiasm aroused on their behalf among devotees of landscape, especially Rousseau in *Julie, ou la nouvelle Héloise* (1761), where St. Preux's journey to Julie and Wolmar's house at Clarens is an occasion of marrying the aesthetics of the Elysium garden to the aboriginal wildness specifically of Tinian and Juan Fernandez. It was evidently a popular parallel in the gardening world. Joseph Heely, for example, said that the forest glades of Pope's walk at Hagley resembled "the much-famed ones of Tinian" (Heely 1777, 102). When Smollett's friend Captain Robert Mann saw the view from the Cameron house at Loch Lomond, he cried out, "Juan Fernandez, by God" (Smollett 1993, 257). In neither direction is Walpole's stricture just, since Richard Walter's description of Juan Fernandez is very like Walpole's of Hagley in its enthusiastic recognition of the correspondence between the unrivaled excellence of a real place and Milton's imagined Eden. As for Rousseau, he had a very just notion of conservation, offering a critique of landscape gardens that shared the principles upon which Walpole himself admired the ha-ha and depreciated the landscapes of painter Claude Lorraine, who was assumed to have provided the model for many English gardens of the prospective type.

In their rapture at reaching land, swooning with scurvy and aching for fresh water and greenery, the sailors of Anson's flagship entered paradise. As he describes their making land, Walter sounds like Satan taking his first view of Eden: "Some particular spots occurred in these valleys, where the shade and fragrance of the contiguous woods, the loftiness of the overhanging rocks, and the transparency and frequent falls of the neighbouring streams, presented scenes of such elegance and dignity, as

---

1 In July 1744, the treasure that Anson had taken from the Acapulco galleon *Nuestra Senora de Cabodonga*, calculated by Walter at almost half a million pounds' worth, was paraded through the streets of London as a show of exotic marvels and national power. Walpole wrote to Charles Hanbury Williams, "The town has been entertained this week with Anson's Acquapulca triumph: I saw it in profile from my window: and a trumpery sight it was" (Walpole 1937–83, 30:53). When he set about to read the narrative of the voyage, he found it such an improbable romance that he referred to Anson afterwards as "Admiral Almanzor" and "Admiral Amadis" (35:284, 37:550), and declared it was as true as the stories told by "his predecessor Gulliver" (9:55).

would with difficulty be rivalled in any other part of the globe" (Walter 1776, 120). As for the landscape of the temporary settlement on the island, Walter presents a glade within a theater of vegetation equal to the best effects of Stowe and Hagley:

> The piece of ground he chose was a small lawn, that lay on a little ascent, at the distance of about half a mile from the sea. In the front of his tent there was a large avenue cut through the woods to the sea-side, which sloping to the water with a gentle descent, opened a prospect of the bay and the ships at anchor. This lawn was screened behind by a tall wood of myrtle sweeping round it, in the form of a theatre, the slope on which the wood stood rising with a much sharper ascent than the lawn itself; though not so much, but that the hills and precipices within land towered up considerably above the tops of the trees, and added to the grandeur of the view. There were, besides, two streams of crystal water, which ran on the right and left of the tent, within a hundred yards distance, and were shaded by the trees which skirted the lawn on either side, and compleated the symmetry of the whole. (Ibid.)

Joseph Heely beholds at Hagley a scene composed of exactly the same textures as these witnessed by Walter on Juan Fernandez: "a lawn, ample as fair, sweeping in a bold descent from the foot and forming itself into an easy level below, embosomed and grouped by the lovelist trees that ever graced the turf," and likewise he is moved to identify it as paradisal by quoting from Milton (Heely 1777, 102). On the milder and more pastoral island of Tinian, the relation of lawn to woodland is more balanced, and the landscape features more strongly marked, but the paradisal model is still clearly evident, when Walter says the following:

> For the prospect of the country did by no means resemble that of an uninhabited and uncultivated place; but had much more the air of a magnificent plantation, where large lawns and stately woods had been laid out together with great skill, and where the whole had been so artfully combined, and so judiciously adapted to the slopes of the hills, and the inequalities of the ground, as to produce a most striking effect, and to do honour to the invention of the contriver. . . . We were going to take possession of this little paradise. (Walter 1776, 306)

Piercy Brett's illustrations of Walter's text do justice to the blend of landscape and wilderness he is admiring (figs. 11 and 12). The first adjusts the natural wildness of the hinterland to the demands of the civil spectator in the foreground, much as Walter accommodates his description of

FIGURE 11 Piercy Brett, "A View of the Commodores Tent at the Island of Juan Fernandes." Engraving, 1748. From Richard Walter, *A Voyage round the World* . . . (London: W. Bowyer, 1776). By permission of Princeton University Library.

FIGURE 12 Piercy Brett, "A View of the Watering Place at Tenian." Engraving, 1748. From Richard Walter, *A Voyage round the World . . .* (London: W. Bowyer, 1776). By permission of Princeton University Library.

the subtleties of the island to Milton's woodie Theatre, and could easily bear a legend from *Paradise Lost:*

Betwixt them Lawns, or level Downs, and Flocks
Grasing the tender herb, were interpos'd,
Or palmie hilloc, or the flourie lap
Of some irriguous Valley spread her store. (4.247ff.)

The second emphasizes the approach of nature to art, with the breadfruit and the coconut palms framing the view down the colonnade. And just as Milton despairs of an art fit to represent scenes of such surpassing natural beauty ("But rather to tell how, if Art could tell, / How from that Saphire Fount the crisped Brooks, / Rowling on Orient Pearl and sands of Gold, / With mazie error under pendant shades / Ran Nectar" [4.246–50]), providing instead a very mannered summary, so does Walter's despair at giving an adequate idea of it all to the reader introduce a picture as studied and as artful in its way as the "crisped brooks" that roll on orient pearl and sands of gold through Milton's Eden. He describes wood and water so beautifully perplexed they match Walpole's praise of William Kent's best effects, where rude wastes are conjoined with theaters of foliage, and streams are half concealed "by thickets properly interspersed" (Walpole 1931, 47). On Tinian, the hint of a grand design is improved by the remains of its previous population: "square pyramidal pillars . . . five feet square at the base, and about thirteen feet high, and on the top of each of them there is a semi-globe, with the flat surface upwards" (Walter 1776, 311). These remains of a vanished population, illegible as anything but nonspecific signs of absence, are like the tokens of "aboriginal" history at Stowe or the Gothic ruin at Hagley in recalling an immemorial past: "Nothing but the dumb stones," as Melville remarked in a parallel situation in the Marquesas (Melville 1964, 178).

   The enjoyments afforded by these verdant amphitheaters are always destined to change into more solemn moods, or more agitated feelings, once their spectators cross the boundary and penetrate the thick cover. That is the moment, for example, when the satanic prophecy is completed, and death, disease, and disgust supplant the amenities and delights of the terrestrial paradise; when Bougainville, Cook, and their redactors deliver their elegies on the theme of corrupted innocence. But there is often encountered an acute personal crisis in which the experience of being out of the world strikes the former spectator with a terrible sense of loneliness and danger. The melancholy of castaways is the simplest manifestation of this reaction; but it is always more complex when it follows on delight, and voyagers find themselves miserably placed in a landscape they formerly viewed so securely. No one explores this transition more fully than Melville in his *Typee* (1846), where his narrator describes in great detail how the verdurous wall is crossed, and how feelings of paradisal simplicity and joy can change into terror, chiefly arising from the enforced adaptation of his body to local customs, including tattooing and cannibalism. Then his Happy Valley turns into the Savage Island, and his charming friends into fierce cannibals, rather like Crusoe's island, which veers between a dreadful prison and a happy desert in proportion as his self-preservation is threatened or assured. In Walter's narrative, the reaction is not so fierce, but when the *Centurion* is blown from its mooring in a typhoon, and the crew face the likelihood of becoming actors in the woodie Theatre, then their sensations are far from flattering: "Their desponding thoughts could only suggest to them the melancholy prospect of spending the remainder of their days on this island, and bidding adieu for ever to their country, their friends, their families, and all their domestic endearments" (Walter 1776, 321). Their former paradise is measured now in nothing but privations, and being out of the world is not modified by any sense of also being in it until the boat makes its reappearance (fig. 13).

In dialogues resembling Othello's with Desdemona, Rousseau's St. Preux informs Julie that he has been on Anson's expedition, and found paradise at Juan Fernandez, "a desert and delightful island, which afforded an agreeable and lively representation of the primitive beauty of nature . . . an asylum to innocence and persecuted love" (Rousseau [1803] 1989, 2:28 [3:28]). At Tinian, "a second desert island, more unknown, more delightful still than the first," he has fancied how sweet it would be to spend the rest of his days in exile there; but instead he has been caught up in "the attempts of human industry to disengage a civilised being from a solitude where he wants nothing, and plunge him into an abyss of new necessities" (2:29 [3:29]). He appears to be referring to Anson's efforts at Tinian to lengthen the small Spanish barque, the only vessel left to escape in after the loss of the *Centurion*. Human art is best exercised, according to St. Preux, in recreating the conditions of these islands, as Julie has done in her Elysium garden, a disguised orchard so thickly surrounded with trees that as soon as he enters it, St. Preux feels he has dropped from the clouds: "I thought myself in the most wild and solitary place in nature, and I appeared as if I had been the first mortal who had ever penetrated into this desart spot . . . seized with astonishment, and transported at so unexpected a sight, I . . . cried out in an involuntary fit of enthusiasm,

Anson voit revenir son Vaisseau que l'orage avoit jetté bien loin dans l'Ocean Indien.

FIGURE 13 "Anson voit revenir son Vaisseau que l'orage avoit jetté bien loin dans l'Ocean Indien" (Anson sees the return of his ship, which the storm had tossed a long way over the Indian Ocean). Anonymous engraving, 1795. Frontispiece to volume 4 of Jean Pierre Berenger, *Collection de tous les voyages faits autour du monde* (Paris: ch. Fr. Dufart, 1795). By permission of the National Library of Australia.

'O Tinian! O Juan Fernandez! Eloisa, the world's end is at your threshold'" (2:132–33 [3:132–33]). By showing St. Preux that hers is not in fact a botanic garden, for no exotics grow there, and by pointing out that no expense has been incurred to make the natives thrive ("It cost me nothing—How! Nothing!—No, nothing" [2:134]), she invites the enthusiast back across the border he was about to cross, crying to him, "Farewell Tinian! Farewell Juan Fernandez! Farewell all enchantment! In a few minutes you will find your way back from the end of the world" (2:135; see Grove 1995, 231–33; Thacker 1977, 41–47; Spate 1988a, 196). She fetches him back from the marooned condition the *Centurion*'s crew briefly experienced on Tinian, and instead of a hard and fast distinction between nature and art, Julie teaches her former lover to relish a ha-ha; and their subsequent oscillations of mood remain, therefore, within the mutual limits of the well in and the well out. This successful reining in of enthusiasm introduces a discussion of the merits of an Elysium garden compared with a larger prospect. Wolmar says, "The taste for perspective and distant views proceeds from the disposition of men in general, who are never satisfied with the place where they are. . . . Here we have no prospect, and we are very well satisfied without any" (Rousseau [1803] 1989, 2:153). St. Preux agrees, confessing that the garden at Stowe has displeased him by the fatiguing and opulent ornamentation of its large spaces, where "erected ruins, temples, old buildings; and different ages, as well as different places, are collected with more than mortal magnificence" (2:156). All three opt in the end for the shaded and bounded space that alternately opens and shuts a window on the illimitable.

The experience of Anson's crew on Juan Fernandez provoked another fiction, Abbe Coyer's *A Supplement to Anson's Voyage round the World* (1752). In it he explores the allure of artifice, just as Rousseau's studies the allure of pure nature. Coyer uses Walter's narrative to make a distinction between taste and patriotism in order to point the georgic moral that "a Train of ridiculous Absurdities inevitably attend upon false Taste" (Coyer 1752, iv), for arts and sciences are to be cultivated "only as Instruments of public Good" (vi). He picks up the story from the landing when the British, bluff and coarse-grained, start inland for the center of Juan Fernandez, where they discover a wonderland inhabited by slender Francophone connoisseurs who spend their days ravished with delight at a succession of artificial curiosities. Indeed, everything in this country called Frivoland is made for delight, nothing for use. The fruits of the country are mere representations, beautifully colored but inedible; the trees are elegant but too brittle to climb or to shape; the horses are too frail to bear a rider; and the birdsong is so exquisite it is inaudible. The simple Britons have to adjust their needs to a place where "Baubles of every sort, elegant Cabinets and gawdy Equipages" are esteemed, and workmen labor to manufacture "a Hundred little paltry Pieces of Furniture . . . a Thousand worthless Gimcracks, that are the Wear of a Day" (29).

The Comptroller of Fashions, Anson's host, reveals the origin of this frivolity in the Mississippi Scheme, the French version of the South Sea Bubble. "I was at Paris in 1719, when the World was possessed with a Madness of bartering Gold for Paper" (Coyer 1752, 21), he confesses. Having lost everything in the speculation but his passions ("which it was out of my Power to gratify"), he plans to ship a cargo of tinsel goods to Peru. His vessel is blown off course and lands at Juan Fernandez, where the inhabitants, evincing a taste for taste, are soon inducted by the castaways into artificial pleasures of every kind. "What Pains it costs," reflects the Comptroller of Fashions, "to form a Nation" (23), thinking of the effort needed to become exquisite as a people; and the sturdy Anson wrinkles his Gothic brow in disapproval.

Coyer's judgment appears to be the same as Bolingbroke's, namely that the primitive virtue impelling the true Briton has nothing to do with bubbles or false ensigns. Like Julie, he warns against the reveries and voluptuous sensations that completely metamorphose a desert island into a paradise, or a garden into the image of a desert island. Nevertheless, the infatuation of the Frivolians, and their reduction of all experience to a standard of taste, is a fair account of aesthetics of patriot solitude and of arrivals at desert islands, whether it is Bolingbroke presenting the je ne sais quoi of the miraculous patriot king, Cobham perpetually multiplying the Gothic attractions of his garden, Walpole finding the Gothic Temple adorable, or Walter greeting Juan Fernandez as though it were Milton's Eden. Assuming that Coyer had no wish to write an unprovoked satire against his own nation, and was in fact responding to what he perceived as the exaggerated beauties in the account of Anson's landfall, his *Supplement* must have been intended (as Diderot's later) to get the "ocean of fantasy" into perspective. With ironic urbanity he asks the English not to behave like the French, and to take their discourse of aboriginal simplicity seriously as a guide to reason and common sense.

The irony is undermined, however, by the artifice of patriotism itself, which talks of aboriginality without any memory of an origin, makes copies of bad copies, and in a theater of vegetation exhibits a pantomime of pure sensation, or what Milton called "taste after taste upheld with kindliest change" (*Paradise Lost* 5.336). Coyer's worldliness gets stuck in the

artifice of the "country," and like Gulliver in the land of the Houyhnhmns, he is forced to accumulate negative instances of frivolity, modernity, and corruption because the rhetoric of patriotism, always traversing
the boundaries between historical and ideal referents, cannot provide an
unequivocal image of virtue or innocence. No one could ever wish, really,
to become a Spartan or a forest German, just as no one ever wished to become a horse. Every urbane appeal Coyer makes to the world on behalf
of natural virtue carries him back from patriot simplicities to the multifarious extravagances of the Frivolians, just as Gulliver's love of inhuman
virtue causes him obsessively to particularize its opposite. In the end, the
things Coyer locates in the landscape of Juan Fernandez are no different
from the factitious things interspersing the garden walks of Kew, Hagley,
and Stowe, as Walter had already hinted. As these curios are not signs of
virtue or of vice and, strictly speaking, represent nothing, Coyer's satire itself is Gothicized, gathering simulacra for the sake of gathering them, and
evincing the same preoccupation with exquisite sensations as the British
patriots when they turn their minds toward nonentities.

His satire emerges, therefore, as something else—an embarrassment
of contrary particulars, the fruit of his attempt to affirm the value of patriotism by lengthily denying its opposite—until the two extremes meet.
This is the authentic language of patriotism and of the desert island. In
both, a negative presence haunts the view over the ha-ha and across the
limit, a barrier between the "country" and the world that is alternately
elided and magnified. Tacitus praises the Germans for what they do not
possess ("They have no house to inhabit, no land to cultivate, nor any domestic charge or care" [Tacitus 1731, 2:340]), for thus "they have accomplished a thing of infinite difficulty, that to them nothing remains even to
be wished" (2:349). Gonzalo greets his desert island with a list of what it
will not contain, his overture to a theme of privative virtue: "Bourn, bound
of land, tilth, vineyard, none; / No use of metal, corn, or wine, or oil" (*The
Tempest* 2.1.150–51). He calls it executing things by contraries, a technique
again employed (with a slightly different inflection) in the outline of paradise on Crusoe's island: "A Place, where as I had no Society, which was
my Affliction on one Hand, so I found no ravenous Beast, no furious
Wolves or Tygers to threaten my Life, no venomous Creatures or poi-
sonous, which I might feed on to my Hurt, no Savages to murder and devour me" (Defoe 1972b, 132).

Contraries can be turned against the state of nature ("In such condition, there is no place for Industry, because the fruit thereof is uncertain:
and consequently no Culture of the Earth; no Navigation, nor use of the

commodities that may be imported by Sea; no commodious Building; no Instruments of Money . . . no Knowledge of the Face of the Earth; no Account of Time, no Arts, no Letters; no Society" [Hobbes, 1968: 186]), or against civil society when the free spirit prefers the condition of having "no Necessity for Dissimulation . . . or feign'd Affection to his Mortal Enemies; no Wife in a Foreign Interest, no Danger to apprehend from his Children; no Plots to unravel, no Poison to fear, no popular Statesman at Home or cunning Courts abroad to manage; no seeming Patriots to bribe, no insatiable Favourite to gratify . . . no divided Nation to please, or fickle Mob to humour" (Mandeville 1924, 1:316). Contraries can reveal a terrible poverty ("There were no Trees, Shrubs, or Grass to be seen . . . I saw there was no Harbour here . . . a place where there was no shelter . . . we searched for Water, but could find none, nor any Houses, nor People, for they were all gone" [Dampier 1703, 118–44]); or a noble austerity ("destitute of arms, of horses, and of homes" [Tacitus 1731, 2:349]). In the valley of the Typee, Tommo inventories, like Gulliver, the wealth of its wants: "There were no foreclosures of mortgages, no protested notes, no bills payable, no debts of honour in Typee; no unreasonable tailors and shoemakers . . . no duns of any description . . . no poor relations . . . no destitute widows, starving on the cold charities of the world; no beggars; no debtors' prisons; no proud and hardhearted Nabobs in Typee" (Melville 1964, 146).

I labor the point because this figure of speech, called litotes, organizes all encounters with utopia and paradise. "How tenuous," Michael McKeon has observed, "must be that secret sanctuary of truth, distinct both from romance and from too confident a historicity, which is defined by the metacritical act of double negation" (McKeon 1987, 110, 118). The secret walled sanctuary has been identified by Stephen Greenblatt, with help from Elizabeth McCutcheon, as utopia, the classic occasion for that affirmation of a thing by stating the negative of its opposite—such as the "Welcome!" mat that reads "Not Unwelcome." (Greenblatt 1980, 23). Thus in Thomas More's *Utopia*, the food is not meager, the buildings are not mean, the clothes of the inhabitants are not unbecoming (McCutcheon 1977, 266). In *Paradise Lost*, Satan, the first voyager to find a new world, gazes at a landscape whose excellence is comparable with nothing that is known, and can be expressed only as a tiered litotes:

Not that fair field
Of Enna, where Proserpin gathring flours
Herself a fairer Floure by gloomie Dis

Was gatherd, which cost Ceres all that pain
To seek her through the World; nor that sweet Grove
Of Daphne by Orontes, and the inspir'd
Castalian Spring, might with this Paradise
Of Eden strive; nor that Nyseian Ile
Girt with the River Triton . . .
Nor where Abassin Kings thir issue Guard,
Mount Amora. (4.268–80)

Whether the sanctuary is natural or artificial, the negative never quite succeeds in sealing the barrier; so that litotes operates like the ha-ha to encourage traffic across a border defined on the one side by the world at large, and on the other by what is not the world, the "country" of contraries. Tacitus's Germans, therefore, are noble in proportion as they lack things of the world, while Dampier's aboriginals are disgraceful in the same degree. Crusoe can never quite make up his mind whether wanting nothing is a good thing or a bad. Gonzalo's and Coyer's island paradises are said to be attractive on account of what they lack; and here is Pedro Fernandez de Quirós talking of his New Jerusalem in a sprawling litotes that supplies all wants with the expectation of civilized arts:

I am able to say, that a land more delightful, healthy and fertile; a site better supplied with quarries, timber, clay for tiles, bricks for founding a great city by the sea, with a port and a good river on a plain, with level lands near the hills, ridges and ravines; nor better adapted to raise plants and all that Europe and the Indies produce, could not be found. No port could be found more agreeable, nor better supplied with all necessaries, without any drawbacks; nor with such advantages for dockyards . . . nor with forests more abundant in suitable timber good for futtock timbers, houses, compass timbers, beams, planks, masts and yards. Nor is there any land that could sustain so many strangers so pleasantly . . . I have never seen, anywhere I have ever been, nor have heard of such advantages. (Quirós 1904, 271)

[Puedo decir con razon que tierra mas apacible, sana y fertil de sos frutos; ni sitio de mayor aparejo de canteras, maderos, y barro para teja, y ladrillo para fundarse una muy grande ciudad, junto al mar y a puerto y a un bien rio en un llano con llanas cerca de sierras, lomas y quebradas; ni de mayor aparejo para criar, plantar y sembrar de todo cuanto produce Europa y las Indias juzgado por la disposicion de lo dicho; ni de puerto

mas alegre ni mas airoso con todos los requisitos menesterosos para serlo,
sin de presente con ocersele contrarios; ni de tantos astilleros, fondo a
pique o de menos para fabrica de grande suma de naos do todos portes;
ni de monte mas abundante, de muy trabadas maderas, buenas para li-
gazones, curvas, busardas, forcajes, altos, gruesos y derechos arboles para
tablas y todos mas tiles y vergas; ni tierra que por si sola pueda luego sus-
tentar a tantas gentes extranjeras y tan regaladamente si bien se considera
lo excrito; ni que tenga lo que esta tiene tan junto, tan a la mano y a vista
de su puerto, y cerca siete islas que bojean dosa en tas legnas al parecer de
las mismas calidades, y que tenga tantas tan buenas snales para ser bus-
cado y hallada sin bajios ne tropiezos, y casi a medio camino y otros ter-
cios islas conocidas con gente y puertos adonde se puede hacer escala,
no la he visto en todo cuanto he andado ni he tenido tal noticia. (Quirós
1876, 341)]

He uses the same contraries as Gulliver in order to reach exactly the opposite point of view. Similarly, in his tour through the Highlands, Johnson organizes a series of litotic judgments around copious negative cata-
logs of circumstances "of no elegant recital." Thus "the inhabitants were
for a long time perhaps not unhappy" because "that which is not best may
be yet very far from bad' (Johnson 1984, 43, 81, 49).

Litotes is provoked by perfect and radically imperfect spaces alike, and
as well as breaching the divisions between what is and what is not acceptable, it sustains a mood that is correspondingly mixed. The pleasures, ec-
stasies, enthusiasms, and reveries enjoyed in viewing rural solitudes or
desert islands are never unambiguous. Undelighted, Satan eyes a scene of
all delight; and rather crossly, Coyer's Anson studies the exquisite superfluities of Frivoland. Between them, Dampier and Tacitus explore the
extremes of emotion caused by the sight of abject poverty, and Robinson
Crusoe experiences the pains and pleasures of wanting nothing. When
privation is next door to warmth and food, Johnson's imagination is impressed with "a delightful contrariety of images" (Johnson 1984, 59). In
1610, a visitor to Virginia wrote of these mixed feelings in a paradisal situation, and warns his reader not to slight their contrary appearances as
lies: "If any man shall accuse these reports of partial falsehood, supposing
them to be but Utopian, and legendary fables, because he cannot conceive
that plentie and famine, a temperate climate and distempered bodies, fe-
licities and miseries, can be reconciled together, let him now reade with
judgment, but let him not judge before he hath read" (Marx 1964, 34).
Only within the shadow of a utopian "full poor cell" is it possible to taste

the promise implicit in despair, as when Antonio tells Sebastian in *The Tempest*,

O, out of that no hope
What great hope have you! No hope that way is
Another way so high a hope that even
Ambition cannot pierce a wink beyond. (2.1.237–40)

When St. Preux enters Julie's Elysium garden, confounding its delightful thickets with his memories of Edenic landfalls on Juan Fernandez and Tinian, his wonder is oddly blended with unease when his ex-lover tells him, "It cost me nothing—How! Nothing!—No, nothing" (Rousseau [1803] 1989, 3:134). The word chimes with his entry into an Eden that he has already left. Similarly, Thomson, replete with the delights of summer, could find himself going through a barrier and footing it paradoxically "to the Brink of dreary *Nothing*" (Thomson 1981, 76 [2:335]). Staring at the double zero of two druidic circles, one enclosing the other, Johnson felt none of the secure expansion of fancy that funerary memorials usually provoked in him on his travels in the North; instead, the evils of dereliction rushed upon him: "It is nothing," he shouted at Boswell (Johnson 1984, 243).

With this in mind, I want briefly to consider Cook's arrival at Dusky Bay as exemplary of the views, rhetoric, and feelings of patriots in paradise. When he paused there, punctuating his two great reconnaissances of the Antarctic, Cook's crew were suffering from scurvy, and his stay in Dusky Bay was lengthened to give his sailors a good chance recovery (Holmes 1984, 67n. 1; Watt 1979, 130). Richard Pickersgill gives a picture of a scurvied crew straining to catch a glimpse of land that closely resembles Walter's, especially in terms of the idealization of the view: "Every body that was able to crawl on the masts and yards got up to satisfy their longing senses of a sight almost forgot, whilst those who were not able, importuned the others as they came down for a description. . . . What a charming sight was this sound to us; what a variety of beautifull landskips did it afford" (Pickersgill 1984, 67–68). He was particularly charmed with the mooring that was to be named after him, "one of the most inchanting little Harbours I ever saw, it was surrounded with high Lands intirely cover'd with tall shady trees like an amphitheatre; and the sweet swelling Notes of a number of Birds made the finest Harmony" (68). His harbor was made the subject of one of William Hodges's finest *plein air* oils, in which a single figure trudges over a gangplank made by a fallen tree, moving from the amphitheater of a primeval forest to the

FIGURE 14   William Hodges, *Pickersgill Harbour, Dusky Bay.* Oil painting, 1773.
© National Maritime Museum, London, Admiralty House Collection.

domestic comfort of the *Resolution,* whose spars and gunwale form the right-hand border of the composition (fig. 14). It is a maritime ha-ha joining the nonworld of a woodie Theatre to the world of the ship, linking savagery to all the advantages of civilization. Every impression of importance at Dusky Bay will traverse these two points.

Cook's first impression of the bay is expressed in a litotes, as if anticipating a terrestrial paradise: "The shores and Woods we found not destitute of wild fowl, so that we expected to injoy with ease what in our situation might be call'd the luxuries of life" (Cook 1961, 112). A little later he was more negative, as if the natural abundance had failed to flatter his sense of being out of the world. Forlornly, he said that it "exhibits to our view nothing but woods and barren craggy precipices, no meadows or Lawns are to be seen nor plains or flatt land of any extent" (133). During the interval, he made the crossing between the world and the country, briefly transforming the wilderness into an estate, and organized sporting expeditions with such enthusiasm that his exploration of the region reads like a field diary. It includes the adventure of Goose Cove, an episode in an antipodal *Swallows and Amazons* in which the sportsmen's boat gets adrift, and they make a fire, cook some fish, and "[lay] down to sleep having a stoney beach of a bed and the canopy of Heaven for a covering" (120). These are the coordinates of being well in and well out of the world. First Cook warms to the plenty of the cove, a place he can recognize and expatiate over, like Pope and Bolingbroke in the fields of Dawley, only to be repelled in turn by its wildness and emptiness, finding it difficult to describe, "as it is somewhat singular" (133).

Of his companions, William Wales was the most confident in assimilating the sight of this untouched shore to the model of patriot landscapes. Although eager to declare that "our pleasures were not all merely Ideal," Wales was nevertheless convinced that Cascade Cove is "one of Nature's most romantic Scenes"; to prove it, he quoted at it lines from Summer in Thomson's *Seasons,* beginning,

> Smooth to the shelving brink a copious flood
> Rolls fair and placid; where, collected all
> In one impetuous torrent, down the steep
> It thundering shoots . . . (Thomson 1981, 88; Wales 1961, 782)

Thomson first conceived this scene of the cascade as an allegory of human uncertainty, where the plunge of the water stands for the sudden misfortune that hurls one "down the Hill of Life" (Thomson 1981, 89n). In turning it into pure description, he magnifies the effect of the cascade at Hagley Park, described in Spring:

> There along the Dale,
> With Woods o'erhung, and shag'd with mossy Rocks
> Whence on each hand the gushing Waters play,
> And down the rough Cascade white-dashing fall,
> Or gleam in lengthen'd Vista through the Trees,
> You silent steal. (46)

By establishing the link between a woodie Theatre interspersed with waterfalls and the sublime version of a great English Elysium garden, Wales was rising to the challenge of Walter's elegant picture of Juan Fernandez—a challenge distinctly recognized by the Forsters. George reported at Dusky Bay, "The view of the rude sceneries in the style of Rosa, of antedeluvian forests which cloath'd the rock, and of numerous rills of water, which everywhere rolled down the steep declivity, altogether conspired to complete our joy," only to add, "Such are the general ideas of travellers and voyagers long exhausted by distresses; and with such warmth of imagination they have viewed the rude cliffs of Juan Fernandez, and the impenetrable forests of Tinian" (Forster 1777, 1:124). The joy of an in-world/out-world experience is vitiated by the thought that it is an illusion caused by stress and disease, and by the fear that rude cliffs and impenetrable forests are not really and truly assimilable to a civilized sensibility. Doubtless this uncertainty was aggravated in Johann Reinhold's case by his attack of scurvy, which severely curtailed his patriotic reflections on the mission he had joined. What ought to have been a perfect fit of public spirit within the enclosure of virgin forest is tainted for both father and son by the suspicion that theirs is a morbid and unoriginal enthusiasm. Perhaps Wales was being troubled by similar reservations when underneath his quotation he added, "I dare not write Thomson at the bottom" (Wales 1961, 783). Cook found the cascade too shocking to describe, and was grateful that Hodges was able in a picture to present "at one view a better description than I can give" (Cook 1961, 119).

Hodges produced two images of the cascade. The first is a long prospect up the reach, where the waterfall is half masked by the shrubs and outcrops on the left of the picture *(View in Dusky Bay)*; the second is much more enclosed, divided by a sheet of foaming water, fringed by rugged rocks and wild vegetation, and overlooked by four Maori figures *(Waterfall in Dusky Bay* [fig. 15]). The contrast between these earlier and later versions of Cascade Cove is owing to a shift from a prospective view to a more constricted one, and a sharper sense of its savagery. In the second picture, Hodges represents a shocking collision of water and rock: "huge heaps of stones lie at the foot of this Cascade which have been brought by the force of the Stream from adjacent mountains" (Cook 1961, 119). In this the more sublime of Hodges's two pictures of the cascade, absence and emptiness are suggested by the vast area of the canvas covered with scumbled white paint, a sheer surface matching the effect of the singular force of the water: "lessening down / From infinite perfection to the brink / Of dreary nothing" (Thomson 1981, 76).

Sick of the prisonlike life aboard the ship, Anders Sparrman started out, like his colleagues, being charmed by "little waterfalls and brooks, peeping forth here and there . . . crystal and shining silver . . . a most lovely effect" (Sparrman 1944, 43). He admired the effect of the woodie Theatre: a "dense covering of thickets and trees, foliage and pine needles, in such

FIGURE 15   William Hodges, *Waterfall in Dusky Bay*. Oil painting, 1775. © National Maritime Museum, London, Admiralty House Collection.

profusion that not the smallest patch was left for further adornment by green grass and plants" (43–44). In these descriptions of the primeval and exotic quality of the desert shore of New Zealand, he makes the same effort as Wales and the Forsters to assimilate it to the aesthetics of the Elysium garden. But the mood of pleasurable wonder will not last. The primeval forest and the wild stream prompt an unpleasantly ambivalent sense of how civilization and Eden relate to each other. This unease deepens in the course of their transactions with the Maori family at the scene. After being given an axe, the man indicates by gestures that he will use it to attack his enemies, and Sparrman is led to a series of reflections, beginning with the savage refusal of productive labor ("a toilsome and fruitless clearance of the forest"), partnered by "a deep-seated and filthy taste for bloodshed and the eating of human flesh" (46, 49). He goes on to speculate that the axe's head might have been manufactured from Swedish steel, like that which tipped the weapons of the Vikings; and indeed, "I recognised [in Maori] many of the methods of war and murder of our Gothic Viking forefathers" (49). Then he is provoked to wonder how often in modern Europe cannibalism has occurred, and he recalls that in the town of Gotha, nominally the fount and origin of everything nobly Gothic, a notorious case was discovered (50). The development from ancient savageries to modern virtue makes little sense to Sparrman other than as a history of necessary repression. He is helped toward this conclusion by the tumult of his own feelings during the duck shooting in Dusky Bay. He reports that while holding some wounded birds in his hands, he enjoyed a moment of Gothic lust: "The blood from these warm birds which were dying in my hands, running over my fingers, excited me to a degree I had never previously experienced. . . . This filled me with amazement, but the next moment I felt frightened' (49).

Johann Reinhold Forster expected to write the official history of this voyage, which explains his attuning its episodes to the language and categories of patriotism. But his suspicion that an appreciation of woodie Theatres is a factitious blend of diseased sensations and Richard Walter's prose was deepened when the "prodigious intricacy of various climbers, briars, shrubs and ferns" impeded their plan to clear ground for an observatory. The inconvenient lushness of the temperate rainforest served only "to lower the great idea which our people had conceived of this country" (Forster 1777, 1:127). Like William Wordsworth in the Alps, George talked of woods decaying, never to be decayed, of "young trees, or parasitic plants, ferns, and mosses sprout[ing] out of the rich mould which [the] old timber had been reduced by length of time," a cycle that fatigued him with its purposelessness and seemed typical of this "original chaotic state" (Forster 1772–75, 1:128, 180). The dense cover lost its paradisal aura when it became expressive of nothing but its own anarchic vitality. Johnson felt the same disgust when he found virgin cover near Loch Lomond, the same spot identified by Captain Mann as a Caledonian Juan Fernandez. Instead of the "soft lawns and shady thickets" he had expected, it disclosed "nothing more than an uncultivated ruggedness" (Johnson 1984, 145).

Cook's men started clearing the forest, and conservation was no longer a priority. The sound of axes betokened for the elder Forster the imminent addition of those lawns Cook missed, together with the benefits of civilization promised in de Quirós's vision of the New Jerusalem: "In a word, all around us we perceived the rise of arts, and the dawn of science, in a country which had hitherto lain plunged in one long night of ignorance and barbarism!" (Forster 1777, 1:179; see Glacken 1967, 702–74). It is a vision of what paradise—a commodious emptiness—is capable of sustaining when the multifarious advantages of industry penetrate it; but the corrupting of primitive environments with art—specifically the destruction of forests by axes—is of course what Tacitus, Gonzalo, St. Preux, and Coyer deplore, because it opens up "an abyss of new necessities" (Rousseau [1803] 1989, 2:29 [3:29]). One kind of privation leads to another. Although Johnson explained the original destruction of forests everywhere as "the first effect of plenitude," the outcome was a waste and a vacuity that terrified him (Johnson 1984, 90, 125). Cook and his associates tasted the full flavor of this contradiction at Dusky Bay.

The Forsters tried to insert a mean between the extremes of unimproved nature and the polite arts in the shape of the four Maori depicted by Hodges. As Hodges arranges these savage figures in various poses reminiscent of Greek models (Smith and Joppien 1985, 2:29), so the Forsters supply a pedigree of their nobility, drawn from authorities such as Strabo and Tacitus, designed to exhibit their aboriginal virtue (Glacken 1967, 702–3; Thomas 1997, 81). By fashioning their appearance in the landscape of Dusky Bay in a manner reminiscent of Claude or Salvator, Forster means the Maori in effect to function like the Gothic monuments at Stowe. They are arranged as points of transition between the aboriginal excellence of the Elysian fields and a prospect of civil society. Their patriot virtues are signaled by references to their "savage valour" and by a scene of sentimental translation, which the elder Forster recalled as being unintelligible, and therefore "at least as edifying as great many which are usual in the politer circles of civilized nations, & which here at least passed with a great deal more sincerity & cordiality on both sides" (Forster 1982, 2:249). But there are a number of distressing impediments to this smooth junction between savagery and civilization. Shortly after this sympathetic exchange, the man and his two female companions started fighting with each other (2:258); the next day, the man, having been given a hatchet with which to accomplish some forest clearing, made it clear he meant to use it as a weapon of war. "Thus we see," said Johann Reinhold—drawing a moral more like St. Preux's on the corruption of invented necessities than the one he had planned—"that the natural depravity of mankind immediately applies things, which are intended for relieving him from labour & tedious toils, to wicked purposes, & makes the instruments invented for shortning labour, the tools of cruelty & bloodshed" (2:262).

In this respect, there is not much difference between the savage and the citizen, for after witnessing the staged scene of cannibalism on the deck of the *Resolution* in Queen Charlotte Sound some weeks later, Forster adduced it as proof of the meretricious effects of "all our artificial Education, our boasted civilisation, our parade of humanity & social virtues" (Forster 1982, 3:426). Indeed, George, following Sparrman's line of thought, linked Maori cannibalism to European, recalling a case in Hesse in 1772 of a famished herdsman who lived off the flesh of young boys, a food he found most delicious. His last view of Dusky Bay makes the same point: namely, that traces of improvement render the triumph of savagery even more atrocious ("the shoots of the surrounding weeds will shortly stifle every salutary and useful plant" [Forster 1777, 1:180]). He reverses out of a woodie Theatre from which he has already been expelled.

The rhetorical figure applicable to these in-and-out maneuvers over the ha-ha that joins and divides the "world" and the woodie Theatre is, I have suggested, litotes. It makes its first appearance at Dusky Bay in Cook's mild expectation of enjoyment in a place "not destitute of wild fowl" (Cook 1961, 112). In a similar mood, reflecting on the abundance of fish, William Wales remarked, "Nor was the plenty greater than the variety . . . but there are not wanting Several Sorts that are well known" (787). He builds a bridge between the familiar and the strange again with litotes when he talks of the birds, who have made a ha-ha out of their weapons. "It was not uncommon for them to perch on the barrel of the Gun in our hands, already loaded for their destruction" (787). In his meeting with the first Maori at Dusky Bay, however, Wales's constitutional difficulty with natives and gender comes to the fore, contorting the figure he applied to the two women: "Their features [were] not disagreeable nor in the least masculine; but one of them was rendered barely not frightfull by a large

Wen which grew on her left Cheek" (779–80). J. R. Forster agreed that
the other girl "looked not disagreeable" (Forster 1982, 2:248); and, like de
Quirós viewing the improvable outlines of Vanuatu, he summed up the
utopian transformation of the camp in a litotes: "The polite arts had not
disdained to live on this solitary spot" (2:265). Of the Maori in Queen
Charlotte Sound, his son observed, "Their black eyes [were] . . . not
without expression; the whole upper part of their figure was not dispro-
portionate, and their assemblage of features not absolutely forbidding"
(Forster 1777, 1:211). But when this qualified recognition of humanity is
exposed to savagery that in turn reflects the savagery of Europeans, as in
the feast of human flesh prepared by Cook for the natives, litotes marks
the transition. He said of his colleagues: "Some there were who . . . did
not seem greatly disinclined to feast with them" (1:513).

Nicholas Thomas has said that the Forsters' encounters in Dusky Bay
are remarkable for the degree to which "what was problematic tended to
be paraded rather than disavowed" (Thomas 1997, 80; see Brunt 1997, 281).
The same can be said of Sparrman's, Wales's, and Cook's. Like Pitt, they
explore and elaborate the contradictions of their situation. They spot
what is missing, and imagine how to supply it; and this causes them intense pleasure followed by considerable dismay. It doesn't matter whether
the want of nothing is being blamed or praised, for nothing returns, like
the sheer band of white paint on Hodges's painting, to haunt their bliss.
Litotes is the rhetorical, and the ha-ha the topographical expression of
such an equivocal relation to the world.

There have been two attempts to recover a sense of Cook's original excitement at Dusky Bay. The most recent revisiting of the site tried to restore the view to what it was before Hodges sketched and painted it, to
locate the encompassing "savage" or aboriginal landscape that Cook's
landing and subsequent spectatorship altered, by turning the point of
view inside out and restoring the arena of the bay to the Maori viewpoint
by the cascade (Adams and Thomas 1999, 56). But the enterprise was
ambushed by the history of the place: there is even a horizontal tree in
Pickersgill Harbor. Thomas says wryly, "The site that is so manifestly historic itself bears that history's legacy in exhibiting no view" (20)—a sight-
less site. The earlier restoration effort was a simpler project, but introduced appropriately through the prism of passionate recollection: "For
me so much is agonisingly nostalgic. One will never forget the scenery,
the wilderness, the birds, the crocodile-jawed sandflies" (Begg 1968, 8).
Each enterprise aimed to remove what civil history has made of the original, and to affirm its opposite as something wild and strange. Each was

obliged, therefore, to function like Wales's quotation of Thomson or the Forsters' idealization of cleared ground, by summarizing a scene radically exorbitant to, or deficient in, precisely those virtues its delineation was supposed to celebrate. The introduction to the 1968 edition of *Dusky Bay* identifies this problem when it cites one of the latter-day explorers of the Sound, David Cowan, who referred to the passage over the mountains as "quite a hairy trip." "A charming example of Kiwi meiosis," says the author of the introduction, giving litotes its posh title—and the author himself is titled too, being none other than Viscount Cobham, descendant of the first Viscount Cobham, who tried to locate the principle of civilization in a fair majestic paradise. What is more, his introduction is dated from Hagley Park, the first of the great English landscape gardens to include a Gothic ruin, commencing a long tradition of dialogues conducted between those well in and those well out of the world.

8

Starlings and Parrots;
Keate and Sympathy

We have seen that the native never ceases to dream of putting himself in the place of
the settler—not of becoming the settler but of substituting himself for the settler.
—Frantz Fanon, *The Wretched of the Earth*

"I have delivered my soul into your hands for ever; I breathe with your breath, I see with
your eyes, I think with your mind, and I take you into my heart for ever."

"You thief!" shouted the exasperated Almayer.
Joseph Conrad, *Almayer's Folly*

The histories of sympathy and of navigation are closely entwined. The
more spectacular perils of seafaring provide readers at home with a respite
from the harsh curiosity and sheer incredulity with which they customar-
ily feel obliged to regard the improbable stories of mariners. Distress at
sea is an opportunity to enter compassionately into the spirit of an un-
speakable event, and to take a holiday from disbelief. Reviewing the catalogue of tempests and shipwrecks in his volumes, David Henry demands,
"What heart is so callous, as not to sympathize?" (Henry 1774, 1:vii). "Yes!
All his cares thy sympathy shall know / And prove a kind companion in
his woe," promises William Falconer in *The Shipwreck* (Falconer 1808, 24).
In *The Task*, William Cowper travels along with the mariner, that he
might "with a kindred heart / Suffer his woes and share in his escapes"
(Cowper 1785, 4:114–49). In *The Botanic Garden*, Erasmus Darwin alle-
gorizes this relationship by personifying sympathy as a figure on a rock,
weeping over the general wreck of human hopes:

So should young SYMPATHY, in female form,
Climb the tall rock, spectatress of the storm:

Life's sinking wrecks with secret sighs deplore,
And bleed for other's woes, Herself on shore. (Darwin [1791] 1973, 3:441)

In his narrative of the wreck of the *Wager,* an event not prolific in edifying moments, James Burney nevertheless pauses to recommend it to his reader as worthy of sympathy: "This picture of strenuous unavailing endeavours presents something heroic, and awakens a deep sentiment of sympathy and respect for their distress" (Burney 1803–16, 5:133). The mariner lost overboard when George Anson's *Centurion* rounded Cape Horn provides Cowper with a mirror of his own despair in his poem *The Castaway* (1799). St. Preux's memories of Juan Fernandez and Tinian in Rousseau's *La nouvelle Héloise* (1761) give the sentimental novel a foothold in Anson's voyage, according to O. H. K. Spate, who notes also that the appearances of *A Sentimental Journey* (1768) and *The Man of Feeling* (1771) coincide with the beginning and end of James Cook's first voyage (Spate 1988a, 16). Once the explorers of the South Seas became heroic public figures—and, with the deaths of Cook, Marion du Fresne, and Jean-Francois de Galaup, Comte de La Perouse, martyrs to the rigors of their calling—sympathy for sailors became more than pity for the forlorn and desperate, but something like a ceremonious patriotic act, proof of "The Patriot Throb that beats, the Tear that flows / For others' Welfare, and for other's Woes" (Savage 1962, 230). "In deep accordance to a Nation's woe," Anna Seward takes up the posture of Darwin's Sympathy to sing the death of Cook, shedding "the soft drops of pity's holy dew" for a hero who himself never stinted a tear for the distresses of others (Seward 1810, 2:33, 37). He attracts similar testimonies from Hannah More and Helen Maria Williams, who mourn the loss of his global goodwill: "Thy bless'd philanthropy! thy social hands, / Had linked dissevered worlds in brothers' hands" (More 1853, 5:351).

In their encounters with native peoples, sailors had their own opportunity to join in sympathetic exchanges. The cycle of mock-epic Obereah poems representing the Tahitian noblewoman, Purea, as Dido forsaken by her faithless Aeneas, alias Joseph Banks, commences with her tearful farewell to Samuel Wallis's ship, the *Dolphin,* two years before Banks's arrival. That event was recorded by John Hawkesworth as follows: "The queen once more bade us farewell, with such tenderness of affection and grief, as filled both my heart and eyes' (Hawkesworth 1773, 1:419; see Orr 1994, 212–13). At Cook's cannibal feast in Queen Charlotte Sound, George Forster sees human nature vindicated in the reaction of the Tahitian Mahine: "We found him bathed in tears; his looks were a mixture of

compassion and grief . . . it spoke a humane heart, filled with the warmest sentiments of social affection, and habituated to sympathize with its
fellow-creatures" (Forster 1777, 1:513). The impetuous emotion that leaps
divisions between cultures colors the work of artists too. In William
Hodges's sketch *A Maori Chieftain* (1773), Bernard Smith detects an energy in excess of the visible facts, the trace of "something he could not
have seen." He suggests it was the chief's *mana*, triggering in Hodges a
"sympathetic apprehension . . . a dynamic faculty for the apprehension of
reality" (Smith 1992, 101–2).

Among those who were impelled to cross from one side of the beach
to the other, such as beachcombers and renegade missionaries, sympathy
is often reckoned to be the motive (Pearson 1984, 64). Of William Pascoe
Crook's attentiveness to local customs, Greg Dening says it required "a
certain simplicity but also a certain sympathy for what he saw" (Dening
1980, 142). The largest defection across the beach, the mutiny on the
Bounty, is presented by Byron as a mutual bond: "Each was to each a marvel, and the tie / Of wonder warmed to better sympathy" (Byron 1993,
7:43). It was already agreed that the islanders of the South Seas were by
and large children of nature, ready with "a sympathising tear, and unre-
strained feelings, the tribute and glory of humanity" (Forster 1778, 475).
Any act of sympathy on the beach mingled the noblest instincts of natives
and voyagers.

It is easy to see how sympathy might redeem the mariner whose civil
identity had been spoiled (as Guillaume Raynal and others suggest) by
lengthy sojourns on a corrupting element. On the domestic front, it gave
him a chance of reengaging an audience that enjoyed but did not believe narratives remarkable for egoisms and monstrosities. On his own account, the mariner rediscovered human relationships more pleasing and
altruistic than the exigent bonds of shipboard life. He could fall in love
and exist in charity with everyone. In this festival of maritime sympathy,
the propensity to share the feelings of others makes the beached mariner
a fuse through which the energies of civil society are renaturalized and
purified, and savage virtues are esteemed at their true rate. James Mont-
gomery called it "the circumnavigation of charity" (quoted in Pearson
1984, 30).

This is one way of looking at it. Given the extraordinary difficulty of
encounters on the beach, prone to misunderstanding and sudden violence, the ideal moment of sympathy is hard to isolate, and harder still to
sustain. It might be only the feeling of relief that nothing worse has happened, or the sentimentalization of mistaken signals. Mariners and chiefs

in the Pacific frequently upbraid one another with defections from a standard of friendship that neither side fully comprehends. There are enough
examples of sympathy won and lost there to suggest that the beach tests
cross-cultural intuitions to the breaking point. And if mistakes like these
can happen at the periphery, then the mariner's troubled relation to the
metropole isn't redeemed at all, but merely played out in another register.
In postcolonial treatments of this theme, the complication of the scene of
encounter advertises a flawed global charity that is prompted not by the
kindness of the voyager but his cruelty. In the mythic tale of Yarico and
Inkle, the story of an indigenous female who rescues a European on the
beach and falls in love with him, only to be sold into slavery when he finds
a market (where she fetches a higher price because she is pregnant with
his child), sympathy can do nothing to soothe her agony or restrain his
greed (Hulme 1986, 225–263; Pratt 1992, 90–102). Thus it is that sympathetic spectatorhood battens on misery. As Peter Hulme says, "sentimental sympathy began to flow out along the arteries of European commerce
in search of victims" (Hulme 1986, 229).

Certainly, sympathy itself was an impulse of uncertain provenance.
A. O. Hirschman has argued that it became part of the design to rehabil-
itate the wild passions unleashed in an interest-led economy (Hirschman
1986, 45). At once the most mechanical and the most refined ebullition
of energy, it presented spontaneity as socially attractive and ethically
pleasing. Unlike the propensity for self-preservation, which acts in a very
troubled relation to norms of good behavior, sympathy was instantly as
principled as it was instinctive. It authenticated all the other links that
political philosophers were at pains to assert between the self and society,
between the division of labor and the aesthetic wholeness of consumption, between accidents and intentions, passion and reason (Guillory
1993, 316; Ellis 1996, 155). Like taste, therefore, it combined a selfish and
libidinal tendency with an outcome that was more than merely an alleged
benevolence. And because the proof of the pudding was in the eating, the
paradoxical union of personal pleasure and social utility was brandished
about. Henry Fielding rejoiced in it when he talked of benevolence as a
species of gluttony, "eating with many mouths" (Fielding 1996b, 83).

Although a momentary sympathy might survive Bernard Mandeville's
counterparadox, namely that anyone claiming for their pleasures a social
utility can never be candid, the consistent transformation of an egoistic
into a social impulse ran the danger of losing its self-evidence and becoming a performance. Rousseau's example of Sulla the tyrant, who could
weep at tragic representations of cruelties he daily practiced without any

compunction, shows how weakly and improbably a sociable result is adduced from sympathy (Rousseau 1993, 74). In *Sir George Ellison*, Sarah Scott invents a charitable man out of a Jamaican planter, one whose sympathies are expressed by means of such a tight and complex set of financial transactions that it is hard to tell business and benefaction apart (Scott 1996). Like patriotism, sympathy can mask and even intensify that friendship for the self that really extinguishes regard for the rest of the species (Trenchard 1725, 2:84; Barker-Benfield 1992, 221). Cowper hymns this sinister side of sympathy in his antislavery poem, *Sweet Meat has Sour Sauce:*

> For oh! How it enters my soul like an awl!
> This pity, which some people self-pity call,
> Is sure the most heart-piercing pity of all. (Cowper 1995, 3:16)

In *The Castaway*, the sympathizing first person ends up competing with the man lost overboard. "We perished each alone; / But I beneath a rougher sea, / And whelmed in deeper gulfs than he"—lines used by Virginia Woolf's Mr. Ramsay in his attempts to extort pity from his family.

Sympathy's compromised relation to the market is Samuel Johnson's target when he exposes the cant behind the fashionable concern for Baretti, accused of killing a man and in danger of the noose, by mentioning Tom Davies, who inquired first after Baretti, then recommended a pickle shop: "Aye, Sir, here you have specimen of human sympathy; a friend hanged, and a cucumber pickled . . . you will find these very feeling people are not very ready to do you good. They *pay* you by feeling" (Boswell 1980, 417). Warning Eliza Draper of the hypocrisy of her city friends, the Newnhams, Laurence Sterne, notwithstanding how deeply he was committed to his own experiment with sentimental exchange, sneered, "They *weep*, and say *tender things,*—Adieu all to all such for ever" (Sterne 1965, 309). William Wilberforce thought "these sweet and benevolent tempers . . . are apt to evaporate in barren sensibility, and transitory sympathies, and indolent wishes, and unproductive declarations" (Wilberforce 1958, 82). This is the languid sensibility Adam Ferguson accused of indulging itself with trifles and gewgaws, and flattering "the pretended demands of a sickly and enfeebled fancy" (Ferguson 1995, 256).

In *A Philosophical Enquiry into the Origin of our Ideas of the Sublime and Beautiful* (1757), Edmund Burke wonders whether sympathy belongs to those social passions productive of pleasure, or instead to the passions of self-preservation that result in those modifications of pain he defines as delight. He alerts the reader to the contradictions central to the debate over sympathy and sociability during the eighteenth century. Whether the propensity that draws people to the vicinity of pain is governable by consensual restraint, or whether it is a blast of primitive energy excited but not controlled by scenes of distress, are questions that put sympathy squarely inside the other antinomies of the market. Wearing the same Janus face as self-interest, therefore, sympathy is willing to gesture at the good of others while being good for itself, and it offers no easy way of proving the truth of its claims. It appeals optimistically to the phantasm of an agreed standard, using events in the South Seas as alibis. When Seward asks her muse what power impelled Cook to desert "imperial London's gorgeous domes," she is told "It was Benevolence," which directed him to "Unite the savage hearts, and hostile hands, / In the firm compact of her gentle bands" (Seward 1810, 2:34–35). But like all the other metropolitan institutions tested in the South Seas, sympathy finds in the blurred divisions between a noble and ignoble savagery a mirror that reflects and complicates its own unsteady position between values associated with self-preservation and those attached to sociability. John Millar believed that it was in transcending the demands of self-preservation that the tribal patriarch learns to enter "with more delicate sensibility into the feelings of others, and [to behold] their distresses and suffering with greater sorrow and commiseration" (Millar 1771, 103). But his colleagues Adam Smith and Adam Ferguson prefer to instance scenes of calculated and ferocious torment among Native Americans as exemplary of the interest taken by primitive peoples in another person's feelings. And then they draw unmistakable parallels between those torturous scenes and the operation of sympathy in civil society.

In choosing to write a sentimental tale about a British crew wrecked on a remote island in the Pelew Islands (the Palau or Belau group, situated between the Philippine and Caroline Islands), George Keate was determined to put this matter straight by exhibiting the most natural impulses of human nature as the most socially attractive. He tells of the warm and unstinted feelings shared by the castaways and their hosts, and crowns his story with short life of Lee Boo, the Pelewan prince who came to London and died of smallpox before he could return to his island. But in showing that nature and sociability are the same thing, Keate was obliged to dramatize those mutually repugnant elements of sympathy that had been exposed in a century-long debate concerning its origin and tendency. The debate begins with Shaftesbury and is promptly joined by Mandeville. When Shaftesbury distinguishes between a magisterial sympathy on the one hand, which governs the passions and enters kindly into the concerns of the people, and a popular fury on the other, acting like a contagion ("the disease is no sooner seen than caught"), he opens up a division between rational sociality and mob instinct that he cannot bridge (Shaftesbury 1964, 1:13–14; Mullan 1988, 26). When Mandeville challenges the sociable tendency Shaftesbury and Francis Hutcheson each claimed to find in the natural propensity to share other people's feelings, he outlines what he understood to be the difference between cultural and natural forms of behavior, between what we learn to do and what we cannot help but do—in short, between Shaftesbury's magistrate and the crowd. He explains our reluctance to understand the connection between the two as resistance to the proposition that each of us is immersed in culture, "a taught Animal," pursuing by means of art "the same Self-Preservation for which Nature had before furnished [us] with Anger" (Mandeville 1924, 1:205).

A little later, when David Hume and Smith revolve the question of whether sympathy acts as an immediate communication of feelings between people, as Hume maintains in his *Treatise* (1739), or as a managed presentation of the self to the public, a theatrical display of socially valuable signs of passion, as Smith argues in his *Theory of Moral Sentiments* (1759), they return to the issue of sympathy's double action, both as a physiological drive and as a mode of social organization. The problem is set aside but not solved when radicals such as Thomas Paine, William Godwin, and Mary Wollstonecraft show how the artifice of sympathy humiliates and oppresses its exponents. At the same time, they expose what Burke called "the triumph of the real sympathy" (Burke 1958, 47), the spontaneous recognition of oneself in another, as a usurpation of privacy leading to a terrifying and destructive intimacy. By briefly tracing the stages of this debate, and how elements of it are both deliberately and accidentally manifest in George Keate's *An Account of the Pelew Islands* (1788), I want to examine another side of the issue of self-preservation in the South Seas.

The sociable tendency of compassion had been the subject of unsentimental speculation in the critique of public charities mounted by Mandeville and John Trenchard (see Kramnick 1992, 148–52). In the notorious example of *An Essay on Charity and Charity Schools* (1723), Mandeville supposes a helpless spectator forced to witness a starving pig eating a little child. "To see the filthy Snout digging in the yet living Entrails suck up the smoking Blood, and now and then to hear the Crackling of the Bones," he exclaims, willing to convince his reader that no one could see such a terrible sight and remain unmoved: "Pity would be clear'd and distinct from all other Passions," and there would be no heart so obdurate as not to ache with it (Mandeville 1924, 1:255–56). That is why, he continues, there is no moral distinction to be drawn here, either with regard to feeling called forth, or the person endued with it. The pity felt on such an occasion by a housebreaker, highwayman, or murderer would be no different from the feelings of the most virtuous citizen.

Instinctive pity at the sight of another person's sufferings, as it cannot be resisted, aspired to, or impersonated, brings everyone to the level of a mechanical impulse of the body, natural to the species under certain circumstances, and operating without any inherent moral value. Wicked people experience it as distinctly as good ones. "It is raised in us, when the Sufferings and Misery of other Creatures make so forcible an Impression upon us, as to make us uneasy." Moreover, it is proximity, not any higher principle, that will determine the intensity of discomfort. "It comes in either at the Eye or Ear . . . the nearer the Object is the more we suffer" (256). Steps are taken to allay the agitation, either by intervening to lessen the cause of the suffering ("Thus thousands give Money to Beggars from the same motive as they pay their Corn-cutter, to walk Easy" [268]), or by putting some distance between oneself and the object ("Nature makes no Compliments, when the Object does not strike, the body does not feel it; and when Men talk of pitying People out of sight, they are to be believed in the same manner as when they say, that they are our humble Servants" [266]). But when people are determined to deserve the compliments nature neglects to pay them, then there arises a culture of compassion, a custom of giving and a discourse of charity that pretends to a moral principle and demands public applause. Such charitable folk deceive themselves, says Mandeville, and raise expectations among the poor and oppressed that society has no means of meeting.

Starting in much the same place, with a scene of vivid suffering (gladiatorial contests), Hutcheson notes how peremptorily and effectively the voice of nature makes itself heard. "We mechanically send forth Shrieks and Groans upon any surprizing Apprehension of Evil" (Hutcheson 1725, 238), he asserts. In so doing, we utter a natural language that cannot be affected, misconstrued, or ignored: "Our Misery or Distress immediately appears in our Countenance . . . and propagates some Pain to all Spectators; who from Observation, universally understand the meaning of those dismal Airs." Here a voice "understood by all Nations" speaks to "a natural, kind Instinct, to see Objects of Compassion." Thus compassion is the simplest and most perfect instance of that "generous Boldness and Openness" which accompanies actions impelled by love of the public good

(233). Rather than the private, close encounter imagined by Mandeville ("lock'd up in a Ground-room"), Hutcheson supposes a public arena or a scaffold, "as in the Instance of publick Executions" (239), as the proper locale for these exchanges of sentiments. The moral beauty of the exhibition lies in its remoteness from any private interest, and in the unmistakable meaning communicated and instantly understood in a broad, accessible public space. Unlike pleasures of the bed and the table, which prefer to be hidden, compassionate spectators and suffering objects need not be modest, and can celebrate together in the open air the honorable "Sense of Excellence in a publick Spirit" (225). It is spatially and morally a public act. The urge to relieve the suffering of the victim is excited "without any imagination that this Relief is a private Good to our selves" (239). The instinct of self-preservation is triggered only when it is certain there is no possibility of our helping to ease the circumstances of the sufferer: "then Self-Love prompts us to retire from the Object which occasions our Pain."

The purely mechanical and irresistible susceptibility to another's pain outlined by Mandeville is of little interest to British moral philosophers. Shaftesbury compares it with an infection, and associates it with enthusiasm (Shaftesbury 1964, 1:13). Although Hume begins by saying that reason is the slave of the passions, he eventually installs a medium between them in order to assign the sympathetic propensity a social end (Mullan 1988, 34). While David Hartley is in one sense the most Newtonian and materialist analyst of sympathy, beginning with the vibrationary links between the blood, muscles, nerves, and the medullary substance, he traces it ultimately to a transcendental goal ("All the Pleasures and Pains of . . . Sympathy . . . beget in us a Moral Sense. . . . it appears also, that the Moral Sense carries us perpetually to pure Love of God, as our highest and ultimate Perfection, our End, Centre, and only Resting-place" [Hartley 1966, 1:497]). But Mandeville's example intrigues Rousseau, who uses it in *A Discourse on the Origin of Inequality* (1755) as the basis of his imagined state of nature (and also as proof that even Mandeville's cold subtlety was not immune to the promptings of nature [Rousseau 1993, 74]). Unblinded by *amour propre,* the single individual in Rousseau's primeval forest is defended by two instincts, self-preservation and its corollary, compassion, "a natural repugnance at seeing any other sensible being . . . suffer pain or death" (47). Although Rousseau regards this impulse as the fond of all virtues truly social—generosity, clemency, benevolence—it is not in itself social; nor, when societies arise, does it survive intact. This far he agrees with Mandeville in making a claim for a natural instinct whose impact on our social being is rendered null or oblique by political and commercial priorities. It thrives only when it is private, involving no more than two individuals in a situation that is unique, not familiar or customary, who are sharing feelings that cannot be modified, represented, or imitated.

It is not this instinct Hutcheson wishes to emphasize, although he does not dispute its existence. Instead, he wants to say that the public communication of shared feeling is what proves the social value of sympathy, its being seen to take place by all involved in it. Sympathy is the occasion of a public and socializing moment, not a private alarm. Hutcheson's stress on publicity leads to Adam Smith's theatrical account of moral sentiments, where it is important that the natural language of shrieks and groans be abated to a level consistent with what he calls the "propriety" of public grief, if anyone is to share it in a public place. Only when the noise of uncontrolled agony has been subdued, and suffering has acquired the tragic grace of a performance, is it possible for the circuit of sympathy to be completed, and for spectators and sufferers alike to spot in one another's countenances a picture of the emotion everyone imagines everyone else is feeling. On the moral scale, propriety is proof of self-restraint; and on the aesthetic, it is a measure of representability. Consequently, the applause, attention, and admiration that greets the successful representation of suffering (Smith [1976] 1982, 48–49) testifies as much to histrionic skill as to virtuous self-control. When Smith attempts a distinction between this state of affairs, where the sociability and pleasure of sympathy lie solely in the representability of what is never more than a represented emotion, and a factitious condition he calls "artificial sympathy" (47), he implies the difference between an original and a copy, a natural language and a translation. But in fact, when he talks of public sympathy, it is always artificial. The price paid by Smith for a theater the size of Hutcheson's public square is the elimination from its neighborhood of the genuine voice of nature.

In his section on sympathy in the *Enquiry*, Burke instances both the theater and the square as scenes of public sympathy, assigning greater power to the latter. He imagines what would happen if the public were given a choice between a sumptuous tragedy and the execution of a state criminal: "The emptiness of the theatre would demonstrate the comparative weakness of the imitative arts, and proclaims the triumph of the real sympathy" (Burke 1987, 47). The real sympathy is not the result of representational skill, any more than powerful sentiments are the result of clear language; it comes from the degree of proximity in which a spectator stands to an event terrible enough to deplore, but too compelling not to view. Distinguishing between real and artificial distress, he comes up with this account of the real sympathy:

> I am convinced we have a degree of delight, and that no small one, in the real misfortunes and pains of others; for let the affection be what it will in appearance, if it does not make us shun such objects, if on the contrary it induces us to approach them, if it makes us dwell upon them in the case I conceive we must have a delight or pleasure of some species or other in contemplating objects of this kind. (45)

Considering how carefully Burke elsewhere marks the boundaries between delight (a feeling incident to self-preservation) and pleasure (a sociable passion), it is strange how he fudges the matter here, talking of sympathy triggering "a delight or pleasure of some species or other." His distinction between the self-preservative and social passions is fundamental to his definition of the sublime; and in insisting that they are not modifications of each other, but distinct feelings with their own range of intensities, he means to isolate the sense of the sublime within the subjectivity of a single spectator, even though it may find its most intense experiences in public places. The unsteady phrasing in the preceding passage is evidence of Burke's difficulty in finding a category suitable for sympathy: whether it ought to be the class of social passions that "[have] their origin in gratification and pleasures" (Burke 1987, 40), or the sublime, which generates feelings of delight when the threat of death and pain is eased (38). With no apparent sense of his inconsistency, he recklessly lists sympathy with both, saying that shocking objects are "the source of a very high degree of pleasure" (44), and that the social bond of sympathy is strengthened by "a proportionable delight" (46). Having defined delight as "the sensation which accompanies the removal of pain and danger," superadding the caution, "this delight I have not called pleasure" (36, 51), it ought not to be possible for him to assign delight to feelings of sociability, and pleasure to feelings of self-preservation.

That he mars his own distinction between pain and pleasure, and between the social and selfish sides of sympathy, shows how firmly Burke is jammed in the contradiction between the Mandevillean and Hutchesonian positions. Although he chooses to test sympathy in a public space, he is discussing feelings singular to each individual, that "merely arise from the mechanical structure of our bodies, or from the natural frame and constitution of our minds," and that act in a manner "antecedent to reason" (Burke 1987, 46). But he cannot leave it there. Mechanical sympathy is blended with pleasure because Burke, while believing that it has no necessary social relevance, cannot relinquish a consensual basis for the evaluation of all sensations. Nevertheless, the logic of his "rationale of the passions" (53) is that benevolence is largely an accidental by-product of sympathy, and that feelings of delight experienced in public are not (as Hutcheson insists) directed at the public. Unlike Mandeville and Smith, who from different directions define a culture of sympathy, Burke rejects the case for intermediate delight, where representation and imitation might explain the coexistence of pleasure and pain, for he deliberately removes the most delightful spectacles from the theater to the square, supplanting the weaker pleasure aroused by imitation with the strong delight impressed by the thing itself (49–50).

The instinct for self-preservation, then, ends up as raw in Burke's analysis as it is originally conceived to be in Mandeville's and Rousseau's, its relation to compassion as immediate and mechanical, and its manifestations as inimical to representation. The urge that carries the crowd involuntarily from the theater to the public square indicates that no mediate or artful positioning of the self vis-à-vis a spectacle, or of the performer vis-à-vis the spectators, can bring the event within the framework of social justice, or the government of Shaftesbury's magistrate. It is simply a strong propensity to view a terrible thing. The human object who confronts these spectators suffers with as little forethought as the man in desperate flight who gains a frontier, "breathless, pale, amaz'd" (Burke 1987, 34). Although various gradations of mutual substitution are possible in this situation, generating corresponding degrees of delight between the viewers and the viewed ("moved as they are moved . . . affected as [they are] affected" [44]), there is no rational or demonstrable social principle at work in it, and certainly no translation from nature to art. Burke desires no standard of representability to oversee or justify these gradations of what is always for him a natural language, which explains why the real sympathy empties the theater, the home of representations, and why he values obscure and difficult language as a direct symptom of passion rather than an eloquent and contrived image of it. Unlike Smith, he lodges no consensus or providence in the eye of a supposedly impartial spectator, nor any art in the appeal to such a spectator. The language of nature cannot be turned into a performance, and it cannot acquire the artificial expressions of benevolence with which, according to Mandeville and Rousseau, spontaneous compassion is eventually furnished when it becomes a species of social exchange. In short, it is not a matter of the will, but a sensation aroused by a specific set of circumstances, sustaining delight as long as terror and indifference are kept at bay; and this seems to depend solely (for Burke as well as Mandeville) upon the degree of proximity.

Sentimental and Gothic novels exploit the insights Burke gains on the border between self-preservation and society. In Sterne's fiction, sympathetic exchanges take place within the "world," a semiprivate sphere carefully demarcated from the world at large. In Henry Mackenzie's novels, even this indeterminate margin is removed, and the world at large is shown to be quite at odds with the feelings of the characters and of their sympathetic readers. One of the many narrators who contribute to *The Man of Feeling* (1771) says the story of Harley's death will make the reader "hate the world"—a world that is specified as the sphere of commerce, where self-interest is pursued at the expense of finer feelings, and where politeness is merely "a certain ceremonious jargon, more ridiculous to the ear of reason than the voice of a puppet" (Mackenzie 1967, 10, 39, 133). As ardently as Hutcheson, Mackenzie rejects the pollution of sympathy by self-interest; yet he affords disinterestedness no public place, and denies its expressions any translation into an articulate tongue, relying instead on chokings, gasps, cries, and floods of tears—the unalloyed voice of nature. Being much less peremptory in drawing such distinctions between private and public domains, Sterne is willing to experiment with various social models of sympathy in *A Sentimental Journey* (1768)—sympathy as commercial exchange, sympathy as politeness, sympathy as casuistry, sympathy as imitation, and sympathy as contract—to see if, under pressure, they will yield a core of natural sensation that might be shared without direction from the worldly doctrines of prudence, morality, or art. In fact, most of these experiments fail, leaving the hero as embarrassed as Harley for a public space and a translatable idiom. The story ends midsentence when a contract drawn up in a bedroom results in a gesture that cannot publicly be described. So both heroes are forced to rely on situations that generate sympathy in a manner more like Burke's privately delightful spectacles than like Hutcheson's, Hume's, or Smith's consensual arenas. Later, Mackenzie was to define this isolation as the willful privacy of sentimental novelists: "The *world*, a term which they applied indiscriminately to almost every one but themselves, they seemed to feel as much pride as happiness in being excluded from; and its laws of providence and propriety, they held the invention of cold and selfish minds, insensible of the delights of feeling, of sentiment, and of friendship" (Mackenzie 1786, 3:233).

An index of unworldliness in both novels is the reduction of sentiment to the level of a situation, where an arrangement of proximate things provokes and frames untranslatable feelings. Whether it is clothing, furniture, an ornament, food, or an animal, it can be used simultaneously as the source and object of a sentiment. Mackenzie wrote an essay for *The Mirror* entitled "Of attachment to inanimate objects," in which he describes the nonmodern habits of Mr. Umphraville, who refuses to be parted from an old tree stump in his garden, or his ancient elbow chair. The waving tree branch at the end of *The Man of Feeling* (Mackenzie 1967, 132) and the creaking pendulum in *Julia de Roubigne* (Mackenzie 1805, 113) are emblems aspiring to the sheer materiality of the tree stump and the chair. Like the snuffboxes, gloves, spectacles, crusts of bread, and millinery that contingently focus action and feeling in *A Sentimental Journey*, they serve the purpose of avoiding explanations, representations, or translations of what is happening. They are simply things themselves, in whose presence the voice of nature may intermittently be heard. Similarly, the dogs, horses, mules, and asses that are so frequently encountered by the sentimental traveler emerge, like the dogs and horses in paintings by Sawrey Gilpin and George Stubbs, as creatures symbolic of nothing outside the situations that frame them, enforcing neither a moral nor a lesson. Barbara Heartless finds this out to her cost when she becomes the companion of Mrs. Sensitive in Mackenzie's essay "The unfortunate attendant of a woman of extreme sensibility." She shares a house with "three lap-dogs, four cats . . . a monkey, a flying squirrel, two parrots, a parroquet, a Virginia nightingale, a jack-daw, an owl," and is instructed by her mistress (who "can understand their looks and their language from *sympathy*") to accommodate herself to the feelings of these creatures. She is bidden to "scratch the heads of the parrots . . . laugh to the monkey, and play at cork-balls with the kittens." But she discovers that this sympathy has no social corollary at all, for Mrs. Sensitive "has no pity on us, no sympathy in the world for our distresses. . . . ordinary objects of charity we are ordered never to suffer to come near her" (Mackenzie 1788, 3:193–94). Her household pets are sufficient as objects of feeling; and like Mandeville's dying infant, or Burke's target of the real sympathy, they subsist without a representing a social value. They are part of the sum of spontaneous feelings provoked within a given situation. "Love, you see, is not so much a SENTIMENT as a SITUATION" (Sterne 1983, 475).

How animals stimulate and reflect sympathetic feeling is an important part of the debate, to which I will return. It is important to emphasize here that the attention paid by Sterne and Mackenzie to the adventitious circumstances in which feelings are generated and exchanged, alters the terms on which sympathy will be handled by later novelists. It is going to be more private—"Nature is shy, and hates to act before spectators" (Sterne 1967, 131). It is not necessarily going to be benevolent; and while remaining close to nature, its spontaneous demonstrations will not be incompatible with the desire to triumph over the other party, or at least to dominate the situation. Mary Wollstonecraft distinguishes between the cult of sensibility, which she characterizes in language close to Ferguson's, and sympathetic energy, "this subtle magnetic fluid, that runs round the whole circle of society . . . not subject to any known rule" (Wollstonecraft 1960, 69). In an effort to understand the politics of this unregulated force, Tom Paine asks, "What renders us kind and humane? Is it not sympathy, the power which I have of putting myself in my neighbour's place? How can a monarch have sympathy? He can never put himself in any place but his own" (Paine 1970, 390). By describing the substitution of sympathy as an active displacement, the result of applied power, Paine implies the opposite of what he means to say. For when he traces the descent of monarchies through a sequence of violent usurpations ("next comes a robber chief, who conquers and kills the first [leader], and makes himself king in his stead" [388]), he charts the history of people who have allegedly freed themselves from sympathy in a series of actions corresponding exactly to sympathy by being substitutions, and the placement of themselves in positions occupied by others. In *Caleb Williams* (1794), William Godwin dramatizes the politics of "unexplained and involuntary sympathy" as Caleb and his master become agonizingly familiar with the secrets of each other's heart. This magnetic force, subject to no known rule, is expressed largely in gestural language—writhing faces, pallor, sweat, tears, murmurs, and imprecations—of which the narrative (especially its split ending) is an imperfect translation. Each character is obsessed with his own preservation, which nevertheless he can approach only through the usurped sentiments of the other. Locked in a terrible mutuality from which it is impossible to escape, each is like the starling in *A Sentimental Journey*, crying to the other that he can't get out.

There is no more teasing example of the relation of a creature to the sphere of sympathy than the caged starling Yorick meets in the passage of his hotel the night when he is informed that he is traveling illegally in France, and in danger of being imprisoned in the Bastille. It is an object that seems to announce its own meaning in a natural language, and yet it is hedged around with artifice; it seems to excite the most unselfish feelings, and yet no benevolent action follows. The bird's repeated cry, "I cannot get out," punctuates Yorick's futile attempts to set it free; and in the sequel, his efforts to interpret the starling as an icon of slavery in general keep collapsing into a picture of himself in prison.

The starling comes of a long line of Shandean conversions, in which the tongues of mute creatures are made eloquent. When Tristram meets the ass in Lyons, he says he can fly "from my own heart into his, and [see] what is natural for an ass to think—as well as a man, upon the occasion" (Sterne 1983, 419). On this basis, he can frame conversations from the animal's countenance. But like the starling, the ass is destined not to participate actively in the conversation, nor to be the object of an act of charity, but to be a passive addition to a situation. It is made to eat a macaroon, then it is beaten by someone entering the hotel. After that, Tristram thinks about it no more. Like the meetings with Maria (who is totally mute when Tristram first comes across her), the encounters with the starling and the ass afford an occasion in a public place for a single spectator to enjoy in private the illusion of dialogue with a creature whose human attributes are fewer than his own. This produces a confusion between the private and public realms, matched by a confusion between subject and object positions. Joseph Wright's various attempts to represent the prison scene of "The Captive," veering between an extensive prospect, like Piranesi's, and a narrow, dark enclosure, indicate how confusingly it is pitched between spectacular and intimate dimensions (Bender 1987, 233–38). Once Yorick has made the starling's plight his own, accomplishing the sympathetic substitution "by which we are put into the place of another" (Burke 1987, 44), he performs a translation like Tristram's with the ass, seeming to usurp a nonhuman feeling in order to conduct a dialogue, only to show in the end that the distinction between himself and the bird is intact. Indeed, the starling is restored to the market as an exchangeable and saleable thing, an avian Yarico, passed from hand to hand.

The relation of nature to art is so specious in this episode that the starling remains without any real translatable voice or sociable function. Yet Sterne allows it a language on four distinct levels. Its utterances are described as mere mechanism ("Mechanical as the notes were . . ."); as the voice of nature (". . . yet so true in tune to nature were they chanted, that in one moment they overthrew all my systematic reasonings" [Sterne 1967, 96]); as dialogue in English ("I fear, poor creature! said I, I cannot set thee at liberty—'No,' said the starling, 'I can't get out.'"), and as mere noise ("an *unknown* language"). These levels of language correspond roughly to Mandeville's, Hutcheson's, Smith's, and Burke's notions of expressive sympathy, respectively: namely, as an irresistible instinct, as a public and significant sentiment, as a modulated exchange of sentiments, and as symptomatic obscurity. The second and third levels invite the reader to believe that nature can combine with disinterested impulses in an act of social conscience, insofar as the starling's cry is publicly intelligible and universally appealing. But the first and fourth propose a merely mechanical engagement with a scene of distress whose point lies exclusively in the feelings its single spectator can wrest from it. In the former, the bird represents the true object of benevolence; and in the latter, it constitutes merely the material and objective circumstances in which a sentiment of a certain degree of intensity can take place. As the first and fourth levels begin and end in a narrative sequence barren of any benevolent intervention, it seems more plausible to place the event of the starling in the category of self-preservation rather than the social passions—of delight, as Burke would say, rather than pleasure. This would seem to be the drift of Yorick's claim to have a property in it: "my bird" (99).

Nevertheless, the mechanical notes Yorick mistakes for the voice of nature are heard by virtue of art, not instinct; for when, in a travesty of sympathy, its captor framed the bird's plight in the first person singular, and repeated it until the bird could imitate what was already an imitation of its imagined sentiments, he fitted the circumstances of the cage and the meaning of the cry to a dramatic appeal agreeable to Smith's standard of propriety in the theater of moral sentiments. Thus the starling's phrase is not like the shriek of Mandeville's dying child, even though Yorick's response to it is unpremeditated. That such an imperative sound can decay into an unknown language indicates, however, that it has no intrinsic social value, nor any real origin in nature. It speaks a phrase that was emptied of meaning before it could be learned. Its notes are true to nature only at two removes, and cannot be taken for natural unless they happen to ventriloquize a sentiment appropriate to a fortuitous additional set of circumstances, such as those in which Yorick finds himself at the inn. The starling in its cage is the mobile occasion for pathos, but not in itself pathetic until a spectator puts himself in its place and speaks as it appears to speak. This happy coincidence imparts to Yorick's heart-piercing self-pity a mode of complaint in the first person consistent with propriety.

By means of a semipublic act of sympathy between a man and a bird, a statement gets to be made about a personal predicament that *seems* generalizable, although it isn't. Self-preservation edges out all other considerations. As Yorick says in a parallel situation where what might have seemed a translation resurfaces as self-evident egoism, "I thought I loved the man; but fear I mistook the object—'twas my own way of thinking"

(Sterne 1967, 85). The starling's insignificance as a public sign, confirmed in the course of its subsequent exchanges, where no pathos survives because it has turned into a joke, is a measure of its importance for the moment to a needy ego. Hence its removal to the crest of the coat of arms, where its sole function is to authenticate the identity of its owner: "that bird was my bird."

There is a curious pendant to this scene in the section of *A Sentimental Journey* entitled "The Passport. Versailles," where Yorick describes his efforts to legalize his presence in France. When he meets the Conte de B——, he identifies himself by pointing to the graveyard scene in Shakespeare's play, conveniently lying open on the desk in front of him, and crying "Me *Voici!*" [Sterne 1967, 109]). With this gesture, Yorick makes another sentimental leap into the heart and mouth of a speaking object, this time the human skull being dialogized by Hamlet, and claims it for his own. This turns out to be a mistake, because the count can't get the play out of his mind; he proceeds to make a categorical error that does Yorick's sense of identity no good. He assumes that Yorick has presented himself as an object ripe for sentimental appropriation, as before the starling presented itself to Yorick. His position vis-à-vis the bird is now taken up by the count vis-à-vis himself. "*Et, Monsieur, est il Yorick?* cried the Count,— *Je le suis,* said I.—*Vous?—Moi—moi qui ai l'honneur de vous parler, Monsieur le Compte—Mon Dieu!* Said he, embracing me—*Vous etes Yorick*" (110). Refusing to acknowledge any difference between the skull and the angular figure in front of him, the count ignores all of Yorick's claims for personal identity, and assigns him the same empty role Yorick assigned the starling. Just as the bird is affixed to the escutcheon to blazon the name of its owner, so the passport is given Yorick in the king of France's name, allowing him no other status than that of a factitious personality— the king's jester—who travels from place to place (and the sequel bears this out) speaking by rote. Not until the reunion with Tristram's Maria does Yorick recover his sentimental initiative.

These two incidents glance (like so much of Sterne's fiction) at John Locke, particularly the section of the *Essay concerning Human Understanding* dealing with personal identity. In order to declare the absolute impossibility of sympathy between a human being and a creature, Locke tells the story of a rational parrot that he found in Sir William Temple's memoir of Johan Moritz of Nassau-Siegen, governor of Dutch Brazil. Prince Maurice (as he is called by Temple) arranged to meet this parrot. Supported by two interpreters, one a Dutchman who spoke Brazilian, the other a Brazilian who spoke Dutch, the prince enjoyed a conversation in which he was informed by the bird where it came from, who owned it, and what job it did. As a dialogue, it shares aspects of Yorick's meeting with the starling, and his subsequent conversation with the Conte de B——, and is worth giving in full: "When they brought it close to him, he ask'd it, *D'ou venes vous?* It answer'd, *De Marinnan.* The Prince, *A qui estes vous?* The Parrot, *A un Portugez.* Prince, *Que fais tu la.* Parrot, *Je garde les Poulles.* The Prince laugh'd, and said, *Vous gardez les Poulles?* The Parrot answer'd, *Ouy, moy & je scay bien faire,* and made the Chuck four or five times that people use to make to Chickens when they call them" (Locke 1961, 1:279; Temple 1692, 57–58). Locke's purpose in giving the story is to make a point about personal identity, "what the word *I* is applied to" (Locke 1961, 1:287). It is not applied to a creature without the body of a human being, no matter how apparently rational; nor is it applied to any substance or figure not continuous with those attributes of body and mind of which the human being is always conscious, and, moreover, conscious of as his own: those aspects of himself with which "he sympathises and [for which he] is concerned" (1:282). The parrot, therefore, is a hollow and extended voice of the "I" who taught him to speak, and to arrange his phrases in such a way as to make them look like dialogue—a starling, in short.

Temple's purpose is somewhat different: it is to laugh at Prince Maurice, rather as Prince Maurice laughs at the bird. The young English diplomat is going to get the old Dutchman to recite a well-known tale that will make him look daft: "I dare say this Prince, at least, believed himself in all he told me, having ever pass'd for a very honest and pious Man" (Temple 1692, 59). However, the parrot has already weakened this hierarchy of mockery by insisting that its relation to the chickens is the same as that which humans think they maintain with birds. Its command of human speech includes the sounds men make when they try to mimic the voice of nature, indicating that the parrot controls not only the difference between itself and other birds, but also that between itself and human beings. And it enforces its consciousness of these differences with an assertion of its own identity: "Ouy, moy." "I hold the same position with regard to fowl as you think you hold to me," it implies. "Challenge that, and I can challenge you." The effect is like the reversal Yorick experiences with the count, where he is made to act the starling. Temple tries to make Prince Maurice act the parrot, only to find that the parrot has made them both act like chickens. This challenge must be met, Locke insists, by placing a human, self-sympathizing "I" where a rational bird appears to stand. The real "I" must usurp the false one, and so preserve itself. From different sides, Burke, Sterne, and Locke agree that the sounds of animals, whether articulate or natural, constitute a threat to the self that has to be overcome. But Temple shows that the contest is never simple, and the starling's place awaits anyone who thinks the game too easy.

Keate's thorough absorption in the literature of sensibility, and the position he takes up in the debate over sympathy, mark him off from Hawkesworth, the other literary gentleman ghosting voyages in the Pacific. Like Johnson, Hawkesworth labors under no illusions about the violence implicit both in the appeal for sympathy and in the response to it. As a result, he tends to be very clear-sighted about its limits, both in civil society and at the ends of the world. He wastes no tears over deaths caused in the process of self-defense, and he explains quite coolly the rhetorical techniques that are needed to cause tears to flow (Lamb 1995, 183). Keate, on the other hand, wants to vindicate the nobility of remote savagery by appealing to a metropolitan culture of feeling. In effect, he wants to prove an ethnographic case by expanding the repertoire of fashionable styles of writing. He tells a tale familiar to sentimental authors such as Sterne and Mackenzie—of "a quiet journey of the heart in pursuit of NATURE, and those affections which arise out of her, that make us love each other—and the world, better than we do," (Sterne 1967, 109)—only that the journey is more extensive. Keate goes to the ends of the earth to celebrate a sympathetic encounter between a local population and a group of British sailors, and then he brings a prince of Pelew, Lee Boo, home to the people of Rotherhithe, to show that the bond forged in distant seas was not illusory.

He begins by recalling how sympathy took effect upon the castaways: "Forlorn and melancholy as their lot at first appeared, the gloom it cast over them was soon dispelled, by finding themselves amongst an humane race of men, who were superior to the wish of taking any advantage of their distress; who had hearts to feel for what our people suffered; benevolence to relieve their immediate wants; and generosity to cooperate with them in every effort to work out their deliverance" (Keate 1788, 289). With readers willing to yield to the pathos of the anecdotes supporting these conclusions, Keate can endow nature with a global dimension that unites London and Pelew within the framework of a telescopic philanthropy that Denis Diderot had prophesied ("that chain of union and charity . . . extend[ing] some day . . . from one end of the world to the other" [Diderot 1992, 214]), Seward had sung, and Charles Dickens was to laugh at in *Bleak House*. The belief that sympathy is social everywhere; that the self preserves only the species in preserving itself; and that ultimately compassion annuls the difference between nature and culture, being dominant in the idealization of politeness that G. J. Barker-Benfield has traced from Shaftesbury to female conduct books, and buoyant too in the primitivism derived from Rousseau, it is worth Keate's labor to prove its truth, as it were, in the field. But much is riding on the experiment. To make his story obedient to the moral, Keate has to purge from the appearance of nature any misunderstanding of ethnographic details, such as the habit of the Pelewans of killing their prisoners in cold blood; and he must disguise or moderate the suspicion and impatience among the crew that threatens to break out into war. On both sides of the beach at Pelew, then, he is determined to socialize the more inveterate instincts of self-preservation, and to naturalize culture, by giving prominence to those gestures and actions that are immediately translatable from the language of civil society into the language of nature. In doing so, he enters directly into the no-man's-land already mined by Mandeville.

In his *Account*, Keate is alert to the sentimental possibilities of situations and animals, having learned through his close familiarity with Sterne's work, especially *A Sentimental Journey*, the skill of discovering nature in hidden places, framed by trivial circumstances. He glances sidelong at the merits of his narrative when he imagines the sort of memoir Madan Blanchard (the sailor who chooses to stay behind on Pelew) might have produced after his sojourn, had he not been illiterate: "Investigations of simple nature . . . infinitely more interesting than those of half the ministers and statesmen of Europe" (Keate 1788, 229). "O Nature! It is to thee that I devote myself and dedicate my pen!" Keate cries in his Shandean pastiche, *Sketches from Nature in a Journey to Margate* (1779). "[W]hat dignity, what beauty in thy paintings . . . no false colouring disturbs the design" (Keate 1779, 1.99). The story of the ship's dog, Sailor, a Newfoundland retriever, is exemplary in this respect. Having formed a close relationship with Arra Kooker, a senior chief, Sailor's "various demonstrations of joy" on seeing him ("[he] would, whenever he appeared, bark, jump, leap, and play his tricks" [Keate 1788, 51]) are offered to the reader as a specimen of the voice of nature greeting the child of nature, a high standard of transparency by which to measure the conversion of the Europeans to the principles of simple nature.

Keate has in mind not only the sentimental novel as he composes these scenes. Robinson Crusoe's relation to his dog, cats, parrot, and pet goats, subjects of his ideal commonwealth of one ("It would have made a Stoick smile to have seen, me and my little Family sit down to Dinner" [Defoe 1972b, 148]), are part of Keate's vision of sympathy in an exotic place,

where animals, natives, and Europeans all participate in dialogue. Similarly, Jonathan Swift's Houyhnhmns, who are as puzzled by European
clothes as were the Pelewans, establish for Keate a level of natural and ingenuous behavior shared by horses and savages with respect to hats,
waistcoats, sleeves, gloves, and other artificial extensions of white skin
(Keate 1788, 28). In a conversation with his own horse in *Sketches from Nature,* Keate had confided, "In the wide extent of the animal reign, there
scarce exists an object from which man may not borrow some useful
hint;—thou, my trusty friend, hast offered me no inconsiderable one;—
thou never aimed to appear what thou wast not" (Keate 1779, 2:23).

As the transparency of animals is equal to the transparency of the Pelewans, there ought to be a frictionless exchange between them and the
British, once the latter shed their cultural addiction to artifice and reserve.
Yet the case of Blanchard made a point Keate was not keen to improve,
namely that nature without letters is dumb, and needs instruction if it is
to provide the pictures and the pen-worthy sketches he admires. In fact,
there are two reasons that prevent nature from becoming transparent.
The first is a problem with translation; the second is a problem with what
is translated. There is a curious scene where Arthur Devis, the supercargo,
starts drawing the picture of the wife of one of the chiefs—a loose sketch
of nature—prompting the king, Abba Thule, to do the same. But instead
of Devis's "fancied likeness," close enough to be recognized by his sitter,
the king produces "three or four figures, very rudely, without the least proportion; their heads, instead of an oval, being in the pointed form like a
sugar-loaf" (Keate 1788, 104). Lest the reader be inclined to laugh, Keate
points out that punctilio is being royally observed: "I rather mention it as
a proof of his openness of temper, to let Mr Devis see that he was not totally ignorant of what was meant by it; nor was it less a mark of his con-
descension, in shewing he could very imperfectly trace what the artist was
able more happily to delineate."

It is a signal advantage, Keate means us to see, that these children of
nature are ignorant of art that in Europe "assumes every form and colouring of life" (Keate 1788, 250). Nevertheless, their imitations of things
are not clear images of them; nor, when they see a clear image, do they
necessarily recognize it for what it is. Indeed, when Lee Boo first looks
into a mirror, he cannot believe that the reflection is his own: "He drew
back, and returned to look again, quite, absorbed in wonder" (276). Yet
when Arra Kooker first sees Sailor, he shows that mimicry is a talent understood on the islands, for, "when he wished to be amusing, [he] would

imitate wonderfully well the barking, howling, jumping, and all the various demonstrations of joy of this poor animal" (51). Nor does he stop at animals: "He would frequently try to take off every one of our people in any particularity he had noticed, and this with such great good-humour, that every one . . . was pleased with his pleasantry" (51). Similarly, Raa Kook and his followers imitate all the gestures of devotion they see the Europeans perform at prayers, "following exactly what they saw our people did" (100). Although it is plain Keate expects these examples of mimicry to be understood as signs of reciprocity, proof that the natives are moved as the Europeans are moved, affected by what affects them, the shadows of the starling and of Temple's parrot fall across them. The voice of nature, the degree of spontaneity, and the circumstances that surround these scenes disturb all simple notions of identity, and of the innocence of the sentiments delivered in the first person singular. The position of the "I" has become contestable.

In appreciating on their own account, without any instruction, the humorous resemblance between things themselves and imitations of them, the Pelewans qualify the natural language of the heart. Abba Thule knows what Devis is doing when he copies a face onto paper; and in following his example he may not be guilty of ostentation, but he shows that he understands the difference between an original and a copy. Keate says, "The Changes of the human Countenance are occasionally as quick as the Operation of Thought; and the Rapidity of their Succession can awaken in a spectator such a Combination of Ideas, as to produce almost instantaneously a correspondent Passion" (Keate 1773, viii). Into that instantaneous contagion of sympathy he ought now to insert the possibility of a deliberate adjustment of the frame of one's face when confronting another's. In other words, along with the mechanical and natural instinct to be affected as others are affected—the first and second levels of the starling's voice—he has to include the third, the artificial reproduction of the voice of nature: the same that is heard in Smith's theater of the moral sentiments, in the count's appropriation of the Hamlet-position vis-à-vis Yorick's skull, and in the parrot's imitation of the noises of men who mimic chickens.

The European reluctance to understand the implications of local art is everywhere evident in the *Account,* for example in Keate's awkward reference to Pelewan artifacts as objects "so neatly and curiously wrought by artless hands" (Keate 1788, 332). Nowhere is this reluctance more dramatically exposed than in the treatment of the Malay translator, called Soogle, upon whom the Europeans have relied in order to understand the sentiments expressed by the voice of nature. In fact, like Prince Maurice in his dialogue with the parrot, they have made use of two translators. At the outset, they count themselves lucky to have in their own crew Tom Rose, who can speak Malay to Soogle, who in turn understands the language of Pelew. The language of nature comes to their ears, then, at two removes, just like the piteous cry of the starling and the repartee of that redoubtable parrot. If the natural purity of this translated voice is to be vindicated from the aspersion of art, of being no more than the representation of a representation, then the translators must be the ones guilty of polluting it. On two occasions, therefore, it is alleged that Soogle has been playing politics in his translations, deliberately conveying imperfectly the sentiments of the king in order to advance his own interests. In the first instance, he informs the British, apparently on his own authority, that it is the king's wish they should prostrate themselves in his presence, just like his other subjects. In the second, he draws attention most undiplomatically to the fact that the six muskets promised by the British to the king as a parting gift have not yet been produced. In a footnote, Keate explains, "This artful fellow probably found, that the interest he had with the King had declined in proportion as our people became more necessary to him, and therefore he set his brains to work to awaken distrust amongst them . . . to make the King and our people mutually jealous of each other" (153n). As for the muskets, Raa Kook, the Pelewan general, exculpates the British while rebuking their translator: "They had not spoken with two tongues as he, worthless Malay! had dared to suggest" (221).

Of course, speaking with two tongues is what the Malay has been obliged to do, both by the Pelewans and by the British; and any misunderstanding, no matter how accidental, between two parties knit by all the ties of nature must be blamed on his artfulness. And it is worth emphasizing that he is accused by both sides, as if they had an equal interest in preserving the simplicity of the voice of nature. There may be an equality in the need to pretend to this transparency, but the motives are different. By insisting on the naturalness of their hosts, the British sustain their own compromised sense of superiority, always believing their technology places them above the ignorant Pelewans in a political sense, although morally speaking they are not fit to tie the latchets of their sandals. By affirming the purity of their original sentiments, Abba Thule and his lieutenants are able to test the limits of their power over their visitors by a series of hypothetical demands, which can easily be disclaimed (should they prove troublesome) as mistakes in the translation. Isolated between two powerful groups who intend to exploit the difference between their two tongues while defending a standard of natural candor, Soogle (the star-ling here) pays the price of their duplicity.

In misunderstandings and confrontations between the two sides, for which Soogle cannot be blamed, Keate sticks to the distinction between corrupt art and ingenuous nature, presenting the British as narrow-minded preservers of their selves and the Pelewans as agents of a disin-terested sociability. For no apparent reason (according to Keate), the crew become convinced that Abba Thule means to hinder their departure, and a low point is reached on the scale of sympathy when they plot to kill the king and his two lieutenants, Raa Kook and Arra Kooker. Such a dis-graceful plan causes Keate for the first and only time to separate himself from the plural first person of his narrative: "I must confess that my hand shrinks from the paper, whilst, impressed with horror and pity, I am com-pelled to relate [it]" (Keate 1788, 215). Contrariwise, Abba Thule's high point comes when he understands that the British do suspect him—"mis-trust . . . appeared too strongly impressed on their countenances to escape the quick discernment of the King" (249)—and finally he knows why they have been prevaricating in the handover of the promised weapons. "And can you not confide in me at the last?" he asks, at which Keate exclaims, "Under what sun was ever tempered the steel that could cut such a pas-sage to the heart as this just reproach of the King's—Every individual felt its force, and its truth; —every individual also felt how much his mind had injured the virtues of this excellent man" (250). The murky singular-ities of self-preservation are shamed before the openness of this natural and notable public man: "The people of Pelew, tutored in the school of Nature, acted from impulse alone, they were open and undisguised—Our countrymen . . . were fashioned . . . to suspicion and doubt . . . such is the fatal knowledge the world teaches mankind" (250).

In this story, Keate ignores Sterne's equivocal treatment of the me-chanical impulses and ventriloquized voices of nature that compose a sympathetic situation, favoring a Hutchesonian account of a noble and primitive publicity. Yet Abba Thule's cutting speech, if thoroughly exam-ined, is not a plea made by a weaker party to a stronger, or by a more in-nocent to a more knowing. It opens a passage to the heart because of the threat strongly implicit in it, which he soon makes explicit: "Had I been disposed to have harmed you, I might have done it long ago; I have at all times had you in my power" (Keate 1788, 249). He is saying, "How could you bear to distrust someone so confiding?" but he means, "You had no choice but to trust me, and I made it easy for you to do so." Indeed, his speech recalls to mind the political struggle that has simmered ever since the wreck of the *Antelope,* pitching the castaways, who want only to build a boat and be gone, against the indigenes, who want to fight a war with people of Artingall. The trouble over the six-pounders stolen from the wreck, the Crusoelike fortifications on the shipbuilding beach at Oroolong, the tricky negotiations about the numbers of men and the quantity of weapons and ammunition that might be spared for the campaign, all are unmistakable signs of a very feudal kind of conflict that could only be brought to a successful conclusion by close attention to protocol and by studied diplomatic maneuvers, such as the blackguarding of Soogle.

Despite Keate's rather strained contrast between a feudal scene of investiture ("where the Gothic hall is decorated with waving banners—where mitred prelates assist the ceremony—where the pomp of regal state imposes on the sense" [Keate 1788, 236]) and the actual ceremony in which Captain Wilson is advanced to the "Order of the Bone," the tusk bangle that distinguishes a chief, there is a close parallel between them. Each determines the level of fealty to sovereign power. When Keate goes on to praise the forbearance of the king, who, in seeming to forget the mistrust of his guests, "transmit[s] to posterity a most captivating picture of the forcible, yet mild triumph of virtue" (251), he points indirectly to the coerciveness of sympathetic gestures, and how smoothly they can be adapted (as Paine and Godwin knew) to the exercise of absolute power. Some years later, when Captain Procter felt obliged to refuse "this untutored son of nature" the arms he was demanding, he describes how terribly a look of sensibility could cut a passage to the spectator's heart: "The good old King said, it was well, that I must obey my superior rupack; but he gave me a look so very impressive of disappointment, yet so free from anger, that I confess it quite overpowered me" (Keate 1803 [Supplement], 40). Abba Thule may not have been Devis's equal on paper, but he is unrivalled in his command over the medium of the flesh, and of the faces needed to be put on if his misbehaving guests are to be quelled. As Keate gets closer to this truth, he has no choice but to assume that the king has been copying faces, and that he has learned the look of sadness and joy from the faces of his guests, an immediate transfer of the print and pressure of feeling: "I am happy to find you are happy" (Keate 1788, 260). In this way, he can redeem mimicry from the imputation of art, and ignore the threat lurking in a sympathetic glance. Even while suppressing the evidence of local art, at no point does he consider, even obliquely, that either art or nature could be culture.

There is a parallel instance of European misreading of sympathy in John Liddiard Nicholas's *Narrative of a Voyage to New Zealand* (1817).

Confused by the symptoms of noble and ignoble savagery in the Maori he meets, Nicholas tries to isolate the two extremes, noting that Korrakorra, the chief with whom he is traveling toward the Bay of Islands, operates in apparently opposite registers. In talking of war, "his gestures and manner became outrageous to the very extreme of frenzy; a savage fury took possession for the time of all his senses; his whole frame shook with rage." But when he is reunited with his aunt, Korrakorra weeps uncontrollably, "the big drops rolling down his manly cheeks," so that "it was impossible to remain an unconcerned spectator; and though I mean not to proclaim to the world my own sensibility, I must say . . . that I could not withhold the tear of feeling at this interview" (Nicholas 1817, 1:27, 1:117). Ignoring the resemblances between these two scenes of passion, and placing the one at the bottom and the other at the top of a scale of natural virtue, Nicholas is keen to find out if there is an intermediate stage of mere irritability somewhere between the two. So he tries teasing Korrakorra by throwing wood chips at him, an experiment that goes badly wrong when the chief responds by hurling a lump of pitch at Nicholas, then challenging him to fight. In the course of the struggle, Nicholas fires a pistol, at which his antagonist "became furiously outrageous, jumping and roaring about like the most crazy bedlamite," deaf to Nicholas's explanation that the pistol was deliberately unloaded. But in the midst of his fury there is a sudden transition: "He wept bitterly, and turning all his reproaches against himself, expressed the most poignant regret for having behaved with so much violence, and taken my joke in a serious manner . . . the tears streaming from his eyes. . . . I was distressed by his emotion, and being immediately reconciled to him, we were now as good friends as ever" (424). Presented with a conundrum in the shape of a European who appears to want, and yet not want to fight, Korrakorra resorts to the second of his two expressive modes, and instantly subdues his tormentor.

Although Nicholas wishes to construe this switch of gestures as the triumph of the child of nature over the bloody and tumultuous savage, just as Keate tries to explain the political art of Abba Thule as ingenuous openness, it is plain in both encounters that the cultural preference of Britons for tearful signs of nature allows the local object of attention—the starling or the parrot, as it were—to seize the initiative and sing back. This happens not simply because local culture is being misunderstood as a noble or savage state of nature, but because the proximity of sympathy to aggression, evident even in metropolitan examples, is persistently ignored, treated as its antithesis, never as its counterpart. Whereas it is plain that in Polynesian culture the face of woe is put on in the same way as a tattoo (as Purea demonstrates to the Dolphins), a material addition to a state of powerful feeling that in some sense represents it, like the mimicries of Arra Kooker or the drawings of the king, and that in some sense is consubstantial with it, like the roar of an animal. It cannot have taken long for these islanders to understand that their management of the noise of woe gave them the edge with Europeans, who found it impossible not be overpowered by it, cut to the heart as by a natural force.

At the center of the confrontation on Pelew is a very simple and unsentimental issue of food. The Chinese crew member charged by Captain Wilson with the job of noting the edible plants growing on the main island of Pelew (Koror) reported, like William Dampier of Australia, "This have very poor place, and very poor people; no got cloaths, no got rice, no got hog, no got nothing, only yam, little fish, and cocoa-nut; no got nothing make trade, very little make eat" (Keate 1788, 97). Despite Philip Benger's broad agreement with this estimate, particularly the lack of corn and livestock, Keate comments, "This fellow's description . . . sufficiently showed that he viewed mankind with the eye of a Dutchman, only calculating what was to be got from them" (ibid.). He ignores the two sides of the problem the Chinese and Benger disclose. The first is the impact on a fragile subsistence economy of fifty new mouths to feed. (Half a century later, wrecked with many fewer men on the same group, Horace Holden recorded that huge resources were necessary to feed them and supply them with timber for a boat [Holden 1836, 63]). The second is the anxiety over food endured by castaways who find themselves unable to catch fish (Keate 1788, 148), and incapable of adding anything but the occasional bird to supplement the stores saved from the wreck (a little biscuit, some water-damaged rice, a few hams, and some beef). If a boat was to be built, and the island reduced to its former population, it was necessary to find enough carbohydrate and protein to keep the crew working; and for the most part, their diet could only be supplied by their hosts, chiefly in the form of yams and fish. The only alternative was a war to the death, on the model of the Artingall campaigns, as a good many of Wilson's men foresaw.

There is evidence on both sides of the beach that the situation was becoming difficult. Food was rationed in proportion as the castaways were able offer gifts of the right quality, and to provide weapons and soldiers in war; notable feasts follow, for example, the first two expeditions to Artingall (Keate 1788, 131, 106). But when the visitors were not compliant, they felt it in their stomachs, getting old coconuts instead of new ones (162), or cooked yams instead of raw (221). Although Keate praises the self-restraint of the crew, he records thefts of food among them: hams are stolen and not recovered, and eventually the cook, James Swift, is scapegoated like Soogle, being blamed for spoiling the already spoiled rice and for sharing extra beef with his Chinese assistant (134, 184). In fact, everyone was forced to view the situation with the eyes of Dutchmen, for self-preservation demanded it. Horace Holden quotes Job at the predicament of a castaway slenderly supplied: "All that a man hath will he give for his life" (Holden 1836, 39).

Shaftesbury used the same quotation to express his contempt for the marketable self that rates the value of life only by the pleasures of the senses, and is never ready to part with them but "on the condition of being repaid in the same coin and with good interest into the bargain" (Shaftesbury 1964, 1:82). It is a sophisticated selfishness, he suggested, not a state of nature, because it has lost all loyalty to the species; whereas with him it is an axiom, "That if anything be natural . . . 'tis that which is preservative of the kind itself" (1:74). Perhaps it is the assumed proximity of sympathy to the state of nature that forces it always to be skirting an unflattering view of human instincts. The law of the heart, said Georg Hegel, calques upon a war of all against all, with each individual struggling to maintain the validity of a private rule: "What seems to be public order, then, is this universal state of war, in which each wrests what he can for himself" (Hegel 1977, 227). Perhaps this is the reason that Smith and Ferguson turn to the ferocity of death song as oddly exemplary of the situation of sympathy, "a grand and terrible game," as Joanna Baillie called it (Baillie 1798, 1:7). Yorick finds himself holding the lady's hand in Calais by an unaccountable transition from sentiments of war ("thy hand is against every man, and every man's hand against thee") to those of peace ("Heaven forbid indeed! said I, offering her my own" [Sterne 1967, 39]). Burke is trying to reckon up the savageries implicit in sympathetic exchange when he says in the fourth *Letter on a Regicide Peace* that a heart too soft can harden unless it is supported by a hatred of cruelty: "The pretended gentleness, which excludes that charitable rancour, produces an indifference, which is half an approbation. They never will love where they ought to love, who do not hate where they ought to hate" (Burke 1991, 9:103). Herman Melville said of a Polynesian nation about to be ruined by Christian sympathy, "I can sympathise in the spirit which prompts the Typee warrior to guard all the passes to his valley with the point of his levelled spear" (Melville 1964, 231). On Pelew, the two extremes are always close, and all that prevents them from breaking out into violence is Abba Thule's ability to triumph over the British with a coercive technique they conveniently mistake for the irenic gestures of a natural man.

Keate's interest in these transactions arose from his friendship with Lee Boo, the prince of nature whom he met four years before he published his *Account,* and who died of smallpox in Rotherhithe. Like his father, Abba Thule, Lee Boo was a skillful mimic. Having been enrolled at the local academy, "He amused the whole family by his vivacity, noticing every particularity he saw in any of his school-fellows, with great good-humour mimicking their different manners, sometimes saying he would have a school of his own when he returned to Pelew" (Keate 1788, 348). It is to be expected that Keate would place these skills to the account of nature: "He adapted himself very readily to whatever he saw were the customs of the country, and fully confirmed me in an opinion which I have ever entertained, that *natural* good manners is the *natural* result of *natural* good sense" (349). Keate (like Gulliver) found the same example of simplicity in his horse. Sterne thought he heard it in the starling's notes, and Temple wanted to believe there was nothing more than that in Prince Maurice's dialogue with the parrot.

Whether Lee Boo was responsive purely to natural impulses, or whether he was operating under his father's subtler regimen, he was restricted to a narrow circuit. Not for him the court end of town Omai had traversed with such success. His social consequence arose only from "the singularity of this young man's situation," and his performances were treated as a circus act of "affability and propriety of behaviour," imitated by a savage ignorant of the social value of what he was copying. Keate tries to disguise Lee Boo's role as starling by declaring the genealogy of natural civility, but in telling the reader that, "when he took leave of the company, there was hardly any one present who did not feel satisfaction in having had an interview with him" (Keate 1788, 346), he cannot quite disguise how little initiative lay on the prince's side. He could only please or fail to please, be worth the trouble of going to see, or not. He was being shown as a curiosity, as Gulliver's miniature animals are shown at Greenwich, or as Gulliver himself is shown in Brobdingnag. On the one occasion that he sings his own song, he is not asked to repeat it, "every one's ears [being] stunned with the horrid notes" (349).

There are two moments in this narrative resistant to the presentation of Lee Boo's mimicries as nature. The first occurs when he is asked what he understands by the miniature portrait Keate has had painted of himself; he replies, "Lee Boo understand well—that Misser Keate die—this Misser Keate live" (Keate 1788, 353). Although Keate tries to generalize the prince's observation, just as Yorick tries to generalize the message of the imprisoned starling, the possibility that Lee Boo understands how identical faces comprise a winner and a loser, a self that is preserved and another that isn't, is developed in the sequel. Lee Boo catches smallpox and sees his face in the mirror so disfigured by the disease that he cannot bear to look at it, turning away "as if disgusted by his own appearance" (357). It is the counterpart of the scene where he first saw his reflection, and looked behind the mirror for the other person. Knowing now that he can no longer call his reflection his own, the prince prepares for death. He can't get out.

Back at Pelew, the dog Sailor and Madan Blanchard were pupils in the school of nature. Nothing more is heard of Sailor, but Blanchard turned out a reprobate. Despite being given a list of instructions by Wilson designed to keep him respectable—not to go naked, not to get tattooed—and despite being imagined by Keate to be capable of a fine sentimental memoir, if only he could write, Blanchard ended up a beachcomber who "left off wearing clothes, and was tatooed or marked like the other inhabitants" (Hockin 1803, 13). He set an example nevertheless to John Mac-Cluer, commander of the *Panther*, who deserted his ship to settle on Pelew, having (as he said) "found my situation quite a paradise" (24). When Holden was shipwrecked there, he met Charles Washington, a castaway who had spent so long on the island that he could only speak a broken English (Holden 1836, 56). These are starlings on the other side, trying to adapt to the customs of a primitive culture, and to speak mechanically in an alien tongue to strangers who might find it in their hearts to respond with sympathy. Matthew Flinders, a mariner who had the misfortune to spend many years a prisoner of the French on the island of Mauritius, found in Sterne's bird an apt emblem of this condition. While he was still seeking ways out of his prison, appealing for assistance to Fleurieu, a French academician, he wrote to his wife, "'I can't get out,' cried the starling. God help thee, says Yorick, but I'll let thee out. May Fleurieu feel as much humanity" (Flinders n.d.; quoted in Carter 1987, 200). It was not a very happy parallel to draw.

9

THE SETTLEMENT OF
NEW ZEALAND

And, whereas the Mind of Man, when he gives the Spur and Bridle to his Thoughts,
doth never stop, but naturally sallies out into both extreams of High and Low, of
Good and Evil; His first Flight of Fancy, commonly transports Him to Idea's of what
is most Perfect, finished and exalted; till having soared out of his own Reach and
Sight, not well perceiving how near the Frontiers of Height and Depth, border upon
each other; With the same Course and Wing, he falls down plumb into the lowest
Bottom of Things . . . like a dead Bird of Paradise, to the Ground.
    —Jonathan Swift, *A Tale of a Tub*

This study has examined the variety of ways in which the business of
self-preservation is transacted in the South Seas, at the farthest reaches
from the metropolis. I have tried to write a cultural history of the strains,
nostalgias, and contradictions that occasionally supplant all contractual
links between private interest and the public good, suspending any continuous sense of personal identity and putting in its place a sublime intuition of dislocation and menace, accompanied by feelings of intense
yearning, misery, or delight. During these emergencies in remote places,
where the mood borders on infatuation and the narrative shatters into
moments of je ne sais quoi, the self experiences—with various degrees of
reflective shock—the loss of social will and the invalidation of the moral
sense. Contract, public spirit, sympathy, and all the other means available
to agents of civility for correcting the distortions of rugged individualism,
merely confirm the isolation of the self in a state of nature (often disguised
as a utopia), where contracts are used only to undermine contracts; where
being in the world is understood only be being out of it; and where sympathetic substitution becomes usurpation. These contradictions prove the
truth of Bernard Mandeville's dictum, namely that contraries are best
cured by contraries, and that civil society operates best when it is ignorant

of the forces that convert its inconstancy into order, its vices into virtues. For as soon as the individual becomes conscious of a will to act charitably, he or she inevitably advances the opposite of what is proposed.

That this metropolitan argument in favor of a brisk and heedless consumption of manufactures should find its exemplification in the South Seas is just one more paradox to add to a world already upside down, ethically speaking. If self-interest alone can be relied on to procure the mutual care only love was supposed to bestow, why shouldn't the savage ends of the world offer the center a familiar and congenial image, and the wild improbabilities of mariners reveal the truest things about it? In *Gulliver's Travels*, Jonathan Swift works his irony steadily along this axis. From the romances of the buccaneers, which intersected so nicely with the opulent promises of the South Sea Company, to the subsequent variations played upon a theme of global benevolence, a direct equivalence can be observed between metropolitan practices and experiences in the Pacific. Curiosities garnered in distant lands are lodged in museums, just as the manufactures of London and Birmingham end up in Polynesian collections. Fetishes of the marketplace, like those of the South Seas beach or the Guinea coast, perform the same miracle of materializing a spiritual or abstract idea. No cultural advantage accrues to one or the other, inasmuch as the primitive or remote example does not merely represent or figure a metropolitan practice, but names and effectually is the same thing. A curiosity in a Polynesian hoard of cargo is no different from an accession to the British Museum: it is no more or less significant; it serves the same purpose; it gives the same pleasure. A shaman's infatuation on the beach is the same as an investor's in Exchange Alley, although the reasons for their fits and raptures may differ widely. There is very little real difference to be noticed here, because these are the blended effects of a change in the civil self corresponding to an alteration in the tribal person that leaves both much more susceptible to new impressions than they were before (Taussig 1993, 7–8; Pocock 1999; Aravamudan 1999, Turner 1999).

In this chapter, I want to conclude the argument by examining the background to the settlement of New Zealand, and a little of its later history, both fertile in these center-edge resemblances. I will stretch the limits of the long eighteenth century so far as to include in its outer boundary Samuel Butler's *Erewhon* (1872), published the same year that Te Kooti Arikirangi te Turuki, a warrior prophet, gave up the last of Maori armed resistance to the confiscations imposed on North Island *iwi* (tribes) in the wake of the Land Wars of the 1860s. Butler could not have made a handsome fortune running sheep in the Canterbury province on land alienated from its Maori owners, had it not been for the visionary labors of another prophet, Edward Gibbon Wakefield. Wakefield was a careful reader of Thomas Malthus and an editor of Adam Smith's *The Wealth of Nations* (1836), and he had elaborated a theory of colonization on the basis of what he understood of competition, rent, population, and the value of land. For his part, Butler was an avid disciple of Charles Darwin's theory of natural selection until he decided that natural selection was a tautology ("the survival of those which survive") falsely justifying industrial modes of production (Butler 1933, 27–29). *Erewhon* marks the sea change in Butler's opinions concerning the struggle for life, for in this story of a utopia without machines, there is a prophecy ("The Book of the Machines") of a time when humans will be reduced to the condition of machinate mammals, machine-tickling aphids whose addiction to the comforts of prosthesis, it is foretold, will end in absolute servitude to machines capable of reproducing and reflecting upon themselves.

To appreciate fully the turn of thought in these two pioneers, it is necessary to consider how the line of political economy that leads from Mandeville to Smith continues in the work of Malthus, only to be strangely reborn as natural law when it emerged from the market to inhabit the evolutionary theories of Darwin and Alfred Wallace. This extraordinary inversion of the priority of nature, now understood to obey the law invented by humans for the production and exchange of goods, likewise is looped through these identical South Seas, where the market found its first speculative opportunity, and where disciples of its latest theories will try to re-export it. What is more, the law that undulates between these levels of political economy and nature is the law of self-preservation.

In his doctrine of necessary ignorance, Mandeville shows what manifold advantages arise from not knowing how desire speeds production, or how production satisfies desire. Heedlessness accelerates happiness, but consciousness of how the self contributes to these processes, or benefits from them, actually inhibits pleasure by encouraging mistaken reliance upon forethought. In exploring this contradiction in *The Fable of the Bees*, Mandeville was germinating Karl Marx's idea of history as a force resulting from human activity, but not from human will. By widening the gap between the conduct of commercial life and the ethical values that were supposed to govern society, Mandeville introduced a motive for social innovation, historical change, and sensual pleasure that had nothing to do with Providence or prudence, but arose merely from the myriad trials made by individuals at maximizing their delights. The narrative of such a force is not easy to give. The story Mandeville tells is of a disaster in planning, not a success in aesthetics. Since this disaster stems from a belief in the perfectibility of the species, Mandeville evinces as little respect for utopias as for exemplars of politeness and Societies for the Reformation of Manners.

History is shaped by a force not easily understood except in the failures of those who neglect to adapt to it. Success—if Mandeville himself is a good example of it—lies in a tolerance for paradox, and a relish for the serpentine indirection of the causes of events. In his pamphlet *A Modest Defence of the Publick Stews* (1724), he traces, for example, the dependence of chastity upon lewdness, just as in his *Fable of the Bees* he shows how good springs up and pullulates from evil. I have suggested earlier that this pose of *louche* cynicism veils a paradoxically utopian conception of the market, or at least a degree of personal foresight and critique operating above the level of necessary ignorance. But what this half-knowledge might be, and how it relates to what the human animal is taught and to what belongs to it naturally, Mandeville is never prepared unequivocally to state. His propensity for analysis and explanation never supplants his wonder at the fact that things never turn out as we would have them.

Although, in *The Wealth of Nations,* Adam Smith concedes that the benefits of society derive not from human wisdom but from acting upon desires (Smith 1976, 1:25), he restores something like Providence to human affairs with the touch of the market's invisible hand; nor is he ever so misled by accidental benefactions as to assume that personal ethics are not a matter of rigorous self-control, as the latter section of his *Theory of Moral Sentiments* demonstrates. To this extent, he presents (like Mandeville) an account of the force of the market that is not quite as unfathomable as some of the examples on which it depends. Once it is possible to explain why the Dutch Wars procured by means of heedless animosity what deliberate policy would have recommended but scarcely been able to accomplish, namely the reduction of the naval power of Holland (1:464), history falls into some kind of order, even if the present is inscrutable. And the narrative seems to point to a general improvement of life, for even the desire to be free of the need to work ensures that more work is done, as machines are improved and labor saved and redistributed. The stadial theory of John Millar, leading to a social history of the forces of production, is affiliated with Smith's applied ignorance concerning the origin and development of the market. Failure in Smith's terms amounts to any hindrance to the free play of supply and demand; success is accommodation to the tendency of the market, a process Smith is unafraid to call natural (Parker 1995, 129). His optimism has its basis in his theory of value. As value depends upon the amount of labor invested in the production of commodities, a proportion always exists between the total amount of work done in a nation and the necessaries of life consumed in it, apart from the surplus that is consumed as luxuries. A day's labor will always produce a subsistence for the laborer, provided he can work, and thus there is a limit to what can go wrong in a functioning economy.

Malthus follows Mandeville in contrasting utopian simplicities, such as those he culls from William Godwin's *Political Justice* (1798), with the real state of the case, reducible to his proposition that for the bulk of humanity, the direct pursuit of happiness ends inevitably in misery (Malthus 1970, 137). Although this seems quite at odds with Mandeville's optimism, in fact they are both convinced that there is a sharp distinction to be drawn between the laboring and consuming classes. Malthus cites the surge in consumption among a growing population as the cause of this unhappiness, while Mandeville cites a collapse of demand; but they are agreed that any vulgar solution to the problem of poverty, such as charitable benefactions, will undoubtedly produce an outcome far from philanthropic. It will teach workers to dream of not working so hard; it will persuade those with the least means of supporting them that they can have children (Mandeville 1924, 1:300; Malthus 1970, 98). As for the force that drives these paradoxes, Mandeville might have been less forthright than Smith in calling it natural, but Malthus goes further even than Smith in clearing away all figurative uncertainty from the drive to compete for limited resources—that is, for land—stripping it of any cultural nuance or historical variation in order to declare it a universal law of nature, true at all times and in all places. It is not labor, therefore, that creates value, but land, and the more land individuals cultivate, the greater their chances of survival. He flies in the face of Locke, who had asserted, "'Tis Labour indeed that puts the difference of value upon every thing. . . . And the ground which produces the materials, is scarce to be reckon'd in" (Locke 1960, 339). In effect, Malthus restores civil society to a state of nature; and in explaining why Godwin's utopia is a sheer fantasy of the community of gratified desires, he goes a good deal further than Mandeville in specifying this drive to compete as the law of self-preservation:

This beautiful fabric of imagination vanishes at the severe touch of truth. The spirit of benevolence, cherished and invigorated by plenty, is repressed by the chilling breath of want. The hateful passions that had vanished reappear. The mighty law of self-preservation expels all the softer and more exalted emotions of the soul. The temptations to evil are too strong for human nature to resist. . . . Provisions no longer flow in for the support of the mother with a large family. The children are sickly from insufficient food. The rosy flush of health gives place to the pallid cheek and hollow eye of misery. Benevolence, yet lingering in a few bosoms, makes some faint expiring struggles, till at length self-love resumes his wonted empire and lords it triumphant over the world. (Malthus 1970, 138)

Malthus is describing a world of surplus population—the world he believed he lived in—as necessarily indifferent to all forms of amelioration except the harshest self-restraint or most abandoned depravity; it operates according to laws "inherent in the nature of man, and absolutely independent of all human regulations" (Malthus 1970, 138). History, therefore, is a tale of thwarted desires, usurpations, plagues, famines, and wars—the necessary checks upon the multiplication of the species unmodified by human will. After reading Malthus, Pitt the Younger dropped his bill for extending poor relief to larger families (Young 1985, 29), convinced that good intentions only collaborated in what they sought to avoid. Although the laws of nature dictate in irresistible terms the necessity of a law of property, thus abridging the war of all against all (Malthus 1970, 268), it is hard to avoid seeing property relations in Malthus as a timeless standoff between those who possess something more than their labor power, and those who do not.

Marx was convinced that this naturalization of social and economic law was a trick on Malthus's part to blind his readers to the historical differences in modes of production, and to the specific differences in the relation of the poor to the rich at different periods. "[Malthus] would find in history that population proceeds in very different relations, and that overpopulation is likewise a historically determined relation, in no way determined by abstract numbers or by the absolute limit of the productivity of the necessaries of life, but by limits posited rather by specific conditions of production" (Marx 1978, 276). The paupers fed in a workhouse are not recipients of the same sort of charity as those fed in a monastery. These distinctions chart the movement of "humanity's own process of history" instead of the fantasy of "this natural Malthusian man," actuated at every stage by natural law (277). Humanity may not be able to make history as it wishes, Marx says, but at least humanity makes it.

But it was Malthus's reduction of economic to natural law that appealed so strongly to Darwin and Wallace, codiscoverers of the theory of natural selection. Each announced the importance of Malthus in arriving at the formulation. Darwin said of his *Origin of Species* (1859), "It is the doctrine of Malthus applied with manifold force to the whole animal and vegetable kingdom" (Darwin 1968, 117). In *Natural Selection and Tropical Nature* (1895), Wallace recalls, "I was suffering from a rather severe attack of intermittent fever at Ternate in the Moluccas . . . and something led me to think of the 'positive checks' described by Malthus in his 'Essay on Population,' a work I had read several years before, and which had made a deep and permanent impression on my mind" (Wallace 1895, 20). Thus it is that a mode of thought exclusively adapted to the consideration of self-preservation as a social and economic propensity, contractually harnessed and culturally determined, is metamorphosed into a law of nature governing all living things. Evidence of its universal sway was gathered on the eastern and western rims of the Pacific Ocean, Darwin concentrating on the mainland and islands of the South American coast, and Wallace on the Malay Archipelago, paying careful attention to the Aru Islands, off the coast of Papua New Guinea. As they reconnoitered "the greatest terra incognita that still remains . . . where altogether new and unimagined forms of life may yet be found" (Wallace 1962, 420), they honored those who had gone before. Darwin quotes Woodes Rogers, William Dampier, and William Cowley when he gets to the Galapagos Islands; Wallace quotes William Funnell on the bird of paradise (Darwin 1902, 389, 403; Wallace 1962, 420). At Tierra del Fuego, Darwin tells his sister he is treading classic ground, because Cook and Banks were there before him (Darwin 1945, 80).

It turns out in the middle of the nineteenth century to be no easier to produce a narrative of this terra incognita than it had been a century earlier. The je ne sais quoi makes regular appearances among their notations. Darwin says, "No drawing or description can at all explain the extreme interest which is created by the first sight of savages" (Darwin 1945, 80). When he finds a specimen of the king bird of paradise *(paradisea regia)*, Wallace notes, "The emotions excited in the mind of a naturalist, who has long desired to see the actual thing which he has hitherto known only by description, drawing, or badly-preserved external covering—especially when that thing is of surpassing rarity and beauty—requires the poetic faculty fully to express them" (Wallace 1962, 339). Wallace's reasons for rejecting the Linnaean system, like Philibert Commerson's a hundred years before, lie in the profusion of nature, especially in this part of the world: "Many causes, no doubt, have operated of which we must ever remain in ignorance, and we may, therefore, expect to find many details very difficult of explanation" (Wallace 1895, 4). But these moments of exquisite explanatory failure advertise a more serious narrative breakdown. In Darwin's case, this has been traced by Robert Young to his ultimate failure to produce natural selection as evidence of design, although he believed that he had done so. He wished to propose evolution as a set of variations in species precipitated by the mobility of the earth's surface, such as geological and climatological changes. In this account, Nature is not a personified agent, selecting with foresight, but a chain of second causes guided by a known law (variations best adapted to the environment will ensure survival) answerable to the inscrutable purposes of the first cause and sole architect, God. The law and its remarkable exemplifications are supposed to be the symptoms of design, just like the astonishing complexity of a watch. But Darwin's metaphors let him down. The most peculiar one appears in the chapter of the *Origin* entitled "Struggle for Existence": "The face of Nature may be compared to a yielding surface, with ten thousand sharp wedges packed close together and driven inwards by incessant blows, sometimes one wedge being struck, and then another with greater force" (Darwin 1968, 119). Selection here is the result of a force administered by an invisible hand upon a passive nature; and whether this hand is forging a more perfect sphere, or whether it isn't just another metaphor for a force operating without direction, is left ambiguous (Young 1985, 93, 111; Beer 1983, 68). Has evolution a telos, or is life nothing but a perpetual adaptation to circumstances changed by chance?

Wallace set himself to answer these questions by rehistorizing what Malthus had naturalized, and coming up with a genealogy of the moral sense. Human development, he argues, has transformed the struggle for existence. Survival is no longer ensured by individual competition, but by maintaining a common cause; benevolence is not a sign of weakness but of species strength. "By his superior sympathetic and moral feelings [man] becomes fitted for the social state; he ceases to plunder the weak and helpless of his tribe; he shares the game which he has caught with less active or less fortunate hunters, or exchanges it for weapons which even the weak or the deformed can fashion; he saves the sick and wounded from death; and thus the power which leads to the rigid destruction of all animals who cannot in every respect help themselves, is prevented from acting on him" (Wallace 1895, 184). Once this division has taken place between the natural and the social worlds, an "inherent progressive power" supervenes, quite distinct from the law of the survival of the fittest. Then the refined pleasures of civilization—"the wonderful conceptions of mathematics and philosophy"—become important to the last stage of human development, guided (as he infers) by a superior intelligence (204). The trouble is that humanity even in its most developed aspect participates unwittingly in the struggle for life by causing the extinction of species less developed than its own. As he gazes at the bird of paradise, rapt in the supererogatory glory of its plumage, Wallace meets the full force of this contradiction, that what he is most apt to admire, he is most certainly destined to destroy:

> Such ideas excite a feeling of melancholy. It seems sad that on the one hand such exquisite creatures should live out their lives and exhibit their charms only in these wild, inhospitable regions . . . while on the other hand, should civilised man ever reach these distant lands, and bring moral, intellectual, and physical light into the recesses of these virgin forests, we may be sure that he will so disturb the nicely-balanced relations of organic and inorganic nature as to cause the disappearance, and finally the extinction, of these very beings whose wonderful structure and beauty he is fitted to appreciate and enjoy. (Wallace 1962, 340)

The same bittersweet mood had been experienced by Pedro Fernandez de Quirós, George Forster, Sir Joseph Banks, and Anders Sparrman, and was to be felt again by Robert Louis Stevenson. It is not even a clean paradox of the best combined with the worst that motivates it. Wallace notes that civilization privileges the mediocre rather than the best, "for it is indisputably the mediocre, if not the low, both as regards morality and intelligence, who succeed best in life and multiply fastest" (Wallace 1895, 185). "It is not too much to say, that the mass of our populations have not at all advanced beyond the savage code of morals, and have in many cases sunk below it" (Wallace 1962, 456). Here is a reason, at least, for the extinction of indigenous peoples, which he prophesies with great confidence: "The true Polynesians, inhabiting the farthest isles of the Pacific, are no doubt doomed to an early extinction. . . . A warlike and energetic people, who will not submit to national slavery or to domestic servitude, must disappear before the white man as surely as do the wolf and the tiger" (455). Darwin prophesied the same outcome: "When civilised nations come into contact with barbarians the struggle is short" (Darwin 1901, 283). No matter which way a narrative of human development is constructed from naturalized political economy, it exemplifies Malthus's law of self-preservation.

Between 1827 and 1830, Edward Gibbon Wakefield was a convict in Newgate Prison, where he was serving three years as punishment for conspiracy. In March 1826, he had eloped with Ellen Turner, a young heiress. Having gone through a form of marriage in Scotland, he took her to France, where he was eventually cornered by her relations, and brought to trial. Although the child was still a virgin, her friends were well connected, and Wakefield spent a great deal of money vainly claiming that she had willingly participated in the adventure. It was widely assumed that his views were solely mercenary, although the correspondent of the *Liverpool Mercury* (2 June 1826) was probably nearer the truth in opining that "the lure of enterprise and adventure seems all along to have been his ruling passion" (*Conspiracy and Abduction* 1827, 27). Wakefield came from an impoverished but well-known Quaker family which, in its various branches, seems to have been fond of elopement. His father, Edward, eloped when he was seventeen; his uncle Daniel was lured into marriage by an adventuress; Wakefield himself eloped with his first wife in 1816; and William, his brother, eloped with a Macclesfield heiress. Altogether there were six clandestine marriages among his immediate kin, exhibiting what Richard Garnett, his first biographer, called "a fine irregular genius for marriage" (Martin 1997, 24). Elopements and mock marriage were still an important part of popular culture, and the Gretna Green marriage, involving the crossing of a border in order to turn romance into reality, was a transformation that appealed to Wakefield (O'Connell 1999). In prison, his mind turned from the romance of the Scottish border to Australia, a topic no doubt canvassed quite eagerly in Newgate as the likely destination of so many of its inmates. It was there that he wrote his first treatise on colonization, styled quite incorrectly *A Letter from Sydney* (1829). In it Wakefield paints a vivid picture of colonial life, while asking his reader to recollect, "I am standing, with my head downwards, as it were, almost under your feet" (Wakefield 1929, 30). He was marking out the antipodes as a familiar scene of action while referring to the metropolis as an exotic land of dreams, "a *terra incognita* . . . a far distant and unknown country" (Wakefield 1831, viii).

Briefly, the content of Wakefield's various pamphlets and books was a neo-Malthusian thesis with a utopian solution (Stenhouse 1994). He believed Britain's population had become so large that the struggle for life was being renewed at all levels of society, not just at the most impoverished. Although crime and Chartism were menacing the middle class from outside, from the inside unmarried women competed with each other, in this "the greatest and saddest convent that the world has ever seen" (Wakefield 1849, 75); professional men competed for clients; younger sons competed with younger sons; and finally, capital was competing unproductively with capital (74). What ought to have been a set of calculable social and economic relations was becoming a series of gambles as people took increasingly fantastic steps to make a profit.

Wakefield's solution was to trump these petty dreams with one enormous speculation. His idea was to invest in a colony capable of reproducing the social system of the mother country in a space large enough to alleviate the effects of competition while at the same time giving capital a high rate of return. In 1837, the New Zealand Association was formed with the intention of securing a grant of ten years' sovereignty in New Zealand (Winch 1965, 111). When that move was defeated, the New Zealand Land Company was set up as a joint-stock company, and in a bold move reminiscent of the flamboyance of the South Sea Company the previous century, it issued four hundred shares at twenty-five pounds per share, redeemable in land that was yet to be purchased or settled. *The Times* reported in a rather confused pun (3 February 1838), "Law's South-Sea scheme was a bauble to this" (Hopper 1838, 35–36). By exchanging with Maori a collection of commodities whose diversity bore some resemblance to the conversational resources of Lewis Carroll's walrus and carpenter (pencils, looking glasses, jews' harps, sealing wax), Wakefield was able to claim he had bought from the indigenous owners a territory the size of Ireland; and by February 1840, more than 1,100 settlers (216 first and second class, 909 steerage) were embarked for New Zealand. In effect, Wakefield was forcing the British government's hand. Although very reluctant to do so, it felt obliged to annex New Zealand later the same year in order to prevent uncontrolled emigration, dubious land deals, and serious provocations to the local population. The New Zealand Company emerged in 1841 with one million acres confirmed by a crown grant.

Wakefield was committing a circuit of illegal, or at least nonlegal, transactions: he was issuing stock in a company that had no tradable asset but a speculative land purchase; he was acquiring land for trifles from Maori who were ignorant of the terms of a European sale; and he was arranging for settlement on land in New Zealand which, even if it had been fairly bought, had no basis in law, since the territory lay in a foreign country in which the British crown had declared no interest, and with which it had not yet signed a treaty. As Arthur Thomson observed, "the Company had as much right to sell estates in Spain as in New Zealand" (Thomson 1859, 2:13); and it had no right to settle anyone upon them. But Wakefield, professed enemy to speculation and gambling of any kind, saw nothing wrong in a scheme that ensured a speedy arrival at the realization of what he persistently called a theory, art, or system of colonization. Australia, in his opinion, was the result merely of uncoordinated attempts to shed surplus population, "an immense amount of practice without any theory . . . vast doings but no principles" (Wakefield 1849, 42), among which he held the doings at Swan River to be the most miserable. The Swan River settlement failed in 1829 because there was nothing but land with which to pay labor, which meant that laborers were perpetually metamorphosing into property owners—the theme dominating *A Letter from Sydney*. New Zealand was to be managed differently, according to a plan whose core was the high price of land.

There were various practical reasons for this strategy: it allowed the company to raise a large amount of money from subscribers in order to purchase cheaply a commodity that, when reinscribed on tradable paper, represented a vast capital asset. The high price excluded riffraff from the outset from joining the settlement, since company colonists needed a title to land, in the form of redeemable shares, before they set sail. This guaranteed people of the right caliber ("of the finest sort, in the prime of manhood, of approved moral character, and in good health" [Thomson 1859, 2:13]), and the success of the flotation (one hundred acres and a town lot from the New Zealand Company was reckoned by hopeful applicants to be the equivalent of winning the lottery) kept up a good supply of them. A high price further ensured that speculation by colonists themselves would be dampened, since the profit from the land was already incorporated into its value, giving settlers a powerful motive to stay where they were originally placed, both within the settlement and the social structure. Richard Taylor jeered that land in the Canterbury settlement was costing at least half the price paid by Queen Victoria for her estate at Balmoral (Taylor 1855, 264).

Nevertheless, Wakefield's attachment to high prices followed a line of utopian logic. In its price, land was to bear the value of its improvement. Its history as a developed asset and as an instrument of civilization was telescoped into the single transaction by which it became settleable. Unlike other commodities, whose prices were wooing glances cast in the direction of money, New Zealand Company land knew its value independently of the market. At twenty shillings an acre, it had already acquired the value of its future attributes of fertility, beauty, and community; and in this dehistoricizing of its value lay its virtue in ensuring the sustained civility of those who acquired it. The high price took the land out of time. As Paul Carter points out, "The process of colonisation becomes . . . for Wakefield and his followers a foregone conclusion" (Carter 1987, 211). Wakefield's contempt for the doings at Swan River arose because the land there lost its transcendence and decayed beyond the point of speculation into a primitive form of money. Theory, or system, represented for Wakefield an intelligible symmetry superior to the uncertainty of market forces, an exhilarating ideal quite the opposite of the ignorance of a gambler's dream of riches. To theorize meant forming a plan that was internally coherent and capable of a perfect transition into actuality, an organon from which all incalculable elements—chance, luck, and contingency—had been eliminated. It meant inaugurating an immortal economy unimpeded by shortage and unstifled by excess, whose perfection was declared in a single foundational move, not in blindly lumbering toward an invisible future. Like Prospero, Wakefield was fascinated by the power of spells. He said, "[T]he utmost happiness which God vouchsafes to man on earth [is] the realisation of his own idea" (Wakefield 1849, 33). The happiness he promised his colonists turned on the same rapid correspondence between the idea and the experience of perfection, "a perpetual feast of anticipated and realized satisfactions" (132). J. R. Godley, his collaborator in the Canterbury settlement, said of him, "his large and practical mind was never satisfied except in the realisation in action of the doctrines which it had been the object of his life to propound as theories" (Godley 1863, 5).

Wakefield's settlers had to carry with them everything of England but the soil and the climate (Thomson 1859, 2:13). The limiting factor in the Malthusian calculus—the land whose productive power grows in arithmetical ratio, compared with a population that grows geometrically—is guaranteed a perpetual supply in Wakefield's plan. Nor will it accidentally turn into the means of social revolution, because its sufficient price will ensure an unvarying relation of property to labor. The same objection Marx leveled at Malthus's economics, namely that it supplanted complex historical changes with a universal natural law, he directs at Wakefield's too. Whereas any free colony would encourage the transformation of wage workers into independent producers, here was a plan to export and artificially to preserve the class system of a specifically capitalist mode of production (Marx 1972, 853). The attitudes of a machine culture were to be frozen in a pastoral landscape. But by naturalizing economic law, and transferring the source of value from labor to land, Wakefield was aiming to eliminate the struggle for life. He wrote a fable about this in *England and America* (1834), where, in a dream vision, he meets Robinson Crusoe on his island and congratulates him upon his accumulation of capital, his seeds, tools, and goats. When an earthquake reduces the island to a mere half acre, Wakefield teaches the reader a lesson about the "field of production": "The only way Robinson and his man could get back to high profits and high wages, would be by getting back the land that they had lost" (Wakefield 1967, 79). New Zealand was to be Britain's Juan Fernandez.

In Butler's *Erewhon,* history has stopped much earlier. By banning clocks and watches, and dismantling all machines built in the previous two hundred and seventy years, the inhabitants have suspended life in an eternal preindustrial moment. In the museum, Higgs, the hero, beholds "fragments of steam engines . . . a broken fly-wheel, and part of a crank . . . fragments of a great many of our own most advanced inventions . . . placed where they were, not for instruction, but curiosity" (Butler 1970, 82). His hosts are very disturbed to find their visitor carrying a pocket watch, and instantly take it away. The utopian intention here is to eliminate all human dependence upon machines, liberating the body to autonomous and exquisite development. As well as being great aesthetes, then, the Erewhonians are shocked by physical signs of decay and disease. Indeed, failure to preserve the self is the only crime in Erewhon. Sickness is punished with shame, as well as with fines and imprisonment, attracting the same sort of odium that Malthus believed should always be annexed to poverty. Although dishonesty, fraud, and embezzlement are palliated as sicknesses of a different order, to be condoled with and asked after, it is expected they will be cured. Somewhere between these two points lies pregnancy, an ambush made by the unborn upon the sexual pleasures of the living—a Malthusian predicament somewhat blunted by the birth formulae, in which the child offers elaborate waivers of parental liability concerning any subsequent ill luck it may endure.

The immobilization of history is meant to show human beings at the full extent of their species capacity, unsupplemented by technology. It is middle-class life without machines, and with plenty of land—in many respects similar to Wakefield's New Zealand. Yet it is clear that the struggle for life is still being waged on all class fronts. The treatment of the sick, for example, is justified by the narrator in terms of the survival of the fittest ("the only means of preventing weakness and sickliness from spreading . . . there is no unfairness in punishing people for their misfortunes, or rewarding them for their sheer good luck: it is the normal condition of human life" [Butler 1970, 120]). He compares Erewhonian practice with the Maori institution of *muru:* "The New Zealand Maories visit any misfortune with forcible entry into the house of the offender, and the breaking up and burning of all his goods" (103). Rates of infanticide are on the rise in Erewhon because relations between the living and the unborn, as well as the living and the living, are conducted as a series of injuries and retaliations, suitable to a culture where, as Arthur Thomson and many others said of the Maori, "revenge is their strongest passion" (Thomson 1859, 1:86). Similarly, the Erewhonians' preference for being drawn through life backwards resembles the proverbial wisdom of the Maori concerning the future, which is to be approached with one's eyes firmly on the past ("i nga ra o mua").

Without machines, that is, and without a future, human beings at the limit of their possibilities act no differently from savages. The resemblance between Darwinian principles of evolution and Maori custom resonates with the equivocality of Higgs's mission in Erewhon. His inability to judge whether the demolition of machines in Erewhon has eradicated competition by halting progress, or whether it has simply set new terms for the struggle for life, is part of a piece with his own alternation between a pious desire to convert the Erewhonians, whom he is sure are one of the ten lost tribes of Israel, and his itch to exploit his discovery by blackbirding boatloads of them to the cane fields of Queensland, where they can be worked to death for a handsome profit. His ambiguous commitment is matched by his attitude to the Maori Chowbok, which swings between contempt for the man's spiritless venality and grudging admiration for his exhibition of Christian piety in London, where eventually he goes on a mission of conversion. Chowbok's real name, Kahapuka, translatable as something like Bookshaker or Troubletext, endows him with a shadowy part in the blurring and disorienting of Higgs's narrative. The civilizing savage as counterpart of the savage citizen, the other half of what Higgs cannot, or will not, disclose, Kahapuka brings the threat of reestrangement into this familiarization of the terra incognita.

Butler was in a cleft stick of his own making. He had written, "Every machine of every sort should be destroyed by the wellwisher of his species" (Butler 1915, 185). He based the judgment on the belief that evolution was a mechanical way of thinking about the machine age:

> What made Darwin's views acceptable to English intelligence was the justification of the nature of things, which it seemed to give to English life and policy. The changes to factory production of commodities for world markets had already called forth the exceptional increase in rate of growth of the population, which had already provided Malthus with his text. . . . The age of the machine had dawned, and as mechanical forces seemed supreme, so mechanical explanations seemed alone valid and final. (Butler 1933: 29)

From the bare organism that declares brutally, "I will suck whatever advantage I can from all my surroundings . . . and what I can do shall be the limit of what I will do" (Butler 1970, 201), all the way to the consciousness refined by the machines it has at its command, the same contempt for weakness and the same triumphing in strength is evident. The more things differ, the more they are the same. This seems to be the moral of *Erewhon Revisited* (1901), where, despite the restoration of machines, "deformatories" are maintained that (like the former Colleges of Unreason) teach the paradoxical truths of this upside-down world, including the dictum that "there is no mistake so great as that of being always right" (Butler 1915, 159). Alertness to contrary possibilities, "the everlasting Is-and-Is-Not of nature" (Butler 1970, 146), and a hostility to downright expressions, are strongly marked characteristics of Erewhon at both periods of its development. Higgs says, "It is a distinguishing peculiarity of the Erewhonians that when they profess themselves to be quite certain about any matter, and avow it as a base on which they are to build a system of practice, they seldom quite believe in it" (162). Hypothetics and the cult of Ydgrun alike are designed to open the imagination "to a set of utterly strange and impossible contingencies," and to get away from any simple-minded belief in the efficacy of good intentions (185, 160). The maxim of Ydgrun is "neutral tones are one thing, muddiness is another . . . the losing in deep shadow is one thing, a diffused smudginess is another" (Butler 1872, 144). In this dialectic of contraries, the echo of a utopian litotes can be heard, strangely confounded with the Mandevillean hypocrisies of civil society, each combining to neutralize Butler's arguments for and against Darwinian evolution.

Wakefield's pastoral colony may have resembled Erewhon, but it was intended to transcend the equivocal and contradictory propositions Butler's utopia encourages. A man whose home is located in terra incognita may well recognize the truth of contradictions: for example, that "nothing is more general than exclusiveness," that the good of Australia arises from the wickedness of England, and that the import of labor into a colony dries up the supply of labor (Wakefield 1929, 26, 37, 15). But by virtue of ideas so shapely and powerful they can be converted into realities with a minimum of delay and distortion, this "strange union of contradictions . . . will vanish like a steam-cloud" (38). Downrightness is Wakefield's solution to the problem of Mandeville's half-knowledge, and the uncertain providences of Smith and Malthus. Like Higgs, he laughs at truths that disarm themselves, and at people too stupid to insure themselves against chance. Shares in his New Zealand Company are like a series of original contracts, all designed to build civil society in the South Seas. Wakefield was pitting himself, therefore, against the history of the previous 150 years in this region, where the contradictions of the market had not been banished by their removal to the South Seas, but rather magnified and improved. He was going to show that planning could work, and that migration to a new spot would not result, as Mandeville promised, in a narrative of disappointments. He was going to rewrite *The Fable of the Bees.*

There was no shortage of critics and enemies ready to restore Wakefield's univocal declarations to dialectical unevenness. The missionaries and civil servants who opposed his scheme did so on historical and pragmatic grounds. Pragmatically, they argued that land was being alienated by the New Zealand Company without the free and intelligent consent of the Maori who had title to it, and that this was illegal both as a bargain and as an act of settlement, since it was unauthorized by the crown, and bound to be productive of future disputes. Were the company to make it clear to the Maori that surrender of sovereignty was involved in the sale of land, then, said Dandeson Coates, lay secretary of the Church Missionary Society, "a stop must inevitably be put, *in limine,* to this Utopian scheme" (Coates 1837b, 17). Moreover, they drew on an extensive history of European colonization to show how the damage done to indigenous people by contact with settlers was unlikely to be avoided in this case by Wakefield's plan of conversion and intermarriage. On a broad front, Wallace's prophecies of Polynesian extinction were anticipated as the outcome of Wakefield's scheme. On 9 December 1840, Lord John Russell wrote to William Hobson, "It is impossible to cast the eye over the map of the globe, and to discover so much as a single spot where civilised men brought into contact with tribes differing from themselves widely in physical structure . . . have abstained from oppression and other evil practices" (Coates 1844, 39). Coates wrote, "The colonisation of uncivilised countries by Europeans in modern times, presents one of the darkest pictures of that dark subject—History" (Coates 1837b, [3]). Coates identified gain as "the latent object of the whole speculation": "It is too high wrought, too Utopian, to believe that a miscelleneous body of men will expatriate themselves to a savage land at the antipodes, merely out of a benevolent regard to the civilisation and moral improvement of the Natives" (13). William Williams predicted that miscegenation (Wakefield's policy for racial integration) would amount to no more than Maori forming illicit ties with the degraded and profligate part of the European population, "the vilest scum of the earth," as Samuel Marsden called them (Taylor 1855, 297), until the defining features of their culture and their race were worn away. "What, then, becomes of the boasted philanthropy of the

New Zealand Company," he demanded, "and their liberal consideration of the aboriginal inhabitants of the soil? It becomes, in fact, a fund for the future exigencies and emolument of the Company, when the unfortunate New Zealanders shall have withered before the blast of this treacherous policy" (Williams 1845, 16). Regardless of Wakefield's motives, Arthur Thomson concluded, "The company settlers . . . looked on New Zealanders as the curse of the country, as the only obstacle to their obtaining possession of their lands" (Thomson 1859, 2.43).

Regardless of the merits or faults of this particular venture, Wakefield's opponents entertained historical and philosophical doubts about the translation of a pure idea into a reality, unassailed by indefinite or contrary outcomes. At its simplest, this rebuttal involved treating all utopian discourse as self-evidently divorced from human experience; at its most complex, it involved exposing Wakefield's certainties to a dialectical critique. Godfrey Arabin, for example, derided "the Utopian systems of Wakefield . . . who propagates opinions repugnant to common sense" (Arabin 1845, 55). According to Anthony Trollope, J. R. Godley's letters on behalf of the Canterbury Association revealed "the difference which had been achieved in so short a time by experience between Utopian theory and practical reality" (Trollope 1874, 75). And Coates thought these utopian theories "too high wrought" to be probable schemes of emigration. Indeed, Coates took a dim view of any project that claimed to disperse the darkness of history. When he demanded of the New Zealand Company, "Are these gentlemen prepared to put forward the pretension, that they alone act on principles of religion, and justice, and benevolence, in forming a plan of colonisation? Or, that they alone have the power or the wisdom to controul the course of future events in the execution of their design, so as to ensure to the Natives of New Zealand those beneficial results which they promise to the public?" (Coates 1837b, 9), he had in mind the Sierra Leone Company, whose benevolent and disinterested plans for the repatriation of manumitted slaves had foundered in a morass of misunderstandings, poor logistics, and human nature. It was Coates's opinion that in all charitable endeavors, "there is an incompatibility between objects so prosecuted, and the exercise of coercive authority in the prosecution of them, which cannot be overcome, and which leads unavoidably to loss and failure" (10). And this was owing to "the incessant working of the great principle of strife, which lies deep in human nature . . . the resistless power of the law of self-preservation, which compels the repelling of force by force" (19–20). William Williams believed that "a well-intentioned purpose" was about to be acted upon that would "most speedily terminate in the ruin of the native population" (Williams 1845, 14). Anthony Trollope, having witnessed the latter stages of the government's persecution of Te Kooti, said, "It now seemed our only choice whether we should abandon New Zealand, or put down the Maoris altogether" (Trollope 1874, 27). In effect, Wakefield was being opposed by the same arguments concerning necessary ignorance that Mandeville had initiated, Malthus had naturalized, and Darwin and Wallace were to universalize.

Wakefield was not such a poor dialectician that he could not join this debate on the terms proposed. In answer to Coates, for example, he conceded that the darkness of history includes the destruction of indigenous people, and he asserted that New Zealand "is no exception from, but a very striking and grievous example of the rule laid down by Mr Coates" (Wakefield 1837b, 5). And the reason for this sad state of affairs was that European settlement was already a fact, encouraged by the missionaries themselves, who had benefited largely from grants of Maori land. In which case, he pointed out archly, "the Church Missionary Society itself would have been the unconscious instrument of an inscrutable Providence towards the ultimate destruction of the New Zealanders" (8).

The two questions looming in these bitter debates over the Darwinization of utopian planning in New Zealand recur to the question of consciousness raised by Butler. Is the utopian mind inevitably ignorant of the contradictions it promotes, the purposes it unhinges, and the antagonisms it provokes, and therefore as blindly selfish and destructive in its pursuit of its benevolent pretensions as the organism pushing to its limits (as his opponents supposed Wakefield to be)? Or is it sophisticated enough to recognize, and perhaps even to exploit, the force of contradiction that persists in mocking its projects with their overthrow or antitype? In short, can a utopia encounter knowingly the darkness of history and the struggle for life and still be a utopia?

Coates is undoubtedly the most articulate of Wakefield's critics, and the one who sees as clearly as Butler how the vision of an incorruptible state colludes with the law of self-preservation. As clearly as Mandeville he understands how charity can nurture rancor, and as clearly as Burke he is aware how sympathy can be ambitious and vengeful. He knows as well as Smith and Malthus that good intentions are not demonstrable propositions, or reliable vouchers of virtuous motives and probable effects. Yet along with William Ellis and John Beecham, he worked tirelessly to promote what constituted the British government's official reaction to Wakefield's utopian colony: the Treaty of Waitangi of 1840. "Probably no better step towards civilisation could have been taken at the time," judged Trollope, rather ambiguously, given his own doubts about the history of colonization (Trollope 1874, 11). Hobson could not have got so many North Island chiefs to sign the document without the mediation of missionaries such as Coates's colleague Henry Williams. In collaboration with Lord Normanby and Lord John Russell in London, and James Busby and William Hobson in New Zealand, the representatives of all three missions designed the treaty as a ring fence against the savage utopian thrust of Wakefield's theory.

Coates quoted back the main guarantee of the treaty to the parliamentary select committee that had produced a report in 1844 critical of the ambiguity of its provisions. Having cited the main guarantee to Maori of "'the full, exclusive, and undisturbed possession of their lands and estates, forests and fisheries, and other properties which they may collectively or individually possess,'" Coates went on, "I cannot discern the ambiguity ascribed to this language . . . the language appears studiously large and full, and to constitute an effectual guarantee" (Coates 1844, 14, 21). But according to the committee, "It would have been much better if no formal treaty whatever had been made, since it is clear that the natives were incapable of comprehending the real force and meaning of such a transaction, and it therefore amounted to little more than a legal fiction" (5). Coates then quoted Lord John Russell on the theme of the obscurity of history with respect to the alienation of the land and the extirpation of indigenes: "'It must be confessed, that after every explanation which can be found of the rapid disappearance of the aboriginal tribes in the neighbourhood of European settlements, there remains much which is obscure, and of which no well-ascertained facts afford the complete solution.'" Coates then conceded that promissory language, no matter how studiously large and full, constitutes no guarantee against history. "If the experience of the past compels me to look forward with anxiety to the too probable defeat of these purposes, by the sinister influence of the many passions, prejudices, and physical difficulties with which we shall have to contend, it is, on the other hand, my duty and your own to avoid yielding in any degree to that despair of success which would assuredly render success impossible" (39, 43).

Here he inhabits the logic of Butler's hypothetics ("Strange fate for man! He must perish if he get that, which he must perish if he strive not after" [Butler 1970, 168]), looking forward firmly to a future that annihilates the groundwork of the claim he is making for the imperishable justice of the treaty's articles. He enters into the ignorance of those eighteenth-century political economists who could impute but never demonstrate the connection between a sentiment and an action, or between a declaration and an outcome, because the one was so often contradictory of the other. He enters too into Wallace's ignorance of the history of natural variety, and his inability to tell why the discovery of a beautiful thing should spell the end of it. That is to say, Coates was aware of the Treaty as a utopian document, as fallible in its charitable intentions as the scheme of Wakefield's it was intended to check. But he urged it as the contrary of a scheme he found detestable, establishing the true valence of the is-and-is-not of an ideal space, and liberating its "force of unlimited contradiction," as Louis Marin calls it (1984, xxii). And the fulcrum on which all of these contraries turn is land.

The alienation of the "lands and estates, forests and fisheries" that the treaty had explicitly defended against encroachment led directly to war. In 1844, *The New Zealander* called the crown preemption right (its prerogative of being first purchaser of all native territory and therefore the treaty's chief instrument of fair dealing) "a device to amuse savages." And when Sir George Grey restored preemption in 1846, the same newspaper denounced the move as "the first step towards the negation of the Treaty of Waitangi" (Orange 1987, 126, 105). In 1877, the treaty was duly declared a nullity by Sir James Prendergast, who said of the alienation of Maori land, "The government must be arbiter of its own justice in this regard: its acts in this particular cannot be examined or called in question by any tribunal because there exist no known principles upon which a regular adjudication can be based" (Hackshaw 1989, 112). Here was the ghost of Thomas Hobbes's sovereign power come to haunt the foundation of the colony (Ewin 1992).

At first, Maori attempted to reverse the recent history of land deals, revoking leases and usufructs, and paying back the cattle and horses they had received as payment. Te Kooti was involved in the land redemption movement in the Poverty Bay region during the early 1850s, trying to set aside unfair or misunderstood land sales (Binney 1995, 36). There followed a shift from secular to spiritual politics of land retrieval as "contact" or "adjustment" cults (strictly speaking, there was never a cargo cult in New Zealand) began to focus feelings of loss and anger (Belich 1996, 218–23). In the Bay of Islands and the Hokianga, the areas settled earliest by Europeans, the Papahurihia cult took hold in the 1830s, based on a vision of apocalypse and the promise of a new earth and a new heaven where there are no books and "everything is found in plenty, flour, sugar, guns, ships" (Binney 1990, 1:328). Henry Williams heard the strange whistling voice of the cult's *atua wera* (fiery god), "commanding the people to be

strong and acquit themselves like men" (Williams 1961, 425). Frederick
Maning heard it too, speaking now in the rafters of the meeting house,
now in the ground, of future events that duly came to pass (Maning 1863,
140–48). In 1845, when the war in the north was begun by Hone Heke,
Papahurihia joined him as war priest, or *tohunga,* and at the battle of
Ohaeawai chanted a version of the second Isaiah at the British troops:
"And I will empty my bowels upon them" (Isa. 1:24; Binney 1990, 1:330).

When fighting broke out in 1864 in Taranaki, those involved were
deeply influenced by the teachings of Te Ua Haumene, a prophet whose
millenarian message was known as Pai Marire (Peace and Righteousness).
The fighters were called Hauhau, because they shouted the word *hau,* using it as a kind of sonic missile ("That which is to kill us is the noise 'Hau'
'Hau' which is like the noise of dog" [White 1864; quoted in Clark 1975,
85]). They preferred the deep boom of smooth-bore muskets to the crack
of rifles because it was consonant with the sound of *hau,* the spiritual impulse behind the movements of things and people, now marshaled in defense of the land—"a mad creed," James Cowan called it, "of Death-to-
the-Whites and Maori Land for the Maori Race" (Cowan 1911, 46, 164).
Although Te Ua Haumene insisted that his was a message of peace ("turn
to that which concerns you, to the key of the land which is peace" [Clark
1975, 125]), he heard the angel Gabriel speaking through the decapitated
head of Thomas Lloyd, who had been killed by his followers at Ahuahua,
near New Plymouth, in April 1864. Under this influence he preached explicitly against land sales, and in a vision of September 1862 foretold the
restoration of the birthright of Israel in the land of Canaan. It was an
allegory easily applied to the Hurai (Jews), as his converts called themselves, partly in acknowledgment of the missionaries' claim that they were
of the ten lost tribes of Israel, and partly by way of identifying with an ex-
iled and dispossessed people (Binney 1966, 325; 1990, 1:328). The following year, Kereopa, a Hauhau leader, decapitated the missionary C. S.
Volkner at Opotiki, and in the church ceremonially ate his eyes.

These lurid events served the cause of peace and of the land in the same
way the treaty had served it, or that war serves the purpose of utopia in
the narratives of Thomas More and Jonathan Swift. Te Ua's dream was to
restore the beginning of time (Clark 1975, 116). He meant to achieve this
by abolishing the difference between black and white, by destroying print
culture (Clark 1975, 94; Binney 1990), and by restoring the land to the
people. But to arrive at this millennial equilibrium, the dukes of peace and
of action, named Gabriel and Riki, must first have it out together, sometimes one and sometimes the other to the fore, "though they are indeed

two in one" (Clark 1975, 81, 120). Similarly, the machinery of the Europeans was adapted by Hauhau for millennial ends, though not millennial in itself. The flagstaff of the *niu*, harking back to the wreck of the *Lord Worsley* on the Taranaki coast, which seems to have been the cult's inaugurating sign, was a cross-cultural index of landownership. Hone Heke's challenge to the British focused on the British flagstaff at Russell (Kororareka), which he kept chopping down (Belich 1988, 33). When Mokene Kohere, a chief of the Ngati Porou, challenged the authority of the Hauhau at Turanga, he set up a flagpole in defiance of the *niu* (Binney 1995, 41). But the *niu* was also a wind machine run by the wind man (*hau*-man = Haumene), concentrating the *hau* and releasing its message in the flags whipping from the yardarms, each marked with the mysterious insignia of the sect (fig. 16). *Niu* is a transliteration of the English *news*, and under its influence Haumene's followers spoke either the glossolalial transliterated English of the chants (Hai, kamu, te ti, oro te mene, rauna te niu / Hema, rura wini, tu mate wini, kamu te ti [Come to tea, all the men, round the niu / Shem rule the wind, too much wind, come to tea]) (Cowan 1922, 10), or invented languages for themselves, claiming to speak in "Scotch, German, Italian, Greek and Hebrew" (Clark 1975, 94). Even though these millennial machines sought to reestablish a pretemporal regime, clockwork was important. In *Ua Rongo Pai*, the Hauhau gospel copied by Governor Grey from a captured manuscript, there are included, along with designs for masts and flags, pictures of ratchet wheels connected by chains or belts, like the flywheels of a donkey engine, but in fact identified by Paul Clark as copies of the movements of pocket watches (Clark 1975, 83; fig. 17).

With peculiar exactness, then, the millennial structure of Maori resistance recapitulated the utopian initiatives of their opponents. Like Wakefield, Te Ua Haumene wished to take the land out of time, so that he could redeem his people from the struggle for life; and like the inhabitants of Butler's *Erewhon*, he fetishized the machines he meant to disable. In such a process, land acquires a value that transcends both use and exchange, setting the stage for war. If Wakefield's claims to justice and fairdealing cloaked a series of frauds and overreachings, and if Butler's utopia merely renewed the struggle for life, so Te Ua's message of peace introduced actions of a quite contrary spirit. This state of affairs is formalized to some extent in the dialectic of contraries adumbrated by Coates in his theory of history, here represented by the dukes of Peace and of Action, whose opposite attributes proceed from a single impulse. They are manifest too in the nonsense of glossolalia, an event in the throat defined by

Figure 16   Niu. Anonymous drawing, 1864. Courtesy
Special Collections, Auckland City Libraries NZ.

Michel de Certeau as the linguistic equivalent of the utopian je ne sais quoi and its litotic rhetoric—"a transition from a *can not say* to a *can say,* by way of a *can say nothing*" (de Certeau 1996, 31). On the border of Ere-whon, it is to be remembered, clear ideas are transformed into music, and articulate sounds into noise. Higgs's vision of the golden city on the hill metamorphoses into a vast organ sending out a "storm of huge arpeggioed harmonies," while at the mountain pass, there is a guard of strange bar-baric figures carved from stone that moan hollowly in the wind (Butler 1970, 59, 67). The role of machines is similarly equivocal in the European

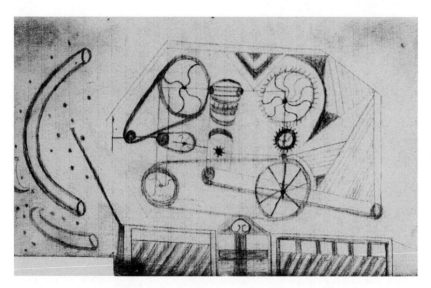

FIGURE 17   Wheel design. Anonymous drawing, 1864. Courtesy Special
Collections, Auckland City Libraries NZ.

utopia and the Maori millennium, insofar as they are instruments of good
that serve the cause of evil. Machines act on behalf of the *hau* and the
land, but at the same time, they measure and preserve the time of a fallen
world.

Although Te Kooti (allegedly named after Dandeson Coates [Binney
1995, 17]) always repudiated the Hauhau movement, notwithstanding his
exile on the Chatham Islands as a convicted Hauhau rebel, much of what
he taught was cognate with this and other millenarian movements in
Polynesia. The group name chosen by his followers was Ringatu, meaning "the raised hand," the Hauhau gesture of invincibility intended to
ward off the bullets of the European soldiers. He passionately pursued the
defense of Maori land undertaken first by Papahurihia and then Te Ua.
The sixth covenant of Ringatu promises the restitution of the land of Canaan: "And the Lord thy God will bring thee into the land which thy fathers possessed, and thou shalt possess it" (71). He had no faith in the
treaty ("impatience would destroy it," he is reported as saying, "and it
would never succeed"): "This is the very reason for our thoughts to seek a
new direction for this land, for the lands and the people too" (461, 278).
He despised the Pakeha trade in land, their hiding their god in money,
and told his people to put the purchase price back where it came from:

"Return the moneys to the bank, the moneys to the bank, for I fear lest this land be bound up, lest this land be bound up" (281). Arthur Desmond said Te Kooti believed "in using the land for the production of wealth, but not in buying and selling it like a pig." He accused the chiefs of profiteering, selling land to enrich themselves (392). In this the Ringatu prophet behaved like Te Ua, and like the shamans of the Mamaia and the Hulumanu, emphasizing chiefly greed as a stumbling block to the people, and an impediment to the millennium.

In fact, the Hauhau and Ringatu faiths were, like other contact and cargo cults in Polynesia and Melanesia, aimed at reinstituting pre-European forms of spiritual government and shamanic possession. The Hauhau leader Titokowaru renewed the ancient ritual of *mawe*, singeing the heart of the first victim of the fight (Cowan 1911, 116). Te Kooti's career accomplished the prophecies of a *tohunga* called Toiroa, made in 1766, three years before the arrival of James Cook (Binney 1995, 71). Although Te Kooti was well read in the Scriptures and a fine penman, he developed, like Te Ua, a growing suspicion of print. A voice told him, "Don't touch any book, because the letters of men are dark, rather I will speak to you." The emphasis on song *(waiata)* and voice induced a strong vein of poetic utterance, also a variety of glossolalial feats (Binney 1999). The ventriloquized squeaking of the Papahurihia *atua wera* (fiery god) and the transliterated chants of the worshippers at the *niu* were joined by Te Kooti's own invented language, "te reo ke," neither English nor Maori, but reckoned by some to be Hebrew (Binney 1995, 69, 134). In Te Kooti's case too, glossolalia is implicated in the unlimited force of utopian contradiction. He was a great speaker of riddles and paradoxes, explained by his biographer in a manner closely resembling Butler's account of hypothetics: "Te Kooti always turned logical relationships upside down, but in so doing he was opening up fresh pathways" (328). He included himself in this riddling, appearing sometimes infatuated like a drunkard or a clown ("he quite forgets himself"), and sometimes like a grave ironist, as in his compliment to Grey: "You teach that troubles may not arise during your days. My word is that your management is very good, is exceedingly good. No man has taught in that manner before. No trouble will now befall us" (106, 305).

After his attack on Matawhero, Te Kooti ordered all the watches seized in the attack to be burned, since they told only "an evil time" (Binney 1995, 123). Such a gesture places him in an interesting relation to his adversaries. Against Wakefield, he stands as a rival theorist of the intrinsic value of land, and its redeemability as a dehistorized paradise by means of a language so peculiarly charged it can alter reality. But it is with Coates's struggle to illuminate the darkness of history that Te Kooti's prophetic intelligence finds its most congenial and yet its most troubling reflection. It was hard for him to give a clear narrative, even of his own achievements, implying that it was only in the doing that it would be known: "Let the story be unravelled face to face, when I reach Waikato . . . who am I, and what is it I long to do" (148). The occasional uncertainty about the stability of Te Kooti's self participates in the excitements known to those crossing borders, like Higgs, whose passion for discovery intersects with a "dreadful doubt as to my own identity" (Butler 1970, 65), or Wakefield's passion for elopement, which made him a stranger in his own land. But like Coates, Butler, Wallace, and Mandeville, Te Kooti could embrace and taste the contradictions of a millenarian position. In Te Kuiti in 1877, he appeared at the meeting house at dawn, his head covered with the feathers of an albatross, in order to tell the people that although goodness belongs to human beings, they will inevitably make it evil (Binney 1995, 303). Impersonating a bird, he spoke as one of those birds of paradise (related to the starling, as it happens [Wallace 1962, 420]) threatened with extinction by the mere presence of Europeans. But what he enunciated was not a cry of alarm or a prophecy of destruction, but one of the very contradictions Mandeville preached, Wallace exemplified, and Wakefield tried to transcend. Everything that Coates feared might happen to Maori was experienced by Te Kooti except the total ruin of his people. He reacted to these injustices and encroachments in ways that linked revenge and "the great principle of strife," as Coates had identified self-preservation, to an alerted consciousness of the limits of resistance and of hope, which was not in itself hopeless. In his case, at least, the consciousness of contradiction abides with millenarian faith.

The same dark history from which Te Kooti and Coates spoke has led in these days to the reactivation of the Treaty of Waitangi, and a reinflation of its language to the dimensions of a full and significant message. Under its terms, past injustices have begun to be remedied, and fresh dreams of utopian cities and millennial harmonies have been dreamt. Whether this is one more stage of an unresolvable conflict over the rights of occupancy of the land, or whether it signals a real advance in the politics of settlement, remains to be seen. But at the moment, if any moral is to be plucked out of the utopian history of New Zealand, and of the reimplication of economic law into narratives of nature and culture that has made it exemplary of eighteenth-century attitudes formed in the South Seas, it would be unable to transcend these paradoxes: that peace depends on conflict; understanding, on a certain amount of ignorance; the sense of space, on a degree of constraint; and the promise of everything, on the threat of nothing.

References

Adams, Percy. 1962. *Travelers and Travel Liars, 1660–1800.* Berkeley and Los Angeles: University of California Press.

———. 1988. *Travel Literature through the Ages.* New York: Garland.

Adams, Mark, and Nicholas Thomas. 1999. *Cook's Sites: Revisiting History.* Dunedin, N.Z.: University of Otago Press.

Addington, Anthony. 1753. *An Essay on the Sea-Scurvy.* Reading, England: C. Micklewright.

Almon, John. 1797. *Anecdotes of the Life of Pitt.* 3 vols. London: n.p.

Anderson, Adam. 1801. *An Historical and Chronological Deduction of the History of Commerce.* 4 vols. London: J. White.

———. 1825. *The South Sea Bubble.* London: Thomas Boys.

Appadurai, Arjun. 1986. *The Social Life of Things.* Cambridge: Cambridge University Press.

Arabin, Godfrey. 1845. *Adventures of a Colonist.* London: J. & D. Darling.

Aravamudan, Srinivas. 1999. *Tropicopolitans.* Durham, N.C.: Duke University Press.

Armitage, David. 1992. "The Cromwellian Protectorate and the language of empire." *The Historical Journal* 35, no. 3: 531–56.

———. 1998. "Literature and Empire." In *The Origins of Empire: British Overseas Enterprise to the Close of the Seventeenth Century,* edited by Nicholas Canny. Oxford: Oxford University Press.

Ayres, Philip. 1694. *The Voyages and Adventures of Captain Bartholomew Sharp.* London: B.W.

Bacon, Francis. 1968. "New Atlantis." In *Ideal Commonwealths,* edited by Henry Morley. New York: Kennicat Press.

Baer, Joel H. 1985. "'The Complicated Plot of Piracy': Aspects of English Criminal Law and the Image of the Pirate in Defoe." *Eighteenth-Century Culture* 14: 3–16.

———. 1996. "William Dampier at the Crossroads: New Light on the 'Missing Years.'" *International Journal of Maritime History* 8, no. 2: 97–117.

Baillie, Joanna. 1798. *A Series of Plays.* 3 vols. London: T. Cadell.

Bakhtin, Mikhail. 1981. *The Dialogic Imagination: Four Essays.* Austin: University of Texas Press.

Banks, Joseph. 1962. *Endeavour Journal of Joseph Banks.* 2 vols. Edited by J. C. Beaglehole. Sydney: Public Library of New South Wales and Angus & Robertson.

Bann, Stephen. 1990. "From Captain Cook to Neil Armstrong: Colonial Exploration and the Structure of Landscape." In *Reading Landscape,* edited by Simon Pugh. Manchester: Manchester University Press.

———. 1994. *Under the Sign: John Bargrave as Collector, Traveler, and Witness.* Ann Arbor: University of Michigan Press.

Barbot, John. "A Description of the Coasts of North and South Guinea." Vol. 5 of *A Collection of Voyages and Travels,* edited by John Churchill and Awsham Churchill. London: J. and A. Churchill.

Barker-Benfield, G. J. 1992. *The Culture of Sensibility.* Chicago: University of Chicago Press.

Barrell, John. 1990. "The Public Prospect and the Private View." In *Reading Landscape,* edited by Simon Pugh. Manchester: Manchester University Press.

———, ed. 1992. *Painting and the Politics of Culture: New Essays on British Art, 1700– 1850.* Oxford: Oxford University Press.

Baugh, Daniel A. 1990. "Seapower and Science: the Motives for Pacific Exploration." In *The Background to Discovery: Pacific Exploration from Dampier to Cook,* edited by Derek Howse. Berkeley and Los Angeles: University of California Press.

Beaglehole, J. C., ed. 1961. *Journal of the* Resolution *and the* Adventure *1772–75.* Cambridge: Cambridge University Press and the Hakluyt Society.

Beddoes, Thomas. 1793. *Observations on Sea Scurvy.* London: J. Murray.

Beer, Gillian. 1983. *Darwin's Plots.* London: Routledge and Kegan Paul.

———. 1996a. *Open Fields: Science in Cultural Encounter.* Cambridge: Cambridge University Press.

———. 1996b. "Travelling the Other Way Up." In *Cultures of Natural History,* edited by N. Jardine and E. C. Spary. Cambridge: Cambridge University Press.

Begg, Charles, and Neil Begg. 1968. *Dusky Bay.* Christchurch: Whitcomb and Tombs.

Belich, James. 1988. *The New Zealand Wars.* Auckland: Penguin.

———. 1996. *Making Peoples: A History of the New Zealanders.* Auckland: Allen Lane.

Bender, John. 1987. *Imagining the Penitentiary.* Chicago: University of Chicago Press.

Berkeley, George. 1953. "An Essay towards preventing the Ruin of Great Britain." In *Philosophical Writings,* 8 vols., edited by A. A. Luce and T. E. Jessop (London: Nelson), 6: 69–84.

Bermingham, Ann. 1994. "System, Order and Abstraction: The Politics of English Landscape Drawing around 1795." In *Landscape and Power,* edited by W. J. T. Mitchell. Chicago: University of Chicago Press.

Best, Elsdon. 1982. *Maori Religion and Mythology.* Wellington, N.Z.: Government Printer.

Betagh, William. 1728. *A Voyage Round the World.* London: T. Combes.

Binney, Judith. 1966. "Papahurihia: Some Thoughts on Interpretation." *Journal of the Polynesian Society* 75, no. 3: 321–29.

———. 1990. S.v. "Penetana Papahurihia." *Dictionary of New Zealand National Biography.* 4 vols. Wellington, N.Z.: Allen and Unwin; Department of Internal Affairs.

———. 1995. *Redemption Songs: A Life of Te Kooti Arikirangi Te Turuki.* Auckland: Auckland University Press.

———. 1999. "Songlines from Aotearoa" in *Quicksands,* edited by Klaus Neumann, Nicholas Thomas, and Hilary Ericksen. Sydney: University of New South Wales Press.

Blackstone, William. 1770. *Commentaries on the Laws of England.* 4 vols. Oxford: Clarendon Press.

Blane, Gilbert. 1785. *Observations on the Diseases incident to Seamen.* London: Joseph Cooper.

Bligh, William. 1784. MS notes on Cook and King. Admiralty Library, London.

———. 1790. *A Narrative of the Mutiny on board the HMS* Bounty. London: George Nicol.

———. 1937. *Bligh's Voyage in the* Resource. Edited by Owen Rutter. London: Golden Cockerel.

———. 1961. *A Voyage to the South Sea.* New York: Signet.

———. 1975. *The Log of the* Bounty, *1787–89.* Guildford, England: Genesis Publications Ltd.

Board of Health of Hawai'i. 1870. "Report on Conditions at the Island of Molokai." Honolulu: Board of Health of Hawai'i.

Bolingbroke, Viscount [Henry St. John]. 1727. *The Craftsman: being a Critique of the Times.* London: R. Francklin.

———. 1735. *Dissertation upon Parties.* London: H. Haines.

———. 1752a. *Letters on the Spirit of Patriotism and the Idea of a Patriot King.* London: Andrew Millar.

———. 1752b. *Letters on the Study and Use of History.* London: A. Millar.

———. 1754. *Philosophical Works.* Edited by David Mallet. London: n.p.

Bolla, Peter de. 1994. "The charm'd eye." In *Body and Text in the Eighteenth Century,* edited by Veronica Kelly and Dorothy von Muecke. Stanford, Calif.: Stanford University Press

Boon, James A. 1982. *Other Tribes, Other Scribes: Symbolic Anthropology in the Comparative Study of Cultures, Histories, Religions and Texts.* Cambridge: Cambridge University Press.

———. 1985. "Anthropology and Degeneration: Birds, Words and Orangutans." In *The Dark Side of Progress,* edited by J. Edward Chamberlin and Sander L. Gilman. New York: Columbia University Press.

Boorstin, Daniel J. 1985. *The Discoverers.* New York: Vintage.

Borland, Francis. 1715. *Memoirs of Darien.* Glasgow: Hugh Brown.

Boswell, James. 1980. *Boswell's Life of Johnson.* Edited by R. W. Chapman. Oxford: Oxford University Press.

Bougainville, Louis de. 1772a. *Voyage autour du monde.* 2 vols. Paris: Saillant et Nyon.

———. 1772b. *A Voyage Round the World.* Translated by Johann Reinhold Forster. London: J. Nourse and T. Davies.

Bourdieu, Pierre. 1977. *Outline of a Theory of Practice.* Cambridge: Cambridge University Press.

Boyle, Robert. n.d. Papers. Royal Society Library, London.

———. 1772. *The Works of the Hon. Robert Boyle.* Edited by Thomas Birch. 6 vols. London: J. E. F. Rivington.

Brantlinger, Patrick. 1996. *Fictions of State: Culture and Credit in Britain 1614–1994.* Ithaca, N.Y.: Cornell University Press.

Bredekamp, Horst. 1995. *The Lure of Antiquity and the Cult of the Machine.* Princeton, N.J.: Markus Wiener.

Brosses, Charles de. 1756. *Histoire des Navigations aux Terres Australes.* 2 vols. Paris: n.p.

———. 1760. *Du culte des dieux fetiches; ou Parallele de l'ancienne religion de l'Egypte avec la religion actuelle de nigrite.* Paris: n.p.

Brown, Janet. 1996. "Botany in the Boudoir and Garden." In *Visions of Empire*, edited by David Philip Miller and Peter Hanns Reill. Cambridge: Cambridge University Press.

Brown, John. 1757. *An Estimate of the Manners and Principles of the Times*. London: L. Davis and C. Reymers.

Brunt, Peter. 1997. "Savagery and the Sublime." In *The Eighteenth Century: Theory and Interpretation* 38, no. 3: 266–86.

Buffon, Georges-Louis. 1797. *Natural History*. 10 vols. London: H. D. Symonds.

Bulkeley, John. 1745. *A Voyage to the South Seas 1740–1744*. London: R. Walker.

Burgh, James. 1764. *An Account of the First Settlement of the Cessares*. London: J. Payne.

Burke, Edmund. 1790. *Reflections of the Revolution in France*. London: J. Dodsley.

———. 1987. *A Philosophical Enquiry into the Origin of our Ideas of the Sublime and Beautiful*. Edited by James T. Boulton. Oxford: Basil Blackwell.

———. 1989. *Reflections on the Revolution in France*. Edited by L. G. Mitchell. Oxford: Clarendon Press.

———. 1991. *Fourth Letter on a Regicide Peace*. In *The Writings and Speeches of Edmund Burke: Volume 9, Book 1, The Revolutionary War, 1794–97*, edited by R. B. McDowell. Oxford: Clarendon Press.

Burney, Frances. 1907. *The Early Diary of Frances Burney 1768–78*. 2 vols. Edited by Annie Raine Ellis. London: George Bell.

Burney, James. 1803–16. *A Chronological History of the Discoveries in the South Sea*. 5 vols. London: Luke Hansard.

Burns, R. M. 1981. *The Great Debate on Miracles: From Joseph Glanvill to David Hume*. Lewisburg, Pa.: Bucknell University Press.

Burtt, Shelley. 1992. *Virtue Transformed: Political Argument in England, 1688–1740*. Cambridge: Cambridge University Press.

Butler, Samuel. 1872. *Erewhon, or Over the Range*. London: Truebner and Co.

———. 1887. *Luck or Cunning as the Means of Organic Modification*. London: Truebner and Co.

———. 1908. *Erewhon Revisited*. London: A. C. Fifield.

———. 1915. *A First Year in Canterbury Settlement and other Essays*. Edited by R. A. Streatfield. New York: E. P. Dutton.

———. 1933. *Evolution for Christians*. London: McLay & Co.

———. 1970. *Erewhon*. Edited by Peter Mudford. London: Penguin.

Byron, George Gordon. 1993. *Complete Poetical Works*. 7 vols. Edited by Jerome McGann. Oxford: Clarendon Press.

Byron, John. 1768. *An Account of the Great Distresses on the Coasts of Patagonia*. London: S. Baker & G. Leigh.

———. 1964. *Byron's Journal of his Circumnavigation 1764–66*. Edited by Robert E. Gallagher. Cambridge: Cambridge University Press for the Hakluyt Society.

Callender, John. 1967. *Terra Australis Incognita*. 2 vols. Amsterdam: N. Israel.

Camoens, Luis Vaz de. 1940. *The Lusiad*. Edited by Jeremiah D. M. Ford and translated by Richard Fanshawe. 2 vols. Cambridge, Mass: Harvard University Press.

———. 1952. *The Lusiad*. Translated by William C. Atkinson. Harmondsworth, England: Penguin.

Campbell, Alexander. 1747. *Sequel to Bulkeley's and Cummins's Voyage*. London: A. Campbell.

Campbell, George. 1766. *A Dissertation on Miracles.* Edinburgh: A. Kincaid and J. Bell.

Carpenter, Kenneth J. 1986. *The History of Scurvy.* Cambridge: Cambridge University Press.

Carroll, Lewis. 1939. *Complete Works.* Edited by Roger Lancelyn Green. London: Nonesuch.

———. 1971. *Alice's Adventures in Wonderland and Through the Looking-Glass and What Alice Found There.* Oxford: Oxford University Press.

Carswell, John. 1960. *The South Sea Bubble.* London: Cresset.

Carter, Elizabeth. 1817. *Letters to Mrs Montagu.* 3 vols. London: F. J. and J. Rivington.

Carter, Harold. 1988. *Sir Joseph Banks.* London: British Museum.

Carter, Paul. 1987. *The Road to Botany Bay.* Chicago: University of Chicago Press.

———. 1998. "Strange Seas of Thought." *Australian Review of Books* (June).

Cascardi, Anthony J. 1992. *The Subject of Modernity.* Cambridge: Cambridge University Press.

Caygill, Howard. 1989. *Art of Judgment.* Oxford: Blackwell.

Certeau, Michel de. 1996. "Vocal Utopias: Glossolalias." *Representations* 56 (fall): 29–47.

Cervantes, Miguel de Saavedra. 1970. *The Life and Achievements of the Renowned Don Quixote de la Mancha.* 2 vols. London: J. M. Dent.

Chambers, William. 1763. *Plans . . . of the Gardens and Buildings at Kew.* London: n.p.

Chard, Chloe. 1999. *Pleasure and Guilt on the Grand Tour.* Manchester: Manchester University Press.

Chatwin, Bruce. 1977. *In Patagonia.* Harmondsworth, England: Penguin.

Churchill, Awnsham, and John Churchill. 1704. *A Collection of Voyages and Travels.* 2 vols. London: Awnsham and John Churchill.

Claeys, Gregory. 1994. *Utopias of the British Enlightenment.* Cambridge: Cambridge University Press.

Clark, John. 1792. *Observations on the Diseases which prevail in long Voyages to hot Countries.* London: J. Murray.

Clark, Paul. 1975. *Hauhau: The Pai Marire Search for Maori Identity.* Auckland: Auckland University Press.

Clarke, G. B., ed. 1990. *Descriptions of Lord Cobham's Gardens at Stowe.* Vol. 26. Stowe, England: Buckinghamshire Record Society.

Clerke, Charles. 1767. "An Account of the very tall Men, seen near the Streights of Magellan, in the year 1764." *Philosophical Transactions of the Royal Society,* vol. 57, pt. 1: 75–79.

Coates, Dandeson. 1837a. *Christianity the Means of Civilization.* London: R. B. Seeley.

———. 1837b. *The Principles, Objects, and Plans of the New-Zealand Association Examined.* London: Hatchards.

———[?]. 1843. "Memoranda and Information for the Use of the Deputation to Lord Stanley." Appendix 4. London: Church Missionary Society[?]. Appendix IV.

———. 1844. *The New Zealanders and their Lands.* London: Hatchards.

Cockburn, William. 1696. *An Account of the Nature, Causes, Symptoms and Cure of the Distempers incident to Seafaring People.* 2 vols. London: Hugh Newman.

Coleridge, Samuel Taylor. 1796. "The Watchman." Edited by Lewis Patton. London: Routledge and Kegan Paul.

————. 1993. *Coleridge's Ancient Mariner: An Experimental Edition.* Edited by William Empson. Barrytown, N.Y.: Station Hill.

Colley, Linda. 1982. *In Defence of Oligarchy.* Cambridge: Cambridge University Press.

Commerson, Philibert. 1772. "Lettre de M. de Commerson." *Supplement au voyage de M. de Bougainville, ou Journal d'un voyage autour du monde fait part MM Banks et Solander.* Paris: Saillant and Nyon.

————. 1977. "Post-scriptum sur l'isle de la Nouvelle-Cythere." In *Bougainville et ses compagnons autour du monde 1766–69,* edited by Etienne Taillemite. Paris: Imprimerie National.

Conspiracy and Abduction. 1827. Liverpool: E. Smith.

Cook, James. 1955. *Journal of the Voyage of the* Endeavour *1768–71.* Edited by J. C. Beaglehole. Cambridge: Hakluyt Society and Cambridge University Press.

————. 1961. *The Voyage of the* Resolution *and* Adventure *1772–75.* Edited by J. C. Beaglehole. Cambridge: Cambridge University Press for the Hakluyt Society.

————. 1967. *The Voyage of the* Resolution *and* Discovery. Edited by J. C. Beaglehole. 2 vols. Cambridge: Cambridge University Press and the Hakluyt Society.

————. 1970. *Captain Cook in the South Seas: Two Letters to Captain John Walker.* Sydney: Library of New South Wales, 1970.

Cook, James, and James King. 1784. *A Voyage to the Pacific Ocean 1776–80.* 3 vols. London: W. & A. Strahan.

Cook, Malcolm. 1994. "Bougainville and One Noble Savage: Two Manuscript Texts of Bernardin de Saint-Pierre." *Modern Language Review* 89, no. 4: 842–55.

Cooke, Edward. 1712. *A Voyage to the South Sea.* London: B. Lintot.

Cooke, George Wingrove. 1836. *Memoirs of Lord Bolingbroke.* 2 vols. London: Richard Batley.

Cowan, James. 1911. *The Adventures of Kimble Bent.* London: Whitcomb and Tombs..

————. 1922. *The New Zealand Wars.* Wellington, N.Z.: P. Hasselberg.

Cowley, William Ambrosia. 1684. The Voyage of William Ambrosia Cowley, Marriner, from the Capes of Virginia to the South Sea. 54 vols. Sloane MS 54. British Library, London.

Cowper, William. 1785. *The Task.* London: J. Johnson.

————. 1995. *The Poems of William Cowper.* Edited by John D. Baird and Charles Ryskamp. Oxford: Clarendon Press.

Cox, Stephen D. 1980. *"The Stranger within Thee": Concepts of the Self in Late Eighteenth-Century Literature.* Pittsburgh: University of Pittsburgh Press.

Coxon, John. 1679. Account of the Intended Voyage from Jamaica. Sloane MS 2752. British Museum, London.

Coyer, Gabriel François. 1752. *A Supplement to Lord Anson's Voyage round the World.* London: A. Millar.

————. 1767. *A Letter to Dr Maty.* London: T. Beckett & P.A. Dehondt.

Crosfield, R. T. 1797. *Remarks on the Scurvy . . . with an Account of the Effects of Opium in that Disease.* London: R. T. Crosfield.

D'Anvers, Caleb [Henry St. John Viscount Bolingbroke]. 1727. *The Craftsman.* 2 vols. London: R Francklin.

Dalrymple, Alexander. 1767. *An Account of Discoveries in the South Pacific previous to 1764.* London: n.p.

———. 1770 –71. *An Historical Collection of Voyages and Discoveries in the South Pacific Ocean.* 2 vols. London: n.p.

———. 1773. *A Letter from Mr Dalrymple to Dr Hawkesworth.* London: n.p..

———. 1775. *A Collection of Voyages chiefly in the Southern Atlantick Ocean.* London: n.p.

Dalton, William. 1990. *The Dalton Journal.* Edited by Niel Gunson. Canberra: National Library of Australia.

Dampier, William. n.d. The Adventures of William Dampier with others who Left Capn Sherpe in the South Seas. Sloane MS 3236. British Museum, London.

———. 1697–1703. *A New Voyage Round the World.* London: J. Knapton.

———. 1707. *Captain Dampier's Vindication of his Voyage to the South Seas.* London: J. Bradford.

———. 1729. *A Collection of Voyages.* 4 vols. London: J. & J. Knapton.

Darwin, Charles. 1859. *On the Origin of Species by means of Natural Selection.* London: John Murray.

———. 1901. *The Descent of Man.* London: John Murray.

———. 1902. *Journal of Researches during the Voyage of the Beagle.* London: John Murray.

———. 1945. *Charles Darwin and the Voyage of the Beagle.* Edited by Nora Barlow. London: Pilot Press.

———. 1968. *The Origin of Species.* Edited by J. W. Burrow. Harmondsworth, England: Penguin.

Darwin, Erasmus. 1789. *The Loves of the Plants.* Lichfield, England: J. Jackson.

———. [1791] 1973. *The Botanic Garden.* London: J. Johnson. Reprint, Menston, England: Scolar Press.

———. 1803. *Zoonomia.* 4 vols. Boston: Thomas and Andrews.

Daston, Lorraine. 1988. *Classical Probability in the Enlightenment.* Princeton, N.J.: Princeton University Press.

———. 1994. "Marvellous Facts and Miraculous Evidence." In *Questions of Evidence,* edited by James Chandler. Chicago: University of Chicago Press.

Daston, Lorraine, and Katharine Park. 1998. *Wonders and the Order of Nature, 1150 – 1750.* New York: Zone.

Davenant, Sir William. 1971. *Gondibert.* Edited by David F. Gladish. Oxford: Clarendon Press.

Davis, J. C. 1981. *Utopia and the Ideal Society: A Study of English Utopian Writing, 1516 – 1700.* Cambridge: Cambridge University Press.

Davis, Lennard J. 1999. "Criminal Statements: Homosexuality and Textuality in the Account of Jan Svilt." In *Narrating Transgression,* edited by Rosamaria Loretelli and Roberto de Romano. Frankfurt: Peter Lang.

Daws, Gavan. 1973. *Holy Man: Father Damien of Molokai.* London: Harper & Row.

Dawson, Richard Harry. 1993. *Imperial Science and a Scientific Empire: Kew Gardens and the Uses of Nature 1772 –1908.* Ph.D. diss., Yale University.

Defoe, Daniel. 1706. *Review of the State of the English Nation,* 3:503. In Defoe 1938, vol. 8.

———. 1712. *An Essay on the South-Sea Trade by the Author of the* Review. London: J. Baker.

————. 1720. *The History of Mr Duncan Campbell.* London: Edmund Curll.

————. 1725. *A New Voyage Round the World.* London: A. Bettesworth.

————. 1728. *A System of Magick.* London: A. Millar.

————. 1860a. *Essays upon several projects; or, Effectual ways for advancing the interests of the nation.* In *Defoe Pamphlets* [a collection of Victorian reprints]. London: Charles Reynell.

————. 1860b. *Jure Divino, a Satire.* In *Defoe Pamphlets* [a collection of Victorian reprints]. London: Charles Reynell.

————. 1927. *The Farther Adventures of Robinson Crusoe.* 3 vols. London: Basil Blackwell.

————. 1935. *A New Voyage Round the World.* New York: Dial Press.

————. 1938. *Defoe's* Review. New York: Columbia University Press for the Facsimile Text Society.

————. 1951. *The Best of Defoe's* Review. Edited by W. L. Payne. New York: Columbia University Press.

————. 1961. *Captain Misson.* Edited by Maximillian Novak. Los Angeles: William Andrews Clark Library.

————. 1962. *A Tour through the whole Island of Great Britain.* 2 vols. London: J. M. Dent.

————. 1963. *The Life, Adventures and Pyracies of the famous Captain Singleton.* London: J. M. Dent.

————. 1972a. *A General History of the Pyrates.* Edited by Manuel Schonhorn. London: J. M. Dent.

————. 1972b. *The Life and Adventures of Robinson Crusoe.* Edited by J. Donald Crowley. Oxford: Oxford University Press.

Delille, Jacques. 1844. *Les jardins; ou l'art d'embellir les paysages.* Paris: Chapsal.

Delumeau, Jean. 1995. *History of Paradise.* New York: Continuum.

Dening, Greg. 1980. *Islands and Beaches: Discourse on a Silent Land, Marquesas 1774–1880.* Carlton, Vic.: Melbourne University Press.

————. 1982. "Sharks That Walk on the Land: The Death of Captain Cook." *Meanjin* 4.

————. 1992. *Mr Bligh's Bad Language.* Cambridge: Cambridge University Press.

————. 1996. *Performances.* Melbourne: Melbourne University Press.

Desmond, Ray. 1995. *Kew: The History of the Royal Botanic Gardens.* Kew, England: The Harvill Press and the Royal Botanic Gardens.

Dettelbach, Michael. 1996a. "Humboldtian Science." In *Cultures of Natural History,* edited by N. Jardine and E. C. Spary. Cambridge: Cambridge University Press.

————. 1996b. "Global Physics." In *Visions of Empire,* edited by David Philip Miller and Peter Hanns Reill. Cambridge: Cambridge University Press.

Diaz, Bernal. 1996. *The Discovery and Conquest of Mexico.* Edited by Genaro Carcia. New York: Da Capo Press.

Dickinson, H. T. 1970. *Bolingbroke.* London: Constable.

Diderot, Denis. 1992. *Political Writings.* Edited by John Hope Mason and Robert Wokler; "Supplement au voyage de Bougainville" translated by Mason and Wokler. Cambridge: Cambridge University Press.

Dryden, John. 1978. *The Works of John Dryden.* Vol. 11: *Plays: The Conquest of Granada,*

Marriage a-la-mode, The Assignation, edited by John Loftis, David Stuart Rodes, and Vinton A. Dearing. Berkeley and Los Angeles: University of California Press.

Dyer, John. 1971. *Poems 1761.* Menston, England: Scolar Press.

Edmond, Rod. 1997. *Representing the South Pacific.* Cambridge: Cambridge University Press.

Edwards, Philip. 1994. *Sea-Narratives in Eighteenth-Century England.* Cambridge: Cambridge University Press.

Egmont, Lord. n.d. Letter to Sir John Perceval. PRO SP 94/253. State Papers, Public Record Office, Kew.

Elias, Norbert. 1982. *The Civilising Process: State Formation and Civilisation.* Oxford: Blackwell.

Elliott, John. 1984. "Journal." In *Cook's Second Voyage: The Journals of Lieutenants Elliott and Pickersgill,* edited by Christine Holmes. Hampstead, England: Caliban.

Ellis, Markman. 1996. *The Politics of Sensibility.* Cambridge: Cambridge University Press.

Ellis, William. 1829. *Polynesian Researches in the South Sea Islands.* 2 vols. London: Fisher and Jackson.

———. 1969. *An Authentic Narrative of a Voyage.* New York: DaCapo Press.

An Enquiry into the Causes of the Miscarriage of the Scots Colony at Darien. 1700. Glasgow: n.p.

"An Epistle from Oberea to Joseph Banks." 1774. London: J. Almon.

"An Essay on the Nature and Methods of carrying on a Trade to South Sea." 1707–46. 140 vols. Vol. Add. MSS. 28. British Library, London.

Ewin, R. E. 1992. "The Treaty of Waitangi and Hobbes' Condition of Mere Nature." In *Justice, Ethics and New Zealand Society,* edited by Graham Oddie and Roy Perrett, 60–72. Auckland: Oxford University Press.

Exquemelin, Alexandre Olivier. 1684. *Bucaniers of America.* 2 vols. London: William Crooke.

———. 1685. *Bucaniers of America (containing the voyage of Captain Bartholomew Sharp).* 2d ed. Edited by Basil Ringrose. London: William Crooke.

Falconer, William. 1808. *The Shipwreck.* London: Cadell and Davies.

Fanon, Frantz. 1963. *The Wretched of the Earth.* Translated by Constance Farrington. New York: Grove.

Fausett, David. 1993. *Writing the New World: Imaginary Voyages and Utopias of the Great Southern Land.* Syracuse, N.Y.: University of Syracuse Press.

Ferguson, Adam. 1767. *An Essay on the History of Civil Society.* London: A. Millar & T. Caddel.

———. [1980] 1995. *An Essay on the History of Civil Society.* New Brunswick, N.J.: Transaction Books.

Ferguson, Frances. 1992. *Solitude and the Sublime: Romanticism and the Aesthetics of Individuation.* New York: Routledge.

Fielding, Henry. 1987. *The True Patriot and Related Writings.* Edited by W. B. Coley. Middletown, Conn.: Wesleyan University Press.

———. 1996a. *The Journal of a Voyage to Lisbon.* Edited by Tom Keymer. London: Penguin.

———. 1996b. *Tom Jones.* Edited by John Bender. Oxford: Oxford University Press.

Fletcher [of Saltoun], Andrew. 1699. *A Short and Impartial View of the Scots Colony's coming away from Darien*. Edinburgh: n.p.

———. 1749. "An Account of a Conversation." In *The Political Works of Andrew Fletcher of Saltoun*. Glasgow: Robert Urie.

Flinders, Matthew. n.d. Letter to wife. In J. J. Shillinglaw Papers, Box 81, La Trobe Library, Melbourne.

Fornander, Abraham. 1878. *An Account of the Polynesian Race*. 2 vols. London: Truebner.

Forster, George. 1777. *A Voyage round the World in the Sloop Resolution 1772-75*. 2 vols. London: B. White.

Forster, Johann Reinhold. 1778. *Observations made during a Voyage Round the World*. 2 vols. London: G. Robinson.

———. 1982. *The Resolution Journal of Johann Reinhold Forster*. 4 vols. edited by Michael E. Hoare. London: Hakluyt Society.

———. 1996. *Observations made during a Voyage round the World*. Edited by Nicholas Thomas, Harriet Guest, and Michael Dettelbach. Honolulu: University of Hawai'i Press.

Foucault, Michel. 1970. *The Order of Things*. London: Tavistock Publications.

———. 1972. *The Archeology of Knowledge*. Translated by A. M. Sheridan Smith. New York: Pantheon.

Fox, Christopher. 1988. *Locke and the Scriblerians: Identity and Consciousness in Early Eighteenth-Century Britain*. Berkeley and Los Angeles: University of California Press.

Franklin, Benjamin, and Alexander Dalrymple. 1806. "Plan for benefitting distant unprovided countries." In *Works of Benjamin Franklin*. London: n.p.

Freeman, J. D., and W. R. Geddes. 1959. *Anthropology in the South Seas*. New Plymouth, N.Z.: n.p.

Frezier, Amédée. 1717. *A Voyage to the South-Sea*. London: Jonah Bowyer.

Friedman, Jonathan. 194. *Cultural Identity and Global Process*. London: Sage.

Frost, Alan. 1988. "Science for Political Purposes: European Explorations of the Pacific Ocean 1764–1806." In *Nature in Its Greatest Extent*, edited by Roy Macleod and Philip Rehbeck. Honolulu: University of Hawai'i Press.

Funnell, William. 1707. *A Voyage round the World 1703–4*. London: W. Botham and James Knapton.

Fussell, Paul. 1977. *The Great War and Modern Memory*. Oxford: Oxford University Press.

Gascoigne, John. 1996. "The Ordering of Nature." In *Visions of Empire*, edited by David Philip Miller and Peter Hanns Reill. Cambridge: Cambridge University Press.

———. 1998. *Science in the Service of Empire*. Cambridge: Cambridge University Press.

Gell, Alfred. 1993. *Wrapping in Images*. Oxford: Clarendon Press.

Gerrard, Christine. 1994. *The Patriot Opposition to Walpole: Politics, Poetry and National Myth 1725–42*. Oxford: Clarendon Press.

Giddens, Anthony. 1991. *Modernity and Self Identity*. London: Polity.

Gigerenzer, Gerd. 1989. *The Empire of Chance*. Cambridge: Cambridge University Press.

Gildon, Charles. 1719. *The Life and Strange Surprizing Adventures of Mr D——
D——*. London: J. Roberts.

Glacken, Clarence J. 1967. *Traces on the Rhodian Shore*. Berkeley and Los Angeles:
University of California Press.

Godley, J. R. 1852. *Self-Government for New Zealand*. London: n.p.

——. 1863. *Writings and Speeches*. Edited by J. E. Fitzgerald. Christchurch: Press
Office.

Godwin, William. 1783. *The History of the Life of William Pitt, Earl of Chatham*. London: G. Kearsly.

——. 1970. *Caleb Williams; or, Things as They Are*. Edited by David McCracken.
Oxford: Oxford University Press.

Gordon, Eleanora C. 1984. "Scurvy and Anson's Voyage." *The American Neptune* 44,
no. 3: 155–66.

Gordon, Thomas, trans. 1728–31 *The Works of Tacitus*. 2 vols. London: T. Woodward.

Grafton, Anthony. 1992. *New Worlds, Ancient Texts: The Power of Tradition and the
Shock of the Discovery*. Cambridge, Mass.: Harvard University Press.

Greenblatt, Stephen. 1980. *Renaissance Self-Fashioning*. Chicago: University of Chicago Press.

——. 1991. *Marvellous Possessions: The Wonder of the New World*. Chicago: University
of Chicago Press.

Grey, Sir George. 1869. "On the Social Life of the Ancient Inhabitants of New Zealand." *Proceedings of the Royal Society*. Vol. 22. London: Royal Society.

Grove, Richard. 1990. "Colonial Conservation." In *Imperialism and the Natural World*,
edited by John Mackenzie. Manchester, England: Manchester University Press.

——. 1995. *Green Imperialism*. Cambridge: Cambridge University Press.

Guillory, John. 1993. *Cultural Capital*. Chicago: University of Chicago Press.

Gunson, Niel. 1962. "An Account of the Mamaia or Visionary Heresy of Tahiti." *Journal of the Polynesian Society* 71, no. 2.

Habermas, Jurgen. 1971. *Knowledge and Human Interests*. Translated by Jeremy Shapiro. Boston: Beacon Press.

——. 1974. *Theory and Practice*. Translated by John Viertel. Boston: Beacon Press.

Hacke, William. 1699. *A Collection of Voyages*. London: James Knapton.

Hacking, Ian. 1975. *The Emergence of Probability*. Cambridge: Cambridge University
Press.

——. 1995. *Rewriting the Soul*. Princeton, N.J.: Princeton University Press.

Hackshaw, Frederika. 1989. "Nineteenth-Century Notions of Aboriginal Title." In
Waitangi: Maori and Pakeha Perspectives of the Treaty of Waitangi, edited by I. H.
Kawharu, 92–120. Auckland: Oxford University Press.

Hakluyt, Richard. 1600. *Voyages of the English Nation*. 3 vols. London: George Bishop.

——. 1907. *The Principal Navigations, Voyages, Traffiques, and Discoveries of the English Nation*. 8 vols. London: J. M. Dent.

Harlow, Vincent. 1952. *The Founding of the Second British Empire*. 2 vols. London:
Longmans.

Harrington, James. 1992. *The Commonwealth of Oceania*. Edited by J. G. A. Pocock.
Cambridge: Cambridge University Press.

Harris, John. 1744. *A Complete Collection of Voyages and Travels*. 4 vols. London:
T. Woodward.

————, and John Campbell (edited and expanded by). 1764. *Navigantium atque Itinerantium Bibliotheca; or, A Complete Collection of Voyages and Travels.* 2 vols. London: T. Osborne.

Hartley, David. 1966. *Observations on Man.* Gainesville, Fla.: Scholars' Facsimiles and Reprints.

Harvey, David. 1996. *Justice, Nature and the Geography of Difference.* Oxford: Blackwell.

Hawkesworth, John. n.d. Notations in the ship log of Samuel Wallis. PRO ADM 55/35, fol. 164. Public Records Office, Kew.

————. 1752–54. *The Adventurer.* 2 vols. London: J. Payne.

————. 1773. *An Account of the Voyages and Discoveries in the Southern Hemisphere,* 2d ed. 3 vols. London: W. Strahan and T. Cadell.

Hawkins, Sir Richard. 1905. "A Voyage to the South Sea." Vol. 17 of *Hakluytus Posthumus; or, Purchas his Pilgrimes,* edited by Samuel Purchas. Glasgow: James MacLehose.

Heely, Joseph. 1777. *A Description of Hagley Park.* London: Joseph Heely.

Hegel, Georg Wilhelm Friedrich. 1977. *Phenomenology of Spirit.* Oxford: Oxford University Press.

Helgerson, Richard. 1992. *Forms of Nationhood.* Chicago: University of Chicago Press.

Henry, David. 1774. *An Historical Account of all the Voyages round the World.* 4 vols. London: E. Newbery.

Herder, Johann Gottfried. 1800. *Outlines of a Philosophy of the History of Man.* Translated by T. Churchill. London: J. Johnson.

————. 1969. *Yet Another Philosophy of History.* Translated by F. M. Barnard. Cambridge: Cambridge University Press.

Herries, Walter. 1700. *A Defense of the Scots Abdicating Darien.* London: n.p.

Herrnstein Smith, Barbara. 1988. *Contingencies of Value.* Cambridge, Mass.: Harvard University Press.

Heylyn, Peter. 1667. *Cosmographie.* London: Philip Chetwode.

Hill, Christopher. 1986. "Radical Pirates?." In *Collected Essays.* Amherst: University of Massachusetts Press.

Hirschman, A. O. 1977. *The Passions and the Interests.* Princeton, N.J.: Princeton University Press.

————. 1986. *Rival Views of Market Society.* New York: Viking.

Hobbes, Thomas. 1651. *Leviathan.* London: Andrew Crooke.

————. 1841. *Philosophical Rudiments.* Edited by Sir William Molesworth. London: John Bohn.

————. 1963. *Behemoth.* Edited by William Molesworth. New York: Burt Franklin.

————. 1968. *Leviathan.* Edited by C. B. Macpherson. Harmondsworth, England: Penguin.

————. 1971a. "Answer to Davenant." In *Gondibert,* edited by David R. Gladish. Oxford: Clarendon Press.

————. 1971b. *A Dialogue of the Common Laws of England.* Edited by Joseph Cropsey. Chicago: University of Chicago Press.

————. 1994. *The Elements of Law.* Edited by J. C. A. Gaskin. Oxford: Oxford University Press.

Hobsbawm, E. J. 1959. *Primitive Rebels.* New York: Norton.

Hockin, J. P. 1803. "Supplement compiled from the Journals of the *Panther* and *Endeavour*." In *An Account of the Pelew Islands*. 5th ed. London: Henry Wilson.

Hodgen, Margaret. 1964. *Early Anthropology in the 16th and 17th Centuries*. Philadelphia: University of Pennsylvania Press.

Holden, Horace. 1836. *A Narrative of the Shipwreck of the American Ship* Mentor *on the Pelew Islands 1832*. Boston: Russell, Shattuck & Co.

Holmes, Christine, ed. 1984. *Captain Cook's Second Voyage: The Journals of Lieutenants Elliott and Pickersgill*. Hampstead, England: Caliban Press.

Hooper, Anthony, and Judith Huntsman. 1985. *Transformations of Polynesian Culture*. Auckland: Polynesian Society.

Hopper, Edward. 1838. Diary. MS 1034. Alexander Turnbull Library, Wellington, N.Z.

Hulme, Peter. 1986. *Colonial Encounters: Europe and the Native Caribbean, 1492–1797*. London: Methuen.

Humboldt, Alexander von. 1907. *A Narrative of Travels to the Equinoctial Regions of America*. 3 vols. London: George Bell.

Hume, David. 1903. *Essays*. London: n.p.

———. 1955. *An Inquiry Concerning Human Understanding*. Indianapolis: Bobbs-Merrill.

———. 1969. *A Treatise of Human Nature*. Edited by Ernest C. Mossner. Harmondsworth, England: Penguin.

———. 1987. *Essays Moral, Political and Literary*. Edited by Eugene F. Miller. Indianapolis: Liberty Classics.

Hurd, Richard. 1911. *Letters on Chivalry and Romance*. Edited by Edith J. Morley. London: n.p.

Hutcheson, Archibald. 1721. "Some Computations." In *A Collection of Treatises relating to National Debts and Funds*. London: n.p.

Hutcheson, Francis. 1725. *An Inquiry into the Original of our Ideas of Beauty and Virtue*. London: J. Darby.

———. 1750. *Reflections on Laughter*. London: B. Urie.

———. 1971. *A Collection of Letters and Essays on Several Subjects*. Volume 8 of *The Collected Works of Francis Hutcheson*, edited by Bernard Fabian. Hildesheim: Georg Olms.

James, Isaac. 1800. *Providence Displayed*. Bristol: Biggs and Cottle.

Jameson, John Franklin. 1923. *Privateering and Piracy in the Colonial Period*. New York: Macmillan.

Jervey, William. 1769. *Practical Thoughts on the Prevention and Cure of the Scurvy*. London: J. Nourse and J. Murdoch.

Johansen, J. Prytz. 1954. *The Maori and His Religion*. Kopenhagen: Minsksgaard.

Johnson, Charles. 1980. *The Successful Pirate*. Edited by Joel H. Baer. Los Angeles: William Andrews Clark Library.

Johnson, Samuel. 1984. *Journey to the Western Islands of Scotland*. Edited by R. W. Chapman. Oxford: Oxford University Press.

Johnstone, Arthur. 1905. *Recollections of Robert Louis Stevenson*. London: Chatto and Windus.

Joppien, Rüdiger, and Bernard Smith. 1985. *The Art of Captain Cook's Voyages*. 2 vols. Oxford: Clarendon Press.

Journal of a Voyage Round the World in the Dolphin. 1767. London: M. Cooper.

The Just Vengeance of Heaven exemplify'd in a Journal lately found by Captain Mawson. 1730. London: J. Jenkin.

Kaeppler, Adrienne. 1978. *Artificial Curiosities.* Honolulu: Bishop Museum Press.

Kames, Lord Henry Home. 1774. *Sketches of the History of Man.* Vol. 1. Edinburgh: W. Creech.

———. 1851. *Elements of Criticism.* New York: Huntington and Savage.

Kant, Immanuel. 1960. *Observations on the Feeling of the Sublime and Beautiful.* Translated by John T. Goldthwait. Berkeley and Los Angeles: University of California Press.

Kaplan, Martha. 1995. *Neither Cargo nor Cult.* Durham, N.C.: Duke University Press.

Kavanagh, Thomas M. 1993. *Enlightenment and the Shadows of Chance.* Baltimore: Johns Hopkins University Press.

Keate, George. 1773. *The Monument in Arcadia.* London: J. Dodsley.

———. 1779. *Sketches from Nature in a Journey to Margate.* 2 vols. London: J. Dodsley.

———. 1788. *An Account of the Pelew Islands.* London: H. Wilson.

———. 1803. *An Account of the Pelew Islands to which is added a Supplement,* 5th ed. London: H. Wilson.

Kelly, Celsus. 1966. *La Australia del Espiritu Santo.* 2 vols. Cambridge: Hakluyt Society and Cambridge University Press.

Kendall, Thomas. n.d. MS journals. New Zealand: Auckland Institute and Museum.

Kidd, Colin. 1999. *British Identities before Nationalism.* Cambridge: Cambridge University Press.

King, J. C. T. 1981. *Artificial Curiosities from the Northwest Coast of America.* London: British Museum.

Kirch, Patrick V., and Marshall Sahlins. 1992. *Anahulu: The Anthropology of History in the Kingdom of Hawaii.* 2 vols. Chicago: University of Chicago Press.

Klein, Lawrence. 1994. *Shaftesbury and the Culture of Politeness: Moral Discourse and Cultural Politics in Early Eighteenth-Century England.* Cambridge: Cambridge University Press.

Koerner, Lisbet. 1996. "Purposes of Linnaean Travel." In *Visions of Empire,* edited by David Philip Miller and Peter Hanns Reill. Cambridge: Cambridge University Press.

Kopytoff, Igor. 1986. "The Cultural Biography of Things." In *The Social Life of Things,* edited by Arjun Appadurai. Cambridge: Cambridge University Press.

Koselleck, Reinhart. 1988. *Critique and Crisis: Enlightenment and the Pathogenesis of Modern Society..* Oxford: Berg.

Kramnick, Isaac. 1968. *Bolingbroke and His Circle.* Cambridge, Mass.: Harvard University Press.

Kramnick, Jonathan. 1992. "'Unwilling to be short, or plain, in anything concerning gain': Bernard Mandeville and the Dialectic of Charity," in *The Eighteenth Century: Theory and Interpretation* 33, no. 2: 148–75.

Laborde, Alexandre. 1808. *Description des nouveaux jardins de la France.* Paris: Imprimerie de Delance.

Lacey, Roderic. 1990. "Journeys of Transformation in Melanesia." In *Cargo Cults and Millenarian Movements,* edited by G. W. Trompf. Berlin: Mouton de Gruyter.

Lafitau, Pierre. 1724. *Moeurs des Sauvages Ameriquains.* 2 vols. Paris: Charles Hochereau.

Lamb, Jonathan. 1994. "Circumstances surrounding the Death of John Hawkesworth." In *The South Pacific in the Eighteenth Century,* edited by Jonathan Lamb, Robert Maccubbin, and David Morrill. Special issue of *Eighteenth-Century Life* 18, no. 3: 97–113.

———. 1995. *The Rhetoric of Suffering: Reading the Book of Job in the Eighteenth Century.* Oxford: Clarendon Press.

———. 1997. "The Medium of Publicity and the Garden at Stowe." *Huntington Library Quarterly* 59, no. 1: 53–72.

———. 2000. "'The Rime of the Ancient Mariner': A Ballad of the Scurvy." In *Pathologies of Travel,* edited by Richard Wrigley and George Revill. Amsterdam: Rodopi.

Latour, Bruno. *We Have Never Been Modern.* Translated by Catherine Porter. N.Y.: Harvester Wheatsheaf.

Lattas, Andrew. 1992a. "The Punishment of Masks." *Canberra Anthropology* 15, no. 2: 69–88.

———. 1992b. "Skin, Personhood and Redemption: The Double Self in West New Britain Cargo Cults." *Oceania* 63, no. 1: 27–36.

Lawrence, Christopher. 1996. "Disciplining Disease: Scurvy, the Navy, and Imperial Expansion." In *Visions of Empire,* edited by David Philip Miller and Peter Hanns Reill. Cambridge: Cambridge University Press.

Lemontey, Pierre-Edouard. 1792. *Eloge de Jacques Cook.* Paris: Imprimerie Nationale.

Lind, James. 1757. *A Treatise on the Scurvy.* London: A. Millar.

———. 1774. *An Essay on the most effectual means of preserving the health of seamen.* London: D. Wilson and G. Nicol.

Lindstrom, Lamont. 1993. *Cargo Cult: Strange Stories of Desire from Melanesia and Beyond.* Honolulu: University of Hawai'i Press.

Litton, Edmund. 1797. *Philosophical Conjectures on Aereal Influences the probable Origin of Diseases, with an unusual Cure in the Scurvy.* London: Thomas Trye.

Locke, John. 1704. *Introductory Discourse containing the History of Navigation. A Collection of Voyages and Travels.* Edited by A. and J. Churchill. Vol. 1. London: A. & J. Churchill.

———. 1706. "A Discourse of Miracles." In *Posthumous Works.* London: A. & J. Churchill.

———. 1960. *Two Treatises of Government.* Edited by Peter Laslett. Cambridge: Cambridge University Press.

———. 1961. *Essay Concerning Human Understanding.* Edited by John Yolton. 2 vols. London: J. M. Dent.

London, Jack. n.d. *The Cruise of the "Snark."* London: Mills and Boon.

Lowes, John Livinston. 1927. *The Road to Xanadu.* London: Constable.

Loyer, Godefroy. 1714. *Relation du voyage au Royaume d'Issyny.* Paris: n.p.

Lund, Roger D. 1995. *The Margins of Orthodoxy 1660–1750.* London: Cambridge University Press.

Lupo, J. 1923. "The Story of Niue." *Journal of the Polynesian Society* 32.

Mackay, David. 1996. "Agents of Empire: The Banksian Collectors and the Evaluation of New Lands." In *Vision of Empire,* edited by David Philip Miller and Peter Hanns Reill. Cambridge: Cambridge University Press.

Mackenzie, Henry. 1786. *The Mirror.* 3 vols. London: A. Strahan and T. Cadell.

————. 1788. *The Lounger.* 3 vols. London: A. Strahan and T. Cadell.

————. 1805. *Julia de Roubigné.* Cupar, Scotland: R. Tullis.

————. 1967. *The Man of Feeling.* Edited by Brian Vickers. Oxford: Oxford University Press.

Macpherson, C. B. 1962. *The Political Theory of Possessive Individualism.* Oxford: Oxford University Press.

Malthus, Thomas. 1970. *An Essay on the Principle of Population.* Harmondsworth, England: Penguin.

Mandeville, Bernard. 1725. *An Enquiry into the Causes of the frequent Executions at Tyburn.* London: J. Roberts.

————. 1924. *The Fable of the Bees.* 2 vols. Edited by F. B. Kay. Oxford: Clarendon Press.

————. 1970. *The Fable of the Bees.* Edited by Philip Harth. Harmondsworth, England: Penguin.

Maning, F. E. 1863. *Old New Zealand.* London: Smith Elder.

Marin, Louis. 1984. *Utopics: Spatial Play.* Translated by Robert A. Vollrath. Atlantic Highlands, N.J.: Humanities Press.

————. 1993. "The Frontiers of Utopia." In *Utopias and the Millenium,* edited by Krishan Kumar and Stephen Bann. London: Reaktion Books.

Mariner, William, and John Martin. 1817. *An Account of the Natives of the Tonga Islands.* 2 vols. London: John Murray.

Markley, Robert. 1993. *Fallen Languages.* Ithaca, N.Y.: Cornell University Press.

————. 1994. "'So Inexhaustible a Treasure of Gold': Defoe, Capitalism, and the Romance of the South Seas." In *The South Pacific in the Eighteenth Century,* edited by Jonathan Lamb, Robert Maccubbin, and David Morrill. Special issue of *Eighteenth-Century Life* 18, no. 3: 148–67.

————. 1998. "Violence and Profits on the Restoration Stage." *Studies in the Eighteenth Century* 22, no. 1: 1–17.

Marshall, David. 1988. *The Surprising Effects of Sympathy: Marivaux, Diderot, Rousseau, and Mary Shelley.* Chicago: University of Chicago Press.

Martin, Ged. 1997. "Wakefield's Past and Futures." In *Edward Gibbon Wakefield and the Colonial Dream.* Wellington, N.Z.: GP Publications.

Marx, Karl. 1972. *Capital.* Vol. 1. Translated by Eden Paul and Cedar Paul. London: J. M. Dent.

————. 1978. *The Grundwisse.* In *The Marx-Engels Reader,* edited by Robert C. Tucker. New York: Norton.

Marx, Leo. 1964. *The Machine in the Garden.* Oxford: Oxford University Press.

Mauss, Marcel. 1990. *The Gift.* Translated by W. D. Halls. New York: Norton.

McCutcheon, Elizabeth. 1977. "More's Use of Litotes in the Utopia." In *Essential Articles on Thomas More,* edited by R. S. Sylvester and G. P. Marc'hadour. Connecticut: Archon.

McKeon, Michael. 1987. *The Origins of the English Novel.* Baltimore: Johns Hopkins University Press.

McNab, Robert. 1914. *From Tasman to Marsden: A History of Northern New Zealand.* Dunedin: J. Wilkie.

McPhail, Bridget. 1994. "Through a Glass, Darkly: Scots and Indians Converge at Darien." In *The South Pacific in the Eighteenth Century,* edited by Jonathan

Lamb, Robert Maccubbin, and David Morrill. Special issue of *Eighteenth-Century Life* 18, no. 3: 129–47.

Mead, Richard. 1794. "A Discussion on the Scurvy." In *A New Method for extracting the foul Air out of Ships*, by Samuel Sutton. London: J. Brindley.

Meek, Ronald. 1976. *Social Science and the Ignoble Savage*. Cambridge: Cambridge University Press.

Melville, Herman. 1964. *Typee*. New York: Signet Classics.

———. 1968. *Omoo: A Narrative of Adventures in the South Seas*. Evanston and Chicago: Northwestern University Press and the Newberry Library.

Meul, Toon van. 1992. "Broadening Millenarianism: The Continuity of Maori Political Practices." *Canberra Anthropology* 15, no. 2: 127–48.

Michell, Mathew. 1741. "A Journal of the Proceedings on board his Majesties Ship the Gloucester 1740-42." Vol. ADM 51/42. Public Record Office, Kew.

Millar, John. 1771. *Essay on the Origins of the Distinction of Ranks*. Dublin: n.p.

Miller, David Philip, and Peter Hanns Reill, eds. 1996. *Visions of Empire: Voyages, Botany, and Representations of Nature*. Cambridge: Cambridge University Press.

Milman, Francis. 1782. *An Enquiry into the Scurvy*. London: J. Dodsley.

Mitchell, W. J. T., ed. 1994. *Landscape and Power*. Chicago: University of Chicago Press.

Moll, Herman. 1711. *A View of the Coasts, Countries and Islands within the Limits of the South-Sea-Company*. London: J. Morphew.

Monboddo [James Burnet], Lord. 1774. *Of the Origin and Progress of Language*. 6 vols. Edinburgh: J. Balfour.

Montagu, Lady Mary Wortley. 1906. *Letters*. London: J. M. Dent and Co.

Montaigne, Michel de. 1711. *Essays*. Tanslated by Charles Cotton. 3 vols. London: Daniel Brown.

Moore, John Hamilton. n.d. *A New and Complete Collection of Voyages and Travels*. 2 vols. London: Alexander Hogg.

More, Hannah. 1853. *Works*. 5 vols. London: Bohn.

More, Thomas. 1910. *Utopia*. Translated by Ralph Robinson and edited by Jenny Mezciems. New York: Alfred A. Knopf.

Morrell, Benjamin. 1832. *A Narrative of Four Voyages to the South Sea 1822–31*. New York: J and J Harper.

Morrison, James. *The Journal of James Morrison*. Edited by Owen Rutter. London: Golden Cockerel.

Muehlhaeusler, Peter, and Rom Harre. 1990. *Pronouns and People: The Linguistic Construction of Social and Personal Identity*. Oxford: Blackwell.

Mullan, John. 1988. *Sentiment and Sociability*. Oxford: Clarendon Press.

Munilla, Martin de. 1966. *La Austrialia del Espiritu Santo*. 2 vols. Edited by Celsus Kelly. Cambridge: Cambridge University and the Hakluyt Society.

Neal, Larry. 1990. *The Rise of Financial Capitalism*. Cambridge: Cambridge University Press.

Neville, Henry. 1668. *The Isle of Pines; or, A late Discovery of a fourth Island near Terra Australis Incognita*. London: Allen Banks and Charles Harper.

Nicholas, John Liddiard. 1817. *Narrative of a Voyage to New Zealand*. 2 vols. London: James Black.

Nicholson, Colin. 1994. *Writing and the Rise of Finance*. Cambridge: Cambridge University Press.

Nordhoff, Charles. 1987 *Northern California, Oregon and Hawaii*. London: KPI.

Novak, Maximillian. 1962. *Economics and the Fiction of Daniel Defoe*. Berkeley and Los Angeles: University of California Press.

O'Connell, Lisa. 1999. "Marriage Acts: Stages in the Transformation of Modern Nuptial Culture." Differences 11, no. 1: 68–111.

Obeyesekere, Gananath. 1992. *The Apotheosis of Captain Cook: European Mythmaking in the Pacific*. Princeton, N.J.: Princeton University Press.

Oliver, Douglas. 1974. *Ancient Tahitian Society*. 3 vols. Honolulu: University of Hawai'i Press.

Orange, Claudia. 1987. *The Treaty of Waitangi*. Wellington, N.Z.: Allen and Unwin and Port Nicholson Press.

Orchiston, Wayne. 1998. "From the South Seas to the Sun: The Astronomy of Cook's Voyages." In *Science and Exploration in the Pacific*, edited by Margarette Lincoln. London: Boydell and National Maritime Museum.

Orr, Bridget. 1994. "Southern Passions Mix with Northern Art." In *The South Pacific in the Eighteenth Century*, edited by Jonathan Lamb, Robert Maccubbin, and David Morritt. Special issue of *Eighteenth-Century Life* 18, no. 3: 97–113.

Outram, Dorinda. 1996a. "New Spaces in Natural History." In *Cultures of Natural History*, edited by N. Jardine and E. C. Spary. Cambridge: Cambridge University Press.

———. 1996b. "The Science of Man." In *Visions of Empire*, edited by David Philip Miller and Peter Hanns Reill. Cambridge: Cambridge University Press.

Oviedo, Fernández de. 1959. *Historia general y natural de las Indias*. Edited by Juan Pérez de Tudela. Madrid: Bueso.

Pagden, Anthony. 1993. *European Encounters with the New World: From Renaissance to Romanticism*. New Haven, Conn.: Yale University Press.

———. 1995a. "The Effacement of Difference: Colonialism and the Origins of Nationalism in Diderot and Herder." In *After Colonialism: Imperial Histories and Postcolonial Displacements*, edited by Gyan Prakash. Princeton, N.J.: Princeton University Press.

———. 1995b. *Lords of All the World*. New Haven, Conn.: Yale University Press.

Paine, Thomas. 1791. *Rights of Man*. London: J. Johnson.

———. 1970. *The Age of Reason*. Harmondsworth, England: Penguin.

Parker, Noel. 1995. "Look, No Hidden Hands: How Smith Understands Historical Progress and Societal Values." In *Adam Smith's Wealth of Nations*, edited by Stephen Copley and Kathryn Sutherland. Manchester, England: Manchester University Press.

Parker, Patricia. 1987. *Literary Fat Ladies: Rhetoric, Gender, Property*. London: Methuen.

Parkinson, Sydney. 1773. *A Journal of a Voyage to the South Seas*. London: Stanfield Parkinson.

Parry, Jonathan. 1989. "On the Moral Perils of Exchange." In *Money and the Morality of Exchange*, edited by Jonathan Parry and Maurice Bloch. Cambridge: Cambridge University Press.

Paulson, Ronald. 1989. *Breaking and Remaking: Aesthetic Practice in England 1700 – 1820*. New Brunswick, N.J.: Rutgers University Press.

——. 1996. *The Beautiful, Novel, and Strange: Aesthetics and Heterodoxy*. Baltimore: Johns Hopkins University Press.

Payne Knight, Richard. 1805. *An Analytical Enquiry into the Principles of Taste*. London: T. Payne.

Pearson, Bill. 1972. "Hawkesworth's Alterations." *Journal of Polynesian History* 7: 45 – 71.

——. 1984. *Rifled Sanctuaries*. Auckland: Auckland University Press.

Pickersgill, Richard. 1984. *Captain Cook's Second Voyage: The Journals of Lieutenants Elliott and Pickersgill*. Edited by Christine Holmes. Hampstead, England: Caliban.

Pietz, William. 1985. "The Problem of the Fetish I." *RES* 9 (spring): 5 – 14.

——. 1987. "The Problem of the Fetish II." *RES* 13 (spring): 23 – 44.

——. 1988. "The Problem of the Fetish IIIa." *RES* 16 (spring): 105 – 21.

Pocock, J. G. A. 1975. *The Machiavellian Moment*. Princeton, N.J.: Princeton University Press.

——. 1987. *The Ancient Constitution and the Feudal Law*. Cambridge: Cambridge University Press.

——. 1998. "Enthusiasm, the Antiself of Enlightenment." *Huntington Library Quarterly* 60, nos. 1 – 2: 7 – 28.

——. 1999. "Nature and History, Self and Other." In *Voyages and Beaches: Pacific Encounters 1769 – 1840*, edited by Alex Calder, Jonathan Lamb, and Bridget Orr. Honolulu: Hawai'i University Press.

Pomian, Kryzstof. 1990. *Collecting and Curiosities: Paris and Venice 1500 – 1800*. Translated by Elizabeth Wiles-Porter. London: Polity.

Poovey, Mary. 1995. *Making a Social Body: British Cultural Formation 1830 – 1864*. Chicago: University of Chicago Press.

Pope, Alexander. 1956. *Correspondence*. 4 vols. Edited by George Sherburn. Oxford: Clarendon Press.

——. 1963. *The Poems*. Edited by John Butt. London: Methuen.

Prakash, Gyan. 1995. *After Colonialism: Imperial Histories and Postcolonial Displacements*. Princeton, N.J.: Princeton University Press.

Pratt, Mary Louise. 1992. *Imperial Eyes: Travel Writing and Transculturation*. London: Routledge.

Prévost, Antoine-Francois. 1746. *Histoire Générale des Voyages*. Paris: n.p.

Public Advertiser. 1773. Correspondent's article regarding John Hawkesworth. Burney Collection, British Library, London.

Public Record Office, United Kingdom. 1709 – 11. Accounts and vouchers of the privateers *Duke, Dutchess*, and *Bachelor*. PRO-C104/161, pt. 1. Public Record Office, Kew.

Pye, Christopher. 1984. "The Sovereign, the Theater, and the Kingdome of Darknesse: Hobbes and the Spectacle of Power." *Representations* 8.

Quirós, Pedro Fernandez de. 1876. *Historia de descubrimento de las regiones australes*. Edited by Justo Zaragoza. Madrid: Manuel G. Hernandez.

——. 1904. *The Voyages of Pedro Fernandez de Quirós*. 2 vols. Edited by Sir Clements Markham. London: Hakluyt Society.

Raban, Jonathan. 1999. *Passage to Juneau.* New York: Pantheon.

Ralston, Caroline. 1985. "Early Nineteenth-Century Polynesian Millennial Cults and the Case of Hawaii." *Journal of the Polynesian Society* 94, no. 4: 308–21.

Raynal, Guillaume Thomas. 1783. *A History of the East and West Indies.* 10 vols. Translated by J. O. Justamond. London: W. Strahan & T. Cadell.

Rediker, Marcus. 1987. *Between the Devil and the Deep Blue Sea.* Cambridge: Cambridge University Press.

———. 1996. "Libertalia: The Pirate's Utopia." In *Pirates: Terror on the High Seas,* edited by David Cordingley. Atlanta: Turner.

Rees, Christine. 1996. *Utopian Imagination and Eighteenth-Century Fiction.* London: Longman.

Reill, Peter Hanns, and David Phillip Miller, eds. 1996. *Visions of Empire: Voyages, Botany, and Representations of Nature.* Cambridge: Cambridge University Press.

Rennie, Neil. 1995. *Far-Fetched Facts: The Literature of Travel and the Idea of the South Seas.* Oxford: Clarendon Press.

Richardson, Samuel. 1985. *Clarissa.* Edited by Angus Ross. Harmondsworth, England: Penguin.

Ricoeur, Paul. 1986. *Lectures on Ideology and Utopia.* New York: Columbia University Press.

Rigby, Nigel. 1998. "Seaborne Plant Transportation." In *Science and Exploration in the Pacific,* edited by Margarette Lincoln. London: Boydell and the National Maritime Museum.

Ringrose, Basil. [1680]. "A Journal into the South Sea." Sloane MS 48. British Museum, London.

Robarts, Edward. 1974. *The Marquesan Journal of Edward Robarts.* Edited by Greg Dening. Canberra: Australian National University Press.

Robertson, George. 1948. *The Discovery of Tahiti: A Journal of the Second Voyage of H.M.S. Dolphin round the World.* Edited by Hugh Carrington. Hakluyt Society, 2d ser., no. 98. London.

Rogers, K. M., ed. 1994. *Restoration and Eighteenth-Century Plays.* New York: Meridian.

Rogers, Woodes. n.d. *Creagh v. Rogers,* distribution of profits and prize money for privateers; entry book of orders. PRO C 104/36, pt. 2:12. Chancery records, Public Record Office, Kew.

———. 1711. Letter to the owners of the *Duke* and the *Dutchess,* 11 February. PRO C104/60. Chancery records, Public Record Office, Kew.

———. 1712. *A Cruising Voyage Round the World 1708–1711.* London: A. Bell.

Roggeveen, Jacob. 1970. *The Journal of Jacob Roggereen.* Edited by Andrew Sharp. Oxford: Clarendon Press.

Romilly, Sir Samuel. 1810. *Observations on the Criminal Law in England.* London: T. Cadell & W. Davies.

Rousseau, Jean-Jacques. 1803. *Eloisa: or a Series of Original Letters.* 4 vols. Reprint, Oxford: Woodstock, 1989.

———. 1993. *The Social Contract and The Discourses.* Translated by G. D. H. Cole and revised and augments by J. H. Brumfitt and John C. Hall.. London: J. M. Dent.

Rowe, Nicholas. 1720. *The Ambitious Step-Mother.* London: J. Darby.

Rymer, James. 1793. *An Essay upon the Scurvy.* London: J. Rymer.

Rymsdyk, John van, and Andrew van Rymsdyk. 1791. *Museum Britannicum.* London: J. Moore.

Sahlins, Marshall. 1972. *Stone-Age Economics.* Chicago: Aldine-Atherton.

———. 1981. *Historical Metaphors and Mythical Realities: Structure in the Early History of the Sandwich Islands Kingdom.* Ann Arbor: University of Michigan Press.

———. 1985a. "Hierarchy and Humanity in Polynesia." In *Transformations of Polynesian Culture,* edited by Tony Hooper and Judith Huntsman. Auckland: The Polynesian Society.

———. 1985b. *Islands of History.* Chicago: University of Chicago Press.

———. 1995. *How "Natives" Think: About Captain Cook, for Example.* Chicago: University of Chicago Press.

Salmond, Anne. 1991. *Two Worlds: First Meetings between Maori and Europeans, 1642– 1772.* Auckland: Viking.

———. 1997. *Between Worlds: Early Exchanges between Maori and Europeans 1773–1815.* Auckland: Viking.

Savage, Richard. 1962. *The Political Works.* Edited by Clarence Tracy. Cambridge: Cambridge University Press.

Scafi, Alessandro. 1999. "Mapping Eden: Cartographies of the Earthly Paradise." In *Mappings,* edited by Denis Cosgrove. London: Reaktion.

Schaffer, Simon. 1994. "Self Evidence." In *Questions of Evidence,* edited by James Chandler et al. Chicago: University of Chicago Press.

———. 1996a. Afterword to *Visions of Empire,* edited by David Philip Miller and Peter Hanns Reill. Cambridge: Cambridge University Press.

———. 1996b. Unpublished paper. Presented July 1996 at the David Nichol Smith Seminar, Australian National University, Canberra.

Schaffer, Simon, and Steven Shapin. 1985. *Leviathan and the Air-Pump.* Princeton, N.J.: Princeton University Press.

Schama, Simon. 1987. *The Embarrassment of Riches: An Interpretation of Dutch Culture in the Golden Age.* London: Collins.

Schrempp, Gregory. 1992. *Magical Arrows: The Maori, the Greeks and the Folklore of the Universe.* Madison: University of Wisconsin Press.

Scott, Sarah. 1986. *Millennium Hall.* London: Virago.

———. 1996. *The History of Sir George Ellison.* Edited by Betty Rizzo. Lexington: University of Kentucky Press.

Seltzer, Mark. 1992. *Bodies and Machines.* New York: Routledge.

Seward, Anna. 1810. *Poetical Works.* 3 vols. Edited by Sir Walter Scott. Edinburgh: John Ballantyne.

Shaftesbury [Anthony Ashley Cooper], Earl of. n.d. Personal memoranda; Shaftesbury Papers, PRO 30/24/27/10, pp. 134, 285, Public Records Office, United Kingdom; PRO 30/24/27/100, p. 59; PRO 30/244/22/4, fols. 153–56; PRO 30/24/24/13.

———. 1964. *Characteristics of men, manners, opinions, times, etc.* Indianapolis: Bobbs-Merrill.

Shakespeare, William. 1987. *The Tempest.* Edited by Stephen Orgel. Oxford: Oxford University Press.

Shapin, Steven. 1995. *A Natural History of Truth*. Chicago: University of Chicago Press.

———. 1996. *The Scientific Revolution*. Chicago: University of Chicago Press.

Shapin, Steven, and Simon Schaffer. 1985. *Leviathan and the Air-Pump*. Princeton, N.J.: Princeton University Press.

Shapiro, Barbara. 1983. *Probability and Certainty in 17th Century England*. Princeton, N.J.: Princeton University Press.

Sheehan, Bernard. 1980. *Savagism and Civility: Indians and Englishmen in Colonial Virginia*. Cambridge: Cambridge University Press.

Shelvocke, George. 1726. *A Voyage Round the World by Way of the Great South Sea*. London: J. Senex.

———. 1928. *A Voyage round the World*. Edited by W. G. Perrin. London: Cassel and Co.

Simson, Richard. [1689]. Observations made during a South-sea Voyage. Sloane MS 86 (672). British Museum, London.

Skinner, Quentin. 1974. "The Principles and Practice of Opposition: The Case of Bolingbroke versus Walpole." In *Historical Perspectives: Studies in English Thought and Society*, edited by Neil McKendrick. London: Europa.

Smeeks, Hendrik. 1995. *The Mighty Kingdom of the Krinke Kesmes*. Translated by Robert Leek. Amsterdam: Rodopi.

Smith, Adam. 1795. *The History of Astronomy*. London and Edinburgh: T. Cadell, W. Davies, and W. Creech.

———. 1976. *An Inquiry into the Nature and Causes of the Wealth of Nations*. 2 vols. Edited by A. S. Skinner, R. H. Campbell, and W. B. Todd. Oxford: Clarendon Press.

———. [1976]. 1982. *The Theory of Moral Sentiments*. Edited by D. D. Raphael and A. L. Macfie. Indianapolis: Liberty Classics.

———. 1980. *Essays on Philosophical Subjects*. Vol. 3. Edited by W. P. D. Wightman and J. C. Bryce. Oxford: Clarendon Press.

Smith, Bernard. 1956. "Coleridge's Ancient Mariner and Cook's Second Voyage." *Journal of the Warburg and Courtauld Institute* 19, nos. 1–2: 117–54.

———. 1960. *European Vision and the South Pacific*. Oxford: Oxford University Press.

———. 1992. *Imagining the Pacific*. Melbourne: Melbourne University Press.

Smith, Bernard, and Rüdiger Joppien. 1985–88. *The Art of Captain Cook's Voyages*. New Haven, Conn.: Yale Center for British Art.

Smith, Vanessa. 1998. *Literary Culture and the Pacific*. Cambridge: Cambridge University Press.

Smith, William. 1744. *A New Voyage to Guinea*. London: n.p.

Smollett, Tobias. 1768–69. *The Present State of all Nations*. 8 vols. London: R. Baldwin.

———. 1979a. *Roderick Random*. Edited by Paul-Gabriel Bouce. Oxford: Oxford University Press.

———. 1979b. *Travels through France and Italy*. Edited by Frank Felsenstein. Oxford: Oxford University Press.

———. 1993. *The Expedition of Humphry Clinker*. Edited by Peter Miles. London: J. M. Dent.

Sobel, Dava. 1995. *Longitude.* New York: Walker.

Sorrenson, Richard. 1995. "The State's Demand for Accurate Astronomical and Navigational Instruments in 18th Century Britain." In *The Consumption of Culture,* edited by John Brewer and Ann Bermingham, 263–77. New York and London: Routledge.

Sparrman, Anders. 1944. *A Voyage round the World.* London: Golden Cockerel.

Spate, O. H. K. 1983. *The Pacific since Magellan II: Monopolists and Freebooters.* Minneapolis: University of Minnesota Press.

———. 1988a. *Paradise Found and Lost. The Pacific since Magellan.* Vol. 3. London: Routledge.

———. 1988b. "Seamen and Scientists: Literature of the Pacific 1697–1798." In *Nature in Its Greatest Extent,* edited by Roy Macleod and Philip F. Rehbock. Honolulu: University of Hawaii Press.

Spilsbury, Francis. n.d. *A Treatise on the Method of Curing the Gout, Scurvy, Leprosy etc.* London: M. Wilkie.

———. 1785. *Free Observations on the Scurvy, Gout, Diet, and Remedy.* Rochester, England: T. Fisher.

Spivak, Gayatri. "Can the Subaltern Speak?" In *Colonial Discourse and Postcolonial Theory.* Ed. Patrick Williams and Laura Chrisman. London: Harvester Wheatsheaf, 1994.

St. Pierre, Bernardin de. 1820. *Paul and Virginia.* London: printed for John Sharpe.

Stafford, Barbara. 1984. *Voyage into Substance.* Cambridge, Mass.: MIT Press.

———. 1996. "Images of Ambiguity." In *Visions of Empire,* edited by David Philip Miller and Peter Hanns Reill. Cambridge: Cambridge University Press.

Starkey, David J. 1990. *British Privateering Enterprise in the Eighteenth Century.* Exeter: University of Exeter Press.

Stead, Jennifer. 1993. "Navy Blues: The Sailor's Diet 1530–1830." In *Food for the Community,* edited by C. Anne Wilson. Edinburgh: Edinburgh University Press.

Steele, Sir Richard. 1955. *The Englishman.* Edited by Rae Blanchard. Oxford: Clarendon Press.

Stenhouse, John. 1994. "The Darwinian Enlightenment and New Zealand Politics." In *Darwin's Laboratory,* edited by Roy McLoed and Philip Rebbock. Honolulu: University of Hawai'i Press.

Sterne, Laurence. 1965. *Letters of Laurence Sterne.* Edited by Lewis Perry Curtis. Oxford: Clarendon Press.

———. 1967. *A Sentimental Journey through France and Italy.* Edited by Graham Petrie. Harmondsworth, England: Penguin.

———. 1983. *The Life and Opinions of Tristram Shandy, Gentleman.* Edited by Ian Campbell Ross. Oxford: Oxford University Press.

Stevenson, Robert Louis. 1890. *Father Damien: An Open Letter to the Reverend Hyde of Honolulu.* Sydney: n.p.

———. 1894. *The Ebb-Tide.* London: William Heinemann.

———. 1911. *Letters.* 4 vols. Edited by Sidney Colvin. London: Methuen.

———. 1947. *Selected Writings.* Edited by Saxe Commins. New York: Books for Libraries Press.

———. 1986. *In the South Seas.* London: KPI.

Stewart, Susan. 1993. *On Longing: Narratives of the Miniature, the Gigantic, the Souvenir, the Collection.* Durham, N.C.: Duke University Press.

Strathern, Marilyn. 1988. *The Gender of the Gift.* Berkeley and Los Angeles: University of California Press.

———. 1992. "Qualified Value: The Perspective of Gift Exchange." In *Barter, Exchange and Value,* edited by Caroline Humphrey and Stephen Hugh-Jones. Cambridge: Cambridge University Press.

———. 1995. "Nostalgia and the New Genetics." In *Rhetorics of Self-Making,* edited by Debborah Battaglia. Berkeley and Los Angeles: University of California Press.

Swift, Jonathan. [1902] 1948. *Gulliver's Travels.* London: Oxford University Press. Reprint, Oxford: Oxford University Press.

———. 1958. *The Poems of Jonathan Swift.* Edited by Harold Williams. 3 vols. Oxford: Clarendon Press.

Tacitus, Cornelius. 1728–31. *Works.* Translated by Thomas Gordon. 2 vols. London: T. Woodward.

Taillemite, Etienne. 1977. *Bougainville et ses compagnons.* 2 vols. Paris: Imprimerie Nationale.

Taussig, Michael. 1993. *Mimesis and Alterity: A Particular History of the Senses.* New York: Routledge.

Taylor, Richard. 1855. *Te Ika a Maui: or, New Zealand and Its Inhabitants.* London: Wertherin and Macintosh.

Temple, Sir William. 1692. *Memoirs of what past in Christendom 1672–1679.* London: Richard Chiswell.

———. 1963. "Upon the Gardens of Epicurus or, Of Gardening." *Five Miscellaneous Essays.* Edited by Samuel Holt Monk. Ann Arbor: University of Michigan Press.

Tennenhouse, Nancy Armstrong, and Leonard Tennenhouse. 1992. *The Imaginary Puritan.* Berkeley and Los Angeles: University of California Press.

Thacker, Christopher. 1977. "'O Tinian! O Juan Fernandez!': Rousseau's 'Elysee' and Anson's Desert Islands." *Garden History* 5, no. 9.

———. 1979. *The History of Gardens.* Sydney: Reed.

Thomas, Nicholas. 1989. *Out of Time.* Cambridge: Cambridge University Press.

———. 1990. *Marquesan Societies.* Oxford: Clarendon Press.

———. 1991. *Entangled Objects: exchange, material culture, and colonialism in the Pacific.* Cambridge, Mass.: Harvard University Press.

———. 1994a. *Colonialism's Culture: Anthropology, Travel and Government.* Princeton, N.J.: Princeton University Press.

———. 1994b. "Licensed Curiosity: Cook's Pacific Voyages." In *The Cultures of Collecting,* edited by John Elsner and Roger Cardinal. Cambridge, Mass.: Harvard University Press.

———. 1994c. "Marginal Power: Shamanism and Hierarchy in Easter Oceania." In *Shamanism, History and the State,* edited by Nicholas Thomas and Caroline Humphrey. Ann Arbor: University of Michigan Press.

———. 1997. *In Oceania.* Durham, N.C.: Duke University Press.

Thomas, Pascoe. 1745. *A True and Impartial Journal of a Voyage to the South-Seas.* London: S. Birt.

Thompson, James. 1996. *Models of Value: Eighteenth-Century Political Economy and the Novel.* Durham, N.C.: Duke University Press.

Thomson, Arthur S. 1859. *The Story of New Zealand: Past and Present—Savage and Civilised.* 2 vols. London: John Murray.

Thomson, James. 1738. *Agamemnon.* London: A. Millar.

Thomson, James. [1972] 1981. *The Seasons and The Castle of Indolence.* Edited by James Sambrook. Oxford: Clarendon Press, 1972. Reprint, Oxford: Clarendon Press, 1981.

Toland, John. 1726. *A Secret History of the South Sea Scheme.* London: n.p.

The Travels of Hildebrand Bowman Esq. 1778. London: Strahan and Cadell.

Trenchard, John. 1725. *Cato's Letters: or, Essays on Civil Liberty.* 4 vols. London: J. Walthoe.

———. 1995. *Cato's Letters.* 2 vols. Indianapolis: Liberty Fund.

Trollope, Anthony. 1874. *New Zealand.* London: Chapman and Hall.

Trompf, G. W., ed. 1990. *Cargo Cults and Millenarian Movements.* Berlin: Mouton de Gruyter.

Trotter, Thomas. 1792. *Observations on the Scurvy.* London: T. Longman.

Turley, Hans. 1999. *Rum, Sodomy and the Lash.* New York: New York University Press.

Turner, Stephen. "A History Lesson: Captain Cook Finds Himself in the State of Nature." In *Voyages and Beaches: Pacific Encounters 1769–1840,* edited by Jonathan Lamb, Bridget Orr, and Alex Calder. Honolulu: University of Hawai'i Press.

United Kingdom. Parliament. 1844. Select Committee of the British. *Report from the Select Committee on New Zealand.*

Valeri, Valerio. 1985a. "The Conqueror Becomes King: A Political Analysis of the Hawaiian Legend of 'Umi.'" In *Transformations of Polynesian Culture,* edited by Tony Hooper and Judith Huntsman. Auckland: The Polynesian Society.

———. 1985b. *Kingship and Sacrifice.* Chicago: University of Chicago Press, 1985.

Vancouver, George. 1798. *A Voyage of Discovery to the North Pacific Ocean and round the World 1790–95.* 3 vols. London: G. G. and J. Robinson.

———. 1801. *A Voyage of Discovery to the North Pacific Ocean.* 6 vols. London: J. Stockdale.

———. 1984. *A Voyage of Discovery to the North Pacific Ocean and round the World.* 4 vols. Edited by W. Kaye Lamb. London: Hakluyt Society.

Vason, George. 1810. *An Authentic Narrative of Four Years' Residence at Tongataboo.* London: Longman, Hurst, Kees and Orme.

Voltaire. 1993. *Dictionnaire Philosophique.* 42 vols. Translated by Tobias Smollett. Paris: E. R. Du Mont; reprint, Austin, Texas: Booklab Inc., 1993.

Wafer, Lionel. 1729. *A New Voyage . . .* Vol. 4 of *A Collection of Voyages.* London: J. E. J. Knapton.

———. 1903. *A New Voyage and Description of the Isthmus of America.* Edited by G. P. Winship. Cleveland: Burrows.

———. 1933. *A New Voyage and Description of the Isthmus of America.* Edited by L. E. Elliott Joyce. Oxford: Hakluyt Society.

Wakefield, Edward Gibbon. 1831. *Facts relating to the Punishment of Death in the Metropolis.* London: J. Ridgway.

———. 1837a. *The British Colonization of New Zealand.* London: J. W. Parker.

————. 1837b. *Mr Dandeson Coates and the New Zealand Assocation.* London: Henry Hooper.

————. 1849. *A View of the Art of Colonization.* London: W. Parker.

————. 1929. *A Letter from Sydney.* London: J. M. Dent.

————. 1967. *England and America.* New York: Augustus M. Kelley.

————. 1986. "England and America." In *Collected Works,* edited by M. F. Lloyd Prichard. London: Collins.

Wales, William. 1778. *Remarks on Mr Forster's Account of Captain Cook's last Voyage.* London: J. Nourse.

————. 1961. "Journal." In *The Voyage of the* Resolution *and* Adventure *1772–75,* edited by J. C. Beaglehole. Cambridge: Cambridge University Press for the Hakluyt Society.

Walker, Ranginui. 1989. "The Treaty of Waitangi as the Focus of Maori Protest." In *Waitangi: Maori and Pakeha Perspectives of the Treaty of Waitangi,* edited by Hugh Kawharu, 263–79. Auckland: Oxford University Press.

Wallace, Alfred Russel. 1895. *Natural Selection and Tropical Nature.* London: Macmillan.

————. 1962. *The Malay Archipelago.* New York: Dover.

Wallis, Helen. 1964. "The Patagonian Giants." In *Byron's Journal of his Circumnavigation 1764–1766,* edited by Robert E. Gallagher, appendix 1: 185–96. Cambridge: Cambridge University Press for the Hakluyt Society.

Wallis, Samuel. n.d. Log of the *Dolphin* around the world. PRO ADM 55/35, fol. 164. Public Records Office, Kew.

Walpole, Horace. 1931. *On Modern Gardening.* New York: Young Books.

————. 1937–83. *Correspondence.* 45 vols. Edited by W. S. Lewis. New Haven, Conn.: Yale University Press.

————. [1766] 1964. "An Account of the Giants lately discovered: In a Letter to a Friend in the Country." In *Byron's Journal of his Circumnavigation 1764–1766.* Edited by Robert E. Gallagher, appendix 3: 200–209. Cambridge: Cambridge University Press for the Hakluyt Society.

————. 1985. *Memoirs of King George II.* 3 vols. Edited by John Brooke. New Haven, Conn.: Yale University Press.

Walter, Richard. 1776. *A Voyage round the World by George Anson 1740–44.* London: W. Bowyer.

Warton, Thomas. 1800. *Essays on Gothic Architecture.* London: J. Taylor.

————. 1802. *Poetical Works.* Edited by Richard Mant. Oxford: Oxford University Press.

————. 1807. *Observations on "The Fairy Queen."* 2 vols. London: R. Dutton and Thomas Ostell.

Watt, Sir James. 1979. "Medical Aspects and Consequences of Cook's Voyages." In *Captain Cook and His Times,* edited by Robin Fisher and Hugh Johnston. Canberra: Australian National University Press.

————. 1991. "Medical Aspects of the Long Voyages of Exploration." In *The Great Maritime Discoveries and World Health,* edited by Mario Gomes Marques and John Cule. Lisbon: Ecola Nacional de Saude Publica, 1991.

————. 1998. "The Medical Bequest of Disaster at Sea." *Journal of the Royal College of Physicians* 32, no. 6: 572–79.

Welbe, John. 1705. *An Answer to Captain Dampier's Vindication.* London: B. Bragge.
————. 1716. John Welbe to Hans Sloane. Sloane MS 4044, fois. 213–17. British Museum, London.
West, Gilbert. 1742. *The Institution of the Order of the Garter.* London: R. Dodsley.
White, John. n.d. MS Journals. White Papers, Alexander Turnbull Library, Wellington, N.Z.
————. 10 May 1864. White Papers, Alexander Turnbull Library, Wellington, N.Z.
Wilberforce, William. 1958. *A Practical View of the Prevailing Religious System.* London: SCM Press.
Williams, Glyndwr. 1973. "'The Inexhaustible Fountain of Gold': English Projects and Ventures in the South Seas 1670–1770." In *Perspectives of Empire,* edited by John E. Flint and Glyndwr Williams. London: Longman.
————. 1994. *Buccaneers, Castaways, and Satirists: The South Seas in the English Consciousness before 1750.* Computer software.
————. 1996. "'To make Discoveries of Countries hitherto Unknown': The Admiralty and Pacific Exploration in the Eighteenth Century." *The Mariner's Mirror* 82, no. 1: 14–27.
————. 1997. *The Great South Sea.* New Haven, Conn.: Yale University Press.
————. 1999. *The Prize of all the Oceans.* London: Harper Collins.
Williams, Glyndwr, and P. J. Marshall. 1982. *The Great Map of Mankind: British Perceptions of the World in the Age of Enlightenment.* London: J. M. Dent.
Williams, Glyndwr, ed. 1967. *Documents relating to Anson's Voyage 1740–44.* Vol. 109. London: Navy Records Society.
Williams, Henry. 1961. *The Early Journals.* Edited by Laurence M. Rogers. Christchurch: Pegasus Press.
Williams, William. 1845. *Three Letters.* London: Church Missionary Society.
Willis, Thomas. 1684. "A Tract of the Scurvy." In *Pharmceutica Rationalis: or, The Operations of Medicines in Humane Bodies.* London: Thomas Dring.
Wilson, Bryan. 1973. *Magic and the Millennium.* London: Heinemann.
Winch, Donald. 1965. *Classical Political Economy and Colonies.* Cambridge, Mass.: Harvard University Press.
Wollstonecraft, Mary. 1960. *A Vindication of the Rights of Men.* Edited by Eleanor Louise Nicholas. Gainesville, Fla.: Scholars' Facsimiles and Reprints.
————. 1992. *A Vindication of the Rights of Woman.* Edited with an introduction by Miriam Brody. Harmondsworth, England: Penguin.
Woodall, John. 1617. *The Surgeon's Mate.* London.
Woodward, Ralph Lee. 1969. *Robinson Crusoe's Island: A History of the Juan Fernandez Islands.* Chapel Hill: University of North Carolina Press.
Woolston, Thomas. 1727. *A Discourse on the Miracles of our Saviour.* London: Thomas Woolston.
Yates, William. 1808–40. Correspondence 12 January 1836. mfm MS 237. Alexander Turnbull Library, Wellington, N.Z.
Young, Robert M. 1985. *Darwin's Metaphor.* Cambridge: Cambridge University Press.
Zavala, Silvio. 1955. *Sir Thomas More in New Spain.* London: Hispanic and Luso-Brazilian Councils.

Index